MALAWI

The Legacy of Tyranny and Shame

WINSTON CHAKUDIKA MSOWOYA

Author: Msowoya, Winston Chakudika
Title: Malawi: The Legacy of Tyranny and Shame
ISBN 978-1-897544-47-1
Copyright (c) 2012, Winston Chakudika Msowoya
Printed in Canada

All rights reserved. No part of this publication may be reproduced, stored in a retrieval system, or transmitted in any form or by any means, electronic, mechanical, photocopying, recording, or otherwise, without written permission of the author and publisher.

All photos and newspaper clippings are from the personal collection of Winston C. Msowoya.

Published by Winston C. Msowoya, Edmonton, Alberta, Canada

Printed by PageMaster Publication Services, Inc.,
11434 - 120 Street,
Edmonton, Alberta Canada T5G 2Y2
Tele: 780 425-9303
www.pagemaster.ca

Comments About This Book

On behalf of the University of Livingstonia Library, and also on my own behalf, I graciously acknowledge receipt of your book which, among other things, provides valuable insights to the history of Malawi in particular, and also Africa at large. Congratulations for producing this piece of work.

Augustine Walter C. Msiska, Ph.D.
University of Livingstonia
Mzuzu, Malawi

Since reading Mr. Msowoya's book MALAWI: The Legacy of Tyranny and Shame, I am still in awe that the news and television cannot begin to show the corruption—and there is a need for the world to know the truth. Through all of this, I hope that his words are the ones that will help Africa start healing. Shift power to the people, take back your culture and traditions, be a proud Africa living without tyranny and shame.

Susan Joyce
Edmonton, AB
Canada

One of the moments that has shaped the history of Malawi is "The Cabinet Crisis" of 1964. Those of us that went to school and college during the Kamuzu Banda era heard a lot about "the rebels" that resulted from that crisis, but did not know exactly how and why it happened. In this book, Winston Msowoya has described in detail the events that led up to the crisis, and what happened during the crisis itself. He was there in Zomba and so his account is first-hand. It is a very illuminating account, and it's just one example of the detailed information that is contained in this book. Instead of just describing the events, he comments on them as well. In the late 1980s, I studied in New Zealand—about as far away from African news as one could get in those days without the Internet. My source of African news was a magazine called *New African*, published in the UK. To my surprise, there used to be news about Malawi too and the main contributor was a certain Winston Msowoya in Edmonton, Alberta, Canada. He used to contribute articles or write letters to the editor. I still remember vividly reading about the murder of an exiled journalist, Mkwapatira Mhango, in Lusaka, Zambia—a murder that was linked to the Kamuzu Banda regime. I could sense that Winston was very annoyed by this blatant atrocity. My point is that Winston, while in exile, has followed and written about Malawi politics for a long time. When I came to Alberta in the 1990s, I met Winston and have known him personally ever since. He has told me many stories about his life in exile around the world, stories that have shaped his life. He is truly passionate about politics, particularly African and Malawian politics. His wife recently "complained" she can't surf the TV channels at home when he is present because it is always tuned to either BBC World News or CNN. The account you'll read in this book is from a man who truly wishes Malawi the best, but cannot understand why some leaders have exploited Malawi instead of developing it.

Dr. Newton Lupwayi

Lethbridge, AB

Canada

Acknowledgements

I greatly desire to acknowledge the untiring support I have received from my wife Jane and my son Martin Vitumbiko during the writing of this book. They were with me through thick and thin and without their moral support my dream for this book would not have come true.

Jane Msowoya   Martin Vitumbiko Msowoya

Table of Contents

FOREWORD vii

PREFACE 1

INTRODUCTION 6

EARLY HISTORY 15

POLITICAL STRUGGLE 26

FEDERATION: RHODESIA AND NYASALAND 57

INDEPENDENCE WITHIN CRISIS 69

AFTERMATH OF THE CRISIS 107

BLEAK FUTURE 136

THE HEIGHT OF REPRESSION 174

THE PATH OF BETRAYAL 221

THE STRUGGLE FOR DEMOCRACY 255

AFRICA IN TURMOIL 316

FOREWORD

While driving with Winston and Jane Msowoya into the mountains of Jasper National Park in western Alberta on the May long holiday weekend of 1997, Winston intently scanned a daily newspaper. The one article that caught his attention described how Laurent-Désiré Kabila had assumed leadership of the Democratic Republic of Congo following the overthrow of Mobutu Sese Seko. As we drove, he scanned and rescanned the article. It claimed his rapt attention. It was then that I first realized that the heart of Winston Msowoya very much resonated with the heart beat of Africa.

My personal knowledge of Malawi up to then was limited. I knew only that it was once a part of British East Africa—the Nyasaland Protectorate—and this I knew because I chanced to find a Nyasaland postage stamp in packet of stamps I received as a Christmas gift while a child many years ago.

As a young man, Winston Msowoya was a harsh critic of autocratic government and soon found it expedient to go into exile in order to avoid the wrath of Malawi's imported President, Hastings Banda. While in exile he remained keenly interested in Malawian affairs, even while pursuing degrees in journalism in a Moscow university.

I first met Winston Msowoya in the early nineties when we were both involved in the planning of a school to be built in Malawi. It was about the time that I also learned that African politics was his first and keenest interest—indeed, upon meeting another countryman their conversation quickly embraced politics.

In this book Msowoya traces the history of Malawi from its colonial status to that of independence. While digressing frequently to developments in other parts of Africa, his principal focus is on Malawi and its leadership following independence. In this regard he expresses deep despair and discouragement. He writes; "The current political and economic crisis engulfing many parts of the Continent are attributed to our leaders' lack of vision and commitment. As soon as these leaders are voted into power, their first priority seems to be to amass wealth and manipulate national constitutions to suit their political agendas. Alas, it is Africa's leaders who have failed Africa." He continues; "Once an African has had a 'taste' of power, he not only wants more of it, but he wants it for life. Dr. Banda, whose footsteps Muluzi seemed to be wanting to follow, was an exemplification of this atrocious African malady."

This position, of course begs the question, Is this only an African trait? Is it not equally true of many other leaders—political, religions, financial? I think it is.

I find it very encouraging, however, to see that there are still those in our midst who cry out against such abuses of power.

The story of Malawi and this man's great love for Africa have been further revealed to me as page by page this book has evolved into the book you now hold in your hands.

Truly does the heart of Winston Msowoya plead, CRY, BELOVED AFRICA.

Warren E. Hathaway, Ph. D.
Edmonton, AB
Canada

PREFACE

This book could have been completed some years back, but the earlier manuscripts were confiscated by Zimbabwe's notorious covert agents in Bulawayo where I was residing (1980-1985) as a political exile. At the same time I was organizing groups of Malawians living and working in Zimbabwe.

Sooner rather than later, the effects of my endeavors caught the attention of the Malawi's repulsive regime through its myriad of covert agents working hand in hand with Zimbabwe's most feared spy agency. Banda protested to his best friend and admirer, octogenarian and corrupt tyrant Robert Mugabe, and forthwith I found myself in deep trouble with the Zimbabwean authorities. My house was searched and the manuscripts were taken away with the promise that these would be returned to me as soon as possible—but I strongly believed that I would not get back my manuscripts. As expected, my prediction proved correct.

Only a few days later I was arrested and put into Grey Prison in Bulawayo and subsequently transferred to Harare's notorious Central Prison. While there, I met a prison warder whom I had met before (name withheld for fear of reprisals) in Havana, Cuba, where I went for training in guerrilla warfare to prepare myself for a long and protracted struggle against one of the most tyrannical and corrupt regimes in the Continent. The warder, at that time, was in the last stage of his military training under the ZAPU PF military wing (ZIPRA).

After so many years of separation, however, our sense of comradeship never evanesced. He helped me in many ways while in the lion's den. One such noble aid was his concerns that the Zimbabwe regime was colluding with Malawi's ravenous covert police to smuggle me out of the prison and covertly deport me to Malawi where I was blacklisted for "high treason" along side Mr. Orton Chirwa, his wife Vera and others. Mr. Chirwa QC was the former leader of the exiled movement (MAFREMO), who with his wife, were serving life imprisonment for their political beliefs and were declared "prisoners of conscience" by the Amnesty International (AI). Mr. Chirwa was also the founder and President of the now discredited Malawi Congress Party (MCP). He was brutally bludgeoned to death in 1994 in Zomba's notorious prison by Banda's murderous thugs.

As things appeared real, the warder asked me what my plans were while in prison, indicating that he was ready to help me in whatever I wished him to do for me. I asked him to go to the Herald Newspaper (ZANU PF-controlled) and see my friend Moletsi Mbeki, the young brother of former South Africa's President Thabo Mbeki, and explain to him my predicament. Indeed, he did just that and Moletsi expressly contacted Mr. Richard Curver of the Amnesty International (AI), London, on this issue of urgency.

Richard Curver forthwith took the matters up with the Zimbabwean authorities and bluntly warned them of the dire consequences should they deport me to Malawi. Having their sinister plan nipped in the bud, I was finally deported to Tanzania where I resided before proceeding to Canada.

In this book, I have endeavored to expose Malawi's successive regimes based on an ethnic doctrine whereby the minority northerners are persecuted and segregated against mostly by the leaders from two provinces (south and central) who command the majority of the population. Even though northerners are in a minority, they represent the nation's intellectual base which had been there since the colonial era due to strong Missionary Institutions. In 2010, the diehard tribalist, and one of the most corrupt in the history of our country, the late President Bingu wa Mutharika, imposed a quota system akin to former South Africa's apartheid system which victimized blacks. In Malawi, this system denies northerners opportunities to enter Universities, Colleges, and Secondary Schools—all because the President personally alleged that students from the north cheat on examinations.

Before Bingu was elected into power, he was Secretary-general of COMESA, for eastern and southern Africa where it is alleged that he misused public funds for personal interest and was therefore unceremoniously fired from his post. His wedding, to a woman 40 years younger than himself, cost taxpayers more than a million dollars. A few months later, towards the end of 2010, he invited his counterparts in southern Africa to attend ceremonies marking the opening of his 50-bedroom house that was reported to cost the poor taxpayers more than US$1.5 million, this in one of the poorest nations in the world. In 2005, he increased his salary from over US $38,200 to $196,200 per annum, a move, heavily criticized by an economic watchdog as unheard of in a country rated among ten of the poorest countries in the world.

Apart from my own country, Malawi, which forms the basis of this book, I have also dealt at some length with exposure of the ills of Africa's leadership in general and in particular Congo, Nigeria, Zimbabwe, Sudan, and Kenya. I have pinpointed where Africa has lost its prestige on the world's stage due to leadership's lack of vision and dire lust for power which tragically plunged the continent into political and economic quagmires of unimaginable proportion. I have also dared to paint much of Africa's leadership as cruel, corrupt, greedy, incompetent, and tribalistic.

As soon as an African leader tastes power, it is hard to relinquish it democratically. This is the time when Armed Forces, Police Forces, and Intelligence Services are corrupted and brainwashed and finally controlled by the Head of State. In turn he is assured of life-Presidency. We have seen that in Zimbabwe. We have seen that in Malawi. And we are seeing that in Uganda.

Indeed, the independence of Africa has brought with it a tragic aftermath. Our people are being killed by government soldiers—soldiers who are supposed to protect them from corrupt and tyrannical leadership. The beautiful and productive soils of our continent are covered with the precious blood and skulls of our own people, even worse than during the colonial era. On the other hand, deadly nuclear toxic wastes are being dumped by unscrupulous western industries on our soils at will—after bribing our so-called leaders with a few million dollars. It is so tragically sad that these leaders stupidly fail to realize the long term health hazards the toxic materials pose to the population—including their own family members.

I have also strongly criticized African leaders for betraying our independence and freedoms in exchange for Chinese economic aid. Fifty years ago, China was a backward nation while at the same time many of our nations were attaining independence. However, our independence has been dogged by bloody tribal conflicts, brutal corruption, incompetence, lack of vision among our so-called leaders, greed, and above all a lack of patriotic zeal. Malawians under the foreign-born dictator, the late Richard Armstrong (Hastings Banda), lived in utter fear and hopelessness for 30 years. They could not even trust their own shadows. Malawi had become like Nicolae Ceausescu's Romania where very little was known beyond its borders and its people were literally treated like slaves by their own government. Popularly known to his subjects as Wamuyaya (the immortal), Hastings Banda was not only the Head of State, but also the "slave master."

I have also revealed the fact that Malawi was involved in the tragic demise of Mozambique's charismatic leader President Samola Moses Machel. President Banda was expressly informed of the deleterious plan a month before the South Africa's apartheid regime carried out the timorous act.

Indeed, I could not betray my moral sense when I realized that we had imported a Frankensteinian monster who would destroy our nation for his own personal agenda. Forthwith I, at the age of 17, made up my mind to leave the country and join my compatriots in exile to fight for democracy and human rights for our people.

On the morning of 19 October, 1964, I called my father and mother to bid them farewell, instantly my mother broke into tears and I said to her, "Mama, when we don't meet again, you know where we are going to meet." My dad took me half way on my journey and in parting words, he said to me, " My son I wish you a safe trip to your unknown destination and remember, only courage, truth and determination can sustain your endeavors. Go well my son, I am proud of you. Fight a good fight not only for your country, but also for Africa."

I returned to my homeland on October 19, 1994 (after 30 years in exile) and after Malawians had collectively liberated themselves from the shackles of fascism. I found my dearest father had died and my mother alive at the age of 75. It would be foolhardy for someone to believe that Africa would perpetually remain in the hands of corrupt and brutal tyrants. The present leadership will soon be swept into the dustbin of political history and the masses will remain for ever to chart their own destiny. MAY GOD BLESS AFRICA.

Chapter One

INTRODUCTION

Deep love for my country and for all of Africa has been my lifelong preoccupation. Throughout my thirty years of exile in Africa, Europe, the Soviet Union (Russia), Cuba, and North American, I have always regarded problems in other parts of Africa, as my own and inseparable from problems in Malawi—my own country. I regard myself as a Pan-Africanist and proud of my African background. Loving Malawi as I do, my inspiration for its future comes from such great men as Kwame Nkrumah, Patrice E. Lumumba, Julius K. Nyerere, Samora Machell, Cheick A. Diop, John Chilembwe, Levi Mumba, Sekou Toure, Steve B. Biko, Amilcar Cabral, Nelson Madiba Mandela, and many others before them.

From deep within my heart I am also obliged to pay tribute to black leaders in the Diaspora such as William Du Bois, Sylvester Williams, George Padmore, Marcus Garvey, Frantz Fenon, Edward W. Blyden, Malcolm X, Martin Luther King, and the list goes on. These great Africans dedicated their lives to the struggle for freedom for the black race throughout the world, indeed, their names are synonymous with liberation of the African people.

The people of Malawi and others in different parts of the continent and around the world have increasingly suffered at the hands of domineering rulers who exercised unprecedented physical and moral injury over their subjects. In Malawi, people were reduced to ciphers—they could not even think on their own. Decent and bright people betrayed their consciences to gain political favors from their leader. This once God-fearing nation was turned into a slaughtering ground for those perceived as ex-ministers' supporters living in exile.

Young men were brainwashed and trained to kill their folks in defense of Bandaism. The Malawian Young Pioneers (MYP), formed by the government to spearhead national reconstruction in the early days of independence, were subsequently turned into Banda's personal "elite" force that was above the law and they abused this liberty to terrorize the whole nation for thirty years.

These misguided hoodlums sold party cards and collected party funds from people by means of vicious force. People could not buy food from markets without producing party cards. Passengers could not travel in public transport without party cards. Old people in the villages had to surrender their chickens, goats, sheep, or cattle if they had no money to buy party cards. Even pregnant women were coerced into buying party cards for their unborn.

For thirty years Dr. Hastings Banda single-handedly dominated the political, economic, and social scenes in the country and presided over a corrupt and kleptocratic regime. His word was a law unto itself. The parliament was obsolete—there were no meaningful debates or discussions on issues affecting the state. As a matter of fact, Banda regarded himself as the most intelligent man in the country and, therefore, his word was always final.

The fact remains that Banda's ascent to power in July 1964 marked the formal beginning of a gory chapter in Malawi's post-colonial history. His 30-year rule was characterized by mass arrests, torture of victims, jailing of people on trumped-up charges, detentions without trial, mysterious disappearances, death whilst in police custody, and many other wanton atrocities. By Amnesty International estimate, tin-pot Banda was responsible for over 15,000 deaths during the thirty-year span of his leadership.

> In common with dictators the world over, Banda tried to conceal the truth about the repressive nature of his dreaded Malawi Congress Party (MCP) regime by: suppressing all venues of democratic expression (be they political, social, or cultural); bringing pressure to bear on

Malawian and foreign media workers through arrests, public beatings, and harassment; and, reducing all news on the national airwaves to oral and visual accounts of the daily activities of the despot. But mostly he sought to divert attention away from his notorious role in Malawi's history by arranging occasional festivities in which he was virtually surrounded by dancing women. It was in that vein that more than US$3 million was spent in a matter of a few hours to celebrate his 60th birthday. The excessive celebrations were reminiscent of similar acts of narcissism by the rogue Idi Amin of Uganda or the brutish Jean Bedel Bokassa who once crowned himself Emperor of the Central African Republic.

During the thirty years of Banda's regime, Malawians were persistently urged to stand behind their "Ngwazi" (hero) under the official slogan of "Ufulu" (independence). In truth his regime was a total mockery of the struggle that led to independence on July 6, 1964. Indeed, the thirty years of Ufulu were characterized as a concerted effort aimed at colonial restoration with Banda as the colonial governor issuing orders from the State House.

All the symbols of Banda's conception of power and his vision of Malawi's future were derived from the colonial past of his ideological upbringing and education. Indeed, the thirty years of his regime were decades of economic, political, and social crimes against the Malawian people.

Banda's legacy has had far reaching consequences that still remain to this day. Dr. Hastings Banda, the first elected President of Malawi, developed a personality cult unrivaled elsewhere in the world. Officially, the people of Malawi were coerced into addressing him as: His Excellency, the Ngwazi, Life President Dr. Hastings Kamuzu Banda. Ironically, people were jailed for simply addressing the president as Dr. Hastings Banda.

He ruled Malawians with impunity and often ridiculed them during public rallies by calling them his people. Usually, the response from his so-called people was overwhelming; women ululating and dancing and men clapping their hands. To Malawians, Banda was more than a political leader. He was, to them, a demigod, Wamuyaya (the immortal), who had been sent by God to lead the Malawian people. In public rallies people were singing, "Zonse Zimene za Kamuazu Banda," which literally means everything in Malawi belonged to Kamuzu Banda—and indeed he took it that way.

His immediate victims were Mbumba za Kamuzu (Banda's women). He used once proud mothers to the fullest. He turned them into dancing robots and shuttled them around. Married or not, these unfortunate women were forced to travel in convoys wherever Banda went. They were treated with contempt and reduced to sex slaves, many being forced to sleep with party officials. Others of the unlucky ones often slept in open spaces or in unhealthy and hazardous environments. All could be separated from their families for weeks or months. Most women returned home diseased and their spouses had no rights to reprimand their wives—fearing reprisals from the party officials. Women were also made to spy on their spouses and as a result there was a great sense of mistrust in the family life. The stratagem worked effectively. For thirty years Banda encountered virtually no grass roots resistance to his obnoxious rule. Women were his most effective tools of repression. Dr. Kenneth David Kaunda, the former Zambian president, once made a remark to the effect that Banda was ruling "zombies." Indeed, the disrespect that Banda showed Malawians defies imagination.

From one of the poorest countries in the world, Banda used to transport these women as far as Europe and Israel for education tours—bearing in mind that 98 percent of them could hardly write and read. The majority of these unfortunate women came from rural areas where poverty and disease were rampant. However, recent political change has not corrected the past wrong. Life in rural areas remains pathetically deteriorated especially for women who were denied opportunities to go to school and instead recruited into dancing groups for political leaders.

Perhaps the most damaging legacy His Excellency, the Ngwazi, Life President Dr. Hastings Kamuzu Banda has left behind is the politics of "divide and rule." Before Banda was imported into the country, Nyasas were among the most united people on the continent. This unity went beyond the borders of their country. In South Africa, they were known as Amanyasa, the same as in Rhodesia (Zimbabwe). Their presence in both countries was deeply felt by local populations.

Following the advent of Banda, and indeed, after the famous September 1964 cabinet crisis, something went dangerously wrong. The people of the north were singled out as enemies of the President and the State and consequently became victims of unprecedented political and economic strangulation. The country became distinctively divided on tribal and regional lines. Perhaps, the most striking instance is the first multiparty elections of 1994 when three major political parties (AFORD, MCP, UDF) were elected on a regional basis. However, politicians within these parties seem to enjoy the status quo, fearing national politics would interfere with their political ambitions.

Even in his grave Banda remains a mysterious man. He claimed to have roots among the Chewa clan of central Malawi and related to Chief Mwase of Kasungu. However, his claims and his true cultural background were two different things. To make things worse, he did not know how to speak Chichewa, a local dialect. Even those who claim to have some sort of blood relationship with him do not know his birth parents—thus prompting the longstanding belief that Banda was truly an impostor.

The struggle for change in Malawi, which had been exclusively carried out by exiles living in neighboring countries, cost many lives which must be remembered if one is to write an authentic political history of our country.

The following are the names of our heroes who either fell in the battle field, were assassinated, or met an otherwise unnatural demise while endeavoring to establish a free and democratic Malawi. Among them are Yatuta Kaluli Chisiza, Dunduzu Kaluli Chisiza, Orton Chingoli Chirwa, Masauko Chipembere, Medison Silombera, Augustin W. Bwanausi, Harry Jonga, Felix Mwaliyambwile, Lutengano Mwahimba, Pemba Ndovi, John Nyondo, Garetta Chirwa, D. Chidawati, David Mzelemeka Nyirenda, Bunda Mhango, William Chisausau Msowoya, Lifford Mkwapatila Mhango, Lawrence, Msawanga, Robert Mlangachalo Karua, Surtie Mwaluwunju, Mapopa Chipeta, Edwin Chabambo, Oliver Munthali, Thipa Msowoya, Kamtekete Gondwe, Harry Bwanausi, Attati Mphakali, and many others whose names do not appear here.

My tributes and recognition are also extended to former exiles who endured untold hardships in foreign lands. These stalwarts did not break down mentally or physically while in their pursuit of freedom and human dignity for their country and countrymen. The following are names which I strongly feel must be remembered for their heroic contribution; Kanyama Chiume, G. Akogo Kanyanya, D. Mundo Mwaubetanya, A. Kapote Mwakasungura, C. Kapote Mwakasungura, Chinduti Chirwa, Hilda Ganji Mhango, James Ganji Mhango, Norman Ganji Mhango, Hess Ganji Mhango, Reginald Ganji Mhango, Jomo Chikwakwa, Willy Chokani, David Rubadiri, George Michongwe, Jando Nkhwazi, Gross Nkhwazi, Thandika Mkandawire, Chimtunga Mhoni, Guy Mhoni, Clement Malama, Hook Kondowe, L. Mahoma Mwaungulu, Joe Mwaungulu, Suzgo Msiska, Machipisa Munthali, Rose Chibambo, Vera Chirwa, Morrie Nkosi, Catherine Chipembere, John Ngai, Vyande Yatuta Chisiza, Kwacha Yatuta Chisiza, Tojo Msowoya, Edward Msowoya, Yaphwantha Chirwa, Peter Muthalika, Thengo Maloya, and many others whose names might have been forgotten.

The history of our struggle for change would be incomplete if I failed to pay tribute to our Catholic Church leaders whose pastoral letters to loyal followers culminated into a national revolt against Banda's brutal regime. And above all, my tributes to sons and daughters of our soil who laid down their lives for the common good of future generations.

So, while 1994 marked the 30th year since attaining independence from Britain, it also marked thirty years of struggle against the neocolonial betrayal of the promises made at that independence. The Ufulu (independence) era epitomizes that betrayal in a way that leaves no ambiguities. Not only because of the scale of the anti-people measures of the last thirty years, but because of the person of Banda himself whose political background remains a mystery now and perhaps for generations to come. Ufulu was therefore, not only a simple mockery, but a tragic mockery of our historic struggle for our country's independence, our national liberation, and the social changes needed to realize social justice for all the people of Malawi.

But it is also a big lesson. People who have won a successful struggle must forever be vigilant against any possible hijacking of their revolution by the enemy through brainwashed agents or turncoats. What Malawians experienced in the thirty years under Banda's evil rule should have transmitted shock waves beyond their borders and awakened peoples' awareness of dangers in other countries. Instead, people in other countries thought what had gone wrong in Malawi could not happen in their own countries.

That judgment was absolutely wrong and misleading. The people of Zimbabwe did the same thing in creating Frankenstein-like monster in whom it was hard to remove or control. Robert Mugabe had learned all the tactics from Banda, whom he so much admired.

Unfortunately, the changes that occurred in 1994, after the first multiparty elections after thirty years of a police state, were fallacious because the people who were elected into power were once Banda's sycophants. They too had been involved in numerous criminal offenses against the people of Malawi and had no vision.

The exiles who spearheaded resistance against Banda's iron-fisted rule were all shut out in the 1994 elections. Under the banner of UFMD and CSR, the exiles were perceived as a spent force who had lived in exile enjoying themselves. To the contrary, there is no jolly life in exile.

Many politicians who had remained at home and worked for Banda blamed the exiles for importing the rogue and then abandoning the masses. However, this sort of propaganda was very effective and many Malawians, unfortunately, equated their suffering with the exiles. I can partly understand their point of view because it took three decades to unseat Banda. But the exiles are unfairly blamed.—the exiles could not effect change from outside Malawi without total support of the masses inside the country.

However, in September 1967, former Home Affairs Minister Yatuta Kaluli Chisiza entered the country with sixteen strong comrades to start a gorilla campaign. Yatuta had hoped that his presence in the country would ignite open revolt. But this did not happen. Chisiza and his comrades were killed after putting up a heroic resistance. More than 300 government soldiers and hundreds of Young Pioneers were wiped out. The government forces were led by foreign commanders from Portuguese East Africa (Mozambique), South Africa (an apartheid regime), and Rhodesia (Zimbabwe).

The aftermath of Yatuta's death created a good deal of fear among the population. This pattern of fear made it practically impossible for exiles to organize supporters inside the country. Since Yatuta's death there have been no further incursions into the country by exiled armed groups. The task of liberating Malawi from oppression and injustices, remained largely a diplomatic offensive which was carried out by exiles.

As a matter of fact, the exiles excelled as a symbol of resistance which had succeeded politically in isolating Banda's regime from the international community. While other world nations were advancing in novel technologies and building their economies for future generations, African nations seem to have hit a stone wall. Our leaders have proved to be more brutal than the former colonial masters. In a continent whose natural wealth is second to none, our people have been reduced to economic slaves while leaders continue to amass unprecedented resources for their own selfish ends.

For how long the people of Malawi can continue to tolerate their state while being cheated of their proper returns is impossible to say. What is needed among all Malawians is the ability and conviction of John Chilembwe to rise and "strike a blow for a common good." Without such notions, our people will be condemned to suffer injustice in silence, since the greatest foe of justice is ignorance itself.

Indeed, thirty years of "police state" should be enough to teach our people a lesson and discourage future citizens from creating illusory Messiahs.

Heroes of Africa

President Joyce Banda became Malawi's first female leader after the demise of former shameful kleptocratic tyrant President Bingu Wa Muthalika in april, 2012. She received overwhelming praise in her debut by refusing that her dying sister be flown to South Africa for medical treatment. She maintained that her sister was no different from other Malawian patients.

Top: Dr. Kenneth D. Kaunda, former president of Zambia and a devoted Christian, ruled his nation with an enormous sense of decency for over 30 years. He also championed Africa's freedom struggle. He stepped down from office a poor man. Bottom: Africa's living and indomitable champion of democracy and Nigeria's Nobel laureate, Professor Wole Soyinka, accepts no compromise in the quest for human dignity. He is also a fervent critic of Robert Mugabe's rogue and corrupt regime in Zimbabwe.

Top: The late former president of Uganda, Milton A. Obote, ruled the nation progressively until removed by rogue Idd Amin in the 1970s. He died in exile, a poor man. Bottom: Former Tanzanian President Dr. Julius K. Nyerere, a Godly Christian, ruled his nation with a sense of morality for more than 30 years and was one of Africa's ardent freedom fighters. He died a poor man.

Top: The late Mozambican president Samora Moses Machel died in a violent airplane crash in 1986. It is widely believed that apartheid South africa colluded with Banda's regime in Malawi to stage the crash. Samora Moses Machel was a brilliant military strategist. Bottom: The late Dr. Eduardo Mondlane, Mozambique's brilliant and intellectual and first university graduate was a charismatic leader of FRELIMO (the Mozambique Liberation Front), was killed by a parcel bomb in Dar es Salaam, Tanzania in early 1969. The bomb was sent by the portuguese organization PIDE.

Top: Rev. John Chilembwe (1873-1915), wife, and daughter—the father of Malawi nationalism. He led the rebellion against British rule and was killed in the battlefield on February 3, 1915. Bottom: Late Dr. Attati Mpakati, former charismatic leader of the exiled opposition (LESOMA). Assassinated in Harare, Zimbabwe by Banda's murder squad in March, 1983.

Top: The late Kanyama Chiume, the first Education Minister who later became Minister of Foreign Affairs after Malawi's independence in 1964. He was Banda's arch-foe and an ardent nationalist. Bottom: Late Augustine W. Bwanausi, former Minister of Social Development and Housing. Died in a mysterious car accident while in exile in Zambia in 1973.

Top: The late Masauko Chipembere and his wife. Chipembere was the former Minister of Education and a leading radical nationalist who died in exile in the United States in 1975. Bottom: Former South African President Nelson Madiba Mandela, the icon of apartheid struggle and beloved son of Africa.

Top: the late Dr. Kwame Nkrumah (1909-1972), the first black President of Ghana and highly acknowledged as the foremost Pan-Africanist of our time. Bottom: Clements Kadali (1896-1951), a Tonga from Northern Malawi, formed the first Trade Union in South Africa in 1919. The first black Nationalist to address the all-white Parliament in racist South Africa in the same year.

Top: The late Lifford M. Mhango, a prolific journalist lying in agony in the Lusaka hospital before he died of a bomb attack on October 13, 1989. Nine other members of his family died with him. Bottom: The late Patrice E. Lumumba, first Congolese (DRC) Prime Minister was killed in January 1961 by foreign sources led by Belgians and America's CIA.

Top: The former Malawi Justice Minister Orton Chirwa and his wife Vera. Both were sentenced to life imprisonment in 1981 and Orton was murdered in Zomba Prison in 1992. Bottom: The late T. D. T. Banda, a former leader of the NAC who strongly opposed the notion of importing Dr. Banda into Malawi from Gold Coast (Ghana) in 1958.

Brothers. Top: The late Yatuta K. Chisiza, Malawi's former Minister of Home Affairs, died in a battlefield in Septermber, 1967. He was the bulwark of the independence struggle. Bottom: The late Dunduzu K. Chisiza, Malawi's former Deputy Minister of Finance and a brilliant economist. He was killed in a faked car accident in September, 1962.

Chapter Two

EARLY HISTORY

Historians and archaeological evidence suggest that Malawi has been inhabited for over 55,000 years. The earliest human remains date from between 4,000 and 10,000 years ago. This finding, together with linguistic evidence, suggest that these early residents were foragers and the ancestors of Twa, Fula and perhaps contemporary Khoisan speakers, such as the San of southern Africa. Bantu-speaking immigrants settled in the area of present-day Malawi between the first and fourth centuries C.E., probably displacing the existing populations. The Bantu migrants relied primarily on shifting agriculture and are thought to have introduced iron-working as they spread through the region during the following centuries. Sometime between the 13th and 14th centuries C. E., a second wave of Bantu migrants, possibly of Shaba and Luba origin, reached Malawi from areas to the north—especially from the region that is the present-day Congo (Kinshasa).

Shifting cultivation, while still practiced in some areas, gave way to more sedentary and intensive forms of agricultural production. This shift, combined with the resulting increase in population density, fostered the development of allied Kingdoms, beginning with the 15th century Malavi (or Malawi) Confederacy. The Malavi Kings formed a Federation of several distinct Kingdoms including the Lundu located in the present-day Shire Valley and the Undi, who lived west of Lake Nyasa (now Lake Malawi). They came to rule over most of the territory that is now known as Central and southern Malawi as well as parts of Mozambique and Zambia. These hereditary Kings came from the Phiri clan, and their principle charge was to collect and store grain as tribute, and to redistribute it during times of famine. These Kings also controlled the trade in ivory and iron materials that were in particular demand among Swahili traders.

Portuguese merchants arrived at the lower reaches of the Zambezi River in the 16th century. Along with arms, ammunition, textiles, and glass beads, the Portuguese introduced manioc (also called cassava). Manioc is a carbohydrate-rich tuber which, unlike millet and bananas, may be stored for significant periods of time. Manioc quickly spread throughout Africa and became one of the dominant subsistence crops.

More immediately, however, Africans in the Zambezi River region were faced with Portuguese efforts to gain control over the river's lucrative gold and ivory trade. In response, Malavi Kings sent troops north to establish alternative routes to the Indian Ocean, conquering a large section of Makua territory in Mozambique. The cannibalism of the Lundi soldiers, in particular, terrorized their neighbors into capitulation. Portuguese troops sent to quell the Lundi in 1592, met with defeat. Ultimately King Kalanga collaborated with the Portuguese to help defeat the Lundu in 1622 in return for unhindered access to the Indian Ocean markets.

Toward the close of the 17th century, Yao and Ngoni moved from the south, acting as brokers of slaves, firearms, and other commodities between Europeans, Swahili, Arab merchants, and various other African suppliers. With its trade monopoly undermined, the Malavi Confederacy disintegrated into numerous independent chiefdoms. Its people fell prey to slave-raiding by the well-armed Yao. In the 18th century a group of Malavi, known as the Chewa, split off and migrated to the west. The Chewa would eventually become the largest ethnic group in modern day Malawi.

The slave trade between the Lake Nyasa region and the Indian Ocean regions such as Mombassa, Zanzibar, Bagamoyo and Kilwa expanded rapidly during the 18th century and early 19th century. Malavi communities continued to suffer from slave-raids by neighboring groups, particularly the Ngoni. By the mid-19th century, Swahili, Ngoni and Yao traders had introduced Islam to the region, and 10,000 slaves were passing annually through the slave depot at Nkhota Kota in central Malawi, then ruled by an Arab sultan. By this time, the merchants had also introduced vast quantities of firearms, making struggles for control over diminishing supplies of ivory and slave labor increasingly violent. The Scottish explorer and missionary, Dr. David Livingstone, remarked on this violence when he first arrived in the region in the 1850s. He and other members of the London Missionary Society established the Livingstonia Mission as well as several mission schools in the northern highlands of Table Mountain, locally known as Chombe. The Livingstonia establishment attracted many Africans from the neighboring countries of Tanganyika (Tanzania) and northern Rhodesia (Zambia) and, of course, it became the cradle of learning in Eastern and Central Africa. Hordes of Malawi's leaders of the independence struggle were educated at the mission.

When Kanyama Chiume was appointed as the first Minister of Education after independence, he contemplated building the Malawi University there so that the establishment could receive an economic and social boost. After the famous 1964 cabinet revolt against Banda, the plans suffered a setback and Livingstonia was left to decay for the simple reason that Chiume was a northerner and the area was located in the north.

The mission won many converts among the groups subjected to slave raids and conquest and they were encouraged to take up legitimate forms of entrepreneurial activity such as cultivating cotton and other cash crops. They also lobbied European government officials to intervene in order to abolish slavery. In the late 19th century other missionary groups also became active in the region; including the Free Church of Scotland, the Dutch Reformed Church of South Africa, and the Roman Catholic Church. Today, approximately 85 percent of the population practices Christianity.

In 1889, the British South African Company (BSAC), headed by John Cecil Rhodes, received a royal charter to exploit Malawi's mineral resources in return for a commitment to hedge Portuguese influence in the region. The crown took control when it created the Nyasaland Districts Protectorate in

1891. Many groups preyed upon by Yao raiders welcomed the British intervention, but the Yao, Chewa and others resisted colonialist Captain Frederick John Dealtry Lugard. He was a notorious colonialist, who was called upon to establish control over the Sultan of Karonga. The Sultan fought to maintain control of his valuable trade in slaves. But, in 1893, the region was renamed the British Central African Protectorate and finally Nyasaland.

No sooner was the country effectively under British control than European immigrants poured in and occupied the land—especially the most fertile areas of the southern Region. In the Cholo District alone, two-thirds of the land was confiscated by white settlers. Cholo has been renamed Thyolo by the former brutal tyrant Hastings Banda to convince his people that he was an authentic nationalist. By 1892, more than 1,600,000 hectares of land had been alienated, that being more than 16 percent of the land area of Malawi. Three quarters of this alienated area, was in possession of eleven big companies, most based in Scotland. Among them were the Central African Company, African Lakes Corporation, A. L. Bruce Trust, and the Church of Scotland Mission which altogether took 500,000 hectares of the most fertile and productive lands of the Shire Highlands. In the northern Region, about 1,100,000 hectares were declared a possession of the British South African Company.

It is not astonishing that Scottish Missionaries and capital followed Livingstone, the Scot, who allegedly said that he went to Central Africa to try to open a path for commerce and Christ. His efforts were indirectly responsible for political intervention of the British which culminated in the establishment of the British Colony of Nyasaland. The religious interlopers were soon to clash with the indigenous peoples. In the words of Professor Mitchell, "The Yaos, having established themselves in the Shire Highlands of Malawi, came into conflict militarily with Bishop McKenzie and Dr. David Livingstone and were later conquered by a British force."

To appreciate how the process of land alienation affected the whole country, we should first understand the original systems of land tenure. Labor was divided according to sex, and the labor force was not then detached from the community as a separate social productive unit. The whole community was a labor unit engaged directly in economic processes, and largely in control of it. The community's inner organizational structure, men and women, children and parents, enjoyed a productive relationship in a democratic sense. Labor was divided for cattle-breeding or agriculture farming. Adult men were responsible for the building of houses, clearing of new lands, herding of cattle, hunting, fishing, and the care of domestic animals. The men also took charge of development, and most importantly, defense. Women, on the other hand, were active in agriculture, planting seeds, weeding, and harvesting in addition to domestic duties.

Before the arrival of the Europeans there had not been any separation of industry from the living environment. The women, for instance, were able to combine their work in the fields with cottage industry. The communal society was self sufficient and averted the need for commodity exchange among and between communities. It was not an economic necessity under these circumstances to be hired as a laborer. The African communalists only needed to exploit the resources within reach to attain the material necessary for subsistence. They could work for themselves for they had no cause to sell (which would enrich a capitalist) so long as they held all the means of production at their disposal—the main one being land. I know this phrase (that is to say, means of production) may drive some readers into thinking that I am a communist. On the contrary, I am not a communist, I am an African socialist with my principles based on an African heritage of communalism.

As the land was expropriated, however, the communal society was destroyed. The concepts of wealth within a communal society with no market economy sharply differed from those of white settlers, who wished to accumulate more despite the fact that they already had money in the banks. As a consequence, they possessed both land and other property of great value. To achieve their goal, they first had to deny the potential black labor force the control of its own means of production—the African soil.

Production within the communal society was motivated by absolute necessity, not by profit. When no community need was in sight—that could be met by future labor—the tendency was to stop working. Usually production ceased when domestic quotas were achieved for certain period. This acted as a builtin limit on output and there was no inherent propensity to evoke continuous work for the sake of accumulation.

In economic terms, the incentive to produce a surplus was lacking. Such an economic system had the effect, not only of keeping the communal societies self sufficient, but also of maintaining a uniform consumption pattern within the community. A yearning to diversity or expand markets could not arise.

The British set out to change that. In his works, Jack Wodd commented thus: "The breaking of this self-sufficiency, the destruction of African subsistence agriculture, became a central aim of imperialists' policy, pursued since the beginning of the twentieth century to this day, for a stable African peasant able to exist independent of European farms and mines, is the last thing imperialism could allow." The British began by issuing certificates of land ownership to give legal recognition to the appropriation of land by Europeans, leaving the African without legal title to his own land. Without land, the African could no longer be self-sufficient. This deliberate policy of the British colonial government aggravated African poverty. Through such ruthless economic persecution or strangulation, the African was coerced to go and sell his labor to a white capitalist. As the fertile land left to Africans diminished, the shifting cultivation system also vanished. The social repercussions of such transition hindered progress of the African people.

What, then, constitutes the alienation of labor? First, the fact that labor is external to the worker (i.e., work is not a part of his essential being), therefore, he does not affirm himself but denies himself—he does not feel content but unhappy, he does not develop freely his physical and mental energy, but mortifies his body and ruins his mind. The worker therefore only feels himself outside his work, and in his work feels outside himself. He is at home when he is not working, and when he is working he is not at home. His labor is therefore not voluntary, but coerced; it is forced labor. Labor is therefore not the satisfaction of a need; it is merely a means to satisfy needs external to it. This alien character emerges clearly in the fact that as soon as no physical or other compulsion exists, labor is shunned like the plague.

By 1936, the land occupied by the white settlers was declared to be British Crown Land. This brought to five-sixths the Malawian territory held by foreign owners. By 1954, more than 211,000 African tenants lived in this European agricultural sector and, 173,000 of these resided in the southern Region. Of the 595,000 hectares controlled by Europeans, only 40,000 hectares were utilized. African labor was used to farm that fraction during the best season which lasted three months. For the remaining nine months, idle land could not be employed productively by the African. The soil was no longer his, and even had it been, he could not employ hired labor like the Europeans because it was the African who served as the source of labor for the settlers' farms. He was destined to be not more than a small-scale peasant, directed to grow certain crops, most often cotton or tobacco (at one time 85 percent in value of Malawi's tobacco was produced by Africans). The Europeans who at first specialized in growing tea, later used the allegation that African cotton and tobacco production was too labor-consuming to be profitable unless they turned their technology to improving quality and yields. The African peasant was denied such benefits, and therefore could not compete in the open market. As the European sector slowly took up cotton and tobacco production, the African peasant was obliged to accept total dependence on the whites who regulated the market supply. The common characteristic of both sectors was that all products were for export. The aim was to keep Malawi's internal market extremely narrow and thereby to create the basis for a mono-cultural economy in which the entire nation's labor force would produce surpluses in a branch that could not be realized on the domestic market and could not be fulfilled by the United Kingdom herself.

This was the beginning of Malawi's economic structure—of total dependence on British capital and initiative. It reduced the socially balanced and self-sufficient indigenous people of Malawi to pawns in a market economy which was to disrupt their traditional pattern of work, leisure and consumption. The problem with market economy, as Marshall A. Sahlins once wrote, is that, "It makes available a dazzling array of products, good things in unlimited quantity and variety, each with its clarion-call price-tag. A man's desires are then inevitably beyond his grasp, for one never has enough to buy everything. Before the judgment of the market, the consumer stands condemned to scarcity and so to a life sentence of hard labor."

One tends to think of ownership and exploitation in terms of complex industrial and mining concerns. There are no industrial developments in Malawi. Instead, exploitation was rampant in the agricultural sector. It was not simply that the European sector engaged African farm labor for token wages, but that the white settlers imposed a feudal bond on people who once occupied the land by historical and tribal right. However, this exploitative system was inherited by political leaders, especially Hastings Banda, after independence.

Overnight, the Africans were transformed into tenants, obliged to give free labor to an alien landlord in return for the right to reside on land which had been arbitrarily taken from them in the name of a remote sovereign. Their labor was demanded by land owners at the peak cultivation period and thereby preventing African peasants from cultivating crops for their own families. The cash crops they were instructed to grow on allocated land could be sold only to the landlord at the price dictated by him. Such arrangements were officially recognized by the colonial government in Malawi under different names—but the differences were only theoretical.

In the southern Region, the system was called THANGATA which means, in local dialect, "Help," but such assistance was extracted from Africans at a cost of determined anti-colonial struggle. In the Central Region there was a visiting system which implied that the African family would stay only for limited times. In practice, the estate owner would provide the African with implements, fertilizer, and perhaps food and other subsidies to help him with crop cultivation until the end of the season when those favors were to be repaid. Very often they were not, simply for the reason that, the price paid by the landowner for the harvest was far too low, so low that it was not only below the market value, but also less than the production cost of the crop.

Once the African was in perpetual debt, he found himself under total subjugation and servitude. He had no union, could not strike, demand price increases, or leave the estate all together. He was driven to political impotence without a whip but by legal enactments—and force if necessary. If he did not work to clear his crop deficit, the landlord could evict his family and prosecute him.

In the crown lands, irrespective of income, an African had to pay poll or hut taxes. The District Administration (Natives) Ordinance of 1912 gave the Resident the power to concentrate the native population where necessary, in organized villages of not less than 20 huts, and to disallow the erection of isolated huts. The African chief, who was traditionally the symbolic head in his society, was induced to be the tax-collector. In 1918, he received ten shillings for every 300 taxes collected for the colonial power. In 1957, approximately 2.9 million dollars was handed over in hut taxes. Evidently, the chiefs did the collecting conscientiously for the more villagers they could extract taxes from, the higher their own annuities. As a consequence more and more Africans were obliged to look for paid employment in order to pay for their taxes. The chiefs were also said to be responsible for administrative work, maintenance of discipline, apprehension of criminals, and so forth. They did not, in most cases, have the consent of their communities to do so.

In the traditional tax of the society, the chief, acting as a kind of banker, used the reserves in a time of dire need only, and then for the equal benefit of everyone in his community. By contrast, the colonial taxation was used to bribe chiefs and to finance a colonial administration in the interests of exploitation.

During the Second World War, compulsory labor was added to the British exploitation of the African population of Malawi. They were coerced to serve in the European agricultural sectors at home and in the military fronts outside Malawi. During the years 1939-1945, more than 35,000 indigenous people of Malawi were serving in an imperialist war, while European settlers who remained in Malawi were able to take advantage of the war situation to compel Africans to labor on their land. Though only a tiny part of the global British Empire, Malawi was exploited to the extremes. Any monetary association between a big and small power tends to act in favor of the first. As in all colonized countries, the currency of the overseas sovereign was foisted on the indigenous people without their wish or consent. The disadvantages are obvious: (a) the reserves are kept abroad, together with foreign exchange, and (b) the colonial country can control expenditure if it wishes.

Britain used this prerogative during the Second World War to acquire what were, in effect, interest-free loans. At that time, military expenditure absorbed a significant part of the Malawi budget. Any economies realized through saving on expenditure, however, had to be surrendered to the British Treasury. Accordingly, at the beginning of 1945, Malawi refunded US$1 million which was three-quarters of the midyearly total budgetary expenditure. A further advantage to Britain, especially when she restored to currency control, was that her colonies could bolster the dollar pool in London.

Whatever the theoretical explanation, the total currency dependence of Malawi on Britain had elevated the former direct colonial rule to neocolonial status. There are several facts to prove this point. The most poignant is the November 1967 devaluation of Malawi's currency which coincided with the English devaluation of its own currency. The problem of monetary and financial exigency must be seen in relation to the overall economic commitments which the Banda regime undertook, especially the export of Malawi's human labor to former apartheid South Africa and former Rhodesia (Zimbabwe) and her pattern of trade which was dominated by reactionary nations. There was no need, from an economic point of view, for Malawi to devalue in 1967 since its economy was already being slowly infused by revenue from those countries which were not even affected by the devaluation. Similarly, when Britain changed to decimal currency on February 15, 1971, Malawi ignorantly followed suit. In place of the former pound, she adopted two new units, the Kwacha and the Tambala. The choice of the former is interesting in that Kwacha, which in Chinyanja and Tumbuka dialects means dawn, once had been a political slogan of both Nyasaland African Congress (NAC) and the dreaded Malawi Congress Party (MCP). But it was Zambia which first adopted the name for her currency, to the embarrassment of the Banda regime. But if Malawi had wished, she need not have waited for the British and Zambian initiative to adopt decimal currency. Logically, it would have been economical for Malawi to make the change during the early years of her independence, thus easing accounting problems in the trade transactions with countries of the world other than Britain.

Since the colonization of Malawi by Britain, the communal agricultural system which was destroyed, has not been replaced by a more highly developed mode of production. It remains half-feudal and semi-capitalist and closely tied to the colonial system of exploitation, keeping the people backward and poor and oblivious to their potential productive and political power.

Chapter Three

POLITICAL STRUGGLE

Seek ye political freedom first and everything will follow unto.
—Kwame Nkrumah

In Malawi, as in many parts of Africa, the political element came into being as a result of colonial domination and injustices that followed.

Before colonialism, slave trade played a very devastating role both physically and mentally among our populations. The rich civilization we inherited from our ancestors, was destroyed with impunity. Families were ruthlessly separated and many Africans were subsequently reduced to subhuman beings.

After slave trade was abolished towards the end of the 17th century, Europeans converged in Berlin, Germany to discuss the partition of Africa into discrete spheres of influence. But it was the infamous Berlin Conference of 1884 that was solely responsible for Africa's present instability. In fact, many people are in the opinion that the Conference was another form of indirect slavery. Ethnic groups were cut off from one another and intertwined societies were destroyed thus paving the way for economic degradation and exploitation. As in slavery, political influence played a brutal role in the minds of our people throughout the Continent.

In a fractured Africa, however, it was simple and easy to dictate terms to us because our strength to resist foreign domination had been vanquished. In view of the fact that today the nations of Europe are striving to create a solid and unified entity, the partition of Africa can now be seen as morally wrong because the division significantly hindered the Continent's advancement politically, economically, and socially.

Today, some argue that African development is possible only on the basis of a radical break with the international capitalist system which has been the principle agency of underdevelopment of Africa over the last five centuries. On the contrary, I strongly believe that the advancement of Africa's economies are part and parcel of global partnership. It would be catastrophic if Africa opts to go it alone against the highly technological nations of Europe and the Americas. In fact, we need each other in order to make world economies beneficial to all the people of this planet.

Mistrust, economic exploitation, and political oppression did not settle well among Africa's populations, hence, their desire to liberate themselves from its colonial yoke. Our people were convinced that only political liberty would eradicate injustices and enhance economic freedom and social justice. However, the outcome has been seemingly disastrous all over the Continent. In the 14th-16th centuries, much of Malawi was ruled by the ancient Munomatapa Empire and the smaller states succeeding it. At that time, the area was a major source of ivory and cotton—and cloth weaving had developed into an important local industry. The growth of nationalism in Malawi was hindered, as in other parts of Africa, by the readiness of the Chiefs to be cajoled into signing documents which they did not comprehend. Chief Kapeni of the Yao, for instance "sold" more than 3,000 acres for a gun, 32 yards of calico, two red caps, and a few other things. With a missionary, he also exchanged 26,000 acres for about 1,750 yards of calico. We can only surmise that chiefs like Kapeni looked upon such exchange as tokens of friendship. They did it in a spirit that, "If friends make gifts, gifts make friends." The settlers and missionaries preferred the view that gifts make slaves. As the class of landless Africans grew, and the colonial government introduced taxation as early as the 1890s in the Shire Highlands, Africans were compelled to work on the estates. The taxation of Africans came to substantially subsidize colonial expenses.

In 1913, more than one million Africans were said to supply about 70 percent of the annual revenue of the protectorate. They also produced the crops grown by the country's approximately 200 missionaries and 100 administrators who had effectively become their masters. If this point, on the eve of World War I, be taken as the time of transition to the most violent phase in Malawi's racial upheaval and injustice, we may as well try to sketch in briefly the events which contributed to it in the light of national consciousness.

It was during this period that Rev. John Chilembwe, the father of nationalism, having established a Mission Station in his District of Chiradzulu, observed all sorts of injustices done to his people by the colonial administration, European missionaries, and plantation owners. In the year of Rev. John Chilembwe's return from the US, 300 Malawi native troops of the Central African Regiment were sent to the Gold Coast (Ghana) to serve in the British Campaign against the Ashanti. Earlier, Nyasa soldiers from Nyasaland (Malawi), had been used as garrison troops and in many campaigns against rebellious tribal elements in Mauritius. Another contingent went to northern Rhodesia (Zambia) to oppose the recalcitrant Lunda chief, Kazembe. In these circumstances, John Chilembwe began to protest against African military recruitment. On behalf of those who lost parents or husbands in the Ashanti war, he demanded compensation for the families of African soldiers killed in action for the defense and consolidation of the British colonial territory. He objected to the Government's policy of forcing widows of such soldiers to pay tax. But his pleas did not stop the deaths of more than 150 of Malawi's native soldiers who fought with the British in the "Mad Mullah" campaigns against Somalis. The Malawi survivors returned to Zomba, the administrative capital in 1904.

The first World War had just begun and Nyasaland bordered Tanganyika (Tanzania), where Germans were recruiting Africans. Chilembwe foresaw the inevitable. Not content to have a million Malawians in servitude to the hundred-odd European planters, two hundred missionaries, and one hundred administrators, the British were willing to embroil their African subjects in a colonial conflict, ostensibly with Germans, but in reality, with black brothers from across the River Songwe, in northern Malawi. In the action of September 9-1,1914 on the border at the northern end of Lake Nyasa (Malawi), about 400 rifles on each side were engaged in heavy fighting. Both sides suffered heavy casualties in the dense forest around Karonga. The King's African Rifles (KAR) of Nyasaland lost 60 men, 49 Africans and eleven whites; the German Army of Tanganyika lost 112, more than a hundred, most being Africans. Tired and frustrated with the injustices meted out to his people, Chilembwe then protested in a long and famous letter published in the local Times, and concluded thus: "Let the rich men, bankers, titled men, storekeepers, farmers and landlords go to war and get shot instead of the poor Africans who have nothing to own and protect in the present world, who in death, leave only chains of widows and orphans in utter want and dire distress, and are invited to die for a cause which is not theirs. We leave all for the consideration of the government and hope that things will turn out well and that the government will recognize our indispensability and that justice will prevail."

As his protests were constantly ignored by the colonial powers, general emotions reached unprecedented heights. To drive his points home, Rev. John Chilembwe physically engaged in an armed struggle in 1915 to protest against injustices and foreign domination. In the course of action, Chilembwe was killed as he was trying to escape into Mozambique together with many of his followers. Although he did not achieve his prime objectives, his heroic demise inspired the people with determination, courage, and patriotism sufficient to spark fresh and concerted resistance to foreign rule and imperialism. It was as Nelson Mandela submitted in his own defense of himself and others accused of sabotage in the Rivonia trial in 1964:

> The time comes in the life of any nation when there remain only two choices; submit or fight. That time has now

come to south Africa. We shall not submit and we have no choice, but to hit back by all means in our power in defense of our people, our future, and our freedom.

Obviously, that time had come to Malawi, too. The myth of Chilembwe lives on and the National Liberation Movement was conceived. That it waited for another World War to pass before giving birth to the Nyasaland African Congress (NAC) can be accounted for by the government in recognizing the principal headman as the only authentic voice of the African people.

The initiative was taken in 1924 by Frederick G. Njilima, son of Duncan Njilima who had been executed for his part in the Chilembwe rebellion, by writing on behalf of the South Nyasa Native Association (SNNA) to the Chief Secretary of the Phelps-Stokes Educational Commission which was at that time visiting Nyasaland:

> We are aware of the fact that education in Nyasaland is in a lower stage than that of any other British possession. We take this opportunity of assuring you that every member of this body is ready to support and follow you to better this condition.[i]

By 1933, there were no less than 15 different associations to keep the few Nyasas with good education contentedly occupied in debate according to the British conventions of the day.

Their Constitutional approaches could not be turned into a genuinely popular mass movement towards radical change, since their membership was limited to the few educated elite. The result was that when the first meeting of Nyasaland African Association was convened by J. F. Sangala in January 1944, it issued a memorandum which unconsciously echoed the standpoint of John Chilembwe before World War I:

> In conclusion, we beg to state that we have served loyally in any war which His Majesty has asked our boys to

---

[i] *The Rise of Nationalism in Central Africa*, by Robert I. Rotberg.

serve and we think this is the time that we should ask for justice so that our boys and girls may enjoy the freedom of being part and parcel of the British Empire. We cannot go on allowing our country becoming a labor centre for the neighboring territories, we must have justice done. We ask you to give us the right to speak for our people, be it in the mission council or in the bodies that govern our country. We have paid the price and it must be compensated accordingly. It is not a question of being ungrateful, but seventy years of patience is a very long time to wait.

Finally, the Nyasaland African Congress (NAC) was inaugurated in October 1944, being one of the first political movements to agitate for self-determination in Central and southern Africa, The various associations were automatically incorporated into the Congress, which undertook to agitate and advocate by just and constitutional means against any discrimination.

They elected Levy Mumba as the first President, and other office bearers were leaders of the same associations: J. F. Sangala, Charles Matinga, Charles Mlanga, Lewis Bandawe, L. S. Mataka and C. C. Chinula. The Congress in turn, created other affiliated associations—for example, The Women's Movement, Trade Unions, and Chiefs' Councils.

The fact that Levy Mumba hailed from the north, our predecessors proved that the politics of ethnicity was not only immoral, but also destructive and unlike the present-day politicians who are guided by tribal or ethnical sentiments. As Levy Mumba and his team phased out due to age and other anomalies, the younger generation stepped in to spearhead the struggle. The task before the Congress was to instill a political con-sciousness into the people for a transitional phase that could create a mass liberation movement capable of fighting for its freedom.

The major problems then facing the Congress were: (a) creating a revolutionary stratagem, and (b) finding a leader from its own ranks to lead the struggle.

Basically, there was no shortage of leadership in the Congress, but power struggles played a destructive role that saw the movement less than effective. Amongst the young nationalists, Orton C. Chirwa was the eldest of them all with brilliant academic achievements earned at Livingstonia (Mumbwe) in Malawi, in southern Rhodesia (Zimbabwe) schools, and at the prestigious Fort Hare University in South Africa. There he met among other people; Nelson Mandela, Charles Njonjo, former Kenyan Attorney General, and Robert Mugabe of Zimbabwe.

Apart from Orton Chirwa there was also Manoah Chirwa, and both men hailed from Nkhata Bay in northern Malawi. The latter was older than the former and with impressive academic achievements. He was a very able politician and a terrific orator, but he was gravely handicapped by a fatal obsession—comfort. He hated radicalism because he thought it might produce riots and lead him and others to prison, or, it might demand his resignation from the Federal Assembly whose membership made him, by the African standard, a rich man—something inconsistent with the country's opposition to Federation.

Manoah Chirwa's involvement in the Federal politics made him an unlikely candidate to lead the Congress. After his fall, T. D. T. Banda (no relation to Hastings Banda) who also hailed from Nkhata Bay, northern Malawi, became the hero of the Congress. Meanwhile, it was understood that Kanyama Chiume and Masauko Chipembere, two leading young nationalists with vast political knowledge, maintained contact with a man they had never seen before—one who lived in America, Britain and Gold Coast (Ghana). This mysterious man used to be known as Richard Willem Armstrong while in the United States, but later on, and for reasons known only to himself, he became known as Hastings Banda and when in Nyasaland, he added the middle name "Kamuzu" to authenticate his nationality.

Squabbles in the Congress persisted and this contributed to a large extent to the movement's inability to effect solid resistance against colonial domination. All this emanated from power struggles among the young nationalists. Meanwhile, time was running out and the political emotions of the people were becoming uncontrollable, hence, the Congress held a small meeting and mandated T. D. T. Banda, a senior official in the Congress, to proceed to Kumasi, Ghana where Hastings Banda was living and practicing his medicine in order to interview him. However, a good number of party officials did not favor the notion of importing a leader they had not seen before.

Despite strong opposition the plan went ahead. T. D. T. Banda left Chileka Airport, Blantyre, in September 1956 for Kumasi, Ghana where Dr. Banda was living. As expected, T. D. T. Banda felt strongly unimpressed with Hastings Banda's lack of political and cultural backgrounds that could enhance the building of a viable movement capable of uniting the people of Malawi for a progressive future. A second disappointment came to T. D. T. Banda when it was discovered that the future leader could not utter a single word in Chichewa (his local dialect). Furthermore, when asked who his parents were and where he was born, he looked pale and refused to answer the questions. This steeled T. D. T. Banda's earlier suspicions about the future "Messiah."

On the political front, T. D. T. Banda wanted to gain an inside glimpse of Hastings Banda's views on Nyasaland and Africa, but still he was vague and not forthcoming with convincing ideas and plans that could be put in place.

Towards the end of September 1956, Thomas Dillon T. Banda left Kumasi, Ghana a disappointed and confounded man. On arrival at Chileka International Airport in Blantyre, Thomas Banda told the reporters that he had interviewed Dr. Banda at length and his conclusions were that he (Dr. Banda) was not the right man to lead the Congress—let alone become the future leader of our nation. On reporting back to his colleagues two days after his arrival, the message was received with a mixture of skepticism and disbelief and T. D. T. Banda was accused of harboring ambitions of leading the Congress himself. Some members of the Central Committee went further by branding him an imperialist dupe. However, he was not cowed down by accusations of such magnitude and he told his colleagues point blank that by importing a leader, who had neither political vision nor cultural background, we are unwittingly committing political suicide and handing over our national pride to an alien monster, the sequel of which would be fatal and calamitous to future generations.

Nevertheless, the top brass of the Congress remained unconvinced with T. D. T. Banda's explanation, but he stood his ground and maintained that Hastings Banda was not the right man to lead the Congress.

T. D. T. Banda, who had become the hero of the Congress after the fall of Wellington Manoah Chirwa and might have become an obstacle to the enthronement of Dr. Banda, fortunately or unfortunately found his name entangled in a financial scandal that got him expelled from the Congress. However, his expulsion did not weaken his determination to oppose Dr. Banda's importation because he was convinced beyond any doubt that an imported leader, who lacked both vision and African culture, would do more harm to the nation than good. T. D. T. Banda went down fighting and eventually he formed his own political party known as The Liberation Party. Basically, that Party's platform was to oppose the importation of Dr. Banda and to fight for Nyasaland's independence. Despite his endeavors to block Dr. Banda's importation, it was at an emergency conference that the Congress resorted to the notion of importing a leader. In early 1957, Dr. Banda who had lived 40 years in a political wilderness in the United States, Britain and Ghana, was officially invited to return to Nyasaland (Malawi) and assume the leadership of the Congress.

By April 1958, the Presidency of the Congress was confirmed or opened to Dr. Banda and on July 6, 1958, the Messiah (Dr. Banda) arrived at Chileka International Airport about 23 km from Blantyre, the country's commercial city. At the airport, the crowd was orderly, but emotions were high. Some of the party officials upon meeting Dr. Banda for the first time, doubted his ethnicity and agreed with T. D. T. Banda's perception. One such leader was Mikeka Mkandawire, from Rumphi West in northern Malawi, who openly asserted that, from his looks, Hastings Banda was not a Nyasa and we had made a grave political mistake that will change our political directions for generations to come and we shall again remember the wise advice of T. D. T. Banda.

Dr. Banda was driven to a house arranged for him in Limbe a few kilometers from Blantyre. As he was settling down, Orton Chirwa jokingly asked him to point to the direction of Kasungu. To the astonishment of everybody who was in the house at that time, Dr. Banda pointed to the south where Malawi shares a border with Mozambique. After being corrected, and told that from where he was Kasungu lies to the north, Dr. Banda cautiously said, "Its been a long time since I left this country and I might have lost track of my geography." Kasungu is supposed to be Dr. Banda's home town in Central Malawi.

News of his arrival spread like a prairie wild fire within the country, but there were some reservations among Nyasas–even from those who worked for his return. The fact that Dr. Banda abandoned his business in Ghana to return home, when called upon, was interpreted by many as a selfless act and proof of his patriotism. Many others maintained that no true patriot could sit idly waiting for a letter of invitation. The late Masauko Chipembere in his memoir, "My Malawian Ancestors," criticized Banda as a "foreigner" who having been absent 43 years and did not have the knowledge of the Malawi people and their aspirations for a good leader. The view that a revolutionary leader might emerge only after extremely complicated and close contact with his people is akin to Marx's concept that, "The educator must be educated."

There were some strong suggestions that Dr. Banda accepted an invitation to return home because he was embroiled in scandals that infuriated his host President Kwame Nkrumah. It was alleged that the diminutive doctor was performing abortions on young school girls and Nkrumah contemplated declaring him persona non grata. In Britain, Dr. Banda was wanted on charges of eloping with somebody's wife by the name of Mrs. E. French. To avoid embarrassment, he had no alternative but to reluctantly accept an invitation to go to the country about which he knew very little.

The young nationalists who dominated the rank and file of the Congress defended the importation of Dr. Banda because in their views, they were convinced that Malawians would respect an elderly and educated leader. Hence, an overwhelming campaign on behalf of the supreme leader was in the making. Dr. Banda was portrayed as the most educated man on the continent, the richest man in the country, and one time it was asserted that he performed medical surgery on one of the royal families in England. Of course, these were the words Malawians wanted to hear. His name was held in veneration throughout the country and in the meantime, the self-styled Messiah slowly but surely consolidated his position in the Congress. This perception, however, was both misleading and hollow because among their ranks, Orton E. C. Chirwa had both of the desired qualities. There was no good reason therefore, for the Congress to even suggest the notion of importing a leader who had no knowledge of the nature of the struggle.

In neighboring Tanganyika (Tanzania), Julius Kambarage Nyerere was younger than Orton Chirwa and had just acquired his M.Sc. degree in economics from Edinburgh University. In northern Rhodesia (Zambia), Kenneth David Kaunda, with Nyasa parents and five years younger than Orton Chirwa, completed Form Two (a Junior Certificate) and qualified as a teacher. The point is, if these two young nationalists could mobilize and command respect among their people, how could Orton Chirwa, a top notch lawyer and Queen's Counsel (QC) as well as being an experienced politician, fail to lead the Congress to independence?

Candidly, Dr. Banda's history has been, to a large extent, very conspicuous and misleading. There are good reasons to believe that Dr. Banda was an impostor. To impress Malawians he cooked up a story, supported by the Congress, that he attended school at Livingstonia Mission in northern Malawi. One day when he was writing his final examination, things somehow went wrong and he was disqualified from continuing with the examination. The invigilator (exam proctor) thought the young Banda was cheating. Upset with the misfortune, he left Livingstonia and, purportedly, traveled on foot through thick forests to Rhodesia (Zimbabwe). At that time we were told he was thirteen years of age.

But, at the age of thirteen, one wonders how he survived the threats of warlike tribes, cannibals, and pernicious wild beasts from Nyasaland through Mozambique and into Rhodesia—a distance of over a thousand kilometers on the often impassable roads or paths of the early 20s. In Rhodesia, we were told that the young Banda settled in Hatley, a small town south of the present day Harare, before proceeding to the Dominion of South Africa. It is true however, that at that time Nyasas trekked to South Africa in search of work, but they traveled in groups and when they approached South Africa, they divided into smaller groups to evade detection or arrests by the authorities. It is therefore hard to believe that the young Banda traveled alone under such perilous circumstances.

Further, if he was accompanied by older people, couldn't he recall even one of them? However, debate on Banda's mysterious trek was brutally curtailed and several lucid Malawians landed in prison when they tried to disprove the authenticity of the story.

As many Malawians began to question the authenticity of his story, the sadistic despot changed the story. This time, his attendance at Livingstonia was erased from the history books. Malawians were now told that Dr. Banda attended school in Kasungu, Central Malawi which he claimed to be his ancestral home. It was alleged that the Ngwazi (Lion), as he was popularly known, attended classes under the tree called "Kachere" where the present-day Kamuzu Academy stands, but he could not mention who his teacher was, let alone any of his classmates. The Kamuzu Academy is a replica of Britain's Eton—an elite institution. At this Academy, Banda wouldn't allow blacks to teach because, according to him, Africans were not qualified enough and did not speak Latin—one of the major subjects at the Academy. He claimed that anybody who could not speak Latin, was not educated, but unfortunately, he himself could not speak the language. The entire roster of staff members were white expatriates drawing exuberant salaries which by far exceeded those of their counterparts (Africans) in other schools and colleges. The Academy cost taxpayers more than US$20 million—funds which Banda claimed came from his own purse.

As time went by, there was an emerging consensus that our politicians had abdicated their integrity by imposing a mendacious leadership on us. The conundrum of Dr. Banda's ethnicity will live with us for generations to come and our children and great grandchildren will never be taught the true story of the cold-blooded despot whose rule destroyed the very fabric of the Malawian society. However, it is strongly believed that Hastings Banda was not his real name. Most probably his authentic name was Richard Willem Armstrong and born outside of Nyasaland (Malawi), presumably in the United States of America.

Some Malawian historians speculate that Dr. Banda might have stolen the name from Mphonongo Banda who went to the States much earlier to study Theology and later became Armstrong's godfather. Most Malawians still ponder whether Banda was really a Malawian. His characteristics and behavior giving little credence to that claim. Generally, Malawians are impetuous, God-fearing and humane. On the contrary, Banda was ruthless, inhumane, and inclined to look down upon others.

There is no single Malawian, be it scholars or otherwise, who knows Banda's parents, his clan, or his childhood life. Cecilia Tamanda Kadzamila, who lived with him for more than thirty years before his demise, could not trace his roots. It is an open secret that Cecilia Kadzamila was a driving force behind Banda's brutal leadership. She lived with Banda as a concubine and wielded immense powers that sent many people, especially the northerners, into concentration camps. Many others lost their jobs on fixed-up reasons. When Banda's health was deteriorating, she and her uncle John Z. Tembo took the control of government affairs.

Having acquired massive wealth through dubious means, Dr. Banda created an illusory dynasty among his so-called tribesmen. However, the issue of Dr. Banda's ethnicity came into prominence soon after the struggle for multiparty started in 1992. It became a criminal offense to discuss or question his roots. Now that he is no more, what disturbs the majority of our people is the direction in which their country is sailing. They are realizing that the people who succeeded him, are people much like him—without integrity, murderers, corrupt tribalists, and diehard opportunists who lack national vision and senses of self-esteem.

After Dr. Banda assumed the leadership of the Congress, served to him on a silver platter, he forthwith created a myth (a personality cult) around himself and impressed his audience with charismatic fervor and a sense of statesmanship. However, the people of Malawi were not lucky enough to foresee that they had welcomed a "Messiah" who would, in the foreseeable future, turn himself into a Frankenstein-like monster. In fact, it was a false start for Malawi.

There was absolutely nothing novel that the so-called Messiah had brought into a promised land apart from two messages that were to become his political rallying call: "I came to Nyasaland to do two things only; (a) to break their stupid Federation, and (b) to bring to you my people your independence." This became the dictator's hallmark message for the rest of his political career and the people of Malawi were left in a long tunnel of darkness as to what would follow after independence.

Clearly and disappointingly, Banda lacked a sense of commitment and dwelt almost entirely on a personality cult that diverted his anticipated leadership from real issues and notions. Before he took over the leadership of the Congress which was formed by others while he was in the political wilderness, political emotions were high and people spoke of physical confrontation with the colonial authorities. Time had ran out and people could no longer wait. They resorted to spontaneous and sporadic violence in the last months of 1958. By early 1959, the colonial government could not control the situation. The Governor intimated that his administration was on the point of abdicating its responsibility unless it was reinforced. European Territorial Forces (ETF) of 6,000 men were then mobilized in southern Rhodesia (Zimbabwe). On March 3, 1959, the colonial authorities declared a State of Emergency and banned the Nyasaland African Congress (NAC) under the orders of the Governor, Sir Robert Armitage.

Under the five-year Economic Plan which was due in three months, airports had been improved for such a contingency and large military planes were able to land. As mass arrests were made, these aircraft flew detainees to the Rhodesian jails of Khami in Bulawayo and Marandellas near Salisbury (Harare). Port extensions on Lake Nyasa (Malawi) allowed the ship MV Ilala, to berth at Nkhata Bay, northern Malawi to also carry prisoners who were ferried from Karonga to Chipoka, southern Malawi.

More than 1,300 members of the Nyasaland African Congress were arrested, from its President down to local branch chairmen and active supporters. Africans clashed with the Armed Forces and the Police. Many arrests were brutal and troops, flown in from Rhodesia, were used to control the population in troublesome areas by employing a good deal of physical violence on villagers rounded up for interrogation. Fifty-one deaths were officially reported and by mid-August 1959, 134 Africans had been convicted and sentenced for periods ranging from six months to ten years for their actions during the emergency.

More than half of the slaughtered civilians were reported in Nkhata Bay, northern Malawi where a colonial District Commissioner John Brock took personal charge in the melee. Astonishingly, John Brock became Banda's personal adviser after self-government—a move that was seen by many as Banda's willingness to turn Malawi into a neocolonial client state.

In its report to the British Government, the Devlin Commission emphasized the popular basis of the demonstrations against the government, stating that it was not open to question. Politicians, chiefs, and peasants in the crowds with their sticks and stones were, in the opinion of the commission and of virtually all observers present during the emergency, united against the Federation and in support of the Congress.

The political awareness of the Malawi masses is borne out by the overwhelming response to the formation of a new movement, the Malawi Congress Party (MCP), to replace the banned Nyasaland African Congress (NAC).

This new political party was formed by Orton Edgar Chingoli Chirwa, QC, one of the few African lawyers in the country and the only Queen's Counsel in Southern, Eastern, and Central Africa. Chirwa became the first President of the new party and showed diligence and leadership acumen during turbulent times.

Mr. Orton Chirwa was the first top leader to be released from prison within a few months of his arrest prompting suspicions among fellow leaders and people at large, especially within the former Executive Committee of the Nyasaland African Congress. M. W. K. Chiume, another of the top leaders and an ardent nationalist, went further by suggesting that Chirwa might have been corrupted by the Colonial agents to confuse and delay the process of independence.

Despite confusion, within two days of the formation of the new Party, 2,000 members were enrolled. By the end of 1959, there were 15,000 and, in early 196, one-sixth of Malawi's population, 500,000 people were registered supporters. While Dr. Banda and some leaders were still in prison, Chirwa continued to prove himself a genuine and competent leader of the Malawi Congress Party.

What was remarkable in this is that without military organization which was denied them, the masses had nevertheless dealt the blow that awakened world opinion. Condemnations from such state leaders as Kwame Nkrumah (Ghana), Julius K. Nyerere (Tanganyika), Sekou Toure (Guinea), Gamal A. Nasser (UAR), and Jawaharlal Nehru of India were unequivocal. "Political prisoners must be released and then the people of Nyasaland should be allowed to decide their own destiny," said these leaders.

After 18 months, Banda was released on the Fools' Day, April 1, 1961 from Gweru prison in Rhodesia and forthwith with due respect and dignity, Orton Chirwa handed the Presidency of the Congress Party to Dr. Hastings Banda. It must be noted, however, that Banda did not play a major role, as we are made to believe, in the freedom struggle of the Malawian People. From the outset, Banda was handed the leadership like manna from heaven. When he arrived in the country, he found the people of Nyasaland in high political emotions and highly organized under the banner of the Nyasaland African Congress and when he came out of prison, he found Malawians had joined the Malawi Congress Party en masse under the able Presidency of Orton Chirwa, proudly and confidently marching toward freedom and independence.

Some lucid Malawians began to wonder whether it was imperative to import a leader who was ignorant of the political and cultural setup within the wide range of African society. However, as days went by, the majority of our people agreed that it was a foregone conclusion that Banda or no Banda, the imposed Central African Federation was going to tumble like the "Berlin Wall" and that freedom and independence were inevitable. But the highhandedness of the Congress itself, discouraged people from airing their grievances in the open.

From the prison in Gweru, Banda came out a completely changed man. His earlier radicalism had waned disappointingly and he behaved very suspiciously. In Gweru, Banda enjoyed the life of a free man. He was given two rooms, one as his bed room and, the other, as a sitting and reading room. I had an opportunity to see these places when our prison truck stopped over in Gweru to take some prisoners to Harare Central Prison. I was incarcerated at Bulawayo Greys Prison because my presence there was deemed subversive because our organization, the Congress for the Second Republic of Malawi (CSR), under the leadership of Kanyama Chiume former Minister of Foreign Affairs in the Banda regime, was attracting overwhelming support from Malawians living and working in Zimbabwe. My articles in the Bulawayo Chronicle under the editorship of Geoff Nyarota, one of Zimbabwe's respected and fearless journalists, critical of the Banda thuggish regime, contributed to my arrest because the Malawi Government launched an official complaint against me with the Zimbabwe Government which was, at that time, trying to cultivate friendly relations with Banda's Malawi despite the latter's collusion with the minority settler regime of Ian D. Smith.

When Banda returned to Nyasaland from his Rhodesian Prison, he was received with a hero's welcome from his people believing that his time in prison had effectively radicalized his political will toward the freedom struggle. On the contrary, he came out a neutralized and indoctrinated Messiah.

He toured the nation giving speeches unheard before. He urged his people not to give trouble to the whites. Malawians had to endure speech after speech that carried absolutely nothing other than self-glorification. His incarceration in Gweru prison became a rallying cry, his previous defiant speeches were no longer there, and people gradually saw Banda dangerously drifting into a submissive trend and treachery.

For the 18 months Banda was in Gweru prison, he considered himself a hero and champion of the freedom struggle of the Malawian people. He made relentless noise about Gweru, though he had been already capitulated to the imperialist machinations. On the contrary, Nelson Mandela, the first black President of South Africa, spent almost thirty years in

Roben Island Prison breaking granite stones, but he has never ever mentioned the words: "When I was in Roben Island...." Generally, the majority of lucid Malawians concede that Gweru was the genesis of the present day political failures in Malawi.

Before the leaders of the Congress were released, the British government had already opened discussions on a Constitution for Nyasaland. Though the Party had advocated a peaceful policy during the disturbances, there were indications that its President would in the future encounter opposition to the perceived moderate stance. The press seized the opportunity to project Banda as a hero of his people and called for his release from Gweru Prison. However, it was possible that his premature release was premeditated, for when he emerged into the limelight he participated in preliminary negotiations with Secretary of State for the Colonies, Ian McLeod. The other leaders of the Congress were deliberately kept in confinement five months more.

Five groups participated in drawing up the Constitution of Malawi: (a) the Colonial Office headed by the Minister of State for the Colonies; (b) the Colonial Government in Malawi headed by the Colonial Governor; (c) the White settlers led by Michael Blackwood with the Nyasaland division of Welensky's United Federal Party dubbed the United Fools Party; (d) the Malawi Congress Party headed by Hastings Banda; and (e) a smaller group called the Liberation Party led by Thomas Dillon T, Banda (no relation to Hastings Banda). The document that emerged from this Constitutional Conference held in London in November 1962, included the following items:

- Financial measures and measures affecting the Public Service may not be introduced into the Legislative Council without the consent of the Governor in his discretion.

- The Governor had a general reserved power to legislate by certifying that any Bill introduced into the Legislative Council had been passed, whether or not it had been submitted to, or received the support of, the majority of the Council.

- The power to assent, or refuse assent, to Bills was exercised by the Governor in his discretion and he could reverse any Bill for Her Majesty's pleasure.
- Her Majesty could disallow any law enacted by the Nyasaland Legislature.

As expected, Sir Roy Welensky sent a telegram to the Secretary of State for the Colonies who had said he would require to be satisfied that the necessary experience in working the Constitution had been gained before recommending a further advance. He concluded thus:

> We can only wait and see how reasonable Banda and Nyasaland interpret the conference undertakings. They have not got off to an auspicious start with Banda's interpretation of the conference as meaning the breakup of the Federation.

Roy Welensky and his party were somewhat suspicious of contacts between Banda and McLeod. Once the United Federal Party settlers in Nyasaland asked the Colonial Secretary if he had formed any opinion about Banda and, "Was he likely to adopt a more reconciliatory outlook?" According to Welensky, McLeod replied, "He had not hitherto met the little doctor, but from reading his speeches he had concluded that Banda was a vain little man and he had not previously understood him, and was astonished to discover that he was completely ignorant about the economic aspects of the government."

Some prominent Malawians, however, began to agree with T. D. T. Banda's perception of the importation of Dr. Banda, who according to T. D. T. Banda lacked qualities of progressive leadership. His release from detention exacerbated his suspicious behavior, prompting frustrations and disappointments. From the time of his arrival in Nyasaland, and having completed almost four years as a resident, the majority of the people did not notice his credibility at all. From prison, his radicalism had been visibly diminished and reduced to a moderate quisling—and signs of dictatorship in him began to show its ugly head. His moderation shocked and frustrated his colleagues to the extent that some even contemplated forming their own political party to challenge him.

What the people of Malawi had seen in him was a Messiah leading them through a long dark tunnel and accompanied by endless rhetoric: "Do not give trouble to the whites and, I came here to do two things and two things alone, to break their stupid Federation and to give you my people your independence." This speech became Dr. Banda's hallmark and he used it during his entire tenure in office. He had no vision whatsoever for a future independent Malawi and that prompted speculations that the political and economic future of an independent nation was at risk of sliding into instability.

Despite Banda's hidden agenda and his weaknesses, the people of Malawi continued to press their demands for self-rule and independence. At that time, Great Britain had principally accepted decolonization as inevitable, and agreed to universal adult voting rights. In the first assembly elections held in April 1961, the Malawi Congress Party (MCP) won a majority of seats and in January 1963, Nyasaland won internal self-governance and Dr. Hastings Banda became its first Prime Minister.

Malawi people were filled with joy and happiness for the occasion they had so long been waiting for. In Rhodesia (Zimbabwe), African nationalists were quick to denounce Banda as an imperialist dupe representing the interests of white hegemony. George Nyandoro and James Chikerema went further describing Banda as an impostor. In response, in his capacity as Publicity Secretary of the MCP, Kanyama Chiume defended Banda as an ardent freedom fighter and warned Nyandoro and Chikerema not to meddle into the internal affairs of Malawi. In the later years, however, the two leading Zimbabwean nationalists, were proved right.

Forthwith after self-governance, Banda showed his true colors. His behavior changed from bad to worse. He started calling his ministers, "My boys" in public rallies and in front of their wives and children. Wherever he went to public gatherings he reminded his people to watch the movements of his ministers and report to the Party Headquarters any suspicious moves. Basically, in his relentless speeches throughout the country, there was no single grain of visionary direction as to what was in stock for the country's future in the wake of the unprecedented rise of his personality cult.

Throughout the period of self-rule, Banda concentrated on building his own image as the liberator of his people and arrogantly continued to frustrate and humiliate his colleagues. It reached a point, however, that some of his ablest rising stars within the Party could no longer brook such degrading humiliation. For instance, Dunduzu Kaluli Chisiza, one of the brightest young nationalists Malawi had ever produced, contemplated forming his own political Party or leaving the country for self-imposed exile in Tanganyika (Tanzania).

When Dunduzu approached his brother and best friend Yatuta Kaluli Chisiza for advice, he was told such a move would give the colonial authorities the needed ammunition to delay the independence process in view of the fact that such a move would also cause confusion in the country. Dunduzu's respect for his brother was unquestionably high and he heeded the vivid advice, but the emotions remained equally high.

With due respect, Dunduzu had emerged as a shinning star joining the ranks of Masauko Chipembere, Kanyama Chiume, Augustine Bwanausi Yatuta Chisiza, Orton Chirwa and many others behind them. He was educated at Livingstonia Mission, the cradle of education in the Rumphi District of northern Malawi and went to Uganda where he joined the prestigious Kings College Budo and passed his Cambridge School Certificate "O" Level with impressive marks and from there went to England where he joined the London School of Economics.

Dunduzu got a prestigious job with the Indian High Commission in Rhodesia. While there, he joined the political struggle against white minority rule. With his brilliant academic achievements, he helped form Rhodesia's first Youth League along side George Nyandoro and James Chikerema. He played an important role in the execution of the movement's goals and aspirations that attracted wide support among African youth that threatened the colonial establishment. Dunduzu's involvement in the Rhodesian political struggle gave him vital experience for the future political struggle in his fatherland, Nyasaland. His stay in Rhodesia was a thorn in the white-men's flesh, hence, he was declared persona non grata in the early 1950s.

Back home, Dunduzu joined the Nyasaland African Congress (NAC) with his brother Yatuta Kaluli Chisiza who had opened a butcher shop in Blantyre, the commercial city. Among the young nationalists Dunduzu, as he was popularly known, proved extremely intelligent and a fiery orator.

After self-government was granted in 1961, Dunduzu was appointed Deputy Minister of Finance by Prime Minister Hastings Banda. The Minister of Finance was a former colonial bureaucrat with limited experience in the field. Realistically, if Dunduzu were to be made the Minister of Finance, he could emerge as the most successful Minister in post-independent Malawi. Of all the rising stars in Malawian politics, Banda feared Dunduzu the most because of his intellectual outlook. Therefore, to appoint him Minister of Finance, was the last thing the tin-pot dictator could have done.

But it was Dunduzu and his brother Yatuta Kaluli Chisiza who saved the life of Dr. Banda in 1958 at Chopi grounds in Blantyre when the Federal troops went to disrupt the meeting that was organized by the Nyasaland African Congress. As the troops were charging through the multitude of people to reach the podium, Dunduzu and his brother Yatuta grabbed the trembling Messiah and rushed him to a waiting car. As one white soldier rushed to deliver a blow, Yatuta dragged the diminutive doctor into the back seat of the car and mounted a daring defense to protect him from being hurt. In doing so, Yatuta was struck in the head by a rifle butt causing oozing blood to cover his face. Thanks to the two gallant brothers, who sacrificed their own dear lives, they saved the life of a brutal monster.

In the Congress, Dunduzu played a pivotal role in mobilizing the masses for future nation-building on socialist principles because he fervently believed that only socialism, based on cultural heritage, would destroy the colonial deep-rooted tendencies of greed and selfishness.

During the period July 18th-28th, 1962, Dunduzu Kaluli Chisiza organized the famous Nyasaland Economic Symposium under the theme: The Temper, Aspiration, and Problems of Contemporary Africa. The paper he presented to the multitude of international delegates set out to provide the background against which the attempt to relate principles of economic development to African economic development should be made. It portrayed the mood, the aspirations, the determination, and the problems of contemporary Africa. Insight into these emotions and problems was deemed essential if foreign experts were to give effective and acceptable advice.

Dunduzu (Du) spoke at length on an African unification that should have meaningful content for the ordinary Africans (and it is these who matter)—an effort must be made to inculcate a political loyalty which is higher than nationalism. A deliberate campaign by nationalist movements to instill regional consciousness, and subsequently Pan-Africanism, into the minds of the masses must be undertaken forthwith.

The vision Du held for the unification of Africa, vividly matched with Nkrumah's vision of continental unity and drew a parallel line against the present notions of the so-called Union of Africa orchestrated by Muammar Gaddafi of Libya after being frustrated and ignored by his fellow Arabs in the dysfunctional Arab League.

In this symposium, Du astonished the highly professional and emotional gathering with his eloquence and the amount of knowledge in political and economic fields. He prophetically warned the delegates about the dangers of investing absolute powers into the hands of a single person. His speech however, was based on issues which the majority of Malawians had in mind. In his highly accomplished book, Africa—What Lies Ahead? Dunduzu repeated his warning shots to his people and Africans elsewhere not to abdicate the reigns of power to single individuals, as this might lead to abuse of powers and eventually to brutal dictatorship. Indeed, he foresaw the dangers of autocracy coming before most of his colleagues, and this obviously made Banda nervous, hence Du became Banda's prime target.

One month after his brilliant and prophetic speech at the Symposium, Dunduzu died in a car accident between Blantyre-Zomba at Nthondwe Bridge in September 1962. His tragic demise shocked the entire nation and most believed the accident was spurious. The circumstances in which he died are very similar to the shocking deaths of Dick Matenje, Aaron Gadama, Twaibu Sangala and David Chiwanga.

All four were senior Cabinet Ministers in Banda's regime. The motive behind the killings, many Malawians believe, was that the former were increasingly disillusioned with Banda's highhandedness in his move to exalt John Tembo, his lifetime henchman, and the uncle to Cecilia Tamanda Kadzamila—the concubine Banda lived with for more than three decades.

The mere fact that Banda did not attend Dunduzu's funeral nor did he initiate an enquiry into his tragic death, speaks volume. One version revealed that he was murdered in cold-blood by Banda's killer-squad in the Malawi Congress Party Headquarters, driven in his own Mercedes Benz car, and dumped at Nthondwe Bridge so that his death would look like he was involved in a car accident.

Though we may speak volumes, Du will not come back. Malawians have been robbed of a talented leader, indisputable visionary, brilliant intellectual and a true son of Africa. Du has indeed been irreplaceable. The politics of novel Malawi, had been dominated by a single person not as a political leader, but as a Traditional Paramount Chief with absolute powers. He ruled Malawians with impunity and disrespect and led the whole nation into a tranquilized and unthinking state.

For the majority of our people, the struggle for nationhood rested in Banda's hands and it was strongly believed that without him, freedom and independence were empty words. Now it is impossible to change the history of a nation. The struggle for our freedom has had some great names that are jealously and deliberately ignored. Masauko Chipembere and Kanyama Chiume are cases in point, their names are synonymous with Malawian politics whether one likes it or not.

In their early 20s, these young nationalists were the focus of our struggle. At the age of 26, Masauko Chipembere (popularly known as Chip) was elected into the Legislative Council with a Nyasaland African Congress ticket. However, he did not feel himself to be much of a newcomer to politics. He had related earlier how the Federation controversy produced an interest in politics in him in his first school year and how at college he specialized in political subjects in his curriculum.

Apart from this academic preparation for playing a role in the liberation struggle at home, he had also taken a keen interest in the political clubs and party branches operating in the college. He joined the South African National Congress (ANC) Youth League as a card-carrying member and was admitted to some of their covert meetings and political study cells. The latter were very educative and gave him a fairly sound appreciation of the political essentials of the African situation. It was in these cells that Chipembere developed his passionate belief in leadership, or at least guidance, by intellectuals in the African revolution.

He also attended processions and public meetings called by the South African Congress. This is what he observed. They had some very brilliant orators down there, whatever else they might lack, and one listening to them cannot resist the impact of their eloquence. It was typical of all greatly oppressed populations—they tend to throw up magnetic leaders and demagogues.

Mr. M. Chipembere met Kanyama Chiume almost fresh from Makerere University College in Uganda. Makerere was then one of the most prestigious institutes of higher learning in Black Africa. Chiume played a significant role in elevating political awareness among other students and Africans at large. In 1952, he was elected Chairman of the Makerere College Political Society and became its mouthpiece. In the same year, he successfully organized the first ever college demonstration against apartheid South Africa on the occasion of the 300th anniversary of the arrival of Van Rieberg and his settler colleagues on South African soils. In 1953, he was elected Assistant Secretary of the Tanganyika Makerere College Discussion Group (the precursor of the Makerere College Tanganyika African National Union (TANU) Branch) under the leadership of Dr. Julius Kambarage Nyerere, first President of United Republic Of Tanzania. Chiume continued to play a leading role in the corridors of Makerere University and was later elected Secretary of the Nyasaland Students' Association, Makerere Branch, and editor of its Magazine The Nyasa.

He worked hand in hand with Professor Yusuf Lule then lecturer in Statistics and Educational Psychology at Makerere (and later President of Uganda) to gather information as a member of the Uganda Education Committee throughout Uganda. The Committee's recommendations brought great educational changes in Uganda. At the end of 1953, Chiume graduated with a Diploma in Education (EA) with physics, chemistry, biology and mathematics as teaching subjects and elected spokesman for the LY's (last year students) at the College Annual Dinner.

From Makerere, he joined the teaching staff at Alliance (Mission) Secondary School (now Mazengo Secondary School) in Dodoma, Tanzania where he taught physics, chemistry, biology and applied mathematics. At the School, Chiume was always at loggerheads with white members of the staff over political issues, and this made him feel that time had come for him to return to his motherland to join the struggle for freedom and independence.

Like his friend Chipembere, Chiume at age 27, was elected, with an overwhelming majority, in 1956 to LEGCO to represent the northern Province. With Chipembere, they formed a formidable alliance and turned the Legislative Council into a political platform propagating nationalistic ideals. Until then, the voice of the African population had been given expression in scantily publicized Congress press statements and in speeches of the two African members of the Federal Assembly, Manoah Chirwa and Clement Kumbikano. These two men were largely regarded as dupes of the Colonial authorities by the population.

The return of Chiume was a blessing by itself for the Congress because the new blood was the engine to revolutionize public consciousness towards the protracted freedom struggles that laid ahead of us. Generally, Nyasaland African Congress was dominated by young brilliant intellectuals such as the Chisiza brothers, Augustine W. Bwanausi, Dr. Harry Bwanausi, Goodale Gondwe, Willy Chokani, David Rubadiri, Shadreck Khonje, Orton Chirwa, Edwin Chibambo and many others. Yatuta Chisiza was in the Tanganyika Police Force and was invited to become the first African Commissioner of Police after independence in 1960, but chose to return home to join in the independence struggle. That he and Chiume abandoned their well-paid jobs in the colonial establishment, was interpreted by many as both selfless and patriotic and unlike Banda who waited for an invitation. In LEGCO, Masauko Chipembere and Kanyama Chiume continued to pummel the colonial administration, but much more publicity would be required if British and world opinion were to be made to militate against the evils we were to combat.

So the speeches in the LEGCO were directed towards three principle objectives:

- To provide much-needed political education to our people by putting forth as convincingly as possible the entire case for independence and to win support for the Nyasaland

African Congress by educating on its policies and activities;

- To draw the attention of the Nyasaland and British Governments towards the manifestations of maladministration so rife in our country and to demand reforms and advancement in all walks of life; and

- To inform the world in general and the British government in particular about our grievances and to enlist their sympathy and support for our demands of self-government and secession from the Federation.

To this end, Hansard became virtually a Congress mouthpiece and sold like hot cakes.

Of all the young nationalists, Masauko Chipembere became a thorn in the flesh of the colonial authorities and spent most of his time in prison. To this effect, he once described life in prison thus: "life in prison without trial, and so far from home, was very bitter. As far as prisons go, their conditions were reasonable but they could not remove from the mind, the bitterness and frustration caused by imprisonment based on hearsay from plain-clothed men and not on charges confirmed in a court of law. This unexplained removal from home, friends, pleasures and family, was greatest when I was declared deposed from the Legislative Council (LEGCO) by the Governor because I was a detainee."

Naturally, when he was released from detention in Gweru, Rhodesia (Zimbabwe), after 19 months, he made some very bitter attacks on the Government and white men generally. Two of his speeches made in this mood, were considered seditious and inciting, and so he was summoned to court to answer these charges. After a tough day of legal battle in which leading London barristers appeared on both sides, he was sentenced on February 10, 1961 to three years imprisonment without the option of a fine and was forthwith brought to the Central Prison, Zomba to do his sentence. The most astonishing and suspicious thing however, was that Dr. Hastings Banda was the Prime Minister, which literally meant he was the Head of the Government, but he did nothing to exonerate Masauko and he (Masauko) completed his 3-year sentence under an African government. To his credit, Masauko came out of incarceration radicalized, visionary and defiant. On the contrary, Hastings Banda came out of his detention apologetic, visionless, neutralized and a sellout.

As Malawians were preparing for a glorious moment with mixed sentiments to welcome their hard-won independence from British rule, Banda slowly but surely, laid foundations for a one-man show in an independent Malawi. First and foremost, his prime targets were his outspoken Cabinet Ministers whom he wanted neutralized before he could consolidate absolute power into his hands. He started by dividing them and pitting one against the other, the strategy of divide and rule. This worked exactly to his advantage. Yatuta Chisiza then Minister of Home Affairs and Kanyama Chiume then Minister of Education, started hating each other. Orton Chirwa then Minister of Justice and Attorney General joined the fracas in isolating Chiume. Orton Chirwa's house in Zomba (the Government seat), was a few meters away from Chiume's, but they did not visit each other nor talk to each other and, yet, all three of these noteworthy leaders came from the same area.

Another of Banda's strategies was based on a campaign of vilification against his closest colleagues. He urged the people of Malawi to spy over his ministers and report any mischief to the party. On countless occasions he berated his ministers in public rallies saying: "I do not rely on these ministers for anything and when you see them accompany me on international trips, they go there as observers, I do the talking." Basically, such divisive and degrading remarks cultivated a sense of anger and mistrust among his closest colleagues who were apparently humiliated in public. Dr. Banda's move was not only to prepare for eventual brutal dictatorship, but also it laid the foundations for future political and economic conflicts at the expense of national unity. Indeed, Malawi is divided along tribal and regional lines now more than during the colonial era. It is a scenario that politicians from densely populated regions of South and Central Malawi condone because in every national election, they emerge victorious. In essence, the road to independence, was not smooth, but full of hopelessness and despair.

Chapter Four

FEDERATION: RHODESIA AND NYASALAND

On April 9, 1953 European voters ratified Federation in a general referendum and inaugurated in September the same year bearing the name of Federation of Rhodesia and Nyasaland (Central African Federation) and G. Huggins became its first Federal Prime Minister with its Headquarters in Salisbury (Harare).

Three countries were involved in the Federation: southern Rhodesia (Zimbabwe); northern Rhodesia (Zambia) and Nyasaland (Malawi). All were British territories. Britain retained ultimate responsibility for External Affairs. Defense, Immigration, European Education, European Agriculture, and Health became the responsibilities of the new Federal Legislature which sat in the southern Rhodesia Capital of Salisbury.

The Federation had a Governor-general and a unicameral assembly elected on two common rolls with qualified franchise. In 1960, there were 44 seats for elected members of any race, eight for Africans, four for specially elected Africans, and three for Europeans responsible for African interests.

The Constitution provided for an African Affairs Board as a standing committee of the Assembly. It consisted of the Europeans representing African interests and specially elected African members from each territory. It had power to make representations to the Federal Assembly, assist a territorial government when asked to, and require any measure which it thought discriminatory to be reserved to the crown. The Federal Assembly had a roll of voters in electoral districts. Both franchises were qualified by both property and educational standards.

As we can see, the amalgamation had a negative impact on the majority of Africans in all three countries. First and foremost, the British government had its eyes on the region's gargantuan resources and markets while the well-being of the black majority was insignificant in the minds of the colonizers—hence, the opposition to the amalgamation. In fact, that opposition to the imposed federation was there even before its official formation because blacks feared they would not be able to achieve self-government within a federal structure dominated by white southern Rhodesians.

The ten-year period in which Malawi formed part of the Federation also consolidated the system of colonial exploitation. There was another fear especially in Zambia and Malawi and that was the racism which was showing its ugly head in southern Rhodesia. There was fear that it might spread its tentacles into their countries. While the notion of federation itself is quite a progressive one, in this case, it served the political and economic interests of the British imperialism. The white landowners in Malawi used the federal structure not only to strengthen their position, but also brought their policies into line with Rhodesia's, where African people had virtually no land rights. But unfortunately, this fear was overshadowed after Malawi attained her independence when the former brutal tyrant Hastings Banda acquired large tracks of land (28,000 hectares) for growing tobacco, tea, and sugar. The workers in these estates were paid "peanuts" and the working conditions were appallingly tragic and worse than those in Rhodesia's white farms.

We have seen that Malawi's economy relied heavily on Britain. During the federal period it came also to rely on Rhodesia. This political and economic enslavement was facilitated by federation. Although the federal structure allowed for division of responsibility between the three Territorial Governments and the Federal Government, it also permitted the major powers to tax personal income, corporate profits, and to levy customs and excise duties payable to the Federal Government. While Territorial Governments retained the right to

POLITICAL STRUGGLE 59

levy certain taxes on their own account, their share in the federal tax receipts was the major source of income. Under the original contract, federal collections of income tax were to be allocated among the territories as follows: northern Rhodesia (Zambia) 17 percent; southern Rhodesia (Zimbabwe) 13 percent; Nyasaland (Malawi) 6 percent. The Federal Government was authorized to retain 64 percent for its own purposes[ii].

Of the three kinds of taxes raising most federal and territorial revenue (company tax, direct income and poll tax, indirect taxes on goods and services), that which claimed the largest contribution from both races, was the tax on corporate profits. The simplest arithmetic can also show that the copperbelt was the financial backbone of the federal fiscal structure. In the financial year 1956-1957, the northern Rhodesian (Zambian) companies paid US$64 million in taxes.[iii]

Only US$22 million of this total was collected by the Zambian government (through its share of federal tax collections and through its territorial surcharge on corporate profits). Thus, the remaining US$42 million, the profit of which came from predominantly African labor, accrued to other Governments. The Federal Government retained US$32 million as its share, a sum amounting to more than 60 percent of its income tax receipts for that year. Clearly, one territory, northern Rhodesia (Zambia), and one industry within that territory, copper, made the major contribution to the whole Federation, and especially to the white racists in southern Rhodesia (Zimbabwe) who dominated it.

While it may be argued that both races help to create the production surplus that was taxed, it may also be said that the

---

[ii] Colin Lays Cranford Pratt. *A New Deal in Central Africa (London)*, p. 83

[iii] Sir Ronald Prain, *East Africa and Rhodesia* (London), November 13, 1958, p. 331

tax represents relatively more for the African in relation to his extremely low wages.[iv]

The African consumer also came to be exposed to the burden of indirect taxation, proportionately high in relation to his limited budget. In the 1955-1956 budget, taxes on low-grade cigarettes, purchased almost exclusively by African smokers, were raised. When custom duties were increased on imported garments in the 1956-57 budget, the Minister of Finance stressed that these duties were aimed at the very cheapest garments. At the same time, prices were rising on consumer goods, and during the Federation period, hut-tax receipts in Nyasaland (Malawi), were increased by US$500,000. These moves highlight the federal policy of aiming to take money from the pockets of the African people in order to dominate and oppress them.

The scope of this chapter does not allow me to analyze the realities of the Malawi economy within the orbit of the Central African Federation since it would require investigating the three economies which formed the Federation (northern Rhodesia, southern Rhodesia, and Nyasaland). But it is imperative to point out that throughout the federal period, the colonists followed a line of development which was to the advantage of southern Rhodesia (Zimbabwe) and exploited to the maximum the human and natural resources of the two partner states of Malawi and Zambia. This tendency was particularly strengthened during the last years of the Federation when mounting opposition from the masses, especially in Zambia and Malawi, prodded capitalists to reap their lucrative profit before the political trend changed.

The demise of the Federation, astonishingly, is accredited by Malawians to one single person, their Messiah, Dr. Hastings Banda, the former bestial despot who single handedly tormented the nation for thirty years. Our nation has a short memory and our history has been corrupted by his suc-

---

[iv] Dr. Attati Mphakati, "Birth of Neocolonial State", *The African Review*, November, 1973, Vol. 3, p. 4.

cessors who clouded the minds of the Malawian people causing them to believe that only Banda came to the rescue of the nation in siege. Malawians have been repeatedly told that while Banda was in a political wilderness in foreign lands, he used to write articles very critical to the Central African Federation. However, not a single piece has been reprinted to prove the case. On the contrary, Rev. John Chilembwe's several letters to the press, critical of colonial domination, have been reprinted in recent years. In a fair analysis of the struggle against the imposed Federation and colonial domination, Dr. Banda has done very little to dominate national history.

It was young ardent nationalists from all three territories, Zambia, Malawi and Zimbabwe who championed the opposition of the Federation long before Banda was erroneously imported into Nyasaland (Malawi). In Zimbabwe, the struggle was spearheaded by militant nationalists such as George Nyandoro, James Chikerema, Tichafa Parerinyatwa, Albert Chitepo, Michael Mawema, and many others. In Zambia, the emergence of Kenneth David Kaunda (born from Nyasa parents), Simon Kapwepwe, Arthur Wina, Sikota Wina, Harry Mwanga Nkumbula, Reuben Chitandika Kamanga, Munu Sipalo, and many others. In Malawi, opposition was led by militant nationalists such as Masauko Chipembere, Kanyama Chiume, Dunduzu Chisiza, Yatuta Kaluli Chisiza, Augustine Bwanausi, Harry Bwanausi, Orton Chirwa, M. Q. Chibambo, Masopela Gondwe, Goodal Gondwe, and many others. In 1953 in the Mlanje District (tea growing area) in southern Malawi, indigenous people revolted against the federal authorities and violent conflict ensued that resulted in many deaths and injuries. There was countrywide resistance that happened in the absence of the so-called Messiah who was, astonishingly, after the demise of the Federation, given the title of the Breaker of the Federation (BOF). It is sad, however, that Malawians allowed themselves to sink so deep that even Banda himself found it incomprehensible.

With the threat of a possible secession of Malawi and Zambia from the Federation to become fully independent African States, all significant economic activities and infrastructures were concentrated in Rhodesia (Zimbabwe)—commencing in the first instance with the gargantuan Kariba Hydro Electric Power Station (a dam on the mighty Zambezi River). It became the systematic policy of Welensky's imperialism to water-down rival projects on neighboring territory. (Roy Welensky was the last federal Prime Minister.) There were, for instance, economic and technical reasons to favor developing, rather than the Kariba Dam, either Zambia's Kafue Project or Malawi's Liwonde-Band Project for power generation. Political considerations of the federal colonialists, however, outweighed these advantages and, despite the claim that economic benefits would accrue to all three territories, the authorities did not even plan for an electric line from say, Kariba to Malawi.

Other ventures indicating the same bias were the extensions to the steel mill foundry at Que-Que, the establishment of a huge chemical plant for fertilizers near Salisbury (Harare), and new machines for copper miners. Indeed, in the light of its function, it would not be rash to suggest that the sole reason the federation had been created was to strengthen the exploitation of Nyasaland and northern Rhodesia in the interests of the capitalists and settlers of Rhodesia. However, to some extent, the people of Malawi got a viable share of the federation, the biggest hospital (Queen Elizabeth Hospital) was built with federal funds in Blantyre, the commercial city. In contrast to that and Banda's zest for building several sumptuous Presidential Palaces in the country for his personal prestige, the majority of his people live in squalor. Banda's construction projects cost taxpayers millions of dollars in one of the poorest countries on our planet. Obviously, the hospital, the only one of its kind in the country, could not otherwise have been built since the earmarked funds were used for personal interests. Amazingly, the current President Bingu wa Mutharika, himself an economist, praised Banda for his contribution to the establishment of a framework for growth and development.

If we can take inter-territorial trade as an example, we find that Malawi was lagging most of the time. Imports into Malawi from Zambia and Rhodesia in 1961 were worth US$18 million and consisted of textiles, clothes, shoes and food products, while Malawi's exports to Rhodesia and Zambia, in the same year, were worth only US$3 million.[v]

Unfortunately, the system of exchange within the three-state Federation enriched only one member, Rhodesia, and robbed the other two member states of both human resources and raw materials, all in order to satisfy the needs of white settlers whose population was expanding drastically.

For all counts, Malawi is an agrarian country producing mainly tea and tobacco. A United Kingdom-based tea buying company, Tetley Group, says Malawi tea is the best in quality the world over and it improves the company's sales. However, the sad part of it is that tea plantation workers are only paid slave wages to sustain their livelihood. Tea in Malawi accounts for nearly 40 percent of the income from all agricultural products. Although Malawi tea was of the highest quality, Malawians were obliged to buy within the home market a third grade tea from Rhodesia at high prices. The "Green Gold" Malawi tea was exported outside the country. Africans received no benefit from this because the tea plantations in the regions of Chipinga-Cholo, Mlanje and Blantyre all belong to white settler capitalists and the factories which process tea, tobacco and coffee belong to the same settlers.

Rhodesia exported to Malawi those products of low quality which could be sold at monopolistic high prices with the aim of strengthening its economic and political domination. The Federal powers also encouraged the immigration of those types of European who had few qualifications to take positions as local clerks and typists in the federal administration and other bureaucracies.

Although the Constitution of the Federation contained no formal limitations to an African becoming a Minister of

---

[v] *East Africa and Rhodesia,* January 24, 1965, p. 448.

Parliament, not until after the first seven years of the Federation's existence in 1959, was an African even nominated to the post of Parliamentary Secretary. This move was undoubtedly made to placate mounting international criticism that the Federation was marching on the same course of apartheid (aparthood) as the south African regime. British imperialists were anxious to convince the world that the policy of partnership between races in the Federation was working. It must not be forgotten, however, that the appointment of an African to such a high post was carefully entrusted to a man who could be relied upon to echo European interests. In other ways, such a person in an African context, was known as "stooge."

The Federal Prime Minister himself had declared, while debating the laws for the Civil Service, that: "It is unrealistic to imagine that Africans are to have the same rights as the Europeans." In practice, the Federal Civil Services were divided into four categories: the first reserved to Europeans, the second mainly for Europeans, but with provision for an African elite, and the third and fourth, for Africans alone. This system existed despite the fact that Chapter 2, Statute 40 of the Constitution explicitly stated that no person could be deprived of the opportunity of joining the Federal Civil Services (FCS) on account of his racial genesis.

The Executive Council (EC) was composed only of white settlers, the representatives of the reactionary and fascist United Federal Party (UFP), whose aim was to eliminate African influence. This government of settlers enjoyed great support from Britain, which surrendered to them the fate of the 7.5 million African people. The settlers were given absolute control over them and their resources when the British Government agreed in 1957 to grant full responsibilities to the federalists in all external dealings. The British Government even went to the extent of defending the Federal government when, in 1959, the House of Commons debated the expatriation of some Labor Opposition members from the Federation as "Prohibited Immigrants," concluding that this action was entirely within the competence of the Federal Government.

The Federal Government passed a series of discriminatory laws as a means of completely dominating (politically, economically, and socially) the peoples of Malawi, Zambia and Zimbabwe. It is significant, however, to know the people who passed these discriminatory laws came to be in the racist Parliament.

There were two categories of voting rights: An "ordinary roll" and a "special roll." The world was made to understand that this distinction did not depend on race, but the composition of Parliament reveals the racial discrepancy. The Federal Parliament, in accordance with Statute (g) of the Constitution of 1953, was composed of 35 members: 26 Europeans and 6 Africans (2 for each territory) and 3 Europeans as so-called representatives of African interests. To qualify as a voter on the common roll, the voter was required to have a yearly income of US$1,440 (or ownership of property equivalent to US$3,000) or yearly income of US$960 (property worth US$2,000) and so on. To qualify on the special roll, a voter was to have a yearly income of US$300 (property US$1,000) or secondary education. The first elections for the Federal Assembly were held in December 1953. Out of 66,979 voters who had registered, only 440 were Africans and none were from Nyasaland (Malawi). It must be noted, however, that it was extremely hard at that time for the majority of Africans to acquire the amount of funds aforementioned because their wages were appallingly low (subsistence allowance) and again, it was also hard for Africans to enter secondary school.

In July 1957, the Federal Assembly (FA) enacted a law to change the Federal Constitution. Under the new Constitution, there were to be 59 Members of Parliament, 44 Europeans and 12 Africans with provision again for three Europeans to represent African interests in the three territories. Since Africans were allowed no active interest in the Federation at all, it was farcical to expect Europeans to protect that which did not exist. That this situation was created and defended by Whitehall was not only a mockery of democracy, but tantamount to dictatorship because even if there had been an honest effort to consider African interests, there were Africans capable enough to represent themselves. The real problem, though, was not merely that of neglecting to promote African interests, but of a Federal setup which exploited, dominated and seized those interests for the enrichment of white settlers, predominantly in Rhodesia.

This injustice is obvious if one considers the obstacles to African enfranchisement. Given the financial criteria for voting, the number of Africans who could qualify was only a few hundred. In 1958, the average annual income of a European was US$2,200, while Africans working in the mines earned about US$160 and those engaged in agriculture less than US$80. It is obvious, too, that with only 35,000 African pupils attending secondary schools in 1959, for instance, even fewer of their elders could meet the educational requirements for voting. These factors allowed the situation to arise whereby the Europeans of the Federation, who were only 3.7 percent of its population, elected 80 percent of the Federal Assembly. Africans, with 95.8 percent of the population, could hardly qualify to vote as long as the Federation existed.

The total voters in 1958, were 88,968 voters, of these, only 1,731 were Africans, less than two percent of all voters registered. In Nyasaland, which led the opposition to the Federation of Rhodesia and Nyasaland, no voter was on common roll. Of the eleven voters with special registration, five were the wives of Africans destined to be handpicked by the Federal Assembly for nomination as African representatives.

The birth of Malawi as an independent state, started with the conflict between the opposition forces of the African nationalism and colonial oppression. It had not been accidental that the first demands of the National Liberation Movement in Nyasaland (Malawi) had been for absolute secession from the Federation, for it was Nyasaland which supplied the emigrants to man the mines of the other two territories. No comparable productive development took place in Malawi while the Federation existed. Instead, Malawi's debts, poverty, ignorance, disease and servitude plagued its people until it became clear that such injustice could not continue. The Federation was disbanded on December 31,1963.

The British claimed that the Federation had been peacefully dissolved: other white settlers in Central Africa accused them of having sentenced the Federation into creating its own death. But for the emerging African nations, the end of colonial rule seemed to be inevitable and irrevocable because of the conflicting social forces it generated. Economic development under British rule or leadership had been sharply contradictory: the paper profits earned by extraction of raw materials had been expatriated, and little was left for the African workers—underpaid, exploited and isolated from their own families. The only development, if one could call it development at all, was the strengthening of their dependence on white patronage.

If it had been allowed to continue, the disparity between the economic and political potential of Africans and Europeans would have grown to proportions already realized in the Republics of South Africa and Rhodesia. The irony is that the disparity did not disappear, on the contrary, it sharpened further in Malawi with the coming of political independence on July 6, 1964. The fact that July 6 was particularly chosen to be the date for independence of Malawi is not a coincidence. It was the date when the Malawian Messiah (Banda) landed at Chileka International Airport after more than 40 years in wilderness; this further reflects the egoist tendency of identifying all national achievements to his personal glory.[vi]

What is most striking is the extent to which Malawians had forgotten their past rich political history and regarded Banda, who had just found political establishments in Malawi that had been deeply entrenched into national societies galvanized by Rev. John Chilembwe's uprising of 1915. Sadly, the political history the majority of our people embrace, starts in

---

[vi] Dr. Attati Mphakati, "Birth of a Neocolonial State," *The African Review*, November, 1973, Vol. 3, p. 1.

1958 when Banda took over the leadership of Nyasaland African Congress (NAC) which had been formed by wise and patriotic leaders when Banda was still an unknown entity and in 1959, when he was given the leadership of the Malawi Congress Party (MCP) on a silver platter. The Malawi Congress Party was formed by Orton Edgar Chin'gioli Chirwa, QC and one of the country's first lawyers. Chirwa was strangled to death in his cell in Zomba Prison by Malawi Congress Party murder squads at the beginning of the 1992 national uprising against Banda's 30-year pernicious dictatorship.

Chapter Five

INDEPENDENCE WITHIN CRISIS

Within two months of Malawi's independence things began to fall apart indicating a very rough and long journey to nationhood. In fact, the people of Malawi did not know what independence could bring to them apart from singing day in and day out about their Messiah. Throughout 1963, a year after Dunduzu Chisiza had died in mysterious circumstances as the first victim of Banda's gangsterism, the Prime Minister's (Banda's) behavior became more that of an insane man than head of government, virtually uncontrolled and unwilling to listen to any one of his colleagues. A few of the more lucid Malawians were of the opinion that things were running amok and that the long awaited independence could end up in upheaval. Though the majority contended that things were going in the right direction, they could also at least see the clouds gathering for the ultimate storm.

Amid still covert crisis or revolt, three key ministers in self-governing Nyasaland: Kanyama Chiume; Yatuta K. Chisiza; Augustine W. Bwanausi were sent by the Prime Minister to Nyika and then on to Kilimanjaro and Arusha regions of Tanzania to study their tourist organizations. At the time Kanyama Chiume held the portfolio of Education Minster, Augustine Bwanausi held Housing and Social Development, and Yatuta K. Chisiza was in Home Affairs. However, there were plans already to establish Nyika, a potentially viable scenery for tourist industry, as a National Park for Malawi. After thirty years of Banda's brutal rule, Nyika was virtually ignored and is still underdeveloped for the simple reason that it is located in the north which Banda perceived to be a bastion of support for the rebel ministers—especially his arch-foe Kanyama Chime. Partly, tribalism and regionalism played a role in the whole scenario.

While in Dar es Salaam, the three able ministers were treated with respect and courtesy which made them more determined than ever before to establish the same sort of relationships at home where Banda treated them as garden or kitchen boys. To their astonishment, Chisiza, though a mere Minister of Home Affairs, inspected a guard of honor for the first time in his life in Dar es Salaam.

At a National Park in Momela, north east of Dar es Salaam, the three ministers had a golden opportunity to discuss at length the looming political crisis and the need to change Banda's negative attitudes and make him fall in line with the rest of Africa in respecting his people and their goals. According to Chiume, the three ministers were prepared to face any eventuality rather than be a party to the treacherous path Banda had taken against Africa's liberation struggle.

Close to independence, things seemed to be worsening. Banda and his closest henchmen; John U. Z. Tembo, Gwanda Chakuamba Phiri, Albert N. Muwalo, M. Q. Chibambo, Gomile Kumtumanje, Aleke Banda, and many others aspiring for ministerial positions, were busy organizing the grass-roots for eventual confrontation with the rebel ministers. Banda had already bribed and corrupted these shallow-minded opportunists to come to his support when the right time comes. For his part, Banda continued with public rallies throughout the country. Now that independence was won, people expected the Prime Minister to tell them what the government would do for the nation, but instead, he dwelt almost entirely on innuendos, insinuations, self-glorification, and disparaging his colleagues. In his view, he wanted to impress the people of Malawi that he, and he alone, championed the struggle against the Federation and colonialism.

The Young Pioneers, a bestial paramilitary organization which was created in 1962 with the help of the Israelis and Portuguese governments, was modernized and put on alert. Unfortunately, the organization's activities were similar to those of Sudan's Janjaweed and Tontons Macoutes of the former rancorous Haiti despot Francois Duvalier (Papa Doc).

They were officially given power beyond that of the police and were used as shock troops to crush opponents of the Banda regime. Before schools, hospitals, clinics and colleges were built, concentration camps and prisons were constructed in Zomba, Lilongwe, and other parts of the country—ready for an intake of political prisoners, real or imagined. Though still the majority of our people were left in the cold, a sense of apprehension began to engulf their conscience.

After the tour of Tanzania National Parks, Kanyama Chiume, Yatuta Chisiza, and Augustine Bwanausi returned home, this time, highly and decidedly determined to hold the bull by its horns. While in Dar es Salaam, Chiume as a Minister for Foreign Affairs negotiated economic assistance with the Chinese (Mainland) Ambassador. At the time China was courting friends among emerging African nations, and in this regard, Malawi was offered 18 million pounds for its development endeavors and Chiume was promised more to come. As a rabid nationalist, Chiume could not have betrayed his nation nor his conscience as Banda did to western imperialism.

Back home when Chiume presented the gift to the Prime Minister Dr. Banda, he was taken aback when he was blatantly told that he should return the funds to the Chinese until further notice. Kanyama Chiume did exactly what he was told. Then, Banda had already developed political hatred toward communism and as such, acceptance of Chinese money could jeopardize his already strong relation with the west. However, only a halfwit and an outdated leader could have refused such amount of aid in an impoverished country in order to appease his western masters. Indeed, the funds could have had a potential viability on Malawi's economic future that had been neglected by successive British administrations. On the other hand, Banda had acquired the first ammunition in anticipation of a revolt by his Ministers.

To this end, it was quite clear that Dr. Banda betrayed the aspirations of Malawians both internally and externally. Dunduzu Chisiza, Yatuta Chisiza, Masauko Chipembere,

Kanyama Chiume, the four bulwarks of the independence struggle affirmed that the independence of Nyasaland was meaningless unless it was linked up with the total liberation of southern Africa. As Nyasaland was totally dependent on Mozambique and South Africa for its outlet, the four rebel ministers sought to avoid using the existing reactionary system to the south and assist our brothers in those unfortunate countries to fight for their freedom. It was encouraging, however, that Banda was temporarily convinced to look north (i.e., to Tanganyika), for that country's route to the sea.

Determined as they were, Kanyama Chiume and Masauko Chipembere left for Tanganyika in February 1963, to negotiate the use of the Mtwara Port for Malawi's trade to the outside world. The late President Julius K. Nyerere, foremost Pan-Africanist after Nkrumah of Ghana, was extremely delighted and assured the two-man delegation of unflinching cooperation and support of the Tanganyika people in our common struggle. From Tanganyika, the Ministers went to northern Rhodesia (Zambia) to discuss the same issue as Zambia was also a landlocked country that relied almost entirely on racist-occupied countries. The then Prime Minister Kenneth David Kaunda of Nyasa parents, was eager to abandon the Lobito-Benguela Railway Systems in Angola which were controlled by the Portuguese. Northern Rhodesia also relied heavily on South African ports through southern Rhodesia. It was therefore agreed in principle to encourage a Zambia-Tanzania-Malawi (TAZAMA) Railway link. While the two-man delegation was touring Tanzania and Zambia, back home, the Prime Minister, Dr. Banda, had covert meetings at Zomba Government House with Mozambican (Portuguese East Africa) top officials from Economic, Transport and Security ministries and a World Bank senior official. Apartheid South Africa and the minority settler regime of Rhodesia were represented by security officials as observers.

The other Malawian Ministers who remained at home at that particular time, had no clue whatsoever that a meeting had been held within their confines and behind their back.

This was a shocking revelation that came only after the covert visitors had been gone for a week. This explains vividly the contempt and disrespect Banda had for his ministers on one hand, and the people of Malawi on the other. This also left a clear message that Malawi had been consigned into the orbit of neocolonialism.

On presenting their findings to the Prime Minister, the two key ministers received a cool shoulder from their boss and were told pointblank to forget about the Chinese-formulated Tanzania-Zambia-Malawi project which, according to his advisers (European expatriates), was a white elephant. Later, Kanyama Chiume and Masauko Chipembere were flabbergasted to learn that the World Bank (an American controlled institution) official had been in Malawi, after they had left for Tanzania and Zambia, and advised Banda to do away with any notion of linking the country's existing system with Tanzania and Zambia. The World Bank official insisted to Banda that a Malawi-Mozambique railway link was a viable solution to the woes of a lacking sea-outlet. It must be noted that these endeavors were carried out amid the East-West cold war which was basically fought in the Continent of Africa.

To add salt to the wound, two months later, the United Nations Economic section experts condemned the Tanzania-Zambia (TAZARA) project as an economic disaster. But at the height of Mozambique's liberation struggle, which the Prime Minister Banda betrayed, the Nacala-Salima Railway link was constantly sabotaged by gallant Frelimo fighters that coerced the reactionary regime of Malawi to turn to the Tanzania-Zambia route to the outside world. TAZARA was fundamentally financed by the Chinese government.

It was not surprising that these treacherous meetings were organized by British expatriates who dominated the armed forces, police, intelligence, civil service and were also a driving force in Banda's vulgar foreign policy. During these covert meetings, Banda was the only black figure surrounded by a white audience such as Michael Blackwood, former leader of the United Federal Party (dubbed United Fools Party) of Nyasaland Branch, as his private secretary. It must also be remembered that Blackwood was the leading opponent of African nationalism and a vicious proponent of the imposed Federation of Rhodesia and Nyasaland: Peter Long, former notorious colonial Police Chief and political adviser, who physically arrested Banda during the March 3, 1959, State of Emergency and John Block: an administrative Adviser. Block was a brutal colonial District Commissioner (DC) who commanded a colonial force that massacred thirty-one defenseless men, women and children at Nkhata Bay in northern Malawi during the March 3, 1959 uprising.

Meanwhile, former Tanzanian President Nyerere, the staunchest supporter of Mozambique's insurgents was preparing to visit Malawi on an official tour of the country. Without any consultation whatsoever with his Ministers, notably Kanyama Chiume as Foreign Affairs Minister, Banda hired a Portuguese contractor to renovate and rewire the Government Lodge at Lilongwe where President Nyerere could spend his nights during his tour of Central Malawi. Banda's covert meetings with the Portuguese fascists and the looming political crisis, made the Ministers horrified and suspicious of Banda's motives, hence, the scheduled visit on September 9, 1964, was forthwith repudiated.

As a result Nyerere never set foot on Malawian soil for the thirty years that the despot was in power— not until after the political change in 1994. Nyerere accused Banda of betraying Africa's struggle for independence. Malawi and Tanzania are close neighbors and both countries share ancestral cultures. As independence drew closer, Banda became increasingly despotic and treacherous. He covertly contemplated inviting President Hendrick Verwoerd to independence celebrations. Verwoerd was the most cold-blooded Boer leader that ever ruled South Africa. He was also murdered in cold-blood by a Parliamentarian Messenger Dimitri Staffendas in 1966. In typical disregard for human respect, Verwoerd once said that God created blacks as hewers of wood and drawers of water for whites and therefore there could be no compromise between white and black. Dr. Banda was also expressly prepared to bootlick racist Ian Douglas Smith of Rhodesia and fascist Antonio Salazar of Portugal as long as he was accepted in the white domain. He reviled his ministers in public as well as in private and made unpopular decisions within their ministries without their knowledge. He instructed the dominant British expatriate Parliamentary Secretaries to spy on his Ministers. He went so far as hiring Rhodesian and South African chefs, bodyguards and covert police because he could not trust his fellow blacks.

Michael Blackwood, apart from being political adviser to the Prime Minister, was also appointed to the important position of Chairman of the Malawi Development Corporation (MDC) and, in addition, to a seat on the Board of the strategic Reserve Bank of Malawi. Astonishingly, Blackwood, a staunch believer of white supremacy, worked devotedly to thwart Malawi's independence. He once praised the Federal authorities for apprehending Banda and his colleagues during the March 3, 1959 State of Emergency. While ministers were required to make an appointment to see the Prime Minister—and this, sometimes, could take weeks or months—European expatriates needed less than two minutes to see Dr. Banda. In reality, such was the extent to which Malawians had to endure humiliation and disrespect in their own country, for thirty years in a police state.

Candidly, close to independence, countless events unfolded indicating that the Malawian leader had already capitulated to imperialist machinations and unwittingly ready to cooperate with brutal empires in the south. In June 1964, a month away from the country's independence, Banda appointed George Jardim, Antonio Salazal's protégé and the Director of the infamous Policia Internacional Para a Defesa Do Estado (PIDE) in Mozambique as Malawi's Consul-General in Lourenco Maraues (Maputo). Kanyama Chiume, as Minister for Foreign Affairs was not consulted and was not aware, leave alone, asked to approve Jardim's appointment. In truth,

Chiume as an ardent nationalist, would not have had anything to do with an apostle of imperialism.

Dr. Banda went far out of his way by firing Dr. Harry Bwanausi one of the first medical doctors in the country for refusing instruction from him to hire Miss Kadzamila's father into medical services for which he was not qualified at all. Dr. Bwanausi was then targeted for arrest, but managed to flee to Zambia where President Kenneth David Kaunda appointed him Director of Medical Services. Miss Cecilia T. Kadzamila was engaged to Augustine Mutambala, but decided to live with Banda as a friend and housekeeper. To gain that status, she was later declared First Lady of Malawi even though they were not officially married. As it turned out, Banda was an Elder of the Church of Scotland which strictly adheres to Christian norms. Not surprisingly, he was excommunicated after the collapse of communism and after being in power for thirty years presiding over one of the most evil regimes on the Continent. However, Dr. Banda emerged as the strongest ally of the western world against communism.

Miss Kadzamila became the most powerful woman in the country, the Kadzamila-Tembo family was Banda's favorite, and was the first choice in receiving overseas scholarships regardless of their qualifications. Many qualified young men and women were turned down in order to give preference to the Kadzamila-Tembo family.

As time was running out, Banda showed no sign of acquiescence to demands by his ministers. He continued to humiliate them everywhere he went in the country. On October 27, 1963, during a ceremony at a party rally held in the City of Blantyre's Central Stadium, Banda was honored by granting him the freedom of the City. This practice, Masauko Chipembere later described as: "The legacy of colonial rule, one of Africa's many blind and meaningless borrowings whose European historical origins have no relevance to Africa." Sadly, on this occasion, Banda devoted only a few minutes to matters concerning the city and spent over two hours berating his own cabinet ministers. He declared repeatedly that he was the boss and that the ministers could not dare, either individually or collectively, to challenge his leadership. If they did, he could crush them all. Such was the treatment meted out to the dignified and popular ministers, some of whom facilitated his return to Nyasaland.

As I mentioned before, Banda had apparently fallen into the hands of imperialists, particularly the British, former colonial power. All these outbursts were the work of M-16 (the British Intelligence Network) which surrounded the Prime Minister. These officers together with those in the civil services, felt insecure in their positions as long as some of the ministers notably Masauko Chipembere, Kanyama Chiume, Yatuta Chisiza and Augustine Bwanausi, who were regarded as radicals, were in the cabinet. They feared that the ministers would soon demand that their posts be "Africanized" (i.e., that they should be replaced by Africans whose political loyalty and dedication to the government could be absolutely significant). These officers also believed that the ministers were potentially, if not actually, communist agitators and could lead the nation into the communist sphere of influence. So their primary objective was to see that the obdurate and popular ministers were dismissed or neutralized. Therefore to achieve this, they had to sow seeds of mistrust and division between Banda and his ministers. To a large extent, this worked. These officers were covering every meeting the ministers addressed. It came to the ministers knowledge that intelligence reports submitted to Banda concerning their activities and speeches were written in such a way as to make the Prime Minister believe that the ministers were building themselves up at his expense, trying to project an image equal to, or higher than, that of the Prime Minister.

That the Prime Minister was receiving distorted reports on his ministers became more apparent during the months heading to independence as he stepped up his campaign to get his own cabinet discredited in the eyes of the people. But nothing could have been more untrue and more mischievous than any allegation that any member of the cabinet was disloyal to Banda at that given time. Indeed, he had no reason at all to fear that any one of the ministers sought to harbor ambitions to replace him. In fact, he was very much senior in age, roughly thirty years older than all but one of the ten of them. The ministers were determined to give him all the support and loyalty he needed to fulfill his duty of leading their young nation to full independence and prosperity. It is, of course, true that by the beginning of 1964, the ministers were already tired of his policies and his increasingly despotic methods, but they hoped to be able to allure him to change, and it was only after failing to bring him to their side, and after the final parting of the ways which came in September 1964, that they were convinced that only his removal from power, would save the nation from polarization.

Apart from the effect of divisive reports submitted to Banda by the British intelligence officers, there was one factor which played a major role in influencing his unbecoming attitudes towards his colleagues. This was his feeling of political insecurity. In fact, he had shown signs of it since his arrival in the country in 1958, and his colleagues had mistakenly believed that with time and with his rise to the position of head of government, he could acquire more self-confidence. Unfortunately, the tragic feeling did not diminish. This is when T. D. T. Banda's perception of Dr. Banda comes in. T. D. T. Banda gravely warned the Nyasaland African Congress (NAC) leadership, which advocated for Dr. Banda's return to Nyasaland, that he lacked political and cultural base in Malawian society after living for more than 40 years in a political wilderness. Suffice it to say, he was right on point.

Dr. Banda had since 1958, repeatedly claimed that he did not fear any of his subordinates, that he was sure of his popularity, that he was the peoples only choice for a leader. That's why he had to return home to Malawi. But he actually returned home through invitation and persuasion. The frequency with which he made these assertions gave his colleagues cause to believe that he was not sure that they were valid and there were many things to confirm this belief.

Exempli-gratia, he gave orders that he alone could be mentioned in political songs and slogans, no minister walking or motoring with him should join him in waving to cheering crowds (an order which was stretched to absurdity). A visiting African Head of State was in for a rude shock while riding in an open car with President Banda. He was bluntly told not to acknowledge the cheers of the crowd because, "The people were cheering for me, not for you." At one stage, a Congolese star-musician Kanda Bongoman was ordered out of the country because he was carried shoulder-high by his fans as this gesture in Malawi applies only to the Ngwazi (Messiah). Since his arrival in 1958, he had always seen his colleagues as actual or potential rivals and had consistently striven to strengthen his own position in relation to them. Some of his public attacks were part of an attempt to cut them down to size.

British intelligence officers studied Banda thoroughly during the anti-colonial struggle and knew his merits and demerits. They were aware of his sense of insecurity and his fear of his colleagues especially Kanyama Chiume and Masauko Chipembere who invited him from self-exile. The officers played on the weaknesses and made him more and more frightened of his colleagues.

Another group that exacerbated Banda's sense of insecurity was senior party activists who had been in the struggle for long period and at one stage in colonial prisons for their political beliefs. These people were a little older than Banda's closest colleagues, but they were not appointed to the cabinet because they lacked formal education. The Malawi Congress Party (MCP) then determined to prove to the British government, and British undercover agents in Malawi, that the new cabinet had men who could hold their own in any debate or discussion of economic, political, and international issues against the British colonial officials who could be working under them.

This did not go well within the party. The men who were left out of the cabinet such as M. O. Chibambo, Gomile

Kumtumanje, Steven Gwanda Chakuamba Phiri, Albert N. Muwalo, and to some extent, John U. Z. Tembo became disgruntled and in years to come, they formed a lynch mob of unprecedented notoriety. These people knew Dr. Banda's fears and anxieties about his closest colleagues, and wanted to ingratiate themselves to him with a view towards promotion. Therefore they tended to tell the despot what they knew he wanted to hear about his ministers. They told the Prime Minister vehement distortions of the ministers' speeches. On one occasion, Chipembere gained access to a handwritten report which had been prepared by a member of the party's youth league on orders from someone higher in the party hierarchy and submitted to the Prime Minister. It purported to be a report of his speech during a tour of one of the administrative areas. Astonishingly, Chipembere could not even recognize his own speech. Such were the despicable intrigues within the party towards independence. Banda seemed delighted in any internal clashes among his ministers. There was much evidence of the all-too-familiar stratagem of pitting them against one another. He would praise one minister lavishly and make insinuations about his colleagues to the extent that his desire to arouse mental jealousy among them became clearly discernible.

On one occasion, the transfer of a department from one Minster to another, was publicly explained by Banda by saying virtually that the latter was more efficient than the former. For a long time the ministers believed that any act of disfavor by the Prime Minister towards one of them, was the result of intrigue by one or more of their colleagues, and the Prime Minister did absolutely nothing to dissuade this sentiment. At one time the Prime Minister was asked to mediate between two groups of ministers which had clashed. After listening to each side, he walked away from both groups, uttering not a word aimed at bringing about reconciliation.

This desire to see disunity fitted into Banda's general pattern already discussed elsewhere in the chapter. The Prime Minister, with his persistent sense of insecurity and his invalid fear of his ministers, was trying to forestall any possibility of their uniting against him. In the words of his arch-rival Chipembere: "He was sure we could topple him if we ganged together." However, it was partly this totally unfounded fear of his ministers that impelled him to make wanton public remarks that sparked the famous 1964 cabinet crises.

In the middle of 1964, and towards independence, the Prime Minister stepped up and intensified his bunkum campaign to discredit his popular ministers. At this particular time, Chipembere was singled out for particularly reprehensible attacks. Although the Prime Minister seldom mentioned names, most lucid Malawians knew Chipembere was the prime target of the wild and divisive remarks and came to express their sympathy and urged him to be patient and not to react. Some even urged him to form his own political party and do away with the illiberal Prime Minister. The reason why Masauko was singled out for these pernicious attacks was that he commanded an overwhelming personal following in the country—in fact very huge support throughout the nation especially the vote-rich region of the south. In the words of Chipembere: "In politics generally, it is not safe for anyone close to the top to have a personal following, but in Malawian politics, it is fatal." It was one thing Banda could not brook and would use any means, fair or fetid, to stamp out. Chipembere took a long time to realize that the Prime Minister resented his gargantuan personal following, but when he discovered it, he emphasized to the closest of his followers that, for the sake of national unity, their loyalty must be to Dr. Banda first, and not to him. This really, dispels Banda's repeated remarks that his ministers were trying to kick him out of power.

On July 6, 1964, Malawi became an independent state but facing a looming crisis. The nation was sitting on a volcano which was ready to explode and spread its destructive lava throughout the nation. To the majority who observed Dr. Banda's dominant position at the independence celebrations, the impending ministerial revolt against his dubious leadership, came as no surprise.

The long and rigorous walk to freedom had been achieved, the people of Malawi had opened a new chapter in the political history of their country, but the remaining distance to establish a just and free society, turned out to be rough and catastrophic. Independence itself was a false start. It was an independence of merely a flag and a national anthem. In reality, the former colonial power retained unprecedented control indirectly or directly over economic exploitation and political dominance that turned President Banda into an overseas Regent. For a good thirty years to come, Malawians were to be transformed into a slave-society that knew no boundaries. The people became virtually tranquilized and unthinking beings, Banda controlled virtually every aspect of life leading to the land of the zombies.

Dr. Banda continued to show signs of naked defiance of his ministers' demands that he change his attitudes towards them and stop his covert meetings with officials from racist-ruled Mozambique, Rhodesia and South Africa who had found a bedfellow to the north of their countries. Disrespect towards fellow African leaders was very evident when he kept Zambia's President to be (Dr. Kenneth David Kaunda and Simon Mwansa Kapwepwe) and Rhodesia's leading nationalists (James Chikerema and George Nyandoro) waiting in a visitors' lounge for two and half hours while he was having a nap with his supposedly private secretary–Miss Cecilia Kadzamila.

It would be fair to note that the Ministers were young men with meritorious academic achievements who had largely created the nationalist movement in Nyasaland and brought Dr. Banda to power. Indeed, they deserved respect in their own rights. But, instead they were frequently irked by the President's despotic and contemptuous manner towards them—but they undoubtedly hoped that after independence things would change for the better. Instead, to a surprising extent, things got worse. The raw material for an exigency was at hand.

On July 10, 1964, four days after the attainment of independence, Dr. Banda left for London to attend the Commonwealth Heads of Government Conference. On his return, he stopped in Cairo to attend a Summit Conference of African Heads of State. The date of his return to Malawi, July 26, had been widely publicized, and a large crowd was ferried by government and party transport to welcome the Messiah at the Chileka International Airport. All members of the Cabinet were present, as well as all leading party officials and singing groups of the Amazon Army (Women) and Youths. The City of Blantyre, the country's commercial hub, was brought to a stand still. All shops, food markets, water systems, schools, and so on, were shutdown and motorists ordered off the roads.

When Banda was invited to address the crowd, he returned to his familiar outbursts. He attacked certain politicians, "especially ministers." He said that now that Malawi had become an independent state, a number of foreign embassies could be established in the country. Some of them would try to subvert the nation and could do so through Malawi politicians. "There were in Malawi ambitious and corrupt politicians who could be easily bought with money to accomplish this end," he rattled. The remark was quite to the contrary in view of the fact that, he himself had already betrayed Malawians and Africa for financial and military favors from white-ruled Mozambique, Rhodesia and South Africa. He called upon his people to watch all African politicians, especially ministers. "Any politician seen frequenting the office or home of any foreign diplomat, had to be reported to me," he roared. In particular, he appealed to members of the Youth League and the Amazon Army (Women's League) of the Malawi Congress Party (MCP) to become his ears and eyes. When they had any report to make to him on any minister or other politician, they could go directly to him. They did not have to send their report through any minister or other leader. They had nothing to fear; he would protect them against any grudge any politician might bear against them. He reminded the people that between him and them, there was a firm bond. He had saved them from the colonial yoke and in turn, they were giving him their unswerving loyalty. He trusted them and they trusted him. While he trusted them, he could not trust the politicians. The links between him and his so-called people were direct and rigid.

In essence, the speech was very divisive and reprehensible and intended to sow seeds of distrust, contempt and dislike for the ministers among the people. A few misguided youths applauded the speech partly as a matter of duty and partly because a method of blackmailing ministers into giving them favors had been created. But the larger part of the crowd greeted these remarks with silence and disapproval. The more elderly people felt that it was in bad taste for the Ngwazi (Messiah) to attack his fellow leaders in public. Those who were ferried from villages wondered what kind of a chief this was who insulted his own counselors in the presence of strangers.

The emotions were high in all the ministers, they were unanimously convinced that Dr. Banda had gone too far and they decided to have a meeting to discuss what action should be taken to bring to an end these unfortunate public attacks. Indeed, it was very wrong for Banda to think that those frivolous attacks did harm only to the political image of his ministers. To the contrary, the damage was being done to the reputation of the country as a whole and to its government in particular. Generally, the attacks portrayed a lack of internal cohesion. They also portrayed the President as a man who did not comprehend the fundamental principles underlying the Cabinet system of Government. After all, he appointed the ministers to, and was retaining them in, his Cabinet because he had confidence in them. He had absolute power to dismiss them if he felt that he could no longer trust them. By retaining them in his cabinet, and at the same time publicly expressing distrust for them, he was indeed, exhibiting a state of mental confusion that ill-becomes the head of a Sovereign State. Perhaps he did not want the ministers in his cabinet, but lacked the courage and self-confidence to dismiss them and hoped that the people could make his task easier by demanding their dismissal. Whatever his motives and reasons, he was by his behavior a lunatic and a moron undermining his own reputation and integrity and that led to the ministers considering it their duty to save him from himself by bringing these points to his attention.

On August 5, 1964, Colin Cameron the only white cabinet minister of Scottish descent and a distinguished lawyer resigned from the government. Colin was the first Minister of Works, Transport and Communications and his resignation was a symptom of the deteriorating political situation in the country. This happened after he and his colleagues had a meeting with Banda as Prime Minister. It appeared that the Prime Minister had had a Preventive Detention Bill in draft for sometime, ready to get it passed by the cabinet and subsequently by Parliament at any opportune moment. Also a new security bill emerged that could consolidate all existing security legislation and provided for preventive detention similar to the notorious Rhodesian Law and Order (Maintenance) Act. Colin, a man of exceptionally high character and deeply dedicated to the well-being of the people of Malawi, bitterly opposed the bill that could turn into an instrument to enable the dictator to jail or imprison, without trial, any persons he considered dangerous to the security of Malawi. This draconian law which could have turned Malawi into a virtual "Police State," had no peace in Colin's conscience. During the struggle for self-rule, he had been virtually ostracized by the white community in Malawi for defending Africans facing political charges in the colonial courts. He was responsible for the acquittal of many Africans who could have been jailed on trumped-up or distorted charges.

Colin Cameron fought this heinous bill with all his might to protect the people of Malawi whom he so respected, but Banda declared that he was determined to go ahead with it come hell or high waters and that those who did not like it could resign. Cameron, with tears of deep sorrow rolling down his cheeks, declared that he had spent the last few years fighting this very type of injustice committed by his own British people on the people of Malawi. He could not support it when it was perpetrated on the Malawi people by their own government. He was resigning. With those words of courage and wisdom, he left the Cabinet Chamber. This clearly shows that the famous cabinet crisis of September 1964 was based on principles rather than a power struggle as Banda and his sycophants made us to believe.

For those who had remained in the cabinet and had not decided to cause a showdown with Banda on the bill, it was a tricky and delicate issue. The people were still bitter about men like Charles Matinga, Manoah Chirwa, Mathews Phiri, Chief Chikowi, Chief Makanjira and many more who were regarded as traitors because they had sided with the colonial rulers during the country's freedom struggle. There had been widespread demands that these men be punished. Those among them who were Chiefs had been deposed, but it had been difficult to punish those who were businessmen or farmers, for example. In fact, in private, Banda had always told his ministers that he could detain some of these men after independence. In the ministers' judgment, if they had opposed the bill right away, Banda could have gone to the people to denounce them for interfering with his intention to make the country safe by punishing the "Capricorns" (a Malawian term for stooge). Indeed, Banda could have an easy victory over his rivals and this could have created difficulties for them to confront Banda on more favorable issues. Instead, they merely pressed him to temporarily withdraw the bill so that more harsh parts of it could be studied thoroughly and, if necessary, amended. He agreed to this request. However, this in itself, was a victory. Never had the ministers ever made the despot withdraw a measure on which he felt strongly. They were therefore further encouraged in their determination to get him to change his position.

Enough was enough. The ministers for a long time had to endure humiliating insults and degradation for the sake of unity and stability of the nation, but time had ran out. They had decided to seek an immediate audience with Banda. As expected, he was extremely reluctant to see them as a group and suggested they come one by one. His ever-present fear of people "ganging together" manifested itself once more. However, the ministers tried for several occasions to bring pressure on the President through constitutional means to change his ways, but to no effect. Eventually, Banda reluctantly agreed to see them as a group. With unexpected courage and unity, they confronted the beast head on August 26, 1964, two weeks before a historic showdown. At this meeting, the ministers with unprecedented courage and candidness pointed out to him all the implications and likely consequences of the type of speech he had made at Chileka Airport on his return from Cairo. The Minister portrayed a high standard of eloquence that Banda could not match. He looked confused and disoriented when the ministers put up a gallant stand against the despot that had humiliated them for so long. The fear of a violent reaction from him vanished especially since during the discussion he, to their astonishment, lost his poise in the face of their barrage of arguments and objections against his Chileka speech. At times he even appeared to be incoherent. This part of the story marked a turning point both in their relations with Banda and in the political history of the nation.

After much prevarication, Dr. Banda said that albeit he did not agree that he had been wrong to make that type of speech, since his colleagues objected to it, he promised that he would not make such a speech again in the future. That was apparently the sign of change of heart after bitter clashes over issues of concern. The Ministers had not only discovered that it was possible for them to overcome their differences and rivalries which Banda had tried to fan, and that they could unite on matters of principle. But they had also discovered that when, and if, they got united in pressing him for change to his wrong methods and policies it was possible for them to get him to change.

They finally resolved that in the future they must not allow Dr. Banda, or any other person or issue to divide them, and that to ensure lasting unity among themselves, all their decisions must be made after thorough discussion as a group.

Though too late, the ministers made other significant decisions. One of them was that since their own excessive praising and glorifying of the autocrat had contributed immensely to his feeling that he knew everything and need not consult anyone, in future they must tone down their praise of the monster. Another decision was that they could use their new strong position and psychological victory to get Dr. Banda to change certain specific aspects of internal and external policy.

The second and much more bitter clash, which was to lead to a final split, was over the following policies: Hospital Fees; Africanization of Civil Service; Banda's relation with racist-ruled Mozambique, Rhodesia and South Africa; and his highhandedness. On Africanization and his relations with evil regimes in the south, he totally refused to compromise and offered to resign. To the surprise of Banda himself and the people alike, the ministers who had strongly criticized the President's leadership, did not want him to resign and it was left that they could produce their complaints in writing. Shortly afterwards, Banda's whole attitude hardened and he decided to fight it out with the ministers. In essence, the ministers had lost the first battle with Banda.

However, the situation was heading to a boiling point. The ministers, on the other hand, strongly felt that time had come for a courageous attempt to save Malawi for the people of Malawi and for Africa. They aired their views on a number of issues already mentioned in the chapter. At this last encounter, a heated debate ensued; tempers were lost. Instead of the usual three hours, the meeting lasted seven hours and reconvened several times during the next few days. Banda was still committed to his obnoxious policies that would in the future turn Malawi into the laughing stock of the world and a political leper in Africa. He adamantly refused to let down his fascist Portuguese, racist South Africans, and settler Rhodesian friends, as well as the British expatriate officers, the source of his strength. He had promised to retain their jobs for many years to come. So he offered to resign rather than accept the demands.

The nation at this stage still had a British Governor-general representing the Queen. His functions were purely ceremonial and his powers purely advisory. The man who then filled the post was Sir Glyn Jones. To be candid, he had been a liberal and played a part in hastening the coming of self-rule. He was a much respected man among the people, but was ineffectual. He disagreed with Banda's dictatorial ways and had himself on several occasions been treated by Banda rather like a junior officer. When Banda went to tender his resignation, Sir Glyn Jones took a line which illustrates the inappropriateness of applying European concepts, unmodified, to African situations. He told Banda that at least on the need for consultation, the ministers were quite right, but urged him not to resign. He said in such a situation what the Prime Minister had to do was to call a Parliament and seek a vote of confidence. If he were defeated, he could and should resign; but if he won, he could continue with his policies and compel the ministers to resign if they were still in disagreement with his policies. Meanwhile, one of his closest henchmen, Aleke Banda, came with a report that he should not resign because according to him (Aleke Banda, no relation) the broad masses of the country were solidly behind him. This, and the Governor-general's advice, resolved Banda's determination to fight for his political survival.

Unfortunately, what the Governor-general did not realize was that Parliament in Malawi was a rubber-stamp of President Banda and had been so for the entire thirty years that he had been in power. As Head of the Malawi Congress Party, he had nominated all that Party's candidates for elections to Parliament, except for the few men whom he could not have dared to leave out of the list of candidates because they were popular in their home front. All MCP candidates owed their nominations to him. Since the opposition parties had all been disbanded for various reasons, the foremost being intimidation. Because all MCP candidates had been elected unopposed, Parliament was full of deadwood parliamentarians who owed their seats to Dr. Banda. They could not obviously pass a vote of no confidence in him; they were too grateful to him and looking forward to the day when their loyalty would be rewarded with elevation to the cabinet. However, most of these parliamentarians were semiliterate, a circumstance which would not put them in a position to acquire decent opportunities.

After seeing the Governor General, Banda sought advice from men within the Party; he saw a few men from the layer of leaders just below the ministers; a group to which reference has already been made. For obvious reasons, they strongly advised him not to resign but rather to expel the ministers. One of these phony advisers, Gomile Kumtumanji later ended up in Banda's jail after rising to the position of second in command and heir apparent. He faced capital charges for allegedly masterminding a wave of mysterious murders which lasted one and a half years and nearly wrecked the government. Kumtumanji died in prison without even being brought to justice.

On September 7, 1964, Dr. Banda dismissed three of the most brilliant ministers and a junior minister: M. W. Kanyama Chiume (Foreign Minister); the late Augustine Bwanausi (Planning and Development); Orton C. Chirwa (Justice and Attorney General); and Rose Chibambo (Junior Minister, Minister of Social Development). Three others resigned in sympathy with their dismissed colleagues. It was indeed, a high profile principle. They were: the late Yatuta Kaluli Chisiza (Home Affairs); William Chokani (Labor); and Masauko Chipembere (Education). John Msonthi who had been reinstated in his post (Trade and Industry) after his dismissal in July, for reasons nobody knew including Msonthi himself, also resigned–but withdrew his resignation after twenty-four hours and Dr. Banda accepted him back in the cabinet. Msonthi died a mysterious death while serving in Banda's government.

Masauko Chipembere, the most popular and loved leader in the country was in Ottawa, Canada attending the Third Commonwealth Education Conference (CEFC) when these unfortunate things happened. There was a sense of uneasiness among the supporters of the Ministers as to where Chip (as he was popularly known) would stand. As a man of high integrity, he could not abandon his courageous and articulate colleagues. On receiving the news from his colleagues, he forthwith left Canada for Malawi to join his comrades in a fight that could either save or break Malawi. Dr. Banda had sent a government driver to pick up Chipembere from Chileka Airport in Blantyre. As the driver approached him, he banged the door of the government Mercedes-Benz and went to a waiting car that had gone to welcome him. His wife was in the same car. The Minister of Finance, John U. Z. Tembo, whose niece was Dr. Banda's concubine as well as housekeeper and who was one of the President's favorites, did not resign. In fact, he had withdrawn from the growing controversy at an early stage and was a staunch supporter of the despot. On arrival Chipembere tendered his resignation.

As advised by the Governor-general, Banda summoned an emergency meeting of Parliament to seek a vote of confidence. The meeting took place on September 8-9, 1964. For reasons I have already stated, President Banda got it without difficulty. The debate on the motion lasted two days, fortunately Chipembere arrived in time to take part in the debate the second day. The motion was couched in words that merely confirmed the need for unity and discipline in the Malawi Congress Party. The rebel Ministers supported the motion, but severely criticized Banda in the debate on other issues and policies. To be fair, Banda was a good Parliamentary debater, albeit he tended to be more at home before an excited crowd of supporters and admirers. But at this particular time, he was no match for some of the rebel Ministers.

On the first day of the debate, Dr. Banda arranged for a system of loudspeakers to relay speeches to the large crowd outside the Parliament–hoping to impress and win the crowd over to his side. I was among the crowd that day, together with a number of other youth. The oratory of Kanyama Chiume, Augustine Bwanausi, Yatuta Chisiza, Willie Chokani, Orton Chirwa and Rose Chibambo who spoke on the first day was such that the crowd wildly applauded their magnificent speeches and there was dead silence when Banda and his henchmen spoke. At times, there were wild jeers and boos. Two men standing beside me, shouted "chisilu" (i.e., a fool or an idiot).

The following day, on September 9, the loudspeakers were therefore ordered removed, but the crowd swelled. It was encouraging, however, to see that the crowd in Zomba (the Administrative Capital) as in most other places was in sympathy with the rebel ministers and its applause reflected this sympathy. This time as Chipembere arrived at the Parliament Building, he was wildly cheered by the crowd and carried shoulder-high. When Banda arrived minutes after, he was violently booed and called Mchona (a man who had been out of his country for long and had lost touch with his people).

In Parliament, Chipembere went straight to the backbenches where his colleagues settled. He was enthusiastically cheered by his colleagues and when a word was whispered to the crowd outside the Parliament, the crowd went wild with jubilation–the women ululating jovially. The now ex-ministers put up a brilliant patriotic fight in the Parliament that well reflected the peoples' desire for real freedom and justice in their newly born state.

In their defense, the rebel Ministers put their case thus;

Yatuta Chisiza said: "If you (House of Parliament) believe that I am a traitor by pointing out what I consider to be pinpricks, in my view, with a view to going ahead and building our nation, then brothers and sisters, I am ready to hang this minute." Yatuta received a standing ovation from his colleagues after his speech.[vii]

Augustine Bwanausi said: "There in East Africa I notice the extent of Africanization..., Whatever happens, there is bound to have some influence, some impact on our country."[viii]

Willy Chokani said: "Some members of this House have complained that some of the civil servants are still stooges. Many people are forgetting to point out that certain (many of them) Europeans who opposed us, men who were directors of manpower in 1959, are possibly now, men who are trying to rule us. This must not happen in the post independence period."[ix]

Here, Chokani had hit right on the point. White expatriates especially British, dominated the Malawi civil service for the coming three decades and enjoyed life they had not experienced during colonial rule.

The aura of reverence which surrounded Banda, venerated in song and praised by misguided members of Parliament during the crisis, is difficult to explain. He had been remote from the political and social struggle of his people which began long before his birth. While their blood soaked the soil of Malawi, Dr. Banda absorbed the culture, conventions and customs of the west, he himself had said: "By culture, race, origin, background, I'm an African, Mchewa (his tribe), by education I belong to the west. I admire the Europeans in the west: the British, the Americans, the French, the Germans, the Portuguese.... I like them all."[x]

Even though he claimed to be a Mchewa, he could not speak the local dialect—even if his life depended on it. His be-

---

[vii] Source: Yatuta K. Chisiza, *Hansard* (Zomba) September 8, 1964.

[viii] Source: A. W. Bwanausi, *Hansard* (Zomba), September 9, 1964.

[ix] Willie Chokani, *Hansard* (Zomba), September 9, 1964.

[x] H. Banda, *Hansard* (Zomba), December 2, 1968.

havior and background were totally different from Chewa society.

While his affection for Europeans allowed him to excuse their reflections upon his ability, Banda could not tolerate criticism from his countrymen. In October 1970, he was host to his former political adversary of the Federation period, Roy Welensky who had tirelessly tried to forestall independence. The former Colonial Secretary responsible for the Constitution, Ian McLeod, who died the same year, was mourned officially in Malawi and is honored by a street bearing his name at Zomba. The most striking thing is that Dunduzu K. Chisiza, whose patriotism and contribution to the freedom struggle of our country was unquestionable, was never honored, nor did Banda attend his funeral in September 1962. Surprisingly, McLeod had earlier expressed his opinion that Banda was "ignorant about the economic aspects of government."

On September 10, 1964, the crisis had taken another turn. Banda made sure that the speeches by the rebel ministers were read by as few people outside Malawi as possible, therefore he expressly ordered that no copies of the official verbatim report of the debate (Hansard) leave Malawi. A few were smuggled out, but most overseas libraries which had other Malawi Hansards, do not have the issues covering this debate, that is to say, Hansards for the period 8th-9th September 1964.

During the days that followed, efforts were made by various persons both black and white, including the Governor-general, to bring about reconciliation. But they were frustrated by Banda's insistence that certain "Rebel Ministers" should be excluded from reconciliation talks and that they should stop making public speeches stating their side of the story while he himself toured the country denouncing the rebel ministers as traitors. The rebel ministers totally rejected these conditions. The result was that his misguided supporters and the rebel ministers', after listening to conflicting versions of the causes of the split, began to clash and fight in the streets of Zomba (the former Administrative Capital City) and in the suburbs of Blantyre (the commercial hub of the country).

The clash that I was personally involved with was near the Zomba Government Hospital on September 11, 1964. I, and my group supporting the rebel ministers, engaged Banda's hoodlums who had earlier been transported into Zomba from different rural areas to intimidate and harass civil servants who unanimously supported the rebel ministers' cause. As we were throwing bricks and stones at each other, a government Mercedes Benz car appeared and a group of my friends apparently recognized the occupants as Albert N. Muwalo and Gwanda Chakuamba Phiri, Banda's newly appointed cabinet ministers and diehard supporters. While some of our friends were engaging Banda's supporters, I and a group of youths gave chase to the car. It was heading for Blantyre, but at the junction, the road had been blocked by a wall of supporters of the rebel Ministers and the two of Banda's henchmen were coerced to leave the car and run towards the hospital. We gave chase and caught up with Gwanda Chakuamba Phiri. He tried to put up a resistance in order to defend himself, but could not halt the deluge of stones pounding his head and face. He fell to the ground, but still the youths kicked him right and left. One of his eyes was apparently damaged and the face was wholly covered with blood. I thought he had died and thought to myself, "Why does this fool endure such humiliation in defense of that rogue?" Meanwhile, Muwalo had sneaked into a hospital ward and concealed himself in a patient bed. But he was discovered and punched in the face several times before the police saved him. Both men later fell out of Banda's favor. Chakuamba Phiri ended up in prison for eleven years and Albert Muwalo was hanged, hitherto, for unknown charges.

By now the Governor-general, after officially being informed that the Parliament had given Banda a "vote of confidence," advised the Army and Police, which were, and continued to be, commanded by Britons for three decades, to support President Banda. However, the General Governor's advice was needless because it was part of the conspiracy to dominate and control the Army and Police for the interest of the former colonial power. The same machinations had backfired on three newly independent East African States (Kenya,

Uganda, Tanzania). Junior officers in all countries led simultaneous army mutinies that ended British dominance. In Malawi, the story was different. The National Army had to endure inferior status before British Officers for a long period. In a controversy which centered on such questions as Africanization of their own jobs and abolition of inequality between black and white, the choice for the ex-colonial British Officers was an easy one. They were inevitably going to back the man who stood for preservation and perpetuation of the Europeans' privileged position. They carried with them the then politically insulated and uninformed African soldiers.

With the intervention of the army, the fate of the confrontation became a foregone conclusion. For the time being, at any rate, the rebel ministers had lost the battle for the second time. In the prophetic words of Masauko Chipembere, he summarized thus: "In African politics, especially in the decade of the sixties, any man who was supported by the army stayed in power or rose to power; he who was opposed by the army no matter how popular he was, stayed out of power, if he was lucky; if he was not, he stayed elsewhere–in jail, in exile, or in a cemetery."

But the seeds of internal strife had been sown. Even more than before, Banda felt rather insecure in his position. All leading supporters of the rebel ministers who did not succeed in escaping to Zambia or Tanzania, were detained at the notorious Dzeleka Concentration Camp (dubbed Auschwitz) and Maula built soon after Banda was swept into power in the 1961 elections. This was his first priority before schools, clinics, or other institutions. Their continued detention embittered their many relatives and friends and led to more agitation against the government which had been virtually turning to places like apartheid South Africa, Portuguese-controlled Mozambique, and racist Rhodesia for protection. It was a vicious circle which could be broken only by Banda himself admitting his blunders and courageously accepting a return to the 1964 setup.

It is extremely sad that more than 95 percent of Malawians have not been told the truth about the genesis of the famous cabinet crisis unique to African politics. All that the majority of the people know hitherto, is that the rebel ministers and Tumbukas (people from the north) plotted to kill Banda and take over the leadership. In the days to come, Banda added more ammunition into his arsenal. This time he accused the rebel ministers of selling the country to red-China. Amidst the East-West cold-war conflict, President Banda hoped to win favors from his masters, the west. Indeed, both lies worked to his advantage. The west, at the helm of the British government, started to meddle directly or indirectly into Malawi's internal affairs

On the advice of his British intelligence officers, President Banda distorted the whole issue. It turned therefore, that the nation was divided into two groups; the educated, who comprehended very well the issues at stake, and the uneducated who could not have any single clue on the prevailing situation—they were just carried by the current. These people were used to intimidate and neutralize the supporters of the rebel ministers. The present national leadership comprised mostly of Banda's former henchmen, are misguided opportunists, people without vision and principles. These are the people who either through jealousies or ignorance, play down the history of the crisis that changed the political landscape of our country that would take generations to fully realize. Admittedly, both the educated and uneducated acknowledge the fact that the post-independence cabinet was the envy of Africa. It was comprised of the brightest and ablest young men and women Malawi ever produced. The late President of Tanzania, Dr. Julius K. Nyerere, summed it up thus: "Banda lost one of the most capable cabinets on our Continent, it's Africa's loss." Boys and girls in our high schools referred to the rebel ministers as a "Cabinet of Geniuses." Such was the national morale, people thought they had been robbed of their national pride.

Banda and his ignorant supporters throughout the crisis maintained that the rebel ministers and their supporters, especially those from the north (Tumbukas), conspired to kill him and take over the leadership. I have mentioned this elsewhere in the chapter. President Banda had good reasons to hide the truth from his people because he had engaged himself in activities which were contrary to what he had been preaching during the colonial struggle. I am taking this opportunity to inform my fellow countrymen in detail what was the genesis of the crises that made the rebel ministers (some of whom played an important role in inviting Banda into Nyasaland) break away from him;

On internal policies:

(a) Dictatorship. On becoming the Chief Minister or Prime Minister, Banda became increasingly despotic. He bluntly rejected the principle of consultation. In several public pronouncements, both in Parliament and outside, he declared that he made and would always make all the decisions. He said that consultation merely confused a man. If you listen to many conflicting opinions you often ended up more confused than you had been before. Thus, decisions affecting the ministries were, on most occasions, made without consulting the minister concerned and often behind his back. What was more frustrating was that while consultation with his ministers was rejected, the President quite frequently consulted British expatriate officers.

(b) The priority within the Cabinet, was the development of the country. It was agreed therefore that a certain amount of sacrifice or tightening of the belt was imperative. To this effect, the rebel ministers supported the introduction of a graduated tax based on incomes, and the ministers themselves had to pay the highest taxes among the African people.

Dr. Banda suggested a 25 percent reduction in the ministers' salaries, and they accepted that. They had gone further and demanded that they cease having free housing and must, therefore, pay rent and at a higher rate than that paid by their people in the civil service. Sadly, Banda had gone even further. He had decided on a draconian reduction of salaries of all African Civil Servants. To this effect, he had appointed a British aristocrat by the name of Thomas Skinner to make a survey of the salary structure in the African civil service. His report received bitter opposition from the rebel ministers and it was one of the reasons why these gallant sons of our soil, parted with Banda. It was this report that made the "recommendation" for the reduction. However, the Skinner Commission was hilarious. It recommended what Banda had already told his rebel ministers that he was going to do. Using the same arguments that the British officials had used for many years before his return from self-imposed exile, he, astonishingly and unpatriotically, declared that such benefits as government-provided housing were wrong for African Civil Servants, but right for European Civil Servants. He idiotically argued that African standards of living did not justify the existing "inflated" salaries. But in fact, an African's salary under the extended family system, was shared with all his uncles, nephews, sisters, brothers, aunts, in addition to his parents, wife and children.

Relatives would come to the town or city from the village to spend weeks or months with their salary-earning cousins and leave him in heavy debt. Moreover, African standards of living were not as low as Banda imagined them to be. This is where T. D. T. Banda comes in. He strongly warned his colleagues of the consequences of importing a leader who lacked an African background. In short, Dr. Banda had no single respect for Malawians let alone Africans. He once said openly that he was more British than the British themselves. Many African civil servants had children in fee-paying secondary schools. In spite of the fact that African civil servants' salaries were low, Dr. Banda had earlier raised the salaries for European civil servants threefold. But the effect of reducing African salaries so soon after raising European salaries was to widen the gap between white and black incomes. As we can see, this is what the rebel ministers, as the authentic representatives of their people, refused to accept and Banda called them traitors.

(c) Sadly, this discrimination between European and Africans was characteristic of Dr. Banda's way of life. At his Party residence (the residence was bought by Nyasaland African Congress (ANC) after he had failed to raise funds on his own in Blantyre) he had a seating room in which he received only Europeans, including officials working under his ministers. Africans were invariably received in the inferior seating room, except for selected visiting dignitaries. When an African visitor had a call of nature, he was shown the toilets at the servants' quarters, a European or white was shown the bathroom inside the residence. At one time, Banda told one of the Ministers that, "I trust whites; they never lie." However, Dr. Banda, the man who had declared on the day of his arrival in 1958 that he had come to bridge the gap between the races, was doing things contrary and thus widened that gap. In general, Banda treated whites with tremendous respect and dignity, Malawians were treated with ridicule and indignity.

(d) Another demonstration of Banda's lack of understanding of African life, caused by fake roots and by the aloof and aristocratic life he led, came when he imposed hospital fees on the people who had throughout the colonial era never been made to pay for government medical services. The amount he imposed was small, but considering the peoples' per capita income of US$50 and the long distance most of them had to walk to the nearest hospital or clinic, the three-Malawi-penny fee was a heavy burden which prevented many people from taking their fever-stricken children to clinics. In fact, he did not care what happened to Malawians so long as he protected his own life. When I was growing up, I was flabbergasted to see people struggle to break the impact of poverty, and yet for many occasions Banda asserted that when he arrived in Nyasaland he found many people walking half-naked. This was an insult and unsubstantiated statement from the man who had arrived from his political wilderness with absolutely limited possessions. In fact, the majority of Malawians were better off during the colonial era than they are today. From the outset, Banda's leadership philosophy was that "familiarity breeds contempt." A leader must live above the people. He must be different from them. They are proud of him when they know that he is someone different and exceptional. This is exactly how he treated the people of Malawi. He had no respect for them, nothing but contempt and ridicule.

(e) But while these sacrifices were being demanded of the people in the name of "tightening the belt" for the sake of development, life at the President's official residences was full of luxury. He had a large number of attendants and guards who were treated like serfs and paid from national coffers. Wherever he went he was accompanied by a large convoy of vehicles, each carrying several youths and women fed and paid from national funds. He owned several expensive cars. Even before independence, he had ordered the putting up of more official residences, and at least two places were already being cleared or surveyed for that purpose. At the time of his death, he had left behind four palaces and numerous official lodges some of which he had never used. The first Palace (Sanjika) cost the taxpayer US$24 million. It is rated as Africa's most expensive Presidential Palace—yet located in a country where per capita income is the lowest in Africa.

(f) It was widely acknowledged that through British reluctance to train Africans for the assumption of responsible positions in the public service, there were not enough Africans with the skill and experience to replace all European officials as soon as the country achieved her independence. But Dr. Banda had himself often said that the best way to train a man to do something was to let him do it, even if he burns his fingers in the process. "The best way to learn how to swim is by swimming and not by climbing mountains," he concluded. So it had been agreed that the government would Africanize all those posts for which able Africans were available—the government had began to do just that gradually, but steadily. Suddenly and treacherously, the puppet leader changed his mind and was beginning to prefer extensive retention of his masters, the British colonial officers, many of whom were, to say the least, hostile to the rebel ministers whom the officers branded as rabid nationalists. And they were also hostile to the very concept of African independence and sought every opportunity to circumvent our national aspirations.

In Gold Coast (Ghana), the then Prime Minister Dr. Kwame Nkrumah, foremost Pan-Africanist of our time, thought of a clever way of easing out the British civil servants. Many were given contracts to train Ghanians to take over important positions in their departments. However, this was not the case in Malawi where its Prime Minister put the whole trust on the former colonizers.

On Foreign policies:

As on domestic policies, foreign policies also played a crucial role on the cabinet crisis. As I have mentioned in previous pages, the rebel ministers were ardent nationalists and widely versed in international issues especially the African liberation struggle. There was no way that they could compromise their deeply rooted conscience on white racist regimes of southern Africa. They wanted to maintain decent relations with other independent African nations and East-West Nonalignment policy.

(a) Though Malawi was an independent state, its foreign policies were dictated mostly by the former colonial power, the British Government. At a later stage, apartheid South Africa assumed the leading role. This had an enormous impact on the nonalignment policy that had been agreed upon and which had been one of the Party's main planks during the election campaign of 1961, prominently furthering its manifesto. Before independence, Banda had not caused great concern, apart from some criticism of communism made during a purely academic debate of the Zomba Debating Society. He had begun to establish contacts with Communist-China through the Chinese Embassy in Tanzania to neutralize the effects of Malawi's strong historical western links. After independence, however, the balance was no longer maintained, with Banda leaning more and more to the former colonizers—the west.

(b) What made the rebel ministers even more frustrated was the growing fraternization with the evil regimes of apartheid South Africa, racist Rhodesia, and brutal Mozambique (Portuguese). However, geographical position necessitated a certain amount of caution in the country's relations with these regimes, but it was needless for Malawi to become a political ally of these foes of Africa. Indeed, Malawi needed continued Portuguese permission to use the Mozambique Railways and the Port of Beira for her external trade. It was also true that thousands of Malawians went to South Africa and Rhodesia to seek work. But it was a mutual-benefit set up. Portugal could not close her Railways and Harbor to Malawi's massive fee-paying traffic without doing harm to her own economy in Mozambique, nor could workers, some of whom were highly skilled and experienced, without wrecking their economies. Ironically, it was not necessary for Malawi to become a quisling of the anti-African liberation struggle. It was tragic for Banda to align himself with these evil regimes. However, it soon became apparent that Banda was merely too much of a European in his outlook to keep close to the white company that ruled southern Africa. "During his forty-three years abroad, he had ceased to be an African in everything but skin color," Chipembere said. Indeed, T. D. T. Banda's prophetic vision could have saved our nation from this shame which had been around us for thirty years.

(c) The treatment meted out to other African nations and in particular to the former dysfunctional continental organization, the Organization of African Unity (OAU), confirmed Banda's attitude towards Africa's endeavors. First and foremost, he had the greatest contempt for them; his treatment of some of the visitors these African nations sent was rather discourteous and un-African. He ridiculed the OAU's efforts to liberate southern Africa, and not only refused to take part, but actually tried to undermine Africa's morale for this struggle. He refused to give even that limited degree of asylum and assistance to African refugees from southern Africa which the United Nations permitted. As I have already asserted, this was part of a foreign policy dictated by foreign reactionary powers bent on disrupting Africa's march to freedom. The Malawi government's relations with other African states were then, of course, at their worst. No black African State had any Embassy in Malawi, while there were Embassies from practically every West European country and the United States. In addition, apartheid South Africa and Rhodesia were represented in Malawi at the ambassadorial level. Both countries were regarded as archenemies of the African liberation struggle. Nationalist China, Japan, and Israel had also embassies in Malawi—but no African country had.

Realistically, these were the sole reasons why the rebel ministers resolved to part with President Banda two months after the attainment of independence. The issues covered the whole political, economic, and social spectrum of the state and were not issues related to opportunism or power-hunger on the part of the rebel ministers. They were issues related to the aspirations of the people of Malawi on the one hand, and Africa as a whole on the other. It was therefore a patriotic duty of the rebel ministers to defend these aspirations on behalf of the people they diligently represented.

These were issues of national and continental interests and were presented with courage and in good faith. The ministers knew of the consequences to their personal life, but were ready to face them for the good of their country and Africa. It was therefore a stance motivated by principles and not greed or otherwise. It is, therefore, my obligation to contribute in my small way this vital information which had been expressly denied or hidden from the majority of our people for the last four decades–in order to undermine the credence of the famous Cabinet Crisis of September 1964.

The present leadership, most of whom had been part to this ugly and shameful trend, did not have the courage or clout to tell the truth about what had happened or what was the cause for the crisis because they are jellyfish, people with no vision who betrayed their own conscience for money and material wealth. Indeed, they lost their souls.

Astonishingly, it seems that the present leadership does not grow. On his ascendancy to power in May 2004, Dr. Bingu wa Mutharika renamed Lilongwe International Airport, "Kamuzu International Airport." In the first multiparty elections in May, 1994, after thirty years of one-man brutal rule, the former disgraced President Bakili Muluzi renamed the Airport from Kamuzu to "Lilongwe International Airport." Despite his moral weaknesses, Bakili Muluzi tried to discourage Kamuzuism in the hearts of Malawians who had been living under the culture of hero-worshipping for three decades. He also refused demands from the leader of the opposition Malawi Congress Party (MCP), John U. Z. Tembo, to erect the mausoleum over Banda's grave.

Bingu wa Mutharika agreed to construct the mausoleum without even bringing the issue to the Parliament for approval. Multimillion dollar construction at the time of an acute food shortage in the country and the grinding poverty among our people fully explains the type of leadership Malawians will have to endure for decades to come. For the man who brutalized, ridiculed, physically and mentally enslaved the people of Malawi for thirty years under a "Police State," and nakedly betrayed the African redemption struggle, to be rewarded with such high profile symbol is hard to believe. President Bingu wa Muthalika and his brother were coerced to leave the country in the 1964 political crisis and had lived in exile for three decades. Dr. Bingu returned to his homeland after multiparty democracy was introduced into the country. Why then this, the looniest of evil men?

In addition to Kamuzu Airport and the infamous mausoleum, Banda had been honored on several national structures: a Kamuzu school of nursing, a Kamuzu highway; Kamuzu barracks, Kamuzu stadium, Kamuzu procession road, Kamuzu academy, and the list goes on and on. In reality, Banda was a demigod to Malawians, they adored and respected him despite his utter disrespect for them, he called them his people and they responded with pride and jubilation. But for many lucid Malawians, the mausoleum is a symbol of injustice, betrayal and oppression under a regime bent on tyranny and misguided policies and principles.

Chapter Six

AFTERMATH OF THE CRISIS

The September 1964 crisis came as a complete surprise to the people of Malawi who had placed their entire hope in Dr. Banda's leadership. Indeed, the aftermath of the crisis left people numb and in shock and in state of hopelessness, wondering what future lies ahead.

In spite of this, however, the rebel ministers, in good faith, made what amounted to a final attempt to discuss the situation with the President. A meeting was arranged through the good offices of the Governor-general for September 21, 1964. On Saturday, September 19, Messrs. Chipembere, Chokani, Bwanausi and Yatuta Chisiza assembled in Blantyre, nominally at a cocktail party at one of their prominent supporter's house, L. Chaponda a business man, to which members of the Malawi Congress Party and the press were invited. The usual speeches were made. On hearing of this gathering Banda condemned it as a "covert meeting" and, as a consequence, refused to see the rebel ministers. They in turn, issued a press statement pointing out that their desire for reconciliation had been thwarted by Banda who had twice refused to see them. After this, no further vehement efforts at reconciliation seemed possible as it became clear that the whole issue, having been debated in Parliament, was now to be hawked about the country as a whole at the cost of a dangerous and ever-widening rift.

Soon after the cocktail party had begun, the situation changed and led to security concerns. The rebel ministers then decided to abandon the party for the sake of peace, law and order. Dr. Banda and his henchmen notably, Aleke Banda, John Tembo, Albert Muwalo, Gwanda Chakuamba Phiri, Gomile Kumtumanji and Richard Chidzanja had organized hoodlums under the leadership of Aleke Banda, Commander of the government-sponsored militias (the Young Pioneers), who were transported by government trucks from rural areas to the city of Blantyre. These rogues started harassing and intimidating people who were simply peaceful supporters of the rebel ministers. Within a few minutes, residents of Soche Township, the biggest township then in Blantyre, responded with concerted resistance and the nearby townships of Zingwangwa and Chimwankhunda joined the melee. The hired hoodlums were soon outnumbered ten to one. Six people were reported dead and several dozens injured. Those who were captured confessed that they were promised jobs and money if they beat up supporters of the rebel ministers.

On seeing blood and the dead bodies of innocent people, Augustine Bwanausi and Willie Chokani left the place and headed for the Republic of Zambia. The remaining colleagues and Banda began holding public meetings in various parts of the country. As the contestants warmed to the task, their attitudes hardened and their speeches became more and more vitriolic. Banda obviously became convinced, partly by the adulatory advice of his immediate entourage and partly by the disputable evidence of the large crowds that were coerced to greet him, that he had the overwhelming support of the country behind him. As a result, he showed less and less disposition to make even the smallest gesture of compromise. On the contrary, having dismissed his rebel ministers from the Party Executive, he then suspended them from the Party, forbade the use of the Party Machine to arrange their meetings, and banned members of the Party from attending them. This action, coupled with his increasingly offensive attacks on his former colleagues (in which he described them as a "pack of hyenas") and implying that they were seeking to murder him, only added further bitterness to the situation. The tone of the rebel ministers' speeches, particularly Chipembere, grew more and more bitter towards Banda and his white backers. This was an ominous sign for the future since of all the rebel ministers, Chipembere had by far the greatest popular following in the country. In fact, he was by far more popular than Banda himself. Towards the end of September 1964, Chipembere told a newspaper reporter that he was under pressure to form a new Party but this he was resisting in the interest of national unity. Ominously too, Chipembere's position took on a distinctly anti-European tone. He had good reasons for this; Chipembere and his colleagues, and indeed most educated Malawians, strongly agreed that Europeans, especially the British community, were behind the crisis which had torn the nation apart.

As the public debate unfolded, it became clear that, as had been anticipated, large sections of the uneducated public opinion throughout the countryside were solidly behind Banda. Some of the rebel ministers had little local support at all; even the northern Region which was supposed to be the anti-Banda opposition lacked any potential force. This was in part due to the fact that the majority of educated northerners were in the south working in government offices and in other sectors. In fact, the key to the situation appeared to lie in the southern Region and particularly around Ft. Johnstone (Mangochi), Blantyre-Limbe and Zomba. The reason for this was first that this area contained the bulk of the so-called "educated classes" for whom many of the policies and arguments of the rebel ministers had a distinct appeal; and secondly that it was the region in which Chipembere's influence was overwhelmingly strongest. Support for the rebel ministers in Central Malawi was pathetic, not because they were villains, but because Banda hails from Central Malawi and as such, he was regarded by Chewa-speaking people as their godfather and besides, the policies that were the centerpiece of the whole crisis, were beyond their comprehension.

Though the heat of the public debate tension gradually increased, it was not until the week following Saturday, October 3, 1964, that the first concerted physical clashes took place and law and order appeared for the first time to be in danger. The cause of the disturbances was undoubtedly the expectation that Chipembere's followers would assemble in Blantyre on Sunday to hear him speak after the first planned meeting was prematurely cancelled. There was also a growing determination on the part of the dreaded Malawi Congress

Party to put on a show of force against the dissident "civil servants." This took place in Limbe, Blantyre's sister city. About 400 Youth Leaguers led by a dozen of Young Pioneers, said to have come from Cholo and allegedly traveling to Lilongwe, had to stop in Limbe due, as they asserted, to a petrol shortage. They were accommodated at the Farmers Marketing Board (FMB) Hall. This aroused the resentment of the local residents and a fray developed in which all the windows of the Hall were shattered and some 40 people were injured, but no death was reported. The following afternoon Chipembere was to have held his meeting in Soche Township between Blantyre and Limbe, but it was banned on the grounds that the necessary police permission had not been obtained. Nevertheless, Chipembere did put in an appearance and spoke for a few minutes to a well-disciplined crowd of some 2,000, gathered outside the house where he was staying. He told them he could not hold his meeting, but would do so the following Sunday and he gave them a pointed resume of what he would then say. As he finished speaking, gangs of Banda's Janjaweeds (militias) arrived again in government trucks or lorries, heavily armed with clubs, iron bars and spears and attacked the peaceful audience. The response was swift and bloody. There were again about 30 casualties. The riot act was read by a police officer and the crowd dispersed.

As violence spread, a big tree had been put across the Blantyre-Zomba Road, 20 km from Zomba by a gang of some 200 government militias who manned this road block from the early hours of Sunday in an endeavor to prevent Chipembere, other rebel ministers, and their supporters from reaching Blantyre for the meeting which had been previously banned. However, Chipembere was already in Blantyre with other colleagues. All vehicles were stopped, and although few police were present under a young and inexperienced European officer with a radio car, they made no attempt to intervene. This clearly proves that the ex-colonial power, and its highly charged expatriates, were behind the crisis and on the side of their puppet Hastings Banda. Instructions had been given from Banda's office not to harass or prevent whites from driving through.

But in the evening there were some violent incidents in which two cars were burned, one of them a Mercedes Benz belonging to Orton C. Chirwa, the rebel Minister of Justice. Thanks to his competent and courageous driver who reversed direction at a terrifying speed and enabled Chirwa and his wife Vera to make a dramatic escape. The couple traveled in darkness for about 25 km and ended up in the Chiladzulu District—avoiding aggressive wild animals. In Chiladzulu they were received by Edwin Chibambo the husband of Rose Chibambo herself an ex-rebel Minster. Chibambo was the government District Commissioner in Chiladzulu, but a staunch supporter of the rebel ministers while his brother McKinley Chibambo was a diehard henchman of Hastings Banda. He fled to Zambia with his wife where he died a defiant nationalist amid increased violence orchestrated by Banda himself and his cohorts.

Heads of the Diplomatic Mission in Malawi (all of them westerners) were briefly the guests of Dr. Banda at a mass rally and cocktail party in Lilongwe, having been flown there by special plane. Banda, undoubtedly wished to demonstrate to the Heads of Diplomatic Mission the vast popular support he enjoyed among his tribal groups in the Central Region. This he did convincingly, though the enthusiasm shown there for him contrasted oddly with the road blocks throughout the country and the events of the following weeks in Zomba and other towns. And when Banda addressed the Heads of Diplomatic Mission in a private "audience," his attitude of overconfidence and inflexibility seemed, in the light of the developing situation in the Capital, further misleading and disingenuous.

On the night of Sunday, September 27, 1964, a gang of Malawi Young Pioneers, fed on drugs and marijuana, some of them from the road blocks, moved into Zomba and stayed at the Malawi Congress Party Headquarters, a small building in the African Market area. In the morning they tried to eject the traders from the market and to intimidate the reputedly pro-

Chipembere civil servants on their way to work. Their motive behind this, presumably, was to teach them some kind of lesson. The civil servants reacted sharply and armed themselves with sticks and iron bars. Open clashes resulted in the Congress Party Headquarters and store for the local MCP chairman being burned down. The Malawi flag was brought down and put on fire. Two of the leaders of the Youth League were also nearly killed from their beating injuries. The Police, including the mobile force (riot squad), were frequently engaged, but no arrests were made. In the afternoon, one of Banda's new Ministers, Gomile Kumtumanji, addressed a public meeting in Zomba Community Hall. I attended the meeting with some friends, all of us being diehard supporters of the rebel ministers. We were shocked and flabbergasted to hear the Minister declaring at the top of his voice that the Tumbukas (people from the north) wanted to kill our Ngwazi (Messiah) and take over the leadership. Indeed, the remark was inappropriate and inauspicious at that given time and it sent a divisive message throughout the country that inflamed tribal sentiments and continued to permeate Malawian politics for the ensuing thirty years.

The week of September 29, 1964, started quietly, but a lunchtime rumor that government sponsored militias were coming to Zomba to attack the African families in those locations. This brought the civil servants rushing from their work armed with every sort of cudgel. There was a good deal of excitement and tension, but there was only one clash in which an unidentified man was attacked and killed. This happened before my eyes. The man was innocent and reacted in panic, and that foolish reaction led to his attack by the rebel ministers' supporters. It was apparent, however, that apart from the civil servants who were themselves staunch supporters of the rebel ministers, pro-Chipembere supporters had now come into Zomba from other areas to support the civil servants against hoodlums who had been organized by the government under Banda's instructions.

AFTERMATH OF THE CRISIS 113

The events of Wednesday 30, 1964, confirmed this impression, for by that morning, the general intimidation was such that the entire African community in Zomba, refrained from going to work. They all wore white bands on their wrists to indicate that they were not Banda's Janjaweeds (militias) and they all carried clubs and cudgels. The situation became somewhat confused in the sense that Banda's hired rogues also wore white bands and infiltrated the pro-Chipembere community and extracted some vital information which was then transmitted to Banda's camp. All shops were closed and eventually government departments also closed down. Large crowds gathered in the market area, with the supposed purpose of defending Zomba against an attack by Banda's recruited thugs from nearby neighborhoods. The situation was tense and explosive. Instead of intervening to restore peace, law and order, astonishingly, the army and police stood by, one company of troops being on "immediate notice." However, the army and the company of troops being on police duty were both officered by junior British officers who were strong supporters of Dr. Banda's puppet regime. During this state of turbulence, not a single minister was in Zomba and, for all intents and purposes, the elected government of the black people appeared to have abdicated its responsibilities in the capital of Zomba. Surely, the independence that the Malawian people had anxiously waited for was in name only—in reality, the country was still in the hands of the British authority with Banda as its quisling. The Army Commander, Governor-general, Police Commissioner and Senior Officials, all of them British expatriates, were left in charge of the day-to-day running of the government business. It was, however, unfortunate that the majority of uneducated Malawians could not see or detect the involvement of British expatriates under instructions from the home government. The few educated people who realized that Malawi had expressly become a neo-colonial state, could not voice their disapproval in fear of their lives and livelihood in a country steadily and slowly on the course to a form of Gestapoism—and those who dared voice their feelings, either ended up in prison, a grave yard, or fled the country.

On the late afternoon of September 30, the leaders of the Civil Servants in Zomba demanded to see a minister. The only one who could be contacted in Blantyre refused, on a flimsy excuse, to show up himself in the capital. Youens, a devious expatriate Permanent Secretary in Dr. Banda's Office, was sent to the African Market to try to reassure the people that all would be well if they returned to work. Having a dubious reputation among African civil servants, the crowd was in no mood to listen and his words were largely lost amid the din. It must be noted, however, that Youens and Peter Long, the notorious Police Commissioner, were the masterminds of the whole crisis targeting the rebel ministers who were a thorn in their flesh and regarded by the former colonial power as radical nationalists who could establish a bridgehead with African liberation movements in southern Africa. Again, though this effort was praiseworthy in itself, it raised suspicions in a situation of this kind. An expatriate official should manifestly act on behalf of African ministers by involving himself directly in this internal political dispute. However, there were some liberal expatriates who resented the involvement of their kinsmen in the internal affairs of an independent state and advised them to be as unobtrusive as possible and to help Africans to be openly associated with any major decisions or policies. For the Malawi army and police to remain dormant in this national crisis that threatened the sovereignty of their young nation, and to look askance as young and inexperienced British officers took charge of the delicate situation, was both unpatriotic and misguided. It was, indeed, part of the colonial policies to keep the army and police misinformed so as to easily manipulate them in such crisis. Moreover, the army and police forces were created in such a way that academic qualifications did not exist or matter at all. For instance, the first Armed Forces Chief Major-General Matewele was an illiterate man who served as a courier in the Second World War. Matewele was elevated to Major-General from Private soldier when he blew up a parked Lebanese aircraft which had been hijacked and landed at Malawi's Chileka International Airport—then the biggest airport. Instead of releasing the aircraft and detaining the hijackers, President Banda ordered its destruction. With such unqualified military officers, there was an ample likelihood that these officers would become servile and serve the interests of foreigners.

In the early years of independence, few young educated people enlisted in the armed forces. Among those who did were two brothers, Hansley Ndovi and K. Ndovi who successfully passed the Cambridge School Certificate with a first grade pass. Their presence in the Army were resented for two major reasons: first, they were Tumbukas from the north who were suspected to be anti-Bandaism, and secondly, being educated, they were knowledgeable and could spread anti-Bandaism sentiments within the armed forces and create a nucleus for an eventual military putsch. It came as no surprise to them, and other members of the educated elite, that their services were unceremoniously terminated and then placed in detention for years for reasons even the authorities didn't understand. In the police force, Sweetman Kumwenda was recommended by a notorious police chief, Peter Long, to become the first Police Commissioner after his retirement. Sweetman Kumwenda was recruited by the Zanzibar revolutionary government led by Abed Aman Karume after violent revolution led by John Okelo of Uganda and his supporters of the Mozambican origin (Makondes). The choice of Sweetman Kumwenda was not accidental. Abed Karume's mother hailed from Malawi in Nkhota-kota District in Central Malawi. Kumwenda played a prominent role in training the Zanzibar police force after the revolution.

After the contract, Kumwenda returned to Malawi to prepare himself to take over from Peter Long, the colonial expatriate. The appointment of Sweetman Kumwenda into such a powerful position did not impress Dr. Banda. First, Sweetman Kumwenda was a northerner and secondly he was a brilliant individual with vast experience in a police force. A few days or weeks before his installation as a police chief,

Kumwenda died a mysterious death and doctors were not permitted to perform a post-mortem to determine the cause of the death. However, it was discovered later that Kumwenda was poisoned—his blood contained a good amount of dangerous poison. The post-mortem was performed covertly by expatriate doctors whom Banda believed would not do things behind his back. Sweetman Kumwenda's position was handed over to Kamwana, a Chewa speaker, who had limited experience with a police force.

Fearing backlash, Banda tried to recruit young and semi-educated men into the army and police force. As under the colonial administration, the army personnel and police officers swore to pay allegiance only to the President himself, and not to the nation. In this way, they remained a misguided force that was ultimately used by Banda to suppress his own people and to protect his own political and economic interests. However, it is not astonishing that after independence, all of the continent's armed forces were directly controlled by the State House and therefore used with precision to undermine national freedoms at all costs. As I have indicated elsewhere, any African leader who is supported by the armed forces, no matter how unpopular he is, is assured of being in power for the rest of his life.

Most of the violent activities were centered in Zomba, the administrative capital. The core of workers in this small town were civil servants—there were no factories or industries. The remaining population consisted of a small business community, dependents of civil servants, and few Asian shops. It was not surprising therefore that the overwhelming majority in Zomba supported the rebel ministers because, in their mind, the ministers spoke the language they understood and they regarded Banda as the representative of yet another system of oppression, "Neocolonialism"

In October 1964, things started to cool down. The Malawi Rifles which was wholly controlled or dominated by young British officers moved quietly into the African residential area. The majority of civil servants were clearly delighted to see them, as there was no sign of any government ministers, including Banda himself, in Zomba. Some commented that this was an opportunity for the rebel ministers to stage a bloodless coup had it been the case that the majority of black soldiers were progressively informed and politically knowledgeable. The civil servants willingly laid down their homemade weapons and returned to work after a month of lawlessness and mistrust. The recalcitrant few were quickly disarmed, and twelve arrests were made. The police and troops were on patrol that day, mainly as a reassurance to civil servants that the government-sponsored militias would not attack their homes. This brief period of violence, appeared to have ended at least for the moment in the capital of Zomba, where it originally started. In the capital alone, 75 people were injured, most of them Banda's hired rogues. Five were killed, three buildings and seven flags destroyed by fire, and six cars damaged. Zomba forthwith returned to normal, but mistrust and fear still remained because the entire control for law and order had been left in the hands of British expatriates while no African minister dared show his face in Zomba. This contradicts Banda's cohorts who maintained that their boss was popular among the majority of Malawians. If, indeed, Banda enjoyed the support of the people, it was through coercion and ignorance which was rampant in the country. It must be noted that the provocation of the violence in Zomba and Blantyre-Limbe was undoubtedly ascribed to Dr. Banda personally and to his henchmen. They used the Malawi Youth League and the Malawi Young Pioneers to foment disorder and then accused the rebel ministers and their supporters of inciting violence and lawlessness.

The attacks on civil servants and other citizens, deemed to be from Chipembere supporters in Zomba, were personally initiated by President Banda using G. Kumtumanji the newly appointed southern Regional minister. Because Banda studiously ignored what was happening and never returned from his northern tour to assume command, Malawians embraced a very uncertain future in their newly independent African State. There were also disturbing reports that Banda refused to accept police reports about the true genesis of the unrest and preferred the sycophantic explanation of his own advisers that all the trouble was due to the disloyalty of the African civil servants.

On the afternoon of October 2, 1964, Chipembere and Yatuta Chisiza addressed what could be the last meeting at Zomba Government Secondary School which was attended by thousands of people. Chisiza spoke first and his speech was frequently interrupted by wild cheers and men and women clapping their hands and ululating. Chisiza told the audience that the independence the people of Malawi fought for, had been handed back to the former oppressors by Hastings Banda for his own personal interest. People in the crowd could be heard shouting, "dispatch him back to London." Chisiza further warned his supporters that the struggle to regain their lost freedom and dignity might be long and costly, because the enemy they were fighting was not Banda—he was only being used as a puppet—but freedom and victory were inevitable in the long run.

Chipembere reiterated what Yatuta Chisiza had said and stressed the need for unity and vigilance because Banda and his henchmen would try to divide the people for their own advantage. Chipembere cited as an example the remarks made earlier by Regional Minister Gomile Kumtumanji that northerners were conspiring to liquidate Hastings Banda in order to take over the leadership of the country. Chipembere condemned this as cheap and dangerous propaganda that might plunge the nation into turmoil. He emphasized that their differences with Banda were not just ethnicity or personal ambitions, but rather nationalist principles and African dignity of which Banda was ignorant and unconcerned. He went on to strongly warn against Banda's closest henchmen, Aleke Banda, Gwanda Chakuamba, Albert Muwalo, Gomile Kumtumanji and John Tembo. They were told not to trust Banda, for even one day, or they will find themselves either in a grave or prison. As for John Tembo, he made a remark that created laughter among his audience. He prophetically said that

Tembo would be spared in the sense that his niece, Cecilia Kadzamila, was Banda's partner. Apart from Tembo, the four men did not go far with their education, but at least they had a grasp of politics, but betrayed their conscience for political favors and material wealth. Throughout his speech, people were attentive, cheerful and in high spirits. There were sharp contrasts between Banda and his former colleagues. While his colleagues appeared to focus on vital issues and ideals, Banda dwelt on self-glorification—repeating speeches he had delivered way back in 1958 when he arrived in Nyasaland from his political wilderness. He said; "I came to Nyasaland to do two things, to break their stupid federation and bring you, my people, independence." This was his hallmark speech for the thirty years he was in power. After the crisis, he focused on character assassination, accusing his former colleagues of conspiring to kill him.

Chipembere continued with vigor and tenacity to deliver home speeches that revolutionized the minds of his supporters. He warned them that Banda had sided himself with European expatriates to derail the aspirations of the people of Malawi in their effort to help their brothers and sisters in southern Africa who were oppressed by minority racist regimes and instead to turn Malawi into a playground for reactionary forces against African winds of change. I was standing near a gentleman whom I recognized as being a policeman, but he was in civilian clothes. I was not sure if he was on an errand mission for the government. But from his outlook, I was convinced that he was one of us, but trying to protect his position. At one point, he interrupted Chipembere's speech and said in a loud voice: "Only a bullet through his (Banda's) head would end this naked betrayal." People burst into instant and tumultuous response, "Destroy the old traitor." Chipembere ended his remarkable speech amid wild cheers by warning his supporters not to be complacent—Banda might be a fool, but the people behind him were not. His victory, however, would mean long and brutal suffering of the African people at the hands of neocolonialists and their collaborators. Chipembere's prophetic words not only proved a reality, but also opened a new chapter in Malawi's political history for the coming thirty years of savage one-man rule. This was, perhaps, the last public meeting addressed by Chipembere and Yatuta Chisiza.

The final episode in this part of the story was the restriction of Chipembere to his home on the lake shore northeast of Fort Johnston (present day Mangoche). It had, by this time, become absolutely clear to the administration that, even if it was Banda and his unruly followers who were provoking the violence, there was no chance of the situation returning to normal until Chipembere, with his large popular following and his capacity to unite public support against the government, had been put under some restraint. The same day on September 30, 1964, after Chipembere had spoken to a well attended meeting in Zomba, Banda as the Head of Government, signed the Restriction Order in Kasungu, his home district, and in the early hours of the following day, a company of troops moved to Fort Johnston. They were greeted in a friendly manner by the local population and encountered no trouble. Chipembere was not at home when the police called early that morning, but on Friday, he subsequently sent them a message and accepted the order with good grace. There had so far been no public reaction to his confinement, largely due to Chipemere's own instructions to his followers.

Meanwhile, Kanyama Chiume, one of the leading nationalists and an independence bulwark, managed to address meetings in Rumphi and Livingstonia (Mumbwe) in the northern region—two areas located within his constituency. Both meetings went on well and were well attended by enthusiastic crowds who had come from rural precincts to hear their representative. It was an opportunity for Kanyama to explain to his constituents why he parted with Banda, the man he had so lavishly praised. At Mumbwe, he strongly warned his audience not to trust Banda as he had betrayed their aspirations and dreams. He explained to the cheering crowd how Banda abdicated the hard-won freedom to a bunch of former colonizers both in Malawi and London. He also warned his supporters not to cave into Banda's tactics of divide and rule, and described him as a dangerous tribalist who would divide the nation on tribal grounds for his own political gains. But he cautioned in a thrilling remark: "He can fool the people some of the time, he can fool some of the people all the time, but he cannot fool all the people all of the time." His audience jumped in the air and cheered wildly in response. In closing his speech, he warned his supporters not to be complacent and expect that the struggle to regain their dignity would take a long time because Banda was just being used by imperialists to undermine their freedom and independence. From Mumbwe, Kanyama headed for Rumphi, his Constituency Headquarters where he was scheduled to address another rally. Things went badly. News had been leaked that the newly appointed Regional Minister M. Q. Chibambo in the company of dozens of Young Pioneer militias were planning to disrupt the meeting and possibly harm Kanyama Chiume. Forthwith, Kanyama changed his mind and decided to proceed to Fort Hill (Chitipa) in the extreme north of the country. A few miles from Rumphi, the car battery failed and he and his colleagues in a VW car were forced to park beside the road while a colleague traveled to Rumphi to buy a new battery. While waiting for their colleague to bring the battery so that they could continue with their mission, Chibambo, the new Minister for Regional Affairs—in a convoy of three government Land Rovers laden with about twenty ugly looking thugs—passed the parked car which Chibambo had recognized as being Kanyama's car.

The colleague returned with a battery and soon the car was fixed ready for the unpredictable journey. Before even the car was started, one Land Rover (plate number MG.735) with Chibambo and six militias inside passed by heading in the opposite direction. Chibambo, undoubtedly, was on a surveillance mission to find out whether Kanyama had made a U-turn. The other two Land Rovers were parked in waiting and had already started organizing villages against Kanyama and his colleagues. Mind you, these villagers were fed up with lies against the rebel ministers and were ready to do anything wicked to harm Kanyama and his colleagues. Soon Chibambo returned, by then Kanyama and his colleagues had left the spot heading north to Fort Hill driving at 120 km/h on the unpaved road. The villagers were even told the color and plate number (RU 13) of the car so that they could not miss it. About midday, Banda spoke on Radio Malawi denouncing Kanyama and telling his people that he (Kanyama) was fleeing the country and must be apprehended and if he resists, "You know, my people, you can do whatever you deem fit for traitors, this is war and not cricket." It must be noted however, that throughout the crisis, Banda and his henchmen were telling people that Kanyama and his colleagues were planning to kill the President and take over the leadership. This sort of obnoxious propaganda attracted the attention of uneducated people, largely in rural areas. Chibambo and his gang of Janjaweeds (militias), exacerbated the situation by telling the mobs that Kanyama was running away after having failed to assassinate the Ngwazi (Messiah). People waited along the road for hours holding ndukus (clubs), spears, iron bars or whatever their hands could carry. They were waiting for a red VW, plate number RU 13. Traveling past at a speed of 120-130 km/h, the stone-throwing mobs missed their target each time they made an attempt, but shouts of "traitors" could not be missed.

    Meanwhile, Chibambo and his gang were waiting at the Ft. Hill Police Station. At around 4:00 PM, Kanyama and his colleagues appeared and the police officer stopped the car to warn them of the prevailing situation in the area. Words of Kanyama's impending arrival had spread like prairie fire. Soon the mobs of unruly people arrived and surrounded the car. The police officer had to call for reinforcements as the crowd became uncontrollable. As the car arrived at the police station, the officer advised the two persons who were with Kanyama in the car, Nkharamba Kaunda and Hudson Mbuluwundi Mhango, to get out of the car. Kanyama was then advised to drive slowly through the gate into the police compound. As he was driving, he asked the police officer whether he was under arrest. The officer told him that it was for his own safety as Chibambo had organized the people to harm him. Meanwhile, his two colleagues were roughed up by the mobs, kicked, punched, and shouted at, but were not seriously hurt. After seeing the rough situation, Chibambo and his government-sponsored hoodlums left, in hopes that the people left behind would finish the job. On his way back, Chibambo reorganized road blocks manned by government militias and local Janjaweeds (thugs) and local rogues with stern instructions to manhandle Kanyama and his colleagues when they showed up at the road blocks.

By this time, the police station was surrounded by a still larger crowd marshaled from villages and armed with machetes, spears, clubs, and iron bars. They were there until midnight to make sure Kanyama didn't escape. The police officer pleaded with them to return to their homes as Kanyama and his friends were under arrest and waiting to be driven to Zomba for interrogation. On hearing these words, the men chanting "Ngwazi Ya Muyaya" (Banda is immortal) and "to hell with Kanyama" started to leave one by one for their homes.

In the early hours of the morning, two officers came to the police station and found that the mobs had left the besieged station. After serving breakfast to Kanyama and his colleagues, the officer warned that they had received reliable information that the road back to Rumphi or Chitipa-Karonga were dangerously manned by government-sponsored thugs. It was not safe for them to travel east or south. Kanyama, therefore, suggested that they would drive north to the Tanzanian border if necessary. The officers had no objection to that and suggested they should hit the road while the mobs were still at their homes. At 3:30 AM they left the police station and the two courageous officers driving the police Land Rover followed behind them to ensure their safety. After more than 75 km or so, and close to the Tanzanian border, the officers gave them a signal to stop and, indeed, Kanyama stepped on brakes. They came out of their vehicles and hugged each other with parting warm words from both sides. Kanyama Chiume thanked the young officers for their patriotic and courageous undertakings which might have jeopardized their lives and positions. From their side, the police officers thanked Kanyama for his selfless sacrifice for the sake of his beloved motherland and Africa, and further assured Kanyama that their little contribution was directed to the ongoing struggle for real freedom and dignity of the African people. "We know our lives could be in danger for helping you, but that would be the price for freedom," declared the two officers with tears in their eyes. On October 17, 1964, Banda announced on Radio Malawi that Kanyama had ran away and fled to Tanzania after he had failed to kill him. By October 20, 1964, Kanyama and his colleagues arrived in Dar es Salaam, Tanzania and were received with respect and courtesy by President Nyerere and the government of Tanzania. The rebel minister had to spend the next thirty years in exile before he was able to return to his motherland in 1994.

Kanyama's flight of escape had left three of his colleagues back in Malawi, Yatuta Kaluli Chisiza, Orton C. Chirwa and Masauko Chipembere. Yatuta, who was lying low at his Chitimba home in northern Region, was joined by Orton Chirwa from his hiding place near Chipembere's home in Malindi—where he (Chipembere) was under house arrest or restriction. Messrs. Chokani and Bwanausi and Rose Chibambo were already in northern Rhodesia (Zambia). The intensity of Banda's campaign of violence against the rebel ministers coerced Yatuta and Chirwa into fleeing to Tanzania to join Kanyama Chiume.

After a month Chipembere broke loose from his restriction and assembled a rebel force of over 400 strong men who had been covertly trained by Medson Silombera, a WW II veteran and Chipembere's comrade-in-arms. The force overran the Ft. Johnstone police station in a thunderous attack and then set out for Zomba military headquarters which were overwhelmingly controlled by British reactionary expatriate officers who were solidly behind President Banda. On reaching Shire River, the ferry was on the other side. Forthwith the word reached military headquarters and the troops were sent to confront the rebels, and forthwith some of the rebels were dispersed, but some regrouped, reached the outskirts of Zomba, and made daring attacks on two police stations. It is said that had the rebels crossed the river and marched up to Zomba—the story could be different. However, at that point, it seemed the immediate crisis had ended. Banda had won the struggle in the cabinet and parliament, and it appeared the puppet head of government had the upper hand in the country as a whole.

On May 21, 1965, Banda announced that Chipembere had "ran away" to the United States of America. It is still a mystery how Chipembere left Malindi, traveled through Zomba, and boarded a flight at Chileka Airport in Blantyre—a distance of some 100 km. In Dispatch No. 3, dated February 3, 1965, from the British High Commissioner in Zomba, D. L. Cole, and received by the Commonwealth Relations Office on March 5, 1965, Cole asserted: "The threat had been contained and Chipembere was in hiding. Banda kept in picture, but expatriate officials took the initiative and President Banda commended them for job well done. Army conduct and discipline impressive. Police less so. No evidence of any external assistance to rebels. Despite the small scale of the rebellion, it came uncomfortably close to success. Foiled by swift counteraction of British-led security forces." The High Commissioner added that, "These events demonstrate wide spread disenchantment, the needs for Malawi's small army to become fully deployed to cope with even a minor rebellion and Banda's dependence for his security on expatriate British officials and officers. Banda, however, still likely to get majority in any entirely free elections, but needs to counter widening gulf between his government and most of educated Africans." Reading this statement by the British representative in Malawi, leaves no doubt that the British Government was directly involved into the internal affairs of a newly independent nation. In reality, Banda was not acting for the interests of the Malawian people, but rather, as a front for international imperialism bent on creating client-states such as Malawi, Congo, and Kenya. It is absurd, however, for the British High Commissioner to talk about free elections. History now records that there were, in reality, no free elections in Malawi during the thirty years of Banda's power.

Dispatch No. 5 from the British High Commissioner in Zomba on July 1, 1965, stated thus: "Following Chipembere's attempted coup, political and security situation uneasy, but on May 21, 1965, Banda announced that Chipembere had "ran away" to the United States. Ministers were suspicious, pondering either neglect or collusion. The public was confused. Rebels seem to lose heart, but resumed sporadic attacks. No threat unless external (assistance forthcoming). Chipembere's motives unclear. Comeback not to be discounted. Situation now eased and repressive measures relaxed, but no hint of reconciliation with rebel leaders. Possibility remains of assassination being considered as the last resort by other ministers. Her Majesty's Government should continue to support Banda; no satisfactory alternative and no obvious successor." From this narration, one may conclude that the rebel Ministers not only fought an African despot, but also well organized neocolonialists in the background.

The revelation in the dispatch that the situation was eased and repressive measures relaxed was a complete lie and a bold distortion of the situation in the country by Banda's masters to convince the international community, especially the western powers, that peace and order prevailed in Malawi. In fact, repressive measures had escalated and many supporters of the rebel ministers were arrested, brutally beaten, and their homes burnt.

Following Chipembere's departure, Banda presented the Penal Code Amendment Bill. He said that there was nothing new in the bill and the purpose for presenting it was simply to clarify the law of treason. He told the house that it had become necessary to clarify the law of treason because of the events that happened in Ft. Johnstone previously. He warned that anyone found guilty of treason would receive a mandatory death sentence, but he added that before a death sentence was applied, the executive authority would allow the court to consider an appeal for clemency. This was a deliberate move to entrench draconian laws to intimidate political dissidents.

Meanwhile, the departure of Chipembere did not ease his struggle to defeat the neocolonialist regime which was heavily protected or defended by the British expatriate community in the country. Under the leadership of Medson Silombela, former World War II fighter, the struggle continued, but was confined to the Ft. Johnstone area only. Silombela and his force staged daring onslaughts on government installations, police posts, and Young Pioneer camps, for example. Even though the effectiveness of Silombela's efforts were not a threat to Banda's regime, the fact remained that the despot had no support in the Ft. Johnstone district and it took the President several years before he could set his foot there.

Searching for Silombela was like looking for a needle in a haystack, but after a year of intense military operations supported by racist South African special forces, Silombela was finally captured in the house of his girlfriend. It was strongly believed that the woman betrayed him for a lump sum of money. Capturing Silombela was a great relief for Banda because Ft. Johnstone was the only hotbed within his puppet administration. On February 12, 1966, Banda went to Radio Malawi and delightedly announced the capture of his archenemy and warned his subjects that they would soon see Silombela's legs "dangling" in public. After two months of a fake trial for his part in the rebellion, Silombela was found guilty of murder and possession of dangerous weapons. However, the majority of the people in the country were not astonished by the verdict, they in fact, expected the consequences. In essence, the trial was conducted in an unfair manner. The accused was found guilty even before the trial began. With the treason law which had just been amended to suit Banda's agenda, Silombela was sentenced to death by public hanging. At that time the judicial system was still in line with (that is to say, patterned on) the British system and almost all of the officers in the system were British expatriates. But these expatriate officers offered absolutely nothing to defend the impartiality of the justice system which, admittedly, the British Society upholds in veneration.

There was a sense of disbelief among the majority of people in Malawi when Silombera was hanged publicly in complete disregard for human decency. The message was simple and clear that Malawians would not see the light at the end of a long tunnel for thirty years to come. The style of the execution was in part to instill fear among the population on one hand and it was a warning to the rebels that Banda was untouchable on the other. However, after the execution of Silombera, dissident activities seemed to slow down and many rebels fled the country. Those who did not, were either arrested and imprisoned without trial or they disappeared mysteriously.

By this time it was obvious that Banda could launch a massive campaign to discredit his former able ministers in view of the fact that all of them had fled the country for their safety. In fact, before they left the country, there were plans to form an opposition party to be led by Masauko Chipembere. The Party was to be known as Pan-African Democratic Party (PDP), based on democracy, integrity, and Pan-Africanism. This made Banda and his cohorts nervous and they resolved to thwart the move by using unprecedented brutal violence and indiscriminate intimidation among the citizens. Several attempts had been made on the lives of almost all the rebel ministers—hence their decision to flee the country.

In his first countrywide tour following the crisis and starting from the north, Banda told his audience that the rebel ministers planned to kill him and bring into the country Communist China. He avoided addressing fundamental issues that led to the national crisis such as; Africanization, hospital fees, government highhandedness, his close ties with racist minority regimes in southern Africa, and his disrespect for his colleagues. Most of the people who attended his rallies were largely uneducated, coerced into attending, and politically naive to his calculated lies all of which worked to his advantage. He wanted to portray to his audience that he, and he alone, brought independence for the country and the destruction of the Federation of Rhodesia and Nyasaland. However, the people of Malawi had no chance to hear the other side of story from the rebel ministers because, as I have stated before, their movements were closely restricted and their lives were in danger and practically threatened by government sponsored militias who roamed the streets and localities throughout the country.

Indeed, the accusations by Banda that the rebel ministers were conspiring to assassinate him and overthrow his regime, were absolutely false and concocted. They lacked any apparent validity. The suggestion that they wanted to murder him, at that time, seemed sheer lunacy. In essence, most of their efforts to change things for the better, were initially carried out along constitutional lines and they made no apparent attempt to organize a popular violent revolution against Banda's regime which was steadfastly bent on dictatorship. Moreover, there seemed no reason to doubt that the rebel ministers were genuine in their expressed desire that Banda should not resign. The fact that the only passionate initiatives to bring about a reconciliation came from them tends to confirm that. Admittedly, in their public meetings, as distinct from their parliamentary speeches, they took an increasingly anti-Banda line but the tone of their speeches was matched to the full by those of President Banda. He never gave any sign of conciliation or compromise at all. The allegation of a Chinese "plot" seemed even more improbable. As a matter of fact, Kanyama Chiume had been in contact with the Chinese Embassy in Dar es Salaam and doubtless they offered him aid—a fact that Kanyama himself did not conceal. It was economic aid that Malawi desperately needed to develop the nation after more than seventy years of British brutal negligence. As then the Minister for External Affairs, Kanyama had dealings with the Chinese with the full knowledge of President Banda. Accordingly, Banda's campaign to discredit his former colleagues did not focus on ideas, substance, and policies, but rather, it dwelt on personal attacks and vendettas. On the other hand, what little opportunity was granted the rebel ministers to speak to their supporters was used to focus on ideas, substance and policies which the newly independent nation should adopt on its long journey to nationhood.

There was no evidence at all that the Red Chinese had moved from the stage of ordinary diplomatic enticement to that of active subversion. When the British High Commissioner, Cole, wanted more information about the plot, Banda could not offer any and shied away from the subject. But the President did not drop his accusations and continued to tell his ignorant audiences that the rebel ministers were selling the country to the Red Chinese. Despite the fact that the British High Commissioner failed to prove the allegations, Banda's rhetoric had listening ears in the western capitals and they made sure that Malawi couldn't get away from their grip.

The British Government and its allies, having gathered much information on Malawi, were very worried about the political "winds of change" blowing across Africa. They regarded the famous cabinet crisis as a threat to western interests—they did not regard the crisis as merely a family squabble. They were right deep in it. In their view, they believed the genesis of the crisis dwelt much deeper. They saw it as a battle over the way in which Malawi was to be governed in future. It had been a battle between paternal pro-western despotism and the new African nationalism. This, however, had been the real issue. The rebel ministers had been imbued with all the beliefs of the typical African nationalism. The Europeans were therefore completely misguided into believing that the rebel ministers were anti-European and had looked to independence to provide them with the opportunity to take a fully responsible part in the governing of their country as well as in Pan-African affairs. Indeed, the rebel ministers had wanted to give Malawi a truly African image. This is what the western imperialists did not want to happen in Malawi.

Their ambitions ultimately, were balked at by the westernized and brainwashed despot who gave them no authority, no power, no responsibility, no respect and condescendingly referred to them as "my boys."

In his closing remarks, the British High Commissioner in Malawi, D. L. Cole, in his dispatch to the Commonwealth Relations Office (CRO) dubbed as Her Britannic Majesty's Government (HBMG), Ref. CAO 41/3/06 copy No.55 dated November 12, 1964 (and intercepted by Kanyama Chiume) had this to say: "Is the crisis now over? At first sight, this might seem to be the case. Dr. Banda has undoubtedly won the first rounds in the cabinet, in the parliament and in the country. At the same time, the nucleus of a vehement opposition remains. It lies in the frustrated ideals and ambitions of the ex-ministers who did so much to create the new state, and who are by the African standards, men of courage, ability, and consequence and who may yet find help and support abroad. It lies in the hopes of the gradually expanding educated classes of Malawi to whom the gospel of Pan-Africanism and the desire to control their own destinies for better or for worse in an African way with Africans in all the directing positions will increasingly appeal. It lies, too, in the perilous economic conditions of Malawi with its corollary as a low standard of living, slow development, and possibly increasing taxation. Chipembere obviously believed that these were factors which, whatever the President did, could eventually remove Malawi from his grip. Perhaps he is right. But Dr. Banda, too, has much, even more on his side. He has vast popular support. He has control of the Party Machine. The whole administration, army and police is in his grasp. He has the respect of the European community. He has courage and resolution. He even still has the attenuated loyalty of some of the rebel ministers. If he plays his cards right and if he is adequately supported by the west, on whose side he undoubtedly is, he can hardly lose. But much will depend on his ability to withstand the corrosive effects of dictatorial power and to show the pliability of outlook, at least on the surface, that can give an African image to his policies and attract the educated classes and perhaps even some of the rebel ministers back into his fold. A little more Africanization; a little less obvious flirtation with the Portuguese; a little more apparent respect for his ministers; a little less open disdain for African ideas; these are the marginal changes which can help to keep him firmly in power."

"But whatever the immediate outcome of this affair, the most serious problems may still be ahead, the economic plight of Malawi which could overturn almost any political regime is one; another is the question of what comes after Dr. Banda (he is not a young man); are we, anyway, bound in the end to get back to Henry Chipembere, Kanyama Chiume and the Chinese, or worse? On these and on the related question of where the British interest seems to lie, I shall speculate in a subsequent dispatch."

"I am copying this dispatch to all British High Commissioners in Africa, to Her Majesty's Ambassadors in Cairo, Pretoria and Addis Ababa and, to the Political Adviser to the Commander-in-Chief, Middle east (Aden), Ian C. D. L. Cole."

It had now become apparent that the British Government, through Cole the first High Commissioner in Malawi, was heavily involved in the internal affairs of an independent nation. Cole had unlimited power and influence on Dr. Banda and his brutal regime. Cole had also strong and close ties with Major-General Lewis, armed forces top-brass, Peter Long Police Commissioner, and L. Youens, Banda's special advisor and suspected M-16 operative. These three British expatriates were de facto powers behind Banda's neocolonialist regime. These are the people who hatched the Cabinet crisis by advising Banda not to heed his ministers' demands to sever relations with minority racist regimes in the south, to refuse the notion of Africanization of the civil service, and to approve no increase of salaries to African civil servants. These Europeans feared that if the able and brilliant ministers remained in the government, their own lucrative positions in the government could be weakened. On the other hand, the new Ministers Banda had appointed lacked integrity and political will and Banda used them as his "house boys." In any matter affecting each ministry, Banda directly dealt with expatriate permanent secretaries who happened to be all British. In other words, the permanent secretaries were more powerful than the ministers themselves. This sort of trend made Malawi's independence counterfeit in the sense that Banda abdicated his responsibilities and consigned the state into covert domination by foreign powers.

In his last dispatch to Commonwealth Relations Office (London) Ref. No. CRO(s)/FO(s)/WH(s) DISTRIBUTION No. 266 dated March 23, 1964, marked "SECRET," and copied to Lusaka, Zambia; Dar es Salaam, Tanzania; Salisbury, southern Rhodesia (Zimbabwe), Cole had this to say:

DETAINEES AND RESTRICTEES

"When I was passing through Lilongwe on Saturday, I heard disturbing allusions to conditions at new detention camp in Dowa. This was subsequently confirmed to me by Army Commander who said that it had just been brought to notice of Military Operations Committee that this camp was being run by Youth League (under direction of four African executive Officers personally selected by Home Affairs Minister (Dr. Hastings Banda), and its inmates brutally treated.

There were authentic stories of beatings, underfeeding, over-exercise, flooding of rooms, prisoners coerced to eat human excreta, etc., Lomax later told me that Commissioner of Prisons (British), was responsible for construction of the camp, but had washed his hands of its running.

Yesterday when seeing Youens on another matter, I mentioned rumors I had heard in Lilongwe and asked whether the camp came under control of Commissioner of Prisons. Youens said it did. I said I was glad to hear this since presumably this meant he was satisfied that conditions in camp were up to required standard. Youens remarked that Youth League had something to do with running of the camp. I referred to recent reports on condition of Ghana detainees and said this was a subject which, if it became known, could easily attract Parliamentary attention at Westminster. After all, it could be argued that British taxpayers were contributing towards costs. Presumably there would be no difficulty about my going to look at the camp, if this were suggested? Youens said: "I get your message"

"I understand that Youens last night raised this issue with Military Operations Committee (MOC) and the outcome is that approach is to be conducted.

It is very difficult to get hold of precise numbers, but Lomax's present estimate is as follows:

(a) Restrictees: About 180, most of them from the northern Region. These were mainly picked up before Ft. Johnstone uprising and include large numbers of civil servants and educated men. There are ominous reports that some of them will shortly be transferred to detention.

(b) Detainees: Dowa 120, Blantyre 120, Zomba 80. Of these, 250 came from the north and are mainly people suspected of being implicated in organized rebellion. Many of them are undoubtedly innocent. Screening is going on. Lomax's view is that at least 40 in Dowa should be released at once. But Banda is proving difficult and unpleasant on this.

Considerable numbers of civil servants, most of them from the north who have felt in danger of restriction, have also left the country. For instance, last week four of the most senior remaining civil servants, namely: Clement Malama, Lutengano Mwahimba, Danwell Mundo Mwambetanya, and Clement Chitepwete Mtawale (Registrar of Cooperatives and Administrative Offices in Ministries of Finance and Development). All four hail from the north. These Officers were dismissed simultaneously and forthwith fled to Zambia. As I said at conclusion of my Dispatch No. 3, this conflict between Banda and educated classes, and consequent "brain drain," is one of most worrying features of present situation with grave implications for development programs. Ministry of Finance has lost four of its six most senior Africans during last year alone. We are studying this further. Reported conditions at detention camps make picture even blacker."

The aftermath of the crisis, could have made Malawians open their eyes. We were made to believe that Banda, and only Banda, knew everything, and therefore, after the crisis things could change for the better. But the people, the majority being uneducated, could not see the implications ahead and did not realize who was behind the crisis and nor the motive behind it? From reading the dispatches from the British High Commissioner, D. Cole, the British had given independence to the Malawian people on one hand and taken it back through Hastings Banda on the other hand. Indeed, there was nothing to celebrate from our independence and freedom and we were blindly and foolishly entering dark days ahead.

Chapter Seven

BLEAK FUTURE

Finally, Dr. Banda emerged victorious over his rebel ministers through unprecedented backing and support by western powers, particularly Britain, the former colonial power. Amid the cold-war conflict, the western democracies could not afford to let slip away its friendship with Malawi which had, under Banda's rule, become a quisling lackey of the western powers.

Dr. Banda steadfastly moved to consolidate the absolute powers that he had longed for and on his way to that goal, Malawians began to feel the effects of a one-man rule. He packed his new cabinet with deadwood ministers and hand-picked parliamentarians who lacked both efficacy and moral obligation. The new cabinet was merely symbolic, the autocrat vested all powers into the hands of the British expatriate Permanent Secretaries leaving his ministers as political statues. This group of devious expatriates was so powerful that it determined both foreign and domestic policies for the Banda regime. In essence, Malawi's foreign policy was dictated from London.

It is in this regard that the people of Malawi lost the battle they had been waging for almost seven decades—the battle to control their own destiny. All in all, Banda had no vision for the newly independent state. He offered both Malawians and Africa for sale for his own interest and those of his expatriate masters. These white expatriates even boasted of having better times than during the colonial era—they became the new masters in a new state. Dr. Banda dominated the reins of power. He established himself as the "Ayatollah Khomeini" of Malawi—answerable to no one. The Parliament had become a one-man show. He had become law all to himself. His ministers had to bow to their knees when entering his office and he treated them as kitchen-boys or messengers. For a number of years, he held several ministerial posts apart from the Presidency— Minister of Agriculture and Natural Resources; Minister of Home Affairs; Minister of Defense; and Minister of Foreign Affairs. He, himself, held the Ministry of Agriculture and Natural Resources position for twenty years. He had special interests in this ministry because it served as a source of funds and materials for his vast commercial farms which he had confiscated from small farm holders.

Dr. Banda exerted a tight grip on his subordinates, particularly his dumb cabinet ministers. Whenever these ministers attended international conferences, speeches were written for them to read at the conference even though, to some extent, they had different views on the issue. They were strictly curtailed from using their own minds. At one stage, the Minister of Trade and Industry, Mr. John Gwengwe went to Mozambique (fascist Mozambique) at the height of Frelimo onslaught, to participate in a conference of Trade Ministers from apartheid South Africa and Settler Rhodesia. After a couple of glasses of fine Mozambican wine, which had started to work in his head, the Minister put aside his written speech which included a passage that praised and encouraged the existing good relations between Malawi and her white-ruled neighbors, and assured the all-white audience that, "Frelimo would rule Mozambique one day."

The all-white participants were stunned at his remarks and the notorious Mozambican Foreign Minister, Antonio Noguera, forthwith phoned Banda to express his outrage and to inform him of his minister's revolutionary remarks. In his response, Banda apologized and demanded his minister's immediate repatriation on the first available flight—under escort and handcuffed. When John Gwengwe landed at Chileka Airport, he was forthwith whisked away by plain-clothed secret agents to an unknown destination and has not been heard from since. In 1992, in Rio De Janeiro, Brazil, Banda's Minister of Agriculture confused his audience at a conference on global environment when he told the delegates that he was thankful to His Excellency Life President Ngwazi Dr. Hastings Kamuzu Banda for teaching his people about agriculture with the result being the country's self-sufficiency in food. Such were the norms for Banda's officials when attending international conferences.

In the Parliament, there were absolutely no passionate discussions or debate and an overwhelming number of these so-called parliamentarians lacked formal education and, therefore, being members of the Parliament, they owed allegiance to Banda and not the voters. Whereas Kanyama Chiume and Masauko Chipembere, way back in the 50s, at the ages of 20 and 21 respectively, were unanimously elected representatives of the Nyasaland African Congress (NAC) in the LEGCO. They kept the majority of white members on their toes by driving home their points of view with eloquence and intrepidity. On the contrary, Banda's parliamentarians were symbolically representing Bandaism, a malignant culture that was well-calculated to embody his tragic vision for the nation's economic, political and social structures. Their sole job in the parliament was to clap their hands when their master stood to speak. They even clapped hands when the despot ridiculed them in one way or the other and showered praises on him day in and day out. That became the hallmark of his despotic rule. The press, which was ruthlessly controlled by the state, extolled his intellectual brilliance, his foresight, and his integrity had virtually converted the majority of our people into docility. He was given such immeasurable titles as: Ngwazi (hero); Mkango (lion); Wamuyaya (immortal); Messiah (the Christ of our day); and the destroyer of the federation. His official title was: His Excellency, the Life President Ngwazi Dr. Hastings Kamuzu Banda. Omitting one of these titles when addressing the President could send someone into prison. In fact many citizens had been harassed by the police and Young Pioneers (the President's personal brutal militias) for addressing the President as President Banda. One citizen was brutally assaulted by a group of Young Pioneers for leaving a MK20 (US50¢) note hanging head-down in his transparent white shirt pocket. (Banda's portrait appeared on all legal tender and in public places all over the country.) This innocent citizen paid a price for disrespecting the Head of State.

A dark chapter had been opened for the Malawian people. They had absolutely nothing to celebrate for their hard-won freedom. The leader they had expected beyond all doubts to lead them to a better life in their newly found nation had become more and more aggressive against the very people who had welcomed him into the country where he knew nobody, knew no culture, and knew no tradition. He was an alien. His ascendancy to power had created enormous hardships, greater than during colonial domination. He ran the nation as his own fiefdom and made Malawians completely cut off from the rest of the world. It was a risk for Malawians to tune into foreign radio stations for news or to possess a typewriter.

To ensure his political strength and survival were guaranteed, Banda turned to women as his political allies. Almost all of these women were illiterate—they could not write or read—and therefore, he used them for his own devious interests. The tin-pot dictator was notoriously paternalistic in his attitude to these unfortunate women. He neither cared for, nor respected these women during the entire thirty years that he ruled the impoverished nation with iron fists. The sad part of it was that absolutely nothing was done to encourage these women to join educational programs or to learn skills in different fields in order to break free from their poverty and drudgery.

Young women normally received little or no education, married early, did far more than their share of agricultural work, and were often left destitute when widowed or divorced. Those women who worked outside the home invariably took low-skilled and low-paying jobs. Very few, if any, achieved real power.

Indeed, all Malawians from all walks of life faced a bleak future. Banda had nothing to offer them to prepare for their decent future and the future of the generations to come. Hitherto, after 46 years of nationhood, the majority of Malawians lived below the poverty line. The gap between rich and poor was, and still is, disturbingly wide. Maybe one of the most obvious manifestations of the malaise affecting Malawian societies during these years was the regular mass rallies held to commemorate events such as the despot's birthday—even though the exact date remains a mystery to the population. The most vulnerable were rural women victims of dire poverty who were shipped into towns and cities in overloaded trucks in their thousands to sing and dance for the Messiah. Banda thought himself as a kind of father figure. He reckoned he was taking care of the country's women, the implication being that they could not care of themselves.

Usually, after performing dances for their "god father," they were paid an equivalent of US$1 (MK 135) after dancing for hours under sweltering heat. Even a slave-master would not have the audacity to pay his slaves such a pitiful amount. At one stage on an official visit to the State of Israel, the President was accompanied by a group of 50 dancing women on a chartered Namibian aircraft that cost the taxpayers US$750,975 to entertain their godfather and the hosts. The total cost for the whole trip amounted to US$3.5 million which, to a greater extent, could have transformed the economic status of these poor women and their families if put into various projects in one of the poorest nations in the world. Before the start of the trip, the women were instructed to carry with them three pairs of Kitenge (cloth bearing Banda's portrait) commonly used by Malawian women to symbolize their loyalty to the Messiah. Equally disturbing, men were coerced into bearing the expenses for these clothes even though most of them earned wages below the poverty level and often also had to sustain their extended families. The fact that Banda and his henchmen sat for more than eight hours a day watching these unfortunate women performing artistic traditional dances, there was a lack of activities in his administration over vital issues. However, these women were mostly illiterate and could not form an authoritative opinion on Banda's motives. He ruthlessly used their ignorance for his own political ego. The once dignified mothers of our country apparently were confident and self-assured that Dr. Banda cared for them. They were immensely proud of their own degradation (that is to say, sacrifice) and could not ponder, even for a moment, what could be their fate when the monster was gone to his final destination. The despot used to praise himself on his great respect for the women of Malawi, but turning these women into a demimonde was not respect at all—it was in fact disrespectful and demeaning to his fellow citizens.

Once dignified women, they were not only used as Banda's dancing tools or robots, but they were also the ears and eyes for the dreaded Malawi Congress Party. Their role was to report anything suspicious to the MCP. They were even instructed to spy on their spouses and neighbors. In this regard, family life was infected with mistrust and moved away from the deep-rooted African tradition of marriage.

Lack of political awareness not only among the majority of women, but also the whole Malawian society in the country, led Dr. Banda to run the country as his personal estate. The woman he had turned into his official hostess slept in his bed as a wife. She took charge as Malawi's first lady and was called officially "mama." Cecilia Tamanda Kadzamila, a former nurse, fulfilled the role of wife to Banda at all state functions even though they were never officially married.

Her close association with Banda, made her the most powerful and feared woman in the country. Economically, she became one of the richest women in Africa second only to the Mama Ngina the former wife of the late Jomo Kenyatta, first President of the Republic of Kenya. To enhance her influence in the country, she formed Chitukuku Cha Azimai Mu Malawi; (Women's Organization of Malawi). The CCAM was in effect, a source of female slave labor at Mama Kadzamila's private disposal. The organization had become one of the most powerful and feared in Malawi—further evidence that the woman was increasingly influencing Banda's thinking. Not only did the organization gain massive membership through coercion, it also had overwhelming influence over the Government. Through this wicked woman, the organization had unlimited access to government resources such as transport, manpower, finances, and the like. The unfortunate women were engaged in farming on Mama's huge tracts of land that were dubiously acquired. They worked on land as slaves and usually under most degrading circumstances. The profits accrued from such labor were channeled to Kadzamila's private bank accounts while the majority of the country's women remained in dire poverty.

As the level of economic imbalance increased, Kadzamila's taste for expensive shopping trips and the building of opulent palaces grew. Several of these places were never used by the wicked couple, yet school children lacked essential facilities such as classrooms, books and qualified teachers to continue with their education. In any nation, however, education is a backbone for a decent and healthier society. The so-called "Mama" had so much acquired the sophisticated tastes of Almeda Marcos, that on one of her several trips to Britain on taxpayer's funds, she bought shoes worth US$25,750, US$3,500 for hand bags and US$7,500 for rings and watches. On her last trip before the national uprising in 1992, she was accompanied by her lifelong partner Hastings Banda and over fifty others (women, secret agents and sycophants) and again in a Namibian executive jet chartered at the cost of US$785,950. They stayed in the most expensive hotels, Claridge's in London and Balmoral in Edinburgh, at US$450-$985 a night while back home, millions of Malawians could not afford two meals a day. As if that was not enough, members of the entourage went on shopping sprees (using public funds) to purchase luxurious items for themselves including videos, fridges, cameras, washers, stereo systems, watches and other luxuries, all of which took 15 vans to ferry the spoils from their hotels to the waiting jet at the airport and another five vans to another plane. The transportation cost of the booty was estimated at US$88,950. As a neocolonialized regime, Malawi received a US$150 million grant annually for economic development from Britain, but only a tiny fraction of this fund reached the most needy majority.

Sixty-five percent of the fund was channeled to defense, particularly to the Young Pioneers (Banda's elite rogues) who terrorized the nation in order to neutralize any quest for dissension. In essence, Malawi was a most favored recipient of western aid in Southern, Eastern and Central Africa—all for its role in the East-West cold war. In a country rated as one of the poorest in the world, the Head of State, in league with sycophants and opportunists, engaged in systematic plundering of Malawi's meagre resources. All the while, the British government turned a blind eye which explains vividly how Banda was viewed by Her Majesty's government during his 30 years of brutal rule. At the end of that trip, the total cost that poor Malawian taxpayers incurred was US$3.5 million, enough to fund more than ten schools in the country. Not only did Malawi lack enough school buildings, but also health care was sadly in pretty bad shape. The AIDS pandemic in Malawi is one of the highest in the continent and yet patients find it difficult to get medication. Some patients travel distances of up to 25 kilometers by foot to attend a clinic. The emergency of the killer disease (AIDS) was detected in the early 80s, but, the regime of Dr. Banda decided to remain silent and ineffective in view of the fact that the revelation could undermine the image and respect of the nation that was dubbed the "Warm Heart Of Africa." Critics of the former Malawi Congress Party government, called it the cold heart of Africa for its thuggery and brutal repression of human rights.

In the dying days of his political career and his virtual domination of absolute power in the land of zombies, a National Convention, the last Dr. Banda chaired in September 1992, was held in Mzuzu, the Capital of northern Malawi and attended by President Robert Mugabe of Zimbabwe, the only foreign Head of State and Banda's most ardent admirer. The resolutions passed at the Convention, albeit not new to the Malawian population, reflected the endless cult of personality that dominated Malawian politics for three solid decades:

(1) Delegates thank God Almighty for the precious gift to the nation of His Excellency, the Life President Ngwazi Dr.

Hastings Kamuzu Banda, who was born in Kasungu. Delegates congratulate His Excellency the Life President for the tremendous development that has transformed the country into a prosperous Malawi.

(2) Delegates applaud and congratulate his Excellency the Life President, Ngwazi Dr. H. Kamuzu Banda for the highly successful private visit he and Mama paid to the United Kingdom earlier in the year. They note with appreciation the love and respect with which the people of United Kingdom received the Ngwazi and Mama.

(3) Delegates welcome the increasing warmth in the relationship between Malawi and Zimbabwe and note with pleasure that the recent visit of His Excellency President Robert Mugabe is indicative of this development.

(4) Delegates thank the President of the United States of America George H. W. Bush Sr. for the visit of the Vice President of the United States of America, Dan Quayle, to Malawi and congratulate His Excellency the Life President, Ngwazi Dr. Hastings Kamuzu Banda, for the friendly relationship between Malawi and the United States of America implicit in such a visit.

(5) Delegates note with appreciation the excellent work that Chitukuku Cha Azimai Mu Malawi (Women's Organization of Malawi) CCAM has undertaken and continues to undertake to assist His Excellency the Ngwazi Dr. Hastings Kamuzu Banda in the socioeconomic development of the nation.

(6) Delegates are angry with the false and malicious reports prepared by the rebel Kanyama Chiume for his subversive activities.

(7) Delegates condemn rebel Kanyama Chiume and angrily refute his false allegations in certain foreign newspapers that Mama C. T. Kadzamila, National Adviser of CCAM was using the Organization's resources for political ambitions and personal gain.

(8) Delegates recognize that the progress and prosperity that Malawians have made since independence, can only be

attributed to the far sighted and wise leadership of His Excellency the Life President, Ngwazi Dr. Hastings Kamuzu Banda under conditions of peace, calm, law, and order. Delegates therefore, reaffirm their absolute loyalty to, and support for, His Excellency the Life President and pledge to uphold the four cornerstones upon which the Party and government are founded, namely; Unity, Loyalty, Obedience, Discipline.

(9) Realizing that neither words nor material gifts can adequately express their gratitude and thanks to his Excellency the Life President for the tremendous economic, political and social development the country has achieved under His Excellency's leadership and believing as we do, that only God Almighty can adequately repay the Ngwazi, delegates unanimously pray to God to give His Excellency the Life President, Ngwazi Dr. Hastings Kamuzu Banda continued good health and long life, so that he continues to give us, "his people," more prosperity.

(10) Delegates are aware of the fact that Malawi Congress Party has been in power for 27 years and has been responsible for all the development that has taken place in the country under the wise and dynamic leadership of His Excellency the Life President Ngwazi Dr. Hastings Kamuzu Banda, the most intelligent person in Malawi. Delegates further noted that Malawi is an island of peace, stability and prosperity, and that Malawians are united and freely choose their party leader every three years and members of parliament every five years. Delegates therefore reaffirm with conviction that the one-party democracy works in Malawi and must not be changed.

(11) Delegates congratulate His Excellency the Life President, Ngwazi Dr. Hastings Kamuzu Banda for the most successful 1991 crop inspection tour and appreciate his love in defying unfavorable weather and muddy conditions as he visits gardens of the ordinary people. Delegates note with gratitude that His Excellency the Life President's crop inspection program encourages and inspires people to produce more food and cash crops.

(12) Delegates praise His Excellency the Life President, Ngwazi Dr. Hastings Kamuzu Banda for putting emphasis on agriculture and for teaching "his people" modern methods of farming. Delegates noted, with satisfaction, reports that the people have harvested a record surplus maize crop. Delegates therefore, wish to reaffirm His Excellency the Life President's appeal to them to grow high-yielding maize varieties.

(13) Delegates highly appreciate and acknowledge that His Excellency, the Life President Ngwazi Dr. Hastings K. Banda is a redeemer and Messiah of our beloved nation, the destroyer of the Federation and defender of women's status. We recognize there is a God in heaven, and we also recognize there is Kamuzu on earth.

LONG LIVE KAMUZU OUR MESSIAH AND WISE LEADER.

However, reading from the excerpts of the last convention of 1992 before Banda was swept into the dustbin of political history in our country, one may deduce that Malawians lived on an outlandish planet walking with their souls in hand and reduced to subhuman beings who could not think for themselves and had yielded their human dignity to a rogue. Though the majority of the convention delegates were people of low moral standards with disappointingly little education, there were some with university degrees who had betrayed their own conscience and dignity for opportunistic reasons. Outsiders, may see these excerpts as frivolous and hollow, but Malawians lived with them for thirty years. Year in and year out, they were subjected to indignity and a culture of personality cult never before seen on the continent–while the current politicians authenticate Banda's notorious legacy as a progressive model that Malawians ought to emulate. However, this trend does not surprise the people of Malawi in view of the fact that most of the present leadership and, indeed, politicians at large, were once Banda's henchmen and sycophants and to a larger extent, tribesmen who lacked political clout and vision. These people are largely unprofessional and would be unable to live a normal life outside politics, in other words, politics is their only means of survival.

Sadly, a lack of progressive leadership in the country promoted ignorance and shortsightedness among the majority of our people, hence, they did not know where they had come from nor where they were going. The fate of their future was left squarely in the hands of a single evil person who cared nothing for their well-being nor for future generations. Not only did the conventions produce laughable resolutions, the parliament was no different. Parliamentarians (all hand picked) were locked up in bitter competition to produce mellifluous words in praising the president day in and day out instead of engaging in the vital issues affecting their constituents and the country as a whole.

One of Africa's last old-style despots, Dr. Banda ruled his subjects with impunity and contempt. The fly whisk, together with the black homburg hat, the dark three-piece Seville Row suits, and the sunglasses were the trademarks of a man who once echoed Bismarck by declaring: "I do things. Let others explain." The diminutive demon who had that touch of magic, kept Malawians on their toes for 30 years. He had neither vision nor comprehensive plans for the future of a nation among the poorest of the world. His culture of the personality cult played extremely well in the country and most of the people explicitly believed that without Hastings Banda Malawi would be the last country to achieve her independence on the continent. However, this baseless perception was also acknowledged by Banda himself by reflecting pleas by young nationalists for his return to Nyasaland to spearhead the struggle for independence. In actual fact, the young nationalists had played a pivotal role before Banda was invited and it was only a matter of time before the British conceded to defeat. The perception that Malawi achieved her independence because of Banda's leadership is therefore false and misguided and must be treated with the contempt it deserves.

As in Kenya where the processes of the national liberation struggle had been entirely associated with the name of

Jomo Kenyatta while sidelining the real freedom fighter–the legendary Dedani Kimathi. In Malawi, the political history was deliberately misconstrued to equate the nation's independence struggle with Dr. Banda's so-called dynamic leadership and thereby sidelining potential political stars with unbroken political records in the freedom struggle of our nation. Among them were; John Chilembwe, Levi Zililo Mumba, James Sangala, Masauko Chipembere, Dunduzu Chisiza, Yatuta Chisiza, Kanyama Chiume, Orton Chirwa, Augustine Bwanausi, Harry Bwanausi, T. D. T. Banda and many other now-forgotten heroes who laid down their lives for the freedom of their people. In his remarkable book, *Not Yet Uhuru* (i.e., not yet freedom), Jaramongi Oginga Odinga, Kenya's foremost nationalist observed thus:

"Many people lost their lives. May they not look backwards. May they make their hard-won independence a reality. The past cannot be forgotten but must be forgiven. It can not be forgotten because it is the past not only of Kenya but of world history."

In Malawi, this was also a tactic by the present inept leadership team, most of whom were not involved or behaved indifferently during the freedom struggle, because diverting our people's attention from the real political, economic and social issues affecting their lives suited their self-seeking ambitions. Indeed, Malawi's culture, based on a personality cult, played a devastating role in the minds of the people. They remained docile and politically backwards for 30 years under a most degrading and oppressive regime without the slightest sense of dissension—finally becoming the political laughing stock of the continent.

The kind of life Malawians endured after the winds had calmed down after Cabinet Crisis and Banda had taken overwhelming control over the country was beyond imagination. In 1974, the President, under international pressure, signed a grand alliance committing Malawi to achieving total immunization of all her children against basic preventable diseases. Worthy as this notion may be, it was somewhat compromised by frequent reports of Banda's Party thugs turning up at health clinics and attempting to intimidate health workers into refusing treatment to children whose mothers could not produce a paid-up party membership card. As I have recorded in previous chapters, it was a grave and catastrophic notion to import a leader who was virtually unknown on his return to Nyasaland in 1958. This mysterious person was by far and large, unprepared to lead the nation to prosperity under democratic norms. The fact remains that the young nationalist leaders succeeded in making Banda into a national hero and then sending him on a countrywide tour to rally support for the struggle. But, perhaps, in their anxiety to bring the struggle to a rapid conclusion, they failed to pay proper attention to early indications that the adulation of the people had gone to Banda's head and that whatever desire he felt for an independent nation was rapidly becoming secondary to his thirst for personal fame and power. To this effect, the entire population, was held in captivity. The "Messiah" the people had hoped could bring the necessary novel notions and national unity upon which to build an ideal foundation for a new nation, instead, started to divide the nation along tribal lines.

In the early 70s, Dr. Banda introduced annual crop inspections—tours, unique in Africa, that gave him an opportunity to demonstrate to Malawians his ability for the dynamic leadership that the people were looking for in an independent nation. As global warming started to effect the patterns of climate, the failures of crops were evident. Mention of any resulting famine was naturally omitted from official reports of this glorified fundraising.

In actual fact, crop inspections were the hallmark of Banda's naked exploitation of his own people—worse than anything that occurred during the colonial era. He also used these occasions to portray himself as a caring and committed leader trying to make Malawians self-sufficient in food production and as he put it, "Most people in other African countries go hungry." This had worked to his advantage in his quest for supremacy in Malawian politics. Moreover, he had the courage to openly tell Malawians at public rallies that he was delighted now to see that his people now had plenty of food—and in sharp contrast to the situation before he returned to his homeland where most people starved due to shortages of food. He attributed this to his wise teaching in agriculture that had produced tremendous incentives among his people of this country, hence: "There was no shortage of food in the country anymore." Such rhetoric, however, resonated among his people and transformed him into an untouchable "Supreme Emperor" who ruled Malawians like dead souls.

His relentless emphasis on agriculture prompted praise upon praise in the tightly controlled national media outlets and national conventions. They were preoccupied with adulation of Banda's successes in agriculture and his portfolio as the Minister Of Agriculture. For almost two decades, Banda's activities gave him unprecedented access to the government's funds, equipment, and facilities for use on his countless farms that employed hundreds if not thousands of workers. These workers were paid slave-wages and under most degrading working conditions—worse than on the former Rhodesian farms of white settlers.

Banda's smooth sailing in Malawian politics over three decades, and without encountering resistance or popular national revolt, was attributed to, first and foremost, timidity of our people because the government pursued tactics of brutal repression and preemptive measures, and secondly, political ignorance among the majority of our people. These two factors played a negative role in giving Banda an upper hand. During his month-long tour of crop inspections, his brutal militias (Janjaweeds) were dispatched to rural areas one month ahead of the tour. The prime reasons were to instill fear over the rural population and to collect forced donations for the President. This practice, generally, was unprecedentedly brutal and unjustifiably carried out by an African leader after the defeat of white oppressors. The militias were driven in government trucks and Land Rovers to different areas and armed with modern automatic weapons. Upon arriving in the villages, and often while high on marijuana (chamba) and other intoxicating substances provided by the government, these unruly thugs could lay their hands on anything; goats, sheep, chicken, eggs, cattle, bags of maize and rice, or money. At one village, for instance in the Mzokoto, Rumphi District in the north of the country where oppression was excessively more brutal than in the central and south where Dr. Banda and the rest of leadership hailed from, these misguided monsters found an 80-year old woman tending to her he-goat and demanded the goat be donated to the Ngwazi (Messiah).

When the unfortunate and innocent old woman, Witness Nyauhango, told the youths that she was intending to sell the goat and use the money for school fees for her two grandchildren whose parents had both died of undisclosed maladies, she was brutally dragged to the ground and her right hand broken in the melee. Her two grandchildren watched helplessly as she was beaten and the goat thrown into the truck. Sadly, this wanton act happened under the watchful eye of Regional Commander R. Nyirongo who happened to hail from the north—very close to Witness Nyauhango's village. Such cases were rampant during Banda's profuse tours of crop inspection especially in the north where people bore the brunt of the dictator's iron-fisted rule and where most of the opposition to his government came from.

The entourage consisted of the dictator's horde of henchmen and cohorts accompanied by dancing groups of women who had left behind children to be taken care of by men. As usual, Mama Kadzamila was beside her lifetime partner. The motorcade of close to a hundred vehicles started from Lilongwe (the capital city) heading north to Karonga. Heavily armed troops were positioned in the front and at the rear of the motorcade. In Karonga, Banda would visit only one small farm where people assembled from early hours of the morning though the redeemer wouldn't appear until late in the afternoon. Some of these people left their homes with empty stomachs and were herded by the militias like prisoners. On his arrival, women would burst into ululation and dancing while the men were jumping and clapping hands. In fact, there was no more to the crop inspection than political activities where District Party officials presented the Messiah with donations acquired from the poor people through unprecedented coercion. These donations would, in part, include; money, cattle, goats, sheep, chicken, tons of eggs—the list goes on and on. At times, the donations reached such an overwhelming level that it created a shortage of transports at which time Banda would instruct his henchmen to obtain an additional fleet of trucks from government ministries within the district he was touring—or from more distant districts. The most disturbing scenario was the fact that these donations taken from the wretched people through force were the most precious possessions these people had and meant for sale to enable them to send their children to school, to buy clothes for extended families, and so on.

For the women who were transported to dance for Banda and his henchmen, it was another doleful story. They were not provided with modest accommodations, in most cases, they were accommodated in churches, public halls and in open spaces–and with no food. At times while Party and Government Officials received handsome allowances, unlucky women were taken by officials as sex-slaves and most of these were married women who had left their husbands and families behind. By allowing such evil deeds to be committed by his sycophants and henchmen, President Banda negated his own religious beliefs as a Church Elder of the Church of Scotland. However, this did not astonish the majority of citizens because the woman Banda was messing around with, Miss Cecilia Kadzamila, was someone's fiancée who had been incarcerated on a trumped-up case in order for the despot to take over the woman he left behind.

The month-long crop inspection tour had devastating ramifications for family values. Some women ended up forcefully married to party officials. One disturbing scenario came to light as a truck driver took the matters to the party headquarters after his wife of five years had been forced to marry the District Chairman of the Malawi Congress Party in Central Malawi after a month of absence from her home during an inspection tour. To his surprise and indeed, to most citizens who had heard of the story, the party officials sternly warned the complainant not to go further with the matter and shut-up his mouth as this could tarnish the image of the Life President, Ngwazi Dr. Hastings Kamuzu Banda and the mighty Malawi Congress Party. Refusing to bow to his own humiliation, the law-abiding citizen found himself in rough hands. He was manhandled by a gang of unruly Banda militias and ended-up in one of several concentration camps under the most cruel conditions that existed in these camps. The innocent citizen had to spend three years of incarceration, leaving behind three young children to be raised by relatives and friends. However, this was not the only case where men were harassed over their wives by party officials—but all the perpetrators of this humiliating injustice went scot-free.

The inspection tours not only gave Banda an opportunity to cement his incredible personality cult, but he also benefited a great deal in economic terms. All the donations were transported to various farms owned by Banda and the money was banked in his personal accounts. It should also be noted that all Malawi Congress Party finances and property were registered under Dr. Banda's name as a "Trustee of the Nation." The inspection tours siphoned millions of dollars from government coffers to foot the bills for gas, food, accommodation, and other expenses. The last inspection tour in 1992 cost the taxpayers US$3.5 million. Indeed, there was absolutely no need for such time consuming adventures for the head of state who was supposed to be engaged in vital issues pertaining to Malawi on one hand and Africa on the other. When his counterparts were meeting in Lusaka or Dar es Salaam to look into problems of southern Africa as far as the struggle for liberation was concerned, Banda was surrounded by dancing women for hours. In a country where a single person controlled the entire government network, the people had no opportunity to participate in issues affecting their country or Africa as a whole. So these crop inspection tours were purely politically motivated to impress the masses of our country into believing that Banda cared for them. Sadly, in this country where 85 percent of whom were illiterate, the stratagem worked for the despot.

The life Malawians lived for the thirty years Banda was in power was, to say the least, degrading and humiliating in the sense that people could not think on their own—they were driven more or less like sheep. After the formation of CCAM in the mid-80s, all donations forcefully collected from poor people during crop inspection tours were channeled to the organization which was becoming stronger, more oppressive and more exploitative in nature. Women were forced to buy Kitenge cloth from Kadzamila's extended businesses. While Banda virtually controlled the Malawi Congress Party funds, his lifetime partner controlled CCAM funds and properties. The corruption within CCAM leadership was so repulsive that donor agencies voiced their disproval of the stated strategies of the false organization. Lifford Mkwapatila Mhango, one of the leading journalists in exile then, took steps to expose Kadzamila and the government's activities in the organization. For instance, the late Mkwapatila Mhango, revealed in one of his several pieces in New African Magazine that the funds for Mozambican refugees, displaced by Renamo thugs (and supported by the Malawi government), were diverted to the CCAM as were trucks, lorries and other relief stuffs sent by donors to the Mozambican refugees through the government of Malawi. However, when you talked of the government of Malawi, you talked of Hastings Banda, for he controlled everything in the country. A good deal of donated stuff was sold by the CCAM and the proceeds were pocketed by Kadzamila. This revelation, however, put Banda and his girl friend in a muddy position and demonstrated the paternalistic tendencies of Hastings Banda and this wicked woman on the Malawian political scene.

Dr. Banda and John Tembo, Kadzamila's uncle, and a former notorious henchman of Banda, were also directly involved in the running of CCAM. In order to authenticate the dubious organization and make it look legitimate, Banda and Tembo resorted to telling lies to the nation—for example, the organization was duly formed to help Malawians and also refugees from Mozambique. On the contrary, the organization had no interests in helping the poor women of Malawi on one hand or the Mozambican refugees on the other. By and large, CCAM was an organization that denied poor Malawians their birthrights and put the organization's interests first before those of the downtrodden masses of our people. People were coerced to work the farms of mysterious owners and if a person refused to work for such farms he or she could end up in a concentration camp. Equally, the general population was also forced to donate money for the organization, cadres went from work place to work place forcing people to contribute money. Those who could not contribute at the end of the month saw their pay cheques reduced to smaller amounts than usual.

In Nyasaland (Malawi), we used to have Thangatha (forced-labor) imposed on the people by the colonial administration. This notorious and inhuman system whereby people, particularly in the congested areas of Cholo and Mlanje, were forced to work for estate owners in return for remaining on land that was originally theirs. Dr. Banda claimed that he ended this humiliating system after Malawi attained independence, but astonishingly, people found themselves working on these mysterious farms under duress instead of cultivating their own pieces of land.

However, the formation of the hated and manipulative CCAM was orchestrated by the President himself to prop up Bandaism in the country along the lines of the dreaded Malawi Congress Party which was virtually controlled by one man while his partner in an illegal marriage became the President of the Chitukuku Cha Azimayi M' Malawi (CCAM). These two wicked and mad lovers together with John Tembo, Kadzamila's uncle, controlled, at will, the destiny of 12 million citizens of our country.

The policies of CCAM were akin to the MCP policies, both being oppressive in nature and deceptive in deed. One soldier, Robert Kaunda, was arrested in 1979 for refusing as a matter of principle to buy for his wife the mandatory Kamuzu cloth or the yearly uniform for the so-called Mbumba Za Kamuzu (Kamuzu's women). While Kaunda was in Dzeleka death camp (dubbed Auschwitz by locals), his wife Edna, was constantly harassed by members of CCAM to go and work on their farms, purportedly owned by an unofficial first lady and to buy Kamuzu cloth which was distributed by a company jointly owned by Banda and his life-companion Cecilia Kadzamila. Through such dubious dealings, the woman acquired unprecedented wealth, thus becoming one of the richest women in the continent on a par with Mama Ngina the former wife of another corrupt leader–and unquestionably a puppet of western imperialists—the late Jomo Kenyatta of Kenya and one of few Banda's bedfellows. For the first five months in the concentration camp, Kaunda endured the same untold conditions as other prisoners including the late Orton Edgar C. Chirwa—founder president of the Malawi Congress Party and Attorney-General and Minister of Justice in the first Cabinet.

Dr. Banda broke all the promises he made during the independence struggle. He promised his people that he would break their stupid Federation and give them freedom. On the contrary, the people of Malawi endured a most humiliating life during the thirty years Banda was in power—perhaps at times worse than during the racists' reigns in Rhodesia and South Africa. In both regimes, Africans were exposed to an inhuman system of apartheid while in Malawi people there were subjected to the same system under different name —"Tribalism"—perpetrated by Banda and his tribesmen against the minority people of the north, the "Tumbukas." However, the demise of the Federation has since been attributed to Banda's efforts by his sycophants. This perception is both misleading and false. Banda arrived in Nyasaland at the time the colonial rulers were about to abdicate the imposed system that had been fought against, right and left, by the people of Malawi under the dynamic leadership of such young nationalists as; Dunduzu Chisiza, Yatuta Chisiza, Masauko

Chipembere, Kanyama Chiume, Orton Chirwa, Augustin Bwanausi, Harry Bwanausi, Chief W. Gomani, M. Q. Chibambo and many others. Not only in Nyasaland were people opposed to this degrading system, but also in northern Rhodesia (Zambia) and southern Rhodesia (Zimbabwe) where the people fought gallantly against the Federation and demanded their own self-rule. In Malawi today, people are taught that their history originates from July 1958 when the mysterious Messiah arrived in the country after some 40 years in a political wilderness. As a result, the majority of our people, especially the young generation, are devastatingly brainwashed, but as an old adage concludes, "You can destroy an effigy but you cannot erase history." All the efforts of the Malawian people to dislodge colonialism and imperialism beginning from 1915, or perhaps even earlier, were disregarded as Banda established himself as "Emperor" of the nation and established a personality cult which largely supplanted the national culture. The title "Ngwazi" which means in my dialect, brave man or lion, was bestowed on him because, corruptly and incorrectly, he was perceived as the destroyer of the Federation. But Banda was not up to that, his cowardice did not merit such a title. During the March 3, 1959, State of Emergency when he and a number of the leading nationalist leaders were arrested, he portrayed low morals completely unbefitting a leader of a nationalist movement. When he, together with; Yatuta Chisiza, Dunduzu Chisiza, and Masauko Chipembere were driven in a police Land Rover to the Chileka International Airport for a flight to southern Rhodesia Prison, Banda physically lost composure and slumped himself on Yatuta's laps throughout the entire 45 minute flight to Salisbury (Harare)—en route to Gwero to start their sentences. To the astonishment of his young colleagues, and indeed his captors, the so-called Ngwazi was not even able to step down from the plane, let alone recognize his whereabouts. This was in Rhodesia (Zimbabwe). Finally, it was Yatuta and his brother Dunduzu who helped the despot down the steps. Dunduzu was coldly murdered by Banda's hired thugs in 1962 at a tender age of 27, while Yatuta was killed in a fierce battle at the

Mwanza-Neno battle in 1967 by joint South African-Rhodesian troops which were called in by President Banda himself.

The sad story of the Malawian political history is that the majority of our people have been intentionally denied the truth of the past by Banda's successors most of whom had been part and parcel of the atrocities committed during his autocratic regime. Banda's personality cult had been deeply entrenched in the minds of the majority of citizens, young and old, and continued to dominate every aspect of life even after his demise a decade ago. For instance, at the Commonwealth Conference in Harare, Zimbabwe, on October 17, 1991, President Banda tripped and nearly fell—largely due to senility. After the Conference he went to England for a medical checkup, but astonishingly the English daily, The Malawi News, carried a story on the front page that His Excellency the Life President, Ngwazi Dr. Hastings Kamuzu Banda, formerly of North Shields and Kilburn, had recently attended church services—but the photograph that accompanied that riveting item of news dated back to 1980. Like Nancy Reagan, he lied about his age. Officially he was born on May 14, 1898, but his real birth date was 21 February 1896. Speculation on the subject was illegal and dozens of Malawians landed in prison for discussing Banda's age. The departure of young and able nationalists from the post-independence cabinet, left a tremendous political and economic vacuum that drew Malawians into a bleak future. The people were denied an opportunity to discuss the future that lay ahead for them, their children, and the generations to come. For the thirty years Banda was in power, the people of Malawi excelled in the field of singing and dancing for their Messiah, day in and day out. Not only did Banda capitalize on the brainwashed masses of our people, but also on educated people who ignored their moral obligations in favor of handouts and lucrative positions.

In a brazen and misguided move, Africa's most ravenous Anglophile—he of Homburg hat, pinstriped suits and fly switch—went on a private visit to England and Scotland for three weeks. At the same time the local daily newspaper, owned by the dreaded Malawi Congress Party, carried malicious and misleading news items each day, declaring that the Ngwazi was resting at his Sanjika Palace after hectic months of hard and exhaustive work. Sadly, however, the majority believed the stories to be true. The absence for so long by the Head of State demonstrated, once again, his confidence in his totalitarian and highly personalized regime. To him, it was living proof that repression can work. He even boasted on several occasions that he could live in London (his second home) and rule Malawi for as long as he desired without risking any damage to his brutal reign. Indeed, it was unusual for any Head of State in Africa to boast about his grip of power over the nation while the Continent was rife with military coups that destabilized governments—some of which were partially progressive. If there is any country in Africa that has suffered humiliation under one-man rule, Malawi is a vivid example. The people of this landlocked and desperately poor nation–where tens of thousands of ragged men run to work each day, pounding along the streets like the Chinese (without bicycles) some fifty years ago–where the rule of-fear was too often masked by their countrified ways and thus producing a funny spectacle. Once, Julie Flint, a prolific British journalist described Malawi as, "The land of the funny and peculiar."

Indeed it was. Malawi was the only country in Africa where people celebrated two birth days, one for the Life President Hastings Banda (the 14th of May each year) and the other, Christmas Day. The former was obligatory where people gathered in stadiums and other venues to witness a Kamuzu Day military parade and traditional dancing. People were herded there in the early hours of the morning by Banda's Janjaweeds (Young Pioneers) and kept there until late evening without food or water. All this, while Banda after inspecting the guard of honor mounted by the Malawi Army, retreats to one of his several opulent palaces, the symbols of his notorious legacy which cost the poor nation more than US$600 million.

More than eighty percent of Malawi's population still live below the poverty line. The infant mortality rate is second in Africa only to a war-torn Somalia. Yet, very little was known about this small nation outside its own borders. When the country did make the news, it was usually in connection with the eccentricities of the bestial despot, Hastings Banda. With his obsession for maintaining the values of Victorian England (men were forbidden from wearing hair long or flared trousers and women from wearing trousers or skirts above the knee), Banda was a figure to the outside world. At the same time, his pro-western policies assured him financial and political support from powerful allies such as Britain, Germany, South Africa, Israel, France and the USA. Yet behind this comic image was the reality of a rancorous rightwing regime which squandered the country's meagre resources on pompous ceremonies and palaces while thousands died from malnutrition and disease or the brutal attentions of the dictator's thugs.

On the economic front, Dr. Banda did not fair well either even though the western capitalist nations kept on praising Malawi as a shinning star of black Africa. The people of Malawi fought for political independence as a means of transforming the country's colonial economy into a pattern which could benefit the majority of our people under a form of socialism based on our cultural heritage. As the move to self-determination was spreading across Africa, Britain in particular, realized the necessity of relinquishing her colonies and of finding other means by which to exploit Africa's gargantuan resources. This came to be known as neocolonialism, and in Malawi it is still rampant. Of the many definitions of the term, probably that of Kwame Nkrumah, himself a victim of neocolonialism when his army officers used by the American CIA overthrew his first civilian government, had this to say:

"The state which subjected to it is, in theory, independent and has all the outward trappings of international sovereignty. In reality, its economic power and thus its political policy is directed from outside. The ramification of neocolonialism is that foreign capital is used for the exploitation rather than for the development of the less developed country. The rulers of neocolonial states derive their authority to govern, not from the will of their people, but from support which they obtain from their colonial masters.[xi]

The fact of the matter was that Dr. Banda had no clear vision for the country and he was ignorant in the field of economics. He strongly believed that Malawi's economic future relied on foreign aid, and when a leader is tied to that mentality, he is obviously bound to be used by aid-givers and on their own terms. Therefore, development was such that Malawi was committed to continued reliance on foreign handouts for her development. In such case, economic growth was not in sight, let alone economic independence. Lacking vision and commitment, Dr. Banda lost credible opportunities to extract potential mineral resources that could work hand in hand with the mainstream agricultural setup. It is, for instance, estimated that there are close to a million tons of untapped bauxite deposits around the Mlanje area in the southern region of the country. Meanwhile, there are modest coal mining activities at the Mchenga Coal Mine in the north of the country, but after more than ten years of activity, people around the area of operations are still stuck in an economic quagmire. They do not have clean water, decent housing, health facilities, schools, road, or other essentials. In general, the north (dubbed as dead north) still remains underdeveloped compared with the other two regions which are favored for development. With its potential national parks and resorts along Lake Malawi, the tourist industry could become a potential foreign currency earner for the poor nation, but there has been, since independence, a failure to develop the industry that could create thousands of jobs for our people. Instead Banda was preoccupied with his own ego. Nyika National Park, west of Rumphi District in northern Malawi has a tremendous capacity for development

---

[xi] Kwame Nkrumah, *"Neocolonialism the last stage of imperialism,"* London, 1965.

due to its pristine scenery (unique in the world) and a wide range of wildlife that could readily attract thousands of tourists each month. The park is also located in the north (as is the Mchenga Coal Mine) where development had been sadly neglected, firstly by the colonial authorities, and then by the successive black governments led by leaders imbued with tribal inclinations from the Central and south of the country. Such disparities, however, are always the recipe for bloody ethnic conflicts such as what has provoked armed conflict in Niger Delta in Nigeria today.

Nigeria, the fourth largest producer of oil and natural gas is creating its own homemade problems. Dubbed the "Kuwait of Africa," Nigerian oil fetches close to US$200 million a day, and yet, the majority of the people are among the poorest on the planet. By far more than half of the oil revenue is diverted into foreign personal bank accounts by unscrupulous politicians and military rogues. Tom O'Neil of the National Geographic in his brilliant article entitled, "Curse of Nigerian Oil" in February 2007 issue wrote thus: "Nigeria has been subverted by the thing that gave it promise, oil, which accounts for 95 percent of the country's export earnings and 80 percent of its revenue." Sadly, Niger Delta, like the northern part of Malawi, is horribly neglected with its people exposed to grinding poverty while its gargantuan oil resources benefit only selected individuals in top positions. Infrastructures that represent colonial relics, are fast crumbling, the state of joblessness is appalling among young people and still worse, 85 percent of the arable land is environmentally obsolete. Unfortunately, as the last resort, the people of Niger Delta, after a hopelessly long wait for their fair share of the oil wealth, have reluctantly resorted to violence under the movement for the Emancipation of Niger Delta (MEND) in order to register their grievances. After more than 40 years of independence, Malawi still relies heavily on foreign aid. Eighty (80) percent of its national budget come from donor countries. In Tanzania, this danger was foreseen and addressed in the Arusha Declaration—that country's socialist blueprint of Tanganyika African National Union (TANU)—and led by the late president and one of Africa's gallant freedom fighters, Dr. Julius Kambarage Nyerere the first president of Tanganyika (Tanzania). The following is part of the declaration embodiment:

"It is stupid to rely on money as the major instrument of development when we know only too well that our country is poor. It is equally stupid, indeed it is more stupid, for us to imagine that we shall rid ourselves of our poverty through foreign financial assistance rather than our own financial resources. We are mistaken when we imagine that we shall get money from foreign countries."[xii]

Even though the intent of the Arusha Declaration was a milestone in Tanzania's economic and political history, sadly it lost its direction on takeoff. The nationalization of private buildings, banks, small butchers owned by local individuals, industries, and the restriction of consumer goods (clothes, shoes, etc.), mushroomed into an unprecedented illicit trade that crippled government revenues. Citizens with resources were discouraged from starting businesses in view of the fact that someone could be summoned by Party officials to explain his or her lifestyle.

The direction Tanzanians undertook to correct the past colonialist economy of exploitation was commendable. Unfortunately, the implementation went terribly wrong—there was also a lack of commitment among the bureaucrats. Orchestrated corruption raised its ugly head to a devastating proportion thus wrecking a once progressive national economy.

In Zambia too, the UNIP government under the leadership of Dr. K. D. Kaunda, embarked on a socialist path under the blueprint of "Humanism." Like Tanzania, the philosophy of humanism did not go far, it collapsed amid corruption, mismanagement, inefficiency and lack of commitment among bureaucrats. These factors were not only the catalysts for fail-

---

[xii] Arusha Declaration and TANU'S Policy on Socialism and Self-reliance, Publicity Section, TANU 1967.

ures, but to a larger extent, the capitalists fought tooth and nail to undermine socialism in the era of cold-war in this strategic region. The failures of socialist endeavors in Malawi's neighbors, gave Banda the needed ammunition to defend his neocolonialist policies. Any attempt to change the status quo in Malawi could meet strong opposition, even sabotage, both on the domestic front and abroad. A political movement away from the traditional defense of private enterprise and ownership of the means of production could damage the relationship with the sources of finance on which Malawi depended. In that circumstance, the regime could be confronted with the dilemma of choosing to carry out a socialist program in one stroke, or to abandon it for fear of failure. The late Oskar Lange wrote that, "Any government intending to introduce socialism in a capitalist economy must go through resolutely with its socialization program at maximum velocity. Any hesitation, any vacillation and indecision would provoke the inevitable economic affliction." "Socialism," Lange continued, "is not an economic policy for the timid." In reality, Fidel's Cuba is a vivid instance of courage and commitment.

The failures of Tanzania and Zambia to establish Socialist States, was used to a greater extent by the powerful capitalist empires to portray Banda's Malawi as a model of capitalism in Africa. Astonishingly, even one of his successors, Dr. Bingu wa Mutharika, himself an India-trained economist, praises the former bestial despot for economic successes. What Dr. Bingu gives as an instance of success is the building of opulent State Palaces which the majority of Malawians have had no access to. Unlike one of the successors, Dr. Bakili Muluzi, Bingu is an ardent admirer of Banda's legacy. In this regard, he has built a multimillion Kwacha (local currency) mausoleum for the late murderous tyrant while millions of our children go hungry, thousands die of curable maladies such as malaria, and thousands more cannot afford medication for HIV infection, or other afflictions. More than 85 percent of Malawians live under the poverty line. But despite consistent positive portrayals of Banda's so-called economic miracles by the western capitalist countries, the fact remained that there was very little progress Malawians could be proud of. It must also be understood that Malawi was the first nation to succumb to the western imperialist influence and to become the first victim of neocolonialism in eastern and southern Africa. Its independence was shamefully compromised. As I have indicated earlier on, both domestic and foreign policies were strenuously directed by foreign powers acting behind the scene.

It was a chorus in the western media that the rest of black Africa must emulate Malawi's economic successes. However, this was misleading propaganda intended to defend their puppet state amidst East-West rivalries and to control newly independent African States. Having been given high marks on economic performance, Dr. Banda himself admitted publicly in October 1984 (during an annual conference for southern Region of his dreaded Malawi Congress Party [MCP]): "No loan, no Malawi." In essence, apart from what had been speculated, Malawi, since the attainment of independence, had been a big recipient of western economic aid although little of it traveled further than Banda's and Kadzamila' pockets.

Much had been said of Malawi's economic miracles especially by his backers in the western capitals, but the fact remained that there was very little economic activity enjoyed by the majority of our people. In 1965 alone, 60,000 Malawians were shipped to work in the mines and factories of Rhodesia and South Africa—a year after the independence of Malawi. In these places, poor migrant workers lived in conditions of slavery. This system was being precipitated by the failure of the government to develop alternative employment in Malawi. To bridge her budget deficits and embark on a road to self-sufficiency and industrialization, Malawi could have exploited the gargantuan water resources of Lakes Malawi, Chilwa, Chiuta and the Shire River, and the mineral deposits now left in the ground. In the case of Shire River, one of

Banda's successors and admirer Dr. Bingu wa Mutharika launched a project in 2006 to turn the river into a waterway for big freighters and barges instead of for potential irrigation schemes which could expedite economic growth and in the industrial sector create more jobs for jobless Malawians who had experience in the mines of South Africa, Rhodesia (Zimbabwe) and northern Rhodesia (Zambia). This could effectively curtail the exodus of Malawi labor power to those countries. Instead, the Malawi government contributed 62,500 Sterling as 38 percent of the cost towards a United Nations Development Program Labor Statistics Unit at Blantyre which aimed to analyze the earnings, savings, skills, and period of repatriation of Malawi's migrant workers. There were two categories: those whose contracts were arranged by the Malawi Government and those who traveled on their own to seek independent employment.

The economic advantages of labor exported from Malawi to the racist regimes of the Republic of South Africa and Rhodesia were:

(1) Laborers from a low income country like Malawi would accept wages below prevailing rates, but above minimum wage scales in Malawi.

(2) The arrival of ready-made workers represented a saving in social services for the racist Republics since such costs as education, pensions, and health were borne by the Malawi government.

(3) Families of migrant workers stayed in Malawi, thereby remaining a social responsibility of the Malawi government, and relieving the racist Republics of the costs of social infrastructure such as housing, schools, hospitals, transport and roads.

(4) Immigrant labor contracts were short-term, lending more flexibility to the racist Republics' African labor supply.

The political windfalls from labor export accrue to both sides:

(1) The readiness of Malawians to accept lower wages than the Africans of South Africa and Rhodesia had a depressive effect on their ability to organize around economic issues. The White regimes therefore, saw the Malawi immigrant laborers as an instrument to neutralize the working class of their own countries.

(2) The short term contract did not allow time for the Malawians to become integrated or initiated into local African politics, and they were segregated into camps or in dilapidated structures where tribal identity was encouraged in order to see the Africans divided and thus more easily controlled by the racist regimes.

(3) The Malawi government was relieved of the political embarrassment and possible consequences of widespread unemployment further clogging the already swollen Malawi labor market.

(4) Malawi was able to use the export of her labor force as collateral in gaining concessions in trade and spectacular gestures such as a 25 million Sterling grant from the racist Republic of South Africa to pay for shifting Malawi's capital from Zomba to Lilongwe (Banda's purported tribal region).

So, there was a high price for a newly independent Malawi to pay for her treacherous policy of "dialogue" with the evil regimes of Southern Africa. The cost of cooperation within the Sterling currency zone of Africa was high for Malawi. There were arguments that the Malawi government gained the foreign exchange earnings remitted by migrant workers to their families in Malawi, and that sum was considerable since well over 80,000 Malawians worked in South Africa alone. It was estimated that in the years 1968-1971, the migrant sector as a whole contributed about 2.5 million Sterling (British) in foreign exchange earnings. However in his analysis of political and economic trends in Malawi under Banda's administration, the Late Dr. G. Attati Mphakali, a prolific economist and former charismatic leader of the opposition the now defunct the Socialist League Of Malawi (LESOMA) and murdered in cold-blood in Harare, Zimbabwe by

Banda's notorious secret agents in collusion with Zimbabwe's secret police, sums thus:

"The propensity to consume luxury commodities retailed through European or Asian owned businesses was so high that it virtually cancelled out the inflow of foreign exchange so far as the African community was concerned. In fact, it could not be rushed to suggest that it was that community, the people of Malawi, who suffer the repercussions, rather than benefits arising from the sale of their labor. They were denied the opportunity of working directly for their own and of being with their families, and by sacrificing that opportunity and contributing to the property of racist regimes, they directly hindered the struggle of Africans elsewhere against apartheid. Not only was the revolutionary spirit of Africans under white oppression and labor exploitation watered down by the presence of neutral Malawians under government sponsored contracts, but in Malawi itself the Congress Party actively discouraged opposition to European interests. This first became evident from the confusion the Congress Party caused in its appeals for calm when the masses rose against Welensky's regime. This betrayal of the uprising weakened the Congress Party's bargaining position when Banda began underhand negotiations on the new Constitution from within Gweru Prison."

While Tanzania and Zambia, the immediate neighbors embarked on socialist paths to institute economic and political equilibrium in their respective countries, in Malawi, Dr. Banda, who believed himself a strong teacher by example, proceeded to demonstrate how a Malawian sufficiently endowed with acquisitive instincts should go about acquiring a gargantuan financial empire amid grinding poverty among his fellow citizens.

The most conspicuous part of his empire was Press (Holdings) Ltd. in which the supreme ruler held 4,999 of 5,000 shares. Reportedly, the remaining share was held by one of his closest henchmen Mr. Aleke Banda (no relation to Hastings Banda).

In the country, much attention had been given to Banda's political legacy, but far less attention had been given to his economic legacy where he had constructed a unique system of personal control meant to be difficult to unravel. The former despot who lacked economic vision had openly and proudly stated that capitalism was the only course his impoverished nation could follow. Other African capitalist states had sought to brush up the image of their economic mode by a whole set of labels: "African socialism," "Ujamaa," "Human capitalism," "Humanism," "Common man's charter," "Authenticity." Some of these labels were put into practice, but with disastrous ramifications. In Malawi, it was simply capitalism. Dr. Banda once told his docile and "rubber stamp" Parliament, "We do not suppress the acquisitive and possessive instinct in Malawi. Instead we encourage it."

The status of Press (Holdings) had baffled many economic analysts and vexed international financiers because, although it was legally a privately owned firm, it generally enjoyed all the privileges of a para-state organization. Dr. Banda himself on many occasions confused matters further by, on one hand, treating the Corporation as his personal property, while on the other, claimed that he held it "in trust" for the people of Malawi.

In fact, the genesis of Press (Holdings) went back to the time of the independence struggle. It was started in the early 60s as part of Malawi Press, which was owned by the ruling Congress Party. For Malawi Press to have access to financial sources, such as banks, it had to be incorporated and financially detached from the Party. The solution was to establish Press (Holdings), whose shares were apparently divided between Banda, as the Party Chief, and Aleke Banda as Editor of Malawi News. It still remains a mystery hitherto whether the original capital came from these two evil Banda's. The two men became the legal owners of what once belonged to the Party, and then, Press (Holdings) became an economic octopus with tentacles in every branch of Malawi's economy. It was again virtually impossible to obtain information on the extent of its activities or its financial status. Even when one looked through Malawi's telephone directory, one found other companies in which Press Holdings had shares—and thus gained a glimpse of this financial octopus. The telephone directory listed no less than fourteen Press Companies.

There were also other subsidiaries which did not have "Press" in their names, but which were known to belong to the conglomerate. One such company was the Peoples' Trading Centre, with department stores, supermarkets and superettes in almost every district of the country. And then, there was the General Farms, reputedly one of the largest individually owned tobacco handling companies. Other reports on Dr. Banda's wealth could be obtained from other company reports in which Press Holdings was a shareholder.

Banda's empire was vast, encompassing breweries, distilleries, food processing industries, textiles, metal products, tourism and hotels, wholesaling and retailing. How the former brutal tyrant had amassed this vast fortune caused Malawians to raise their eyebrows. When he came to the then Nyasaland after, we are told, 40 years of self-imposed exile in Britain, USA and Gold Coast (Ghana), he brought virtually nothing with him apart from one small suitcase that contained three suits and a handful of white-shirts. The Nyasaland African Congress footed all the bills, from his house rental, food, transport, clothing and a monthly allowance of US$65,000. This amount, in the early 60s and in an impoverished country, was just too much for a political Messiah who had come back to liberate his people from colonial oppression and exploitation.

The former brutal tyrant used to announce the profits of his farming activities to the Parliament. In August 1975, he boasted of profits of more than US$15.9 million from tobacco alone. Usually, he accompanied these announcements with appeals to his sycophants to emulate his acquisitive capacity. However, the extent to which he controlled economic activities among his sycophants and senior civil servants alike, this elite was confined to limited economic advancement in a sense that their financial abilities were strictly curtailed in order to neutralize their political strength. Among his henchmen, only John Z. Tembo the notorious uncle of his concubine Cecilia Kadzamila, excelled in economic activities and became one of the richest and most feared Party officials in the country. Dr. Banda was fully convinced that to control his subordinates from challenging him politically or economically, he had to enslave them economically. Indeed, the plan worked to his advantage. Citizens who built houses in cities were required by law to submit copies of transactions to the President's office. The reason behind this draconian measure was to make sure that people were not being bought by foreign money or enabled to carry on revolutionary activities on behalf of the rebel ministers.

Dr. Banda had been the Minister of Agriculture and Natural Resources for more than two decades, a position that gave him unlimited access to the Ministry's technical and research services. He saw no conflict between state and personal interests. When the rebel ministers accused him of running the country as his personal estate, he disarmingly admitted it and said he was "proud" of it. A more glaring example of this relationship between Banda's personal interests and those of the state, was a curious figure in the annual financial reports of the Agricultural Development and Marketing Corporation (ADMARC). For a number of years then, more than US$35 million had been included as "unsecured loan" to Press Holdings Ltd. It was crystal clear that no other Malawian capitalist could even dream of such credit facilities.

Where could a corporation in an agricultural-based underdeveloped economy obtain so many millions of unsecured funds? ADMARC was the linchpin of the Malawi government's relationship with the peasantry. The Corporation enjoyed unprecedented monopoly on the purchases of virtually all marketable peasant produce. The rich farmers on the other hand, had direct access to the world market through the auction floors. ADMARC bought crops from the peasantry at very exploitative prices on the world market. One ramification of this, was the large profits accruing to ADMARC. Between 1983-1987, profit margins on crop trading averaged 32 percent of net sales of crops purchased. In some years, it had been as high as 45 percent. Astonishingly, these profits had not been ploughed back into the peasant sector, but had instead, gone into estate agriculture and industry. Some of it had been given as "unsecured loans" to Dr. Banda. The former despot's use of his profits is a tale in itself. He made lavish "gifts" to the nation. He built the elitist Kamuzu Academy in his tribal district at an estimated cost of US$22 million. He built expensive houses for members of women's league who had excelled in dancing and praising him. Millions of dollars had been spent to ferry dancing and singing troupes of women to his mostly monotonous meetings.

In a country that is plagued by unprecedented poverty, malnutrition, an HIV/AIDS pandemic, malaria, and acute unemployment, it is saddening that the available meagre resources were diverted invariably to projects for the benefit of a single person. It is also very perturbing that majority of Malawians, after the dictator's disappearance, find no fault in his shameful legacy—his catastrophic policies are still applauded even when in his grave. Using State property for his own interests, as the Head of State, was the absolute height of corruption and yet many Malawians remain loyal to his noxious past.

In Malawi, one of the poorest nations in the world, the late eccentric despot Hastings Banda built several State Palaces at a cost of more than US$500 million. These funds that were meant for national economic development could have benefited the well-being of the majority of our people. Banda claimed that the funds for these structures, which have not uplifted the standard of living of the people, came from his purse. All in all, Malawians had been subjected to untold misery sometimes worse than slaves in their own country. Yet, the outside world knew very little about the plight of Malawians. The western democracies in particular, were the strongest supporters and financiers of the most noxious regime in Africa. What the outside world heard was the intensity of the western media trying to portray Malawi, under their lackey, as a model in black Africa–yet, its economy was not sustainable, 85 percent of the population lived below poverty line, the government could not survive on its own without foreign economic aid and, thousands of young able-bodied men left the country each year for greener pastures in neighboring countries such as Zambia, Tanzania, Rhodesia (Zimbabwe), Botswana and the Republic of South Africa. As Dr. Banda lacked vision and commitment for the betterment of Malawi, economic prosperity, political freedom, and social equality were washed down the drain thus allowing the neo-fascist despot and his closest henchmen to run the nation as they pleased. While marching to an unknown destination through darkness and ragged terrain, Malawians were unwittingly heading for a bleak future–one that made them political slaves in the land of their birth where their destiny was virtually controlled by a single person. There was no doubt in their minds that they were practically subjected to conditions of a wretched society under the police state.

Chapter Eight

THE HEIGHT OF REPRESSION

By the mid-1970s Malawi had drifted into a police-state under the leadership of President Hastings Banda who single-handedly ruled the nation for the next 30 years. He controlled virtually every aspect of life thus transforming Malawians into a tranquilized and unthinking state.

After he was deserted by the people who helped him gain power during the independence struggle, he was soon virtually surrounded by a horde of zealous henchmen and sycophants. He not only he ruled the nation, but he literally owned the people and the nation. He was the government. Whatever he said, it was the law of the land. Having emerged victorious over his former able ministers, they were soon scattered as exiles throughout the neighboring states. He proceeded to demonstrate to his subjects that he was their untouchable boss with a mandate to direct their destiny. To Malawians, he was a small-god.

The Malawi Young Pioneers, equivalent to the Janjaweeds in the Sudan or the Tonton Macoute of the former brutal Haitian tyrant Francois (Papa Doc) and Jean-Claude (Baby Doc) Duvalier, were transformed into a unique fighting force loyal only to Dr. Banda. In other words, this force was a militia whose major task was to intimidate, humiliate and brutalize the masses to complete submission. In 1965, Aleke Banda (no relation to Hastings Banda), but a very close henchman to the despot, was appointed as a Commander of the dreaded Young Pioneers. (Mr. Aleke Banda himself had no previous military experience.) Under his command, new military equipment (i.e., guns, walkie-talkies, uniforms, boots, and vehicles, etc.) were imported from apartheid South Africa and Israel and some from Britain and the United States. The budget for the evil force was raised to US$140 million, more than double the amount allocated to the National Police Force.

Thousands of young half-educated men were sent to Israel, apartheid South Africa, and Taiwan for military training. Back home, these misguided young men were effectively used to neutralize and suppress any form of dissenting opinions. Indeed, life for the general public under the imported so-called Messiah became miserable and fearful. The young men were transported countrywide to coerce people to accept and acknowledge Banda's supremacy. The Malawi Congress Party Card was an issue at stake, every citizen was obliged to carry the card wherever he or she went and no age was, for that matter, exempted. Beatings of innocent people and all sorts of humiliation were the order of the day, forcing people not to trust their own shadows. Aleke Banda became very unpopular especially in the north where atrocities and repression were the most numerous and brutal. Aleke Banda himself comes from the north.

Dr. Banda was a delusional fabricator and a pathological intriguer who used his henchmen and sycophants for his own political and economic advantage. After he realized that Aleke Banda had lost ground in the north, his own birthplace, he demoted him and directly appointed another of his loyal henchmen, Gwanda Chakuamba Phiri, as Commander of his militia force. Chakuamba pursued power with a vengeance. He was very ruthless when it came dealing with the north, the region that was perceived as anti-Banda. School children were obliged to buy party cards and parents, besides having to buy party cards, were coerced into displaying Banda badges on their shirts, jackets or dresses. If a citizen was found without a card or badge, he or she could be arrested or roughed up by the militia thugs. Sadly, all these unlawful acts were done with the full knowledge of the Head of State.

As if the power Banda wielded was not enough, his closest henchmen and sycophants ganged up to give him more power to rule the nation. Therefore at it's annual convention in 1970 at Nkhota-kota, Central Malawi, the Congress Party (MCP) resolved unanimously that Ngwazi Hastings Banda be elected Life-President of the Republic of Malawi. To the detriment of our democracy, the country's Constitution was amended accordingly by a rubber-stamp Parliament on November 26, 1970, and the President formally accepted the convention's decision on December 3, 1970. He was sworn in as Life-President of the Republic on July 6, 1971, July 6 also being the date that the Messiah arrived in Nyasaland in 1958 as well as the date Malawi became independent (6th July 1964). The people who campaigned on behalf of the President for this sad and treasonous trend that saw the demise of democracy and human dignity in Malawi, believed that by doing so, their positions and status in the Party and Government were secured and guaranteed. But to the contrary, they willingly and foolishly dug their own political graves.

Instrumental to this wholesale betrayal of the peoples' aspirations were Aleke Banda in the lead, John Tembo of course, Gwanda Chakuamba Phiri, the late Albert N. Muwalo, and Robson Chirwa. Although the Convention represented the people of Malawi as a whole, their views and opinions were in sharp contrast with their representatives' views. They saw miseries and unprecedented abuse of power awaiting them. His election by his henchmen and the narrow-minded horde of delegates at the Convention to lead the Party and government for the rest of his life, gave him, as expected, prodigious power to do anything he wanted to be done whether within the framework of the National Constitution or not. Already the President had wielded unlimited powers in his hands, he was himself the Constitution, the Government, the Law, the Parliament, and the Nation.

During the multiparty campaign in the early 90s, some leaders of the opposition movements (UDF/AFORD), accused Kanyama Chiume, former articulate Minister for Foreign Affairs and an archenemy of President Banda, of being responsible in creating his (Banda's) life-Presidency. Such accusations however, were hollow and malicious and designed to harm Chiume's integrity. They knew very well that Chiume was not repressible, but to be candid enough Chiume did contribute to Banda's arrogance and highhandedness by overpraising the monster, but when he was elected Life-President in 1971, Chiume and his colleagues were already in exile. By all means Chiume and his colleagues could not have jumped onto that treacherous and degrading bandwagon. They were principled individuals driven by undiluted Pan-Africanist ideals. Moreover, the entire leadership of the UDF served in the tyrannical regime of Hastings Banda.

President Banda got what he wanted–a political gift to oppress his fellow citizens who generously welcomed him from his self-imposed exile in 1958. Forthwith, he manipulated the country's judicial system to better support his dubious desires. He created a two-tier judicial system: (a) a High Court System consisting of magistrate courts; the High Court of Malawi, and the Supreme Court of Appeal; and (b) Traditional Courts at Area, District, and Regional levels, and above which is the National Traditional Court. The personnel within this system were largely uneducated, corrupt, primitive, and easy to manipulate into dancing to the tune of the despotic regime.

Sooner rather than later, in a show of force, President Banda made an impromptu trip to Usisya, Nkhata Bay District, Kanyama Chiume's birth place accompanied by a horde of Party loyalists and several government ministers followed by dozens of trucks carrying dancing women and red-uniformed heavily armed militias. Villagers were brutally and inhumanely coerced into attending the meeting which the President was to address. However, there was nothing important or new that the people expected to hear as they were used to his usual wearisome speeches. What shocked the audience was that Banda forced Chiume's father to stand before the multitude of people and disown and castigate his own son Kanyama Chiume. With a smiling face, the old man did what he was told to do, but at that moment, the people made it clear that they were not delighted. There was a "dead silence" that expressed the peoples' disapproval.

Before even the tyrant left the place rather disappointed, a gang of elite militia attacked and destroyed Chiume's house and his belongings. The house was beautifully built with several big rooms which could have been turned into a clinic, library, or guesthouse to generate some sort of income for the village. The rampage, however, did not end there. His herd of cattle at his Chikwina Farm was attacked and slaughtered, just for the sake of it, and his coffee plantation, which was the best in the region or country, was virtually cut-down by government sponsored militias (Young Pioneers). Not only that, Banda went to the National Radio to announce that he wanted Chiume dead or alive. He didn't care what his people might do to him. This sort of witch-hunting and organized murder-squads made it more difficult for Chiume and his colleagues to rally their supporters and explain to them their next move. His election as the Ayatollah Khomeini (Supreme Ruler) of Malawi, made President Banda an omnipotent and uncontrolled monster who considered himself above the law and beyond accountability to the Party, the Government, and the Nation.

After dealing devastating damage against Chiume's Constituency in the northern Region, he directed his militia to the south, this time to Ft. Johnstone (Mangoche)–Masauko Chipembere's home District. Chipembere and Chiume were prominent leaders in the independence struggle and were instrumental in obtaining Banda's return to Nyasaland from his self-imposed exile. Chip, as he was popularly known in the country, was the most popular leader in the country and could have easily and overwhelmingly defeated Banda in any national political contest. In Mangoche, the unruly militias were instructed to attack Jehovah Witnesses who had earlier refused to buy Party cards because of their religious beliefs. The Witnesses stood their ground. They refused to betray their own beliefs amidst unprovoked attacks.

In the melee, more than one hundred members of the sect were brutally slain, 5,000 injured, and more than 30,000 displaced. Their homes were burnt down and properties stolen including herds of cattle, sheep, goats and chickens. More than 20,000 Witnesses crossed the border into Mozambique and some ended up in Zambia and Zimbabwe. The Witnesses had been practicing their faith for centuries in Malawi and during the colonial era, to be fair, they were free to do so. Journalists, mostly westerners were imprisoned and sympathetic expatriates were deported. Eventually, there was not a single journalist resident in Malawi despite the fact that their respective governments overwhelmingly supported and backed Banda's neo-fascist regime.

At times, to be fair, Banda's regime was worse than the apartheid regime of South Africa. Whenever the Presidential motorcade passed, Malawians were obliged to go to the nearest window or sidewalk and wave. It was forbidden to mock or criticize the know-it-all President. It was forbidden to make a photocopy of a newspaper photograph of the President. And any reference to him, must employ the full title: HIS EXCELLENCY THE LIFE-PRESIDENT NGWAZI DR. HASTINGS KAMUZU BANDA. Many people ended up in prison for omitting one of these titles.

The Life-Presidency bestowed on him really transformed Malawians into the political lepers of Africa and the laughing stock of the world. The people of talent and intelligence betrayed their conscience to win political and economic favors from the President. To keep his people amenable and cut them off from the rest of the free world, he refused to introduce television services in Malawi, though he possessed one set for himself. Foreign magazines such as informative NEW AFRICAN based in London, was banned. At times, tuning into the BBC or any foreign radio station could lead someone to prison. Sadly, through this obnoxious and calculated system, the President had managed to shape every aspect of life in Malawi to his own liking, which was that of a paternalistic, omnipotent, human-god. When he spoke to his people (indeed, they were by all means his people), it was in the language of a father speaking to his multiple, slightly stupid children: "Plant your maize seedlings. Work hard. I am proud of you my people."

There had been tyrannical regimes in Africa, but Malawi's was unique in that the people seemed proud of being owned by a fellow human-being. Throughout Banda's thirty years of wanton rule, there were no revolts or demonstrations, nor any form of passive resistance. The doctrine of four cornerstones of the dreaded Malawi Congress Party: "Unity, Discipline, Obedience, Loyalty," had turned Malawians into servile subjects, absolutely semi-human beings who ceased to think for themselves. It was this dubious slogan ("Unity, Discipline, Obedience, Loyalty") that tragically changed Malawi's political landscape. Realistically, the four-word slogan brainwashed the people to the extent that they remained perpetually vulnerable to manipulation and were like politically dead-people. There was neither obedience, loyalty, nor discipline–nothing but slavery and dehumanization. There was no unity either for the people of northern Malawi (Tumbukas). They were severely discriminated against—a pattern which still apparently continues. The President could preach the significance of national unity among his people in his countless monotonous speeches: "There should be no Tumbukas, Chewas, Yaos, Nkhondes, etc., we should all remain united as Malawians." But behind scenes he and his tribesmen orchestrated tribalism and regionalism. The most frequently targeted were northerners whom he and his so-called clansmen perceived as antigovernment. The politics of divide and rule had been Banda's hallmark in Malawian politics ever since he arrived in the country to assume leadership. The first victims were his ministers whom he divided into groups in order to control and manipulate them.

Soon after he was assured of his continued leadership in a Police State, the President ordered the construction of three more concentration camps. These "camps of death and torture" were completed two months before the schedule and cost the taxpayers US$5.6 million—and this in a country rated as one of the poorest in the world. The tender was given to a South African (apartheid) construction company with vast experience in torture facilities. Within one month, all three death-camps (dubbed as Auschwitz) were filled with prisoners who had not been tried in a court of law, though some were tried in kangaroo courts presided over by Banda's hand-picked judges who had absolutely no judicial credibility—some were even former members of his notorious murder-squad. Ninety-percent of the prisoners were Tumbukas from the north and the rest from the two regions, South and Central.

The first intellectuals to be locked up at Mikuyu camp was Professor Jack Mapanje from the English Department of the University of Malawi, followed by a neurosurgeon, Dr. George Ntafu. Both these men of principle were innocent, but both fell victim to their own academic achievements which Banda hated. That same month of their incarceration, the Malawi government hypocritically sent a delegation to Addis Ababa, Ethiopia to attend a Conference on Human Rights and the Malawi government had just signed the charter relative to Article Six which states. "No one may be arbitrarily arrested or detained." Malawi's attitude of the right of free expression, guaranteed in Article Nine, had been an equally derisive fact. Mapanje had not committed any offense to deserve such unwarranted treatment. One of his articulate poems entitled "Of Chameleons and God," was behind his incarceration and was banned while the author was in the Mikuyu death-camp in 1987. His detention, however, was probably intended to pre-empt a further volume of poetry to be entitled, *Out of Bounds.*" Mapanje's poems joined a list of prohibited publications which included *"Not Yet Uhuru"* and works by George Orwell, Graham Greene, Ernest Hemingway and Simone de Beauvoir as well as the Kama Sutra and indeed, just anything the despot thought was subversive in nature.

In a major political trial of the 1970s, one of the counts against the defendant, a former dupe of Banda, was possession of a copy of "Animal Farm." In vain, he pleaded that he had studied it as a required book when in school and had forgotten to throw it away when it was banned. Banda, to state the fact, was a confused and megalomaniacal individual of low intellectual level and out of touch with realities. But his tactics, though treasonous, helped him remain in power—for just as long as he kept Malawians manageable and cut off from the rest of the international community.

Once on a visit to Meharry Medical School in Tennessee, USA where he claimed to have studied, he was presented with a book which in turn he recommended to his servile ministers as suitable reading material. It was later discovered, much to his general embarrassment, that it was already on the Malawi Censorship Board's banned list. Life in Malawi then, especially to right-minded people and those who chose to remain in the country, was unbearable. But with no other choice, some endured such a life by holding to the opportunistic conviction that things could be better for them—but they paid an outrageous price. Opportunism at times leads people to illusive perceptions and eventually, they become slaves of their own making.

The President went even further and banned the Simon and Garfunkel song, "Cecilia." The reason being that his former unpopular "Hostess" was called Cecilia Kadzamila. At one time, a bowdlerized version of the song was circulated, satirizing the domestic life of the President and his partner. As days went by, the unofficial first lady preferred to be known as "Mama" or Tamanda. As consistent rumors circulated in the country that the President was an impostor or foreigner, he expressly directed the Censorship Board to outlaw a song which was highly liked or loved in Southern Africa. That was sung in Chinyanja: "A Phiri anabwela." These words translates thus: Phiri had returned home after a long time from Harare and could not remember where he was born, had found all his relatives had died and he could not speak one of his local dialects. One of the former rebel ministers told me that he began to suspect Banda's roots when he accompanied him to Kasungu, his home district, where he was totally lost and refused to answer any question relative to his background. Myself, though I lived in exile for 30 years and another 14 years in self-imposed exile, I have never forgotten my native

Tumbuka or the extended members of my family, leave alone boyhood playmates.

As his grip on power intensified each day, so too the repression of Malawians the likes of which were unheard of beyond its borders. The new concentration camps he had constructed, in addition to the existing ones, were expressly filled with five to ten new prisoners each day mostly the Tumbukas from the north.

The Kafkaesque nature of the Malawian system was illustrated by the sad and barbaric case of Blaise Machila, a colleague of Professor Jack Mapanje in the English Department of the University of Malawi. He had a long history of mental illness and after Mapanje's arrest, he became distressed and began claiming that it was him who had denounced his friend to the authorities. He was admitted as a voluntary patient to a mental hospital, where he began to criticize Banda's draconian policies which in turn led to his friend's arrest.

The hospital authorities summoned the police. Machila's mental state made him abandon the caution which was usually second nature to Malawians. He consistently repeated his attacks on the leadership. Machila was discharged from hospital, arrested and detained at the notorious Mikuyu prison. That was in January 1988. More than two years later, he remained in servitude, his mental health apparently deteriorated dangerously, and he was perpetually chained and naked.

It was no secret that Banda's power rested upon the systematic suppression of dissents. Candidates for the rubber-stamp Parliament were strictly approved by himself and despite his professed enthusiasm for education, he usually selected candidates of low educational attainment in order to domesticate them mentally and otherwise. The effect was obvious. The Parliament ceased to function democratically, quite unlike the post-independence cabinet which consisted of Malawi's most talented and articulate young nationalists. The first cabinet was put on par with Kwame Nkrumah's cabinet in Gold Coast (Ghana) at the time of independence in 1957.

For instance, in dealing with racist minority regimes of southern Africa, Dr. Banda hypocritically introduced the policy of "dialogue" as a means to resolving the conflict and urged, to no avail, other African States to emulate his treacherous and hollow notion. To his delight, every Parliamentarian and politician at large, knowingly or unknowingly, memorized the word "dialogue" and it partially became a foreign policy landmark.

The fact is that women were made to believe that the MCP government cared about them. There were some, however, who harbored skeptical views of this systematic political control. One such woman was Margaret Marango Banda, a former radio presenter and prominent laywoman in the Anglican Church. She was arrested and imprisoned without trial. Her crime? She openly criticized alleged corruption in the National Women's Organization (Chitukuko Cha Azimai Mu Malawi). The leader of this dubious organization was none other than Banda's hostess—Cecilia Tamanda Kadzamila.

Margaret was arrested in June 1988 on her return from a visit to Britain and was kept in a very poor conditions at Zomba Central Prison—built by colonialists some 70 years earlier. She was 62 at the time and suffered from diabetes and high blood pressure. Nevertheless, she was denied proper medical attention and died. Margaret, like a disproportionate number of political prisoners, came from the north. Under British colonial rule, northerners were better taught in mission schools or institutions with the result that they came to dominate both the Civil Service and the education system after independence. This was, and still is, resented by the Chewa-speaking political elite, John Tembo being that group's leader.

The sufferings of Malawians under the Banda regime were rigorous. Marton Machipisa Munthali, my own cousin, was imprisoned in the first of several death-camps in July; 1966 for allegedly committing subversive activities. He was given a sham trial and sentenced to five years imprisonment, but the government appealed and got his sentence increased to 11 years. When the 11 years had elapsed in 1973, the President would not let him be released. During his imprisonment he was kept in several different death-camps. He was first kept in a condemned cell, ten feet by ten feet in Zomba prison before he was transferred to the notorious Ndzeleka concentration camp. While imprisoned Munthali was brutally tortured and was unable to walk for almost a year—his feet were severely burnt and he had been forced to walk barefooted on broken glass.

His cell did not have a window and his toilet, a bucket, was only removed every five days. Munthali recalled John Savage telling him that Malawi was a neocolonial state where whites still wielded enormous powers and that Banda had more trust of whites than blacks. John Savage was one of six Prison Officers recruited by John Tembo, under Banda's instructions, from apartheid South Africa soon after the latter was elected President for life. The torture chambers in the prison system were in line with South Africa's apartheid system. John Savage, was born of an English father and a Boer (Afrikaner) mother. As his surname implies, he was a brutal savage who had no respect for basic human rights and openly cursed blacks. He was recruited while still working in Rhodesia (Zimbabwe) under the minority regime of Ian D. Smith. There in Rhodesia he was employed as both Prison Guard and Hangman—roles that earned him the name of "Crowbar" for his brutal and wanton methods of torture against African political prisoners. He personally took charge of dozens of hangings of Zimbabwean freedom fighters.

While Machipisa Munthali was in Mikuyu prison, John Savage led a group of twenty men from the Malawi Police Force (PMF)—the most feared and ruthless elite force—from Zomba to Mlowe Village in Rumphi District, north Malawi, a distance of some 500 km. On arrival, they went to Machipisa's house under the escort of a local Village Headman who was threatened if he refused to comply. As soon as they arrived, they forcefully entered the house and dragged out Machipisa's old mother and the rest of the occupants and started looting, taking among other things, expensive suits, shirts, shoes which Machipisa had brought while working in South Africa in the early 50s. John Savage himself stole an expensive Antlantic wrist watch. To the astonishment of the onlookers, Savage ordered his men, black men, to burn down Machipisa's house after the looting. Among the onlookers and bystanders, one young man angered by the unwarranted act of aggression against civilians, wondered how in Malawi, a truly free and independent state, 20 policemen commanded by a Boer (a white man) could carry out such cowardly orders without any shame or a sense of pride. The courageous young man was forthwith apprehended and taken to Mikuyu's notorious prison where he was detained for five years under brutal conditions and without trial.

Dr. Banda, having lived in the US and Britain, the so-called mothers of democracy in the world, had turned Malawi into a hell under the sun. Two female office workers arrested in Blantyre in early 1993, for allegedly being multiparty sympathizers, were mercilessly tortured at Chichiri prison. These women activists claimed that they shared a single bucket which they used as toilet during the night and in the day time used it to carry water for cleaning their cell. In the adjacent cell, one woman inmate was severely assaulted by three prison guards for calling the President "monster" in the presence of their boss John Savage and his colleague. The guards pulled her clothes right up above her waist and then took a pair of pliers and pressed them into her (private parts) until she started bleeding profusely and eventually lost her consciousness. Later she claimed that for the two months she was there in prison, she was regularly discharging pus.

Such was Dr. Banda's naked hypocrisy when it came to women's status in the country. In another cell, measuring 12 feet by 25 feet there were 35 women inmates. They were so many that they had to sleep in two rows next to the wall and face the same direction as there was not enough space to sleep facing different directions.

The "warm heart of Africa," as Banda and his people used to call his police state, was transformed into the "cold heart of Africa" under his leadership. Before the rise of multi-party struggle in 1992, there were 101,500 political prisoners in more than five detention camps. To say the fact, general conditions in Malawi prisons were worse than those in apartheid South Africa and yet, the western democracies remained indifferent about this brutal violation of basic human rights. Some prisoners were subjected to a special punishment regime, that was so-called "Hard Core Program." The Hard Core Program was not only cold-blooded, inhuman and degrading, but seemed to constitute a protracted form of extra-judicial execution. Prisoners under this regime were reportedly kept naked and chained to the floor, given minimal food, denied medical care, and severely beaten. In Ndzeleka and Nsanje alone, 25 prisoners died within one month in 1975 and yet the former OAU and UN Human Rights Division, closed their ears and eyes. Had these people died in South African or Rhodesian prisons, the international community would have likely shouted itself hoarse. In July 1966, two political prisoners who refused to betray their conscience by denouncing rebel ministers, were brutally beaten to death in Mikuyu prison. Yet, the authorities held no inquest into any of these deaths—as required by Malawi law.

Powers of detention under the 1965 Public Security Regulations, were strictly arbitrary. There was no independent review of the reasons why someone was detained. That often led to the whimsical use of detention powers against dissidents. Typical of this draconian security regulation, Dr. Matembo Nzunda, then working at the University Law Department, was detained after a letter of his had been published in the July issue of a Roman Catholic magazine "Moni." In that letter, Dr. Nzunda criticized the arrests of ten women for wearing or selling culottes. Under Malawian law, women were not allowed to wear trousers. Dr. Nzunda and the editor of the magazine were held for two weeks at Chichiri prison. The August issue of Moni devoted its editorial column to an apology for "inadvertently" publishing Dr. Nzunda's letter which it described as "erroneous and misleading." At about the same time, the editor of the government-owned "Daily Times" was briefly detained for publishing a story criticizing the traffic police for allowing an untaxed vehicle, owned by one of Banda's henchmen, on the road.

President Banda ran Malawi almost on par with former Romania's eccentric despot Nicolae Andruta Ceausescu—the two were personal friends. Romania was the only former communist country to have ties with ultra-capitalist Malawi. What did these two demons have in common? "Both were greedy, murderous, and had lust for power—and both were corrupt."

It was not only political dissidents who were victims of Banda's regime, even unpoliticized citizens fell victims of the regime's horrendous records of human rights abuse. One man was detained for buying tobacco from tenant farmers on land owned by Life-President Hastings Banda. Another was held for twelve years because he criticized the President for drawing multimillion dollar "unsecured loans" from state funds. A woman was held for three years at Mikuyu prison because she refused to keep silent about her brother's death while in police custody. Sycophants and henchmen alike, most of whom, unfortunately, are still in influential positions hitherto defend their former master as a clean man who did not engage in corrupt practices when he was in power.

The despotic rule Malawians endured for thirty solid years under one leader had no rival elsewhere on the Continent—and yet the western democracies heaped praise on Banda and described him as Africa's best leader. The legal system was vastly manipulated to suit his dubious desires. For instance, the legal basis for detention without trial in the country was provided for by the 1965 Public Security Regulations, which allowed the President to detain an individual indefinitely "for the preservation of public order."

This placed many people in danger especially those suspected of, or perceived of, being supporters of the rebel ministers. Authorized officers, that included both police and paramilitary Malawi Young Pioneers (Banda's thugs), had the power to arrest and detain any individual for up to 30 days if the person's conduct warranted imposition of a Presidential detention order. In practice, however, this limit was seldom observed and prisoners awaiting Presidential detention orders, which were known as Temporary Detention Orders (TDO), could themselves be detained indefinitely.

Indeed, from the time Banda was proclaimed Life-President in 1971, life became increasingly unbearable, citizens could not trust their own "shadows." Banda's very name bore similarities to a ghost that terrorized people at will. When people went to bed at night, they were not sure whether they would see the sun the following morning. Life was such a terrifying phenomenon it made sons fear fathers, mothers fear daughters, husbands fear wives and everybody feared everybody. Some prominent political leaders who themselves ascribed to T. D. T. Banda's ouster from the Congress for his uncompromising stance against the importation of Dr. Banda, conceded later that he, T. D. T. Banda, was absolutely right, but it was too late to correct the wrong.

The arrival of two more prison crews from apartheid South Africa, approved by Banda himself, exacerbated the conditions and treatment of the prisoners. Inmates were made to sleep upright and back to back, their cells unfit for animals. Cells were often flooded with cold water to make their sleep impossible. In some cells ten to 15 inmates, used one bucket as a toilet and at times the excrete spilled all over the cell. However, there were a number of aspects of the bad conditions suffered by political detainees which appeared to be the consequence of official policy. For instance, the frequent ban on correspondence, denial of reading or recreational materials, the frequent denial of medical attention, and, above all, the imposition of cruel, inhuman, and degrading punishments.

The number one person in charge of prison affairs was President Banda himself aided by the Minister of State John U. Z. Tembo, his most trusted and notorious henchman. Below these two sinful people, were South African Boers led by

John Savage. Black Malawians played a third-party role as they were not trusted by Banda, these were just prison warders carrying orders from their masters. The South African Boers whose hands were drenched with blood of our brothers in South Africa's notorious prisons, were best known for their brutality and arrogance, frequently calling black prisoners "kaffir" or "Monkeys" to the delight of President Banda and his bedfellows. By mid 1973, and in the height of brutal repression, the number of political prisoners swelled to 15,500 and more than half of them were from the north. The six or so concentration camps were dangerously overcrowded, torture and beatings became the order of the day. Prisoners were subjected to electric shock, coerced to drink their own urine, tied by their legs upside-down for hours each day and, those considered hard-core, were denied meals for up to three days.

Ndzeleka along with the Nsanje prison in the far south of the country, had become particularly centers for severe punishment regimes imposed on long-term political prisoners. By far, Malawi's prison conditions were the worst in the continent. At one stage, hundreds of inmate were kept in one small cell which resulted in the deaths of one to two inmates per night. Other prisoners were being tortured by having their genitals squeezed by long-nose pliers. There were also terrifying accounts from the notorious Zomba, Mikuyu, and Maula prisons that cells were smeared with human excrement before inmates went to sleep and cleared out of the cells with their bare hands. When President Banda officially opened the notorious Ndzeleka Prison in Dowa Central Malawi in the mid-60s, he said, "I will keep them and they will rot. And I am going to make sure that in addition to the regular prison officers, we have additional warders (South African Boers) who will know what to do with these fools...they will knock some sense into their heads." Really, such a statement could have only come from a deranged and immoral person who did not respect fundamental human rights.

Not only did Banda's political foes ended up in death-camps, some less fortunate were bundled into sacks and thrown into the crocodile-infested Shire River. On one occasion, the President proudly announced to his rubber-stamp Parliament that, "Political adversaries end up as lunch for hungry crocodiles." For this, the rogue despot actually received a tumultuous standing ovation from his deadwood Parliamentarians. Like his friend and admirer Robert G. Mugabe, Banda was absolutely drunk with power that made him Africa's odd man. In fact, since his arrival in Nyasaland, Banda looked down upon Malawians, he regarded them as shoddy, uncivilized and generally uneducated and for thirty years he called them "my people" and, astonishingly enough, the people responded with a sense of pride at being Banda's property. As the mother of despots, no African leader in the continent has ever used the word "my people" when addressing his fellow citizens—apart from Hastings Banda. President Banda, as one might conclude, had reached a stage where he was absolutely convinced he owned the nation and its people and could do whatever he deemed fit or necessary. All was at his disposal.

Addressing a rally in Kasungu, his adopted hometown, on April 13, 1965, a few months after the famous Cabinet Crisis, he said: "If to maintain political stability I have to detain 20,000 or 100,000 people, I will do it. I want nobody to misunderstand me." True to his word, he detained thousands of Malawians during the thirty years he was in power. As the Head of State, Banda had no respect for the law of the land. He was on several occasions heard saying that: "Anything I say is law. Literally law. It is a fact in this country." Needless to say therefore, there was no need for Parliament or any other law enforcement establishments in the country.

In this chapter, I have put some light on prison conditions as part of a repressive mechanism to dispel western democracies' perception that Malawi was a fine and decent State other African States should emulate. However, it was not covert that Malawi, under Hastings Banda, was a unique puppet state for western imperialism and a South African "Bantustan," that had no independent foreign policy.

Given the low nutritional status of prisoners and poor sanitary facilities, it is not surprising that outbreaks of disease were frequent in the national prisons. Diarrhea, malaria, hepatitis, scabies, and acquired immune deficiency syndrome (AIDS) were all reported to be rife. Even though Prison Regulations made detailed provision for the supervision of prisoners' medical needs by a medical officer, absolutely nothing happened. More than 15 prisoners including Sylvester Phiri, a prisoner of conscience, died of curable maladies in Mikuyu Prison. Phiri died of possible tuberculosis and was buried within the prison's premises without the knowledge of his relatives. The prison regulations also stated that the officer in charge shall release the body of a dead prisoner to his family unless there were overriding reasons, such as public health, not to do so. The fact that dead prisoners were buried within prison compounds or premises, meant not only that families were unable to carry out funeral rites, but also that they could not arrange their own investigations into the death, for instance independent post-mortem examinations. It is sad, but not astonishing, that the majority of Malawians after 11 years of democratic change, knew very little or absolutely nothing as to what went wrong in their prisons. The core reason for this silence is that almost all the people who were in powerful positions hitherto, were the very same people within the notorious system of Hastings Banda's regime and most of them were part and parcel of the brutal atrocities committed against civilians. To illustrate the injustices and atrocities committed by a black government under a black leader, I list some repulsive crimes that most of our people do not have a clue about—even up to this day. Fred Sikwese, then 40 years of age, was a Principal Protocol Officer in the Ministry of Foreign Affairs. That such a position was then held by a northerner was by itself a crime. There was a conspiracy to remove Sikwese from that position and replace him with an unqualified Chewa speaking person. The authorities therefore cooked-up a story that he passed confidential material to the apartheid South African Press which was thought to be damaging to the Banda regime. Sikwese was arrested on February

20, 1986—and in good health at the time of his arrest. He was subjected to brutal beatings, electric shock and often found naked and in leg-chains when his mother and sister paid him a visit at Maula prison, one of the most atrocious. On March 7 (after only a month), he appeared very weak and yellow, as if he was suffering from jaundice. He died on April 10, 1990, after being tortured the whole night. His family asked for his body for a decent and traditional burial, but were refused. Instead, he was buried within the prison compounds without a grain of respect and dignity. To add salt to the wound, his mother at the age of 75, was arrested and detained for crying "subversively" for the death of her only son. The same day Sikwese was arrested, two young men, Frackson Zgambo and Benson Mkandawire, both from the north, were detained without charge at Maula prison. They remained there for three years before being released. Sikwese's sister was later detained without charge at Mikuyu prison for accusing the police for her brother's death. She remained in custody for two and half years without trial.

Alex Kadango, a businessman in Lilongwe, was arrested and detained without charge in March 1972. While in prison he was stricken by malaria and reportedly had been denied medical attention. Kadango was also assaulted by prison warders and at one stage, he lost consciousness. He died in Mikuyu Prison on July 18, 1990. As with his former inmates, he was buried in prison precincts without the consent of his family members. From 1965 to 1994, Malawi passed through an appalling history that its people will not forget for generations to come even though the present leadership still includes most of whom are accused of the past atrocious records. In Mangoche, the former stronghold of former rebel minister Masauko Chipembere, and obviously our national "hero," Katanga Sani was arrested and detained, on January 15, 1991, for helping five young Muslim women who had been arrested for dressing as men as part of a local initiation celebration. The Decency in Dress Act prohibited women from wearing trousers. The crime Sani committed was that he paid the fines on behalf of the poor women. Sani was held incommunicado for more than six-months. After several demands to see him in prison, eventually his family were reluctantly allowed to visit him and found him in good health. After one week, his health abruptly worsened, he began complaining of dizziness and fatigue. It was reliably reported that he endured two nights of brutal beatings and other systems of torture as were the norms in Malawi's prisons. Sani died on October 10, 1992 of head and body injuries and was hurriedly buried the same day in a prison compound against the wishes of his family members. His brother demanded an explanation of his suspicious death, but was rudely told to, "Shut-up or else...." The leadership of the dreaded Malawi Congress Party (MCP) was apparently bent on fascism to intimidate the citizens and it had become a wanton "lynch mob" with desires to remain in power defiantly. This trend, however, led to a general perception that Banda's regime was exceedingly worse than the former colonial administration. Yet, all this blatant abuse of human rights was ignored by the Continent's Commission on Human and Peoples Rights. However, this was not a surprising trend. In Uganda, after the brutal massacres of 30,000 people by the barbaric regime, Idi Amin Dada was unanimously elected Chairman of the defunct Organization Of African Unity (OAU) at its annual seating in Kinshasa, Congo on October 17, 1975—an action that almost split African leaders. The late President Julius K. Nyerere of the United Republic of Tanzania and foremost African statesman and former Zambian President Kenneth D. Kaunda boycotted the organization's deliberations for a while in protest. In his defense, President Nyerere said: "I can not sit beside an African murderer while at the same time condemning Boers in apartheid South Africa for killing blacks."

President Banda used the indifference of the dysfunctional OAU and United Nations Human Rights Commission as support for his crimes against humanity. On July 27, 1975, Yadanga Zolongwe Mhango, then aged 75, was arrested at Chipata border post. He, Mhango, was coming from Zambia where he had gone to visit his son Steven Z. Mhango who had gone to Zambia, then northern Rhodesia, long before Banda's arrival in Nyasaland in 1958. The authorities alleged that Mhango was a supporter of the rebel ministers who lived in Zambia and Tanzania. However, they could not substantiate the allegations. But, they based their case on Mhango's two big suitcases full of expensive clothes and so on. The undercover police at the border maintained that Mhango received money from the exiled leaders to enable him to establish underground cells and to recruit cadres for possible revolutionary struggle.

The most striking scenario was that Mhango never went to school and therefore could not write or read. To him, the accusation was an outright nightmare. He could not comprehend what the undercover officials were talking about. Nonetheless, Mhango was eventually arrested and detained at Ndzeleka prison without trial. Being asthmatic and diabetic, his condition in the prison soon worsened. He was denied medical attention and subjected to frequent torture. He died on August 17, 1975, and his family was not informed for three months. Like most of the prisoners, he was buried within the compounds of the prison. Mrs. N. Msofi Vula, in her 40s, met the same fate when she was returning home from a trip to Zambia to visit her relatives. Mrs. Vula and Mhango both came from the same village in the north.

Before she left Ndola, Zambia, her female friend working with the Malawi secret service based in Malawi Embassy in Lusaka, Zambia, passed false information to her counterparts at Chipata border-post that Mrs. Vula, carrying a Malawian passport, had carried the "kitenge cloth" bearing the portrait of a woman suspected to be Kanyama Chiume's girl friend. (Chiume was Banda's bitterest adversary.) In fact when Mrs. Vula was packing items into the suitcases, her friend was there helping her, and as such, she knew what was in the suitcases. When Mrs. Vula arrived at the border-post of Chipata on August 10, 1977, she was forthwith confronted by a horde of secret police and immigration officials. She was taken into a private room, stripped of her clothes by both female and male officials while others were searching her luggage. In one of the suitcases, they found exactly what they were looking for, "kitenge cloth" with a woman's portrait as described by their undercover agent from Zambia. It must be noted however, that Malawian intelligence service operated in Zambia at will unlike in Tanzania where hundreds of Malawian spies were arrested each month.

Forthwith, Mrs. Vula was arrested and detained in a very small and dirty room for six hours. When the night fell, she was taken half-naked in a Land Rover to Zomba's notorious prison some 250 km southeast of Lilongwe. She was brutally assaulted along the way. By the time she arrived in Zomba, she was half-dead and, sadly, denied medical attention. In the prison, torture and beatings continued unabated. She was frequently subjected to electric shocks to her private parts until at one stage, she fell unconscious. It was at this time the medical doctor visited the prison and ordered her be taken to the hospital for treatment. The prison authorities agreed on the condition that there would be no medical report submitted to anybody whatsoever. After three days of treatment, the unfortunate and innocent lady was handed back to the prison authorities. Two days later, on December 14, 1978, she was released and returned to join her family back in Zambia where she died a week after her arrival. An independent post-mortem in Lusaka, Zambia, revealed that she had died of severe brain damage resulting from heavy blows on her head. Her private parts were medically damaged. Like Mhango before her, she was illiterate and nonpolitical and undeserving of such treatment.

After her arrest, the kitenge cloth issue became political nationwide. Several business people had pressed orders for the same cloth which had been manufactured in the Democratic Republic of Congo (DRC), but to their astonishment, they were warned not to put the cloth in their shops for sale and they were not reimbursed. Those who defied the order had their stock appropriated by the Young Pioneers, the most feared brutal thugs under the President's personal command. These political hoodlums were by all means above the law and only accountable to His Excellency, the Life-President Dr. Hastings Kamuzu Banda. Mind you, omitting one of the titles when addressing the President could lead someone into long-term incarceration.

The campaign to get rid of the kitenge cloth intensified countrywide. Women who were found wearing the cloth, were instantly roughed-up and arrested, some stripped naked if they resisted. The harassments against women were so ruthless that those who owned the cloth were coerced to hide it in their homes and only reemerged 15 years later after the advent of multiparty democracy in 1994.

Another shocking report was that of Matupi Mkandawire. He was an MP for Rumphi West, northern Malawi. He was working in southern Rhodesia (Zimbabwe) and went back home in mid-50s where he joined the Nyasaland African Congress (NAC) and became an active fighter for the independence of his homeland and an ardent foe of the imposed Federation of Rhodesia and Nyasaland—way back before Nyasalanders knew about Hastings Banda (i.e., Richard Armstrong). At the National Convention at Nkhota-Kota in Central Malawi in 1971, when Banda was unanimously elected Life-President of the dreaded Malawi Congress Party (MCP), it was reported that Mkandawire was urged to publicly denounce Kanyama Chiume and his colleagues (rebel ministers), but refused in principle to do so. He bravely told Banda's henchmen that he found no fault with them. Being a northerner in the first place, and a personal friend of Kanyama Chiume, henceforth his life was in jeopardy: he was walking with death on his hands.

In December 10, 1974, Matupi Mkandawire was arrested at his home in Bolero, Rumphi West, by the notorious secret service agents and driven straight to Ndzeleka prison. No charge was read to him and he was detained without trial. While in prison, Mkandawire was frequently tortured, kept for long periods in leg-irons in the "dark cell" and without any natural or artificial light. He was denied food for days and buckets of cold water were, from time to time, thrown at him during the night. Mkandawire's words of defiance earned him the fury of prison warders especially the white Boers from Rhodesia and apartheid South Africa. His last words quoted by one of the warders who happened to come from the north also, were: "No amount of torture, beatings, and starvation will coerce me to ask for mercy, for I have not done something wrong to deserve this inhuman treatment." It is reported that Mkandawire was brutally bludgeoned by one of the warders while exchanging bitter words with John Savage telling him that he had no right whatsoever to torture him with electric shocks. Sadly, the blow was delivered by a black man uttering these words: "A Tumbuka inu ni anthu ovuto," ("You Tumbukas are troublesome people"). Tumbuka is a prominent minority ethnic group from the north which was subjected to systematic harassments by Banda's tribalistic regime. Mkandawire died in prison towards the end of January 1976. His body was transported to his ancestral village, but under strict instructions not to open casket and view the body. A horde of dreaded Young Pioneers and Secret Agents were there to ensure that the instructions were strictly followed.

The names of victims of Banda's regime disclosed in a previous chapter are just a tip of an iceberg. An estimated 15,000 inmates died or vanished in the prisons. A good number were taken during the night, loaded into sacks, and driven to the crocodile-infested Shire River where they were thrown to the hungry beasts. Some were buried covertly within the prison compounds without the knowledge of their loved ones. It is, however, beyond comprehension that the embassies of the powerful nations in Malawi such as the US, Germany, Britain, France, Italy, and others, did not have any access to reports of such macabre abuse of basic human rights by the Malawi government. All these representatives of the so-called western democracies, remained indifferent to the plights of the Malawian prisoners of conscience who endured the most cold-blooded conditions in prisons—even worse than in colonial Portuguese Mozambique and Angola, apartheid South Africa, and settler Rhodesia. But the very same democracies, especially the US and Britain, condemned President Robert

Mugabe for his brutal suppression of human rights in Zimbabwe. However, there is no doubt in my mind that Britain and the US were concerned with the plights of their kith and kin, while in Malawi the victims were wholly blacks.

To cement western influence and support for the despotic puppet regime, Margaret Thatcher, Britain's icon of conservatism, paid an official state visit to Malawi in 1976, at the height of repression in the country and the Soweto uprising in South Africa. Though she was a Head of State visiting Malawi as an independent state, she saw it as Britain's overseas possession with its own national flag and anthem. The British Prime Minister was accorded a highly anticipated welcome at the country's International Airport in Lilongwe. As usual, women were mobilized, traffic was brought to a standstill, shops, schools, food markets and things like that were coerced into closing down. The city of Lilongwe looked almost like a ghost town.

In her two-day state visit, Mrs. Thatcher devoted her time to praising Malawi's leader Hastings Banda. As the Malawian autocrat was widely regarded in western democracies as a staunch anti-Communist who had stamped his absolute authority on the country, Mrs. Thatcher did not raise the issue of human rights abuse by her counterpart. Instead, she described Banda as a model for the rest of Africa. Back home, the Queen praised Malawi's farming achievements. In essence, both perceptions were sets of fallacies. The Queen, however, did not realize the fact that malnutrition among children was the highest in the continent, even lagging behind fragmented Somalia. How could the rest of Africa emulate Malawi's atrocious policies? Coincidentally, while Thatcher was still in the country, two prisoners of conscience died in two separate prisons: Dzeleka and Mikuyu and as customary, the only newspaper in the country the "Daily Times," owned by the dreaded MCP, did not flash the news of such magnitude in its pages, but it was reported that the British Prime Minister was briefed of the deaths by Britain's High Commissioner in Malawi. As expected, Mrs. Thatcher brushed the news aside and continued with her itinerary as though nothing foreboding had happened. Perhaps, the Queen did not have a clue of Malawi's so-called farming achievements and honestly, she could not care what type of life ordinary Malawians lived under. In spite of all the praises, the gravity of malnutrition had not improved in the country. For the 30 years Banda had been in power, yet 80 percent of children suffered from lack of proper diet and 75 percent of the general population could not afford two meals a day. On her departure, the British PM doubled the economic aid to Malawi, which of course could not benefit the ordinary citizens. She also increased the sale of arms to the murderous regime.

During the struggle for freedom and justice in South Africa, Thatcher, strongly opposed the African National Congress (ANC) and described it as a "communist tool." She also remained indifferent to Nelson Madiba Mandela's release from Rubben Island Maximum Prison. In fact, Thatcher inherited Britain's treacherous foreign policy which in its course defended and supported President Banda right from the attainment of self-government when Westminster meddled into the internal affairs of a newly independent state on the pretext of containing the spread of communism. It was indeed, through diluted foreign-dictated policies Malawi had in place, that the former Malawian corrupt tyrant betrayed the liberation movements in Africa and denounced these movements as "communist terrorists" and agitators.

For all of the thirty turbulent years that MCP was in power under the leadership of a single person (who wielded absolute power never heard of before in the continent) all Malawians of good will, would tacitly agree with me that the northerners were singled out as prime targets of the sadistic regime. As a northerner and Tumbuka, I have never ever thought myself as being separated from Lomwe, Yao, Sena, or Chewa for that matter. I strongly regard myself first and foremost as an African. I would, likewise, have condemned the regime if the Lomwe, Yao or Chewa were singled out for unnecessary persecutions. I am prepared to agree to disagree with any different opinion or mind so long as it is for the interest of my country.

I am not, in the things I have written, trying to revive old wounds. Nevertheless, northerners under the MCP regime were regarded as third or fourth class citizens in their own country and to the effect that countless attempts were made to frustrate and abbreviate their opportunities in life as citizens of Malawi. Most strikingly the treatment of teachers in the 70s, whereby those from the north were singled out for repatriation to their home region on the pretext that they spent all class time teaching "Nyau." This was perhaps the last straw in the charade Malawians had ever paraded as unity in the country. "Nyau" is a traditional dance performed by the Chewas of Central Malawi. It had absolutely nothing to do with teachers from the north whereby, "Malipenga" is a dominant traditional dance exclusively for men and Mbotosha for women. To be fair, nationally there were more teachers from the north than from Central and south combined, that meant that there was an unprecedented shortage of teachers in Central and southern Malawi. This had a devastating repercussion on class performance for students in the two regions and a step backward for the future of a nation that relies on its youth.

To add insults to injuries, the government introduced a "quota system" that required students from the north to score 85 percent to qualify for college or secondary school, while their counterparts from the Central and South were allowed entrance with scores as low as 40 percent–astonishingly, both completing the same national examination. The President himself defended that tribalistic notion by saying publicly: "If the government did not introduce this system our colleges and schools would be filled with students from the north." Such a remark by the Head of State was clearly intended to divide the nation for his own political gains. Indeed, under such a negative system, many youth did not have to be brilliant to secure a place at a college or secondary school. So long as the student was the best in his or her district, they would find themselves in the college or secondary school corridors. In essence, by this means of selection, the perpetrators of this evil and divisive system did not even hope to produce first class scientists, mathematicians, chemists, engineers, doctors, and so forth. However, the introduction of such a system did not deter the grim determination of the northern students, as a result, the system acted as a catalyst for hard work and that enabled them to score higher marks than ever before. Some of the students even resolved to change their surnames to sound as if they were from the Central or southern Malawi, so the system did not achieve its sinister desires—apart from plunging the nation into regional groupings. Students from the north made their way in larger numbers and it was an uphill struggle for students from the other two regions to compete intellectually.

President Banda could have acted alone on this shameful and retrogressive notion, but it was highly speculated that as the despot was losing his senses due to senility, his long time partner Cecilia Tamanda Kadzamila and her uncle John Tembo, the most hated politician in the country and an equivalent of Kenya's Biwott for his notoriety, were behind the unpopular scheme. These two people were known to have harbored grudges against the northerners for the simple reason that the northerners were bent on unseating Dr. Banda and his dreaded MCP government. Another glaring instance was the firing of the entire complement of workers in the Vital Statistics Department, eventually detaining them at Zomba Prison without trial. The entire work force comprised of Malawians from the north with brilliant academic achievements. On their release, after a considerable ordeal in the notorious prisons, no reason or reasons were given for their ultimate detention and they were not allowed to return to their former jobs.

The purge of the northerners reached its zenith when most senior civil servants were demoted and some made to retire prematurely to allow those positions to be occupied by Malawians from Central and southern Malawi regardless of their qualifications and some positions were transferred to the white expatriates who dominated the Civil Service after independence. On diplomatic postings, the northerners topped the list at independence, but after the famous Cabinet Crisis of 1964, they were pruned to zero. Sadly, the trend continued unabated in the Muluzi's administration and was further exacerbated under President Wa Mutharika.

The sufferings of the northerners were wholesale, not only that they were subjected to political oppression, but their Region was neglected by two successive governments while the other two regions, Central and South were favored for economic development. Nobody, however, offers reasonable explanations for this imbalance. The people of the north have been in the forefront with their brethren in every major national endeavor, be it the fight against the imposed Federation of Rhodesian and Nyasaland, the struggle for national independence, or the struggle for multiparty democracy. So why are they sidelined on every national issue? Indeed, the treatment of the northerners, if it were in other countries, would have sparked off senseless national bloody conflicts with unprecedented consequences. Perhaps the bloody conflict in Nigeria's civil war (Biafra-Nigeria) and Rwanda's genocide where a million Tutsis perished in a hundred days of slaughter that shocked all mankind, must live as a vivid lesson for African people in the continent.

The long suffering of the people of the north under the Banda regime, drove some people, including myself, to think of succession. The people of the north had the right to seek autonomous power just as the whole nation refused to be coerced into the Federation of Rhodesia and Nyasaland in 1953. A national union must embody not only an understanding of liberty to associate, but also on the question of the north being "dead" and poor. It is also an apparent fact that Malawians have helped develop other neighboring nations in the region. The kind of help was cheap labor at its best until a few years ago and just as the north provided "cheap labor" that has helped to develop the nation of Malawi.

Likewise, the southern Region developed as a region substantially because of cheap Lomwe labor, and labor from the North and Central. In emphasis of my assertion, the first lot of migrant labor from the north was shipped out from Nkhata Bay around 1882 by the father of imperialism in southern Africa, John Cecil Rhodes, to work on the Shire Highlands. The purge of the north, however, had come in different ways and in painful experience. In March 1966, Hastings Banda as the Minister of Agriculture, one of a half dozen portfolios he held–and paid fully for each of them–issued a decree banning the north from growing the moneymaking flue-cured tobacco, while restricting its growth in southern region. At the same time, the central, supposedly his home region, could grow the crop freely. He opened his first tobacco farms in Kasungu and Muchinji. It was no secret that Hastings Banda had formulated a stratagem to divide the country on tribal and regional lines to exert his obnoxious rule. To the utter astonishment of the majority of our people, the corrupt and despotic ruler moved the International Airport, with all its bureaucracy and tons of jobs, from Chileka, Blantyre and the capital Zomba to the Central region. The fact remains that these movements required labor and that labor (cheap labor) came from the south and north, hence, the latter is depopulated and poor after more than 40 years of nationhood. The majority of our people, regardless of where they are coming from, ask this question: "Should we take this divisive issue as a joke or as a vehement problem facing real unity of our nation for the best interest of all our people and generations to come? The problem of Tutsis and Hutus must not be separated from our own. By doing so, we risk placing ourselves on a sea-volcano which will one day explode and send a "tsunami" across the nation the consequences of which would be catastrophic and irreparable for generations to come."

But we can spare ourselves by regarding or treating ourselves as one entity regardless of our political, regional and tribal affiliations as the manifesto of the forerunner Nyasaland African Congress (NAC) envisaged. The Malawi Congress Party (MCP), after the dissolution of the former on March 3, 1959, unanimously adopted this clause, but it was unfortunately sidelined soon after the famous Cabinet Crisis of 1964 to the detriment of our national unity.

After his elevation to the Life-Presidency, Hastings Banda did not waste any time to turn against his own dupes or henchmen who had orchestrated the creation of his position. At this time, and after rebel ministers had been driven into exile, Banda became overconfident that he could neutralize the new ministers without difficulty in view of the fact that they had no political base or support from the masses of our people and they did not excel in the academic world. Soon after the crisis these people willingly organized lynch-mobs against the able rebel ministers and their supporters and fed Banda with malicious lies to win favor from the monstrous tyrant.

The first high ranking official to fall was Aleke Kodanaphani Banda Secretary-General of the dreaded Malawi Congress Party (MCP) and Commander of the brutal militia, the Young Pioneers. As the Secretary-general of the ruling party, Aleke Banda (no relation), was second in command and this did not go well with John Tembo and others—the leaders from the Central and South who were also vying for Presidency in the event of Banda's demise. The man to watch was John Tembo who was very close to Banda due to relations the President had with his niece Cecilia Kadzamila who had unprecedented influence over the President. Aleke Banda was opposed right and left from two camps; John Tembo and Cecilia Kadzamila on one hand, and Albert Muwalo and Gwanda Chakuamba on the other. Of the four contenders, Aleke Banda proved intelligent, balanced and with considerable experience while the other three were bullies, tribalistic and unintelligent, but potentially influential among their tribesmen.

In 1972, Aleke Banda paid an official visit to the Republic of Zambia. At Lusaka International Airport, he was quoted by the Times of Zambia as saying: "I am the heir apparent." Speculation on Banda's succession being strenuously obstructed to, the article therefore gave the President and Aleke's rivals, especially the over zealous and extremely unpopular John Tembo, the ammunition to destroy his political ambitions once and for all. Prior to his visit to Zambia, Aleke Banda then Managing Director of the Press Holdings Ltd., (later known as Press Group), of which Hastings Banda was the Chairman, wrote to his master, questioning the latter's withdrawal of US$5 million from Press Holdings Accounts at the National Bank of Malawi. In his reply, President Banda described the withdrawal as an "unsecured loan" which had been approved by John Tembo, then Chairman of the Reserve Bank of Malawi and uncle to Banda's longtime concubine Cecilia Kadzamila. As Chairman, and later Governor of the Reserve Bank of Malawi (the position that was recommended by the IMF and the World Bank for Austin Madinga a top-notch economist who died of a mysterious death) the institution was notoriously known for its nepotism and inefficiency. On his return from Zambia, Aleke Banda was forthwith removed from his post as Secretary-general of the Malawi Congress Party (MCP)–the second most powerful position in line–and ordered to return to his village where he was placed under house arrest.

A week later, he was expelled from the Congress and arrested shortly afterwards. He was imprisoned at the notorious Pyumpyu prison and thereafter, moved from one prison to another. Aleke Banda was the mastermind for Hastings Banda's elevation to Life-Presidency, with no regrets, he paid the price. He remained in prison without charge for eleven years all the while under inhuman conditions. He was released in 1994 under pressure from multiparty activists whom Aleke sought to liquidate, when he was in power. During the Cabinet Crisis in September 1964, when Banda was confronted by his ministers for his highhandedness and covert dealings with evil minority regimes of southern Africa, Aleke Banda rushed to the Government House to dissuade Hastings Banda from going to the Governor's Residence to handover his letter of resignation after he had succumbed to pressure from his ministers. Aleke Banda told the President that the people of Malawi were solidly behind him and therefore there was no need for him to resign. If Aleke Banda had not betrayed the peoples' aspirations on that day, the history of Malawi could be different. There is no doubt that President Banda had a hand on Aleke's predicament, but the real power behind it, was that of John Tembo and his niece Cecilia Kadzamila—who, herself, had unprecedented influence over the tyrant. These two evil people worked behind the scenes, and under Banda's wing, to usurp power after the latter's impending demise. As a consequence, Aleke Banda's status in the Party and his closeness to the President were apparently seen as real stumbling blocks to their political ambitions, hence, he had to depart. But the pair had to fight two remaining political giants who also stood in their way.

After the downfall of Aleke Banda, Albert Muwalo Nqumayo became Secretary-general of the Malawi Congress Party. According to the MCP Constitution, the Secretary-general could become interim President on the death of the Life-President Banda. Muwalo became the most feared man in the country for his sadistic behavior that led political pundits to conclude that he was not acting alone, Banda must be behind him. According to the insiders, Muwalo's rise in power, had put Tembo and Kadzamila in a shaky position, but Banda assured them not to panic as everything would be okay. The rise of Muwalo had sent shock waves into every household, he was a symbol of repression, to say the least. Women could jam the offices of the Malawi Congress Party in Blantyre and Limbe to see him and report minor conflicts within their homes with their husbands. Once a woman reported that she had been harassed by her man, the latter was forthwith summoned to the Party Headquarters only to be watered-down. In some cases, a man might be detained without valid proof. Muwalo could then use the opportunity to have an affair with the man's woman. This blatant abuse of power by the number two man created an unprecedented culture of mistrust against Banda's regime. In fact, the President had full knowledge of what Muwalo was doing, but was waiting for the right time to flex his muscles. Muwalo was not alone in the executions of these evil deeds. He was in league with his direct cousin Focus Gwede, then top Intelligence Officer in the notorious Secret Police. In fact, Gwede superseded Muwalo in notoriety at some stage and, was nicknamed "Chemical Ali" in reference to Saddam Hussein's half-brother who gassed thousands of Kurds from northern Iraq. Gwede was responsible for imprisoning thousands of innocent citizens, mainly from the north. He personally directed and participated in waves of torture and beatings of prisoners resulting in countless deaths. In reality, these two rogues were more feared than Banda himself, still he gave them a long rope to hang themselves.

In 1977, Albert N. Muwalo was arrested and put on trial for treason. He was accused of conspiracy to overthrow the government by violent means. However, to suggest that Muwalo had the courage of that nature or magnitude raised the eyebrows of the majority of the people. Many strongly believed that the two rogues expressly acted under Banda"s blessings and then turned against them when it was appropriate for him. He was doing all this to pave the way for his favorites. The notorious Secretary-general was committed to Malawi's High Court presided over by unqualified personnel with connections to the Malawi Congress Party. It was obvious, therefore, that the disgraced Muwalo could not expect to receive a fair trial.

During the proceedings, Muwalo looked visibly dejected, broken, confused, and at times tears flowed from his eyes freely. He seemed to know Banda had tricked him and his moment had come. His trial was a mockery of justice in the country where the accused were denied access to an independent representation. However, a case of such magnitude could have required the government side to produce exhibits or evidence to convict the defendant. It appeared therefore that Muwalo was charged on trumped-up evidence and with premeditated motives. Above all, to suggest that Muwalo had planned to assassinate President Banda and overthrow his regime was in itself a defeated lie because Muwalo had no political clout or national support to challenge his boss. One wonders how Muwalo, and his wicked cousin Focus Gwede, might bring down an established institution with a national army, police and unprecedented defensive apparatus firmly controlled by the dictator himself. Like Aleke Banda's case, Muwalo was a sacrificial lamb, and he reaped what he had sowed.

In a hurried and astonishingly few days of trial for such a high-profile case, a conclusion was reached and the verdict was passed. On July 17, 1977, Albert N. Muwalo was sentenced to death by hanging and his cousin Focus Gwede to life imprisonment. However, as for Muwalo, people were not surprised, for them it was a foregone conclusion. But on the other side his verdict sent waves of jubilations–people felt relieved from harassments and unfair treatments. The hangman was hired from Salisbury (Harare) to do the job. From Chileka International Airport, the white hangman was driven directly to the notorious Zomba prison where Muwalo was manacled to an iron-ring on the floor throughout the night. As soon as Muwalo saw the hangman, whom he recognized, he broke into tears knowing that his last breath on earth was but a few minutes away. At about 6:00 AM on July 19, 1977, Muwalo was hanged in an isolated place in the prison and buried in the prison precinct without members of his family in attendance.

The white Rhodesian hangman had his hands drenched in the blood of Malawians. Earlier, he was hired by the same Muwalo when he was the minister in charge of national security to do his dirty job on convicted rebels who had infiltrated the country in September 1967, under the gallant leadership of Yatuta Kaluli Chisiza–former Home Affairs Minister in the Banda regime–with an aim to overthrow the brutal regime of Hastings Banda. Sadly, it was not covert that the hangman had earlier hanged dozens of Rhodesian African nationalists who were captured in Chimulenga battles (liberation battles) in the 70s.

After the dismissal of the rebel ministers in 1964, some of whom were instrumental in Banda's return from self-imposed exile and the downfall of Aleke Banda, Muwalo could have thought twice before drawing closer to the Frankenstein monster. His downfall therefore had absolutely nothing to do with the allegations that he wanted to assassinate President Banda and overthrow his regime. There was a wide range of conspiracies between Banda, Tembo and Kadzamila to get rid of all rising stars who could stand in the way of the latter two towards the country's top leadership contest.

After the fall of Albert N. Muwalo, Gwanda Chakuamba Phiri, another of Banda's closest henchman, was next to be axed. Without sensing the dangers of becoming closer to the tyrant, Chakuamba was appointed Commander of the Young Pioneers (MYP), Banda's paramilitary thugs who were taught to sacrifice their own lives, if needs be, to protect the person, image, and reputation of the President. This loyalty of a personal commitment was demanded of each member of the movement. It was also a collective one per se, small wonder, no matter what the public opinion may be, the Young Pioneers would not listen to anybody (they were above the law) except their Commander In-Chief, who was the Life-President himself.

Banda's new ministers had no political clout. He treated them like his own "kitchen boys." They had no identity of their own. No minister had been permitted to leave his stamp in a Ministry howsoever long he might have served in that Ministry. That was because no Minister was given the chance to exhibit his or her talents to the fullest potential. They were always reminded, sometimes openly and publicly, sometimes by veiled hints and subtle means, not to forget the shadow hovering over them of the omnipresent leader, who ran the country like a "personal estate."

These ministers had no popular support, they were hand-picked individuals with no political clout nor independent minds. After the Cabinet Crisis of 1964, a culture was established that for a minister to express an opinion or notion contrary to the one held by the demigod leader, was to repeat the trend of 1964—it was to rebel or show disrespect to the know-it-all leader. The repression reached such a stage that even his closest henchmen, the ministers (whether in public or private meetings), had to watch everything they said, inside or outside the country. As a matter of fact, even to be reported out of context could lead one into hot waters. Many cabinet ministers and party luminaries lost their portfolios through circumstances that nobody including themselves understood. Throughout his 30-year reign of terror, Banda relied heavily on lies and his own policy of divide and rule to ensure that ministers never acted as a team. That's why they were obsolete and without clout. The rebel ministers on one hand, had clout and had independent minds, while on the other, they could debate impressively and on many occasions, outwitted Banda.

In almost the same year, October 1977, the third closest henchman to Hastings Banda, Gwanda Chakuamba Phiri former Regional Minister for Southern Region and Commander of the hated and criminal Young Pioneers (Banda's personal political hoodlums), was arrested. The crime? He was allegedly found in possession of arms of war. Indeed, the offense amazed all Malawians from all walks of life having known Chakuamba's overzealous loyalty to his master. They couldn't believe he harbored such traitorous ambitions.

Mr. Chakuamba was committed to stand trial in Malawi's High Court on charges of treason. By then, Banda had already corrupted and manipulated the country's Justice System to suit his hidden political agenda. The verdict was obvious. He was found guilty and sentenced to 22 years imprisonment for possession of "arms of war" and planning to overthrow the elected government. Like Muwalo before him, Chakuamba did not show any sign of resistance during the fake trial, instead, he looked visibly shaken, confused, and immobile.

In 1964, during the Cabinet Crisis, Chakuamba and Muwalo were badly beaten up and left for dead by supporters of the rebel ministers for defending and supporting Banda's policies. It is reported that the same Chakuamba danced on

Yatuta Chisiza's body at Queen's Hospital grounds to appease his master (Banda). Indeed, Chakuamba had shown his inhuman instincts by doing things that no sane human being could have done to a lifeless body—no matter what differences existed between them. Yatuta Chisiza was the former rebel Minister for Home Affairs killed in September 1967, in the Mwanza-Neno battle when he and his 16 strong members of his group returned to Malawi to wage a guerrilla warfare. It is reported that more than 300 government troops and Young Pioneers were wiped out in this, one of the fiercest and bloodiest battles in the history of our country. The government soldiers were led by a white Colonel from apartheid South Africa's special Armed Unit. However, the majority of Malawians are still kept in darkness as to what transpired in the Mwanza-Neno conflict. Chakuamba was released in 1994, due to pressure mounted by the exiles, people he tried relentlessly to liquidate on behalf of his former master. He had already been imprisoned eleven years at the time of his release.

Soon after his freedom, thanks to the multiparty activists, he joined the United Democratic Front (UDF), one of the movements for change which had pressed for the release of political prisoners. As unprincipled as he was, hardly two weeks later, he was lured back to the Malawi Congress Party under the leadership of Hastings Banda who incarcerated him for a crime he did not actually commit. It is reported that Chakuamba was offered a lump sum of money to cross back to the dreaded Congress Party with the assurance that he could succeed Banda in the event of his impending downfall.

Chakuamba's cross over to the Malawi Congress Party did not surprise the majority of the people. They acknowledged the fact that Chakuamba had no political muscle to stand on his own. However, Aleke Banda, Gwanda Chakuamba and Albert Muwalo were leaders who attracted very little support nationally apart from their tribesmen. What worried John Tembo and his niece Cecilia Kadzamila in their bid to usurp power after Banda, were the strategic positions this trio held, so, in their narrow-minded opinions they thought if they could remove the three people from those positions of influence, their dreams could come true.

However, the downfall of the trio was conceived by another trio (Banda, Tembo and Kadzamila) as mission accomplished. As repression continued unchecked and many people begin to wonder and complain privately of the way Hastings Banda ran the nation as if it were his personal estate, another group of senior cabinet ministers questioned Banda's autocratic leadership. When he sensed this, the President started to heap influential and powerful positions unto the Tembo dynasty. Tembo himself was given the portfolio of Minister of State controlling the "Security of the State." This was widely seen by the discontented Malawians as a gradual and systematic transfer of power from Banda to his henchman.

As a potential internal conflict was imminent Banda did not want to entertain another version of 1964 Cabinet Crisis. He expressly summoned Aaron Gadama, Dick Matenje and Edward Bwanali, all senior Cabinet Ministers with considerable followings among their tribesmen. Before they were even given an opportunity to speak, Hastings Banda addressed them in his Sanjika Palace. He sternly accused them of aspiring for his position and also accused them of using David Chiwanga and Twaibu Sangala both Ministers in the government for their political ambitions.

As things heated up, the ministers gathered momentum and courage. They accused Banda of highhandedness and suggested that his habit of appointing all members of Parliament be liberalized and that he appoint three candidates for election in each constituency. The most burning and contentious issue was Banda's express desire to appoint John Z. Tembo, whose hands were drenched in the blood of innocent citizens, to act as President while he would be away on sabbatical leave abroad. He also suggested that Cecilia Kadzamila, his longtime concubine and niece to Tembo, could act as Prime Minister. As it were, therefore, the Malawi National Constitution could be open for change to accommodate those two Banda dupes.

But the Ministers could have learned from the past lessons that challenging the obnoxious tyrant could lead to an unprecedented tragedy. It was alleged that after two weeks of a divided cabinet, similar to the 1964 Cabinet Crisis, President Banda and his closest henchman John Tembo, instructed the Police Chief to arrest the four trouble-making ministers. It appeared that the Police Chief did not approve the arrests of the four persons in view of the fact that he could not take direct instructions from the Minister of State John Tembo. However, the plans to liquidate the four ministers had to go on anyway.

On May 17, 1983, at a road block specifically mounted at Likangala Bridge near Zomba the former administrative capital, and near a Catholic Secondary School, arrests were made on Dick Matenje, Secretary-general of the murderous Malawi Congress Party and senior Cabinet Ministers Aaron Gadama, David Chiwanga and J. Twaibu Sangala. All four were chained by the legs and handcuffed and thrown into a government Land Rover and briefly detained at the notorious Mikuyu death camp (Auschwitz) before they were picked up at midnight of the same day by hired hit-men and driven towards the Mozambican border on Mwanza Road. The following day, Banda's controlled Radio Malawi announced that the four Ministers had vanished and anybody with information leading to their whereabouts, should forthwith report to the nearest Police Station. Meanwhile, the three, Banda, Tembo and Kadzamila, the axis of evil knew precisely what had happened to the four ministers.

Between May 18-19, 1983, the government announced that the four ministers had been found dead in a car accident when they were apparently trying to flee into Mozambique. In truth, these people were murdered in cold-blood at Mikuyu Prison by the same hired government thugs who picked them up at midnight. They then drove the dead bodies in government vehicles close to the Mozambican border and put them together in a single car which was positioned as if it had been involved in an accident.

Such was the grip of the Banda regime on Malawi that when it was announced the four prominent politicians had died in a car accident in the remote town of Mwanza, the general conclusion was unanimous, they had been murdered. But many people registered silent protest and the Mwanza incident became a long festering sore, a symbol of the numerous and unprecedented human rights abuses committed by the Banda regime. When the bodies were checked, they were found covered with bullet holes and fractured head skulls. Indeed, in a country where people lived in the lion's den for much of their lives, privately people asked themselves how could the government lose track of its own senior officials for 24 hours until their bodies were discovered in such bizarre circumstances. However, the handling of the funeral rites further convinced the general public that the four ministers were actually murdered in cold blood. Their families were strictly forbidden from opening the coffins to pay their last respects and the bodies were buried unceremoniously to the unprecedented astonishment of the general public.

The brutal deaths of the four people bore similarities to the previous suspicious demise of Dunduzu Kaluli Chisiza one of the brightest rising stars in the country's history. He was Deputy Finance Minister at independence under a white colonial expatriate who held lesser credentials in the economic field. Du, as he was popularly known to his people, was also Secretary-general of the Malawi Congress Party (MCP). Dunduzu was actually murdered in Limbe, Blantyre's twin sister city, in the Party's Headquarters. His body was stuffed into his Mercedes Benz car and driven towards Zomba. The car was left to roll at Thondwe Bridge in a patently fabricated car crash. The fact that Banda did not attend Dunduzu's funeral nor did he order an inquest into his suspicious death, clearly suggested that Banda and his closest dupes had, undoubtedly, committed this heinous crime against humanity.

The advent of a democracy struggle in the mid-90s, rekindled the circumstances in which the four people died. One of the multiparty movement's leaders, Bakili Muluzi, capitalized on the issue and won wide spread support when he was heard to shout: "Remember the Mwanza Four" during his campaigns against Banda and his murderous Malawi Congress Party. Shortly after Muluzi was swept into power in May 1994, he became Malawi's second President in 30 years. To his credit, he commissioned judicial investigations into the Mwanza incident. The lengthy report, about 1,000 pages, concluded that Banda and Tembo ordered that the four men be killed because they were posing a political threat to Banda's rule and more pointedly to Tembo's position as the next ruler. The inquiry also found that the murder-squads carried out the crime using guns, claw-bars and other lethal objects to beat the men to death.

When President Muluzi received the report, little time was wasted in ordering the arrests of Banda, Tembo and the top police chief. The fact that Muluzi had ordered the arrest of the former brutal and corrupt tyrant was by itself a victory for democracy and for justice denied to Malawians over three decades of savage rule. Indeed, it was unique in the Continent that a former Head of State had been arrested to face criminal charges. However, as anticipated, the government, to the disappointment of the general public, lost the case despite vivid evidence presented to court. The reasons for the loss, however, were twofold: (a) The government side was ill-prepared for the high profile case, and (b) lack of funds prevented the government from hiring top notch lawyers to represent it. On the other hand, with massive funds Banda and Tembo had acquired through dubious means, they managed to hire London's most prestigious lawyers who dominated the case throughout the proceedings.

Even though justice had taken its course, the majority of Malawians were disappointed that Banda and his atrocious henchman, John Tembo were off the hook. The anger was visibly there, the mere mention of the two names stirred up blistering and bitter hatred in many Malawians, particularly Tembo whom they rightfully accused of the worst and most repulsive crimes of the Banda era in the 60s to 80s. However the popular anger against Tembo was not surprising. It was John Tembo and his niece, Cecilia Kadzamila, who for more than two decades controlled access to Banda and effectively maintained a harsh rule in Banda's name. Although Banda did not marry the woman officially, she reigned imperiously as Malawi's first lady–even ordering all to stand whenever she entered a room. Furthermore she helped her unpopular, sadistic and ambitious uncle, Tembo, get a foothold in politics and he quickly made his way to the top of Banda's Malawi Congress Party. As the eccentric despot became more elderly in the 80s, Kadzamila and Tembo together ran the nation, easily manipulating the serviles in the Civil Service, Malawi Congress Party, the rubber-stamp Parliament, the Police, some Army Officers, and highly politicized courts.

The fact that Tembo, alongside his master Hastings Banda, dominated Malawian politics unchallenged, he was not, to say the least, an upright person, he was half-witted, unintelligent, a tribalist, and atrocious. As Chief of the Reserve Bank of Malawi, he turned the institution into a tribal entity that produced only mediocre results. This prompted the IMF and the World Bank to lodge formal complaints against Tembo and urged Banda to fire him and appoint the more knowledgeable and brilliant economist Austin Madinga. Through Tembo, Banda is strongly believed to have siphoned off from the poor nation an estimated US$500 million which is stashed in foreign banks. It is part of this ill-gotten money that Banda used to pay for his legal fees to British lawyers during the Mwanza murder trial of four former cabinet Ministers. The sad part of it is that after political change in the country in 1994, his successor Bakili Muluzi could not pursue this matter in order to retrieve some of the ill-gotten funds for the development of one of the poorest nations in the world.

In contrast, Mobutu's successor, D. L. Kabila, as soon as he was swept into power through armed conflict involving Rwandan Tutsis and Ugandan soldiers, tried to retrieve the US$9 billion, Mobutu stole from the Congolese people during his brutal reign. However, some of the institutions agreed to send the funds back to the impoverished Congo, but were held back because Kabila had already involved himself in corruption and scandal reminiscent of Mobutu's administration.

The current President Joseph Kabila, Jr., took the matter from where his late father had left it and was promised by one of the institutions holding Mobutu's ill-gotten money to return US $7 million, but that is the tip of an iceberg.

The fact that the first former Head of State in Africa had been brought to justice for his crimes against humanity, Bakili Muluzi deserve some respect even though Banda won the case on technicalities. Another African leader who deserves respect is President Mwanawasa of Zambia who took the former President Fredrick Chiluba to justice for his past crimes of corruption and mismanagement of public funds. Chiluba handpicked Mwanawasa as Presidential candidate for MMD Movement in the hope that the latter could conceal his past evils and dance to his tune.

The political and economic history of Malawi in the first place has been sad and shameful. It has been, since the arrival of Hastings Banda from his self-imposed exile in 1958, immensely corrupted and manipulated to the extent that a good majority of our people live in unknowing darkness hitherto. It has been crafted so that people are driven to believe that Banda, and Banda alone, championed the independence struggle and without him this could not have been achieved. It therefore turns out that the people have been the victims of atrocious deceit and that will take some time to vanish from their corrupted minds. For the good of our children and many more generations to come, Malawians of goodwill ought to dig deeper and come out with authentic revelations that would prevent our people from committing the same tragic mistakes of heaping absolute power into the hands of a single person or a tiny group of misguided zealots to run the affairs of the State on their behalf. Already, and interestingly, after 30 years of the worst brutal repression and degradation ever seen in the continent of Africa committed by a civilian administration,

Malawians are now applauding Banda's former regime for inculcating discipline in the Malawian society, which they say, led to economic prosperity. Which or what economic prosperity? After more than 40 years of nationhood, Malawi still relies heavily on economic handouts. Malawians hitherto would not distinguish between "discipline" and "fear," and "prosperity" and "poverty." The Malawi Congress Party (MCP) has been always hiding behind the facade of four deceitful party slogans: Loyalty; Unity; Discipline; Obedience. These slogans had taken an unprecedented toll in the minds of our people detrimental to their own political, economic and social freedoms. In his brilliant article in the African Review of 1973, under the title: "MALAWI, THE BIRTH OF NEOCOLONIAL STATE," Dr. George Attati Mphakati, the former charismatic and a brilliant leader of the opposition, the Socialist League Of Malawi (LESOMA), and murdered in cold-blood by Malawian death-squads assisted by the Zimbabwean dreaded Secret Agents, wrote thus: "How long the people of Malawi can continue to tolerate their state, cheated of their proper returns, is impossible to say. What is needed among all Malawians is the ability and conviction of John Chilembwe to rise to strike a blow for socialist victory. Without such ideas, our people will be condemned to suffer injustice in silence, since the greatest enemy of justice is ignorance itself." Indeed, Hastings Banda had capitalized on the ignorance of our people, hence, his successful grip of power for 30 years was unchallenged. This also vindicates Banda's assertion, before his demise, that even if he died, his spirit would perpetually rule this country. Indeed, spiritually, it does.

The readers of this book would notice that I have mentioned the name Hastings Banda many times. I have nothing whatsoever, against him as a person, but whoever writes a book on Malawi's economic, political and social history, must not be tempted to avoid mentioning the name Banda for that would be incomplete and false information because Banda single-handedly dominated Malawi's political, social, and economic spheres for 30 solid years.

Indeed, there was absolutely nothing to celebrate or to be proud of, during Banda's tenure. Malawians paid a high price for embracing a person whose roots they didn't know, but on the other hand, this has taught Malawians a vivid lesson never again to hand over absolute power to an individual. This is the lesson that Africans in other countries must ultimately learn and embrace. However, it is not too late, the forces of progress will triumph over the forces of evil and darkness.

Tyrants of Africa

Top: President Omar El Bashir of the Sudan has killed one million Africans from the south and 500,000 others from the Darfur Region. He is sought by the ICC for crimes against humanity. Center: The late Bernard Bongo (changed to Omar Bongo to assuage the Muslim world) ruled Gabon like his own personal fiefdom for 44 years. He looted US$2.7 billion from oil revenues, his children being the richest in the country. Bottom: President Robert Mugabe, the "Butcher of Harare", has been in power 32 years. He has killed 35,000 minority Ndebeles, siphoned US$5.5 billion from state coffers and destroyed the economy. He is accused of looting tons of Congo's vital resources.

Top: Former marxist Leninist President Yoweri Museveni of Uganda ruled the nation with brute force for 26 years. He and his family are among the richest elite in Africa. Center: Daniel Arap Moi, former Kenyan corrupt tyrant, who ruled that nation with unprecedented brutality for 24 years. He is accused of stealing up to US$2.5 billion from state coffers. Bottom: Former tin-pot despot of Somalia Siad Barre massacred over one million Somalis before he was toppled by rebels. He left the nation bankrupt and polarized. He died in Lagos, Nigeria.

Top: Former self-proclaimed Emperor Jean B. Bokassa of the Central African Republic ruled his poor nation for 30 years. His coronation seat cost taxpayers US$3 million. His soldiers killed 100 students for refusing to buy school uniforms from his girl friend's factory. Bottom: Theodoro Nguema of Equitorial Guinea ruled his oil-rich country for nearly four decades with barbaric force. Together with his family, they looted billions of dollars from oil revenues while his citizens live in dire poverty.

Top: The late Colonel Muammar Al Gaddafi ruled a Stalinist regime for 42 years with a brutal iron fist and stole US$92 billion. He also corrupted many of Africa's leaders. Center: The former corrupt tyrant President Charles Taylor of Liberia is sentenced to 52 years by the ICC for crimes against humanity. He is also accused of stealing millions of dollars from state sources. Bottom: The late General Sani Abacha, Nigeria's former corrupt and ferocious military leader. He killed a number of his critics including Ken Saro Wiwa. He stole billions of dollars from state coffers.

Top: A monstrous thug, the late Idd Amin Dada, who killed millions of Ugandans and plunged the nation's economy into total collapse. A Muslim, he died in Arabia. Center: The former tyrant and corrupt President Annassingbe Eyadema ruled Togo with absolute force for four decades and killed 25,000 people. He siphoned away US$475 million while people lived in brutal poverty. Bottom: One of Africa's obnoxious and corrupt tyrants, the late Mobutu Sese Seko of the Congo (DRC) He stole US$9 billion and killed a million people during his reign of three decades. He was also involved in the death of Patrice Lumumba.

Top: The late demon Hastings Banda (1895-1997) ruled Malawi with a brutal iron fist for 30 years. More than 15,000 people were killed during his repulsive rule and US$ 500 million was stolen from state sources. Center: Mr. John Z. Tembo, was formerly Banda's heir apparent and greatly feared for his brutal notoriety against his rivals. He is related to Cecelia Kadzamila. Bottom: Cecelia Kadzamila was the late Banda's concubine for 31 years. She was also the power behind many of Banda's brutal atrocities against civilians—mainly northerners. These three were popularly known as "the axis of evil."

The late President Bingu Wa Mathalika, Malawi's obnoxious and corrupt tyrant, died April 5, 2012 of a heart attack. He massively looted the nation's coffers and some of the spoils were hidden in his own-built mausoleum. He was Mugabe's overzealous dupe.

Banda's mausoleum, a symbol of oppression and injustice, built by the eccentric despot the late President Bingu Wa Muthalika at a cost of US$1.5 million.

Typical of Malawi's life-style amongst the majority of downtrodden citizens trapped in unprecedented and grinding poverty.

Chapter Nine

THE PATH OF BETRAYAL

It all started soon after Banda was released from Gwero prison in the early 60s. He had been imprisoned for only 18 months while many other African nationalist leaders, elsewhere in Africa, spent decades in incarceration. His early release, however, was due to the fact that the colonialists found in him an ally who could work for their ultimate interests. But when he came from self-imposed exile to Nyasaland in 1958, he gave hope not only to Nyasas, but also to most other parts of Africa also fighting colonial domination. He was indeed the beacon of hope to millions of oppressed Africans who were ready to stand upright and challenge the status quo. There was no doubt, however, that Banda had come out of prison a completely changed man and with completely different behavior that started to amaze his closest colleagues and people at large.

In every political rally he warned his people, as he always called them, to respect the white folks and not to give them trouble. He completely detached himself from the people of Malawi and instead aligned himself with his former adversaries, all to the total astonishment of his supporters.

After self-government, as the Prime Minister of Nyasaland, he visibly showed his true colors. Mozambican and Rhodesian fascist leaders used to covertly visit the country for meetings with Dr. Banda, returning to their respective colonies in the early hours of the morning—also in secret. His ministers learned about the arrival of his covert visitors only after a couple of days or weeks. Banda also paid similar visits—reciprocating earlier visits by his friends. In Mozambique, Banda, the former Presbyterian Church Elder was well received and even entertained by pretty young Portuguese women.

It was a foregone conclusion that Dr. Banda had chosen the path of betrayal over the liberation of his mother Africa. Before the CIA and M16 gained footholds in Malawi, South Africa's Bureau of Secret Services (BOSS) and the Portuguese Policia Internacional a Defesa do Estado (PIDE) had already established themselves in Malawi in order to check the movements of the African Nationalists from neighboring white colonies. South Africa in particular, which viewed Malawi as its greatest ally in Africa, wanted to make sure that Malawi did not fall into the hands of radicals as this could alter the status quo. As a matter of fact, from the early days of self-government, Malawi had already become a "Bantustan province" of apartheid South Africa—apart from being the region's biggest source of cheap labor. One of the major issues during the Cabinet Crisis of 1964, two months after the attainment of independence, was Banda's flirtation with Africa's archenemies of the liberation struggle.

At one occasion, the late Kanyama Chiume was in Lusaka, Zambia, trying to reconcile Zimbabwe's two major factions, ZAPU and ZANU. While there he heard through BBC (Africa News), that Winston Field, Rhodesia's former notorious minority Prime Minister was in Malawi, at the invitation of Dr. Banda, where the two leaders had a cordial private meeting. At the time, Chiume, Malawi's Foreign Minister, was taken to task by ZAPU and ZANU delegations, casting doubts as to whether Chiume was serious enough to carry on with the issue of reconciliation while his President was hobnobbing with their enemy. Chiume was so upset by the news that he caught the first available flight back home to confront his boss. However, Dr. Banda had no good reason to convince Chiume over Field's covert visit. On another occasion, Banda asked Chiume, as the Foreign Minister, to go to apartheid South Africa to deliver a special message to the Prime Minister, the late Dr. Hendrick Verwoerd–one of the most cold-blooded racist leaders South Africa had ever produced. Kanyama instantly and flatly told Banda, he was not in any position to betray his conscience and that he should find another person for the mission.

Since then, Kanyama Chiume and his closest colleagues, men like Masauko Chipembere, Yatuta Chisiza, Augustine Bwanausi, Orton Chirwa, Willie Chokani and Rose Chibambo, were convinced beyond any doubt that Banda had really taken the path of betrayal and something should be done sooner rather than later. Without wasting time, Chipembere, Yatuta and Kanyama were sent by their colleagues to approach Banda and redress the issue of Malawi's relations with minority oppressive regimes of southern Africa before the President became entangled in a potentially political fallout. As expected, Banda gave the three senior Cabinet Ministers a cold shoulder and promised them he would look into their concerns and give an answer later. However, the three ministers left Banda with a sense of distrust and disappointment. He had already made up his mind to jump on an evil bandwagon and he would not listen to anybody. Private visits by senior military and intelligence officials from Mozambique, Rhodesia and apartheid South Africa continued unabated. Apart from Banda's partner, Miss Cecilia Kadzamila, none of his senior cabinet ministers knew of these visits until some time after the fact.

When the famous Cabinet Crisis broke out in September 1964, Malawi's "relations" with oppressive white minority regimes in Southern Africa were at the top of the issues relating to the crisis. The rebel ministers maintained that they would rather sacrifice their all than be found hobnobbing with the oppressors of their brothers and sisters.

What a coincidence? The Front for the Liberation of Mozambique (FRELIMO), which was formed in 1962 (one year after Nyasaland won her self-government) fired its first shots in September 1964, at colonial symbols throughout Mozambique warning the oppressors that the war of liberation had come to their doorstep.

From the early stages of the FRELIMO onslaught, the fight was mainly confined to the Cabo Delgado, Nyasa and Nampula Regions, east of Lake Nyasa and in the extreme north of Mozambique. Meanwhile, PIDE, the Portuguese notorious secret police had already established roots in Malawian soil with its first branch in Blantyre, the commercial city, to monitor the movements of FRELIMO combatants. Their operational offices in Blantyre and Limbe were centers for recruitment of Sena-speaking ethnic group members which are found on both sides, Malawi and Mozambique, to help track down FRELIMO activists along the border areas and towns. Most senior PIDE and military senior officials were issued with Malawian passports which enabled them to travel to neighboring states for espionage activities. However, it proved hard for the spy agency to operate successfully in Tanzania where FRELIMO and hordes of other liberation movements had their headquarters. The Tanzanians had established excellent and sophisticated security and intelligence networks. Many PIDE agents were apprehended and this forced them to change tactics. Instead, Mozambican blacks were sent to carry on the dirty job of espionage along side their Malawian counterparts.

As the struggle intensified, FRELIMO scored success after success against Portuguese forces in collusion with NATO allies. The Bureau of Secret Services (BOSS), South Africa's dreaded secret police, opened its first offices in Blantyre followed by Israel's notorious MOSSAD. The latter was used mostly by the Malawi government to track down local dissidents and provide intelligence information to the neo-colonialist government. In fact, MOSSAD was in overall charge of state security and had sponsored hundreds of young Malawians to undergo espionage and other related courses of training in Israel. But why was Israel readily involved in Malawi's internal affairs? The major reason was to defend and strengthen the Banda regime which was extremely anti-Arab, the archenemy of the State of Israel. Malawi leaders made no secret of condemning Arabs as foreigners colonizing northern Africa and further wanting black Africa to recognize white minority racist regimes in southern Africa.

Meanwhile, FRELIMO continued to record impressive victories over the strong and well equipped Portuguese army in the north that was threatening the Malawi-Nacala Railway line, the life blood of the former. FRELIMO fighters were strictly instructed not to attack and destroy the railway line which had fallen within the confines of their firepower. After two years of fierce fighting, FRELIMO opened a new front in Tete and Zambezi provinces in the southwest of Malawi. This sent a strong message to the Portuguese authorities in Lourenco Marques (Maputo) who wondered how FRELIMO, in a short space of time, had managed to open a new vital and strategic front.

PIDE and the Malawian Army therefore, worked hand in hand to thwart FRELIMO's gains in the new front. In fact, PIDE took the leading role of directing and commanding the troops. There were numerous occasions that FRELIMO combatants were captured and eventually handed over to the Portuguese authorities where they were subjected to brutal and inhuman treatment by these enemies. Some of these fighters met a very cruel demise. They were dropped from heights of 200-300 meters by military helicopters as an apparent tactic to intimidate others. However, that was a gross violation of the Geneva Convention on prisoners of war and a crime against humanity. Despite Malawi's destructive role on Mozambique's liberation struggle, FRELIMO, backed by Tanzania and Zambia in the early stages, continued to bring the war closer to the bastion of imperialism and colonialism.

To ensure his paymasters in Portugal and Lourenco Marques that Malawi would stand side by side with its friends, Banda elevated Jorge Jardim from Malawi's Consul to Ambassador to Mozambique. Jardim was a rich fascist Portuguese with close ties to Antonio Salazar, Portugal's notorious fascist, with enormous political and economic muscles over Angola, Mozambique, Guinea-Bissau and the Cape Verde Islands. Jardim was also a top PIDE official whose hands had been drenched in the blood of the Mozambican African nationalists. It is reported that Jardim, in appreciation of Banda's cooperation with Portuguese authorities, handed Malawi's President a cheque in the amount of US$25 million and promised the traitor an executive jet if FRELIMO was denied passage through Malawian territory. Officially, Malawi did not recognize FRELIMO as a liberation movement, but rather a communist-inspired movement. On one occasion, Banda told his people not to fear FRELIMO as it could not win over the forces of civilization and democracy—thus implying that FRELIMO was a movement of lawlessness and misguided communist agitators, whereas the Portuguese were democratic and law-abiding people.

Sadly, Banda had turned Malawi into a rear base for anti-African freedom, but that did not in any way or form deter the grim determination of the oppressed to fight for their God-given birth rights–freedom and self-determination. Malawi had become a virtual no-man's land for African exiles and political refugees who, as a consequence, had to walk thousands of kilometers into Tanzania and Zambia for their safety.

To show Banda that the people of Africa were determined, once and for all, to liberate their mother continent from foreign domination, Tanzania, Zambia and Botswana formed an alliance called Front Line States to coordinate liberation strategies among the liberation movements in southern Africa. Botswana, geographically, has a common border with powerful South Africa and almost entirely relies on her ports for its foreign trade. Above all, South Africa remains Botswana's vital trade partner with more than 70 percent of its trade finding its way to and from South Africa—but still, Botswana remained uncompromising on the question of the liberation of Africa. Refugees and exiles from both Rhodesia and South Africa were warmly welcomed thereby prompting reprisals from both white minority regimes. On the other hand, Malawi had no common borders with the two regimes and, yet, its commitment to the liberation of Africa remained tepid and treacherous.

At times, PIDE operatives blew up Nacala Railway lines and blamed the actions on FRELIMO fighters. This gave Malawi some ammunition to portray FRELIMO as a terrorist movement bent on lawlessness and lacking political direction. PIDE and BOSS virtually controlled the security and intelligence operations of the Malawi's reactionary regime in a bid to thwart FRELIMO's advance to the south by all means possible, but the war of liberation had by then reached a point of no return. The imperialist forces embarked on desperate moves. In many occasions they bombed refugee camps on Tanzanian soil, sometimes with devastating consequences for both the innocent people of Tanzania and the refugees. In Zambia, Ian Smith's Air Force conducted frequent bombings on the city of Lusaka aiming at the premises of refugees and exiled leaders.

After Banda had appointed J. Jardim, a rich Portuguese fascist to represent Malawi's national interests in Mozambique, a highly charged Mozambican white Military Attaché presented his credentials to President Banda in Zomba in January 1970. Among other activities, the Military Attaché controlled Malawi's Military Intelligence and had special duties to check FRELIMO's movements and activities in Malawi. On top of that, the Military Attaché was a de facto Banda adviser on State Security as the President could not in any way, trust Africans in general. In Africa, if you control the army and police, you are assured of a lifelong Presidency.

Despite Malawi's strategic position, it was hard for FRELIMO to use Malawi as a rear base because the Portuguese had already established a fortification detrimental to FRELIMO's efforts. However, Malawi's sellout attitudes could not stop FRELIMO's quest for freedom and justice. The freedom fighters recorded impressive successes much to the astonishment of the Portuguese forces which had more superior firepower than FRELIMO. The enemy forces had the advantage of NATO's total support in terms of military hardware and financial backing. As the war gained momentum—each day, month, and year—enemy forces changed tactics. They intensified the attacks against Tanzania and Zambia which gave moral and material support to their oppressed brothers under minority domination.

In 1970, after the visit to Malawi by the South African Prime Minister Balthazar Voster, Malawi established full diplomatic relations with apartheid South Africa. This move made Malawi the pariah of Black Africa. However, this idiosyncratic diplomacy, was rewarded with foreign investment and large South African loans to build a new capital in Lilongwe, this regional stronghold and a railway link from the Indian Ocean port of Nacala, made Malawi a virtual South Africa's "BANTUSTAN."

The following year, Banda shocked the entirety of Africa with grandiose claims to the southern parts of Tanzanian territory for Malawi: Mbeya, Iringa, Songea and Mbamba-Bay. In Zambia, he claimed eastern and northern parts—Chipata, Isoka, Mfuwe—as part of extended Malawi. This outburst prompted sharp response from Tanzania where national demonstrations were staged in protest against Banda's provocative claims. At a public meeting organized by TANU, the late President Nyerere described Banda as "Mshenzi" (fool) and an agent of imperialism on the payroll of Africa's enemies. Nyerere warned his people to be vigilant, "Banda could be a fool, but those who were backing him were not." In Zambia, the former President Dr. Kenneth David Kaunda warned Banda not to try to steer unrest in the region in the name of neocolonialism. "Any attempt to grab part of our land will meet with the full force of our defense forces," President Kaunda warned. It is a pity that the people of Malawi, while contributing their meagre resources to the liberation of their neighbors from under the colonial yoke, found Banda betraying their cherished aspirations and turning the chapter backward.

However, despite Banda's chosen path of betrayal, the people of Mozambique after 500 years of brutal Portuguese domination, had reached a point of no return under the dynamic leadership of one of Mozambique's illustrious sons, the late Dr. Eduardo Chivambo Mondlane—the first-Mozambican university graduate. His tragic demise occurred in Tanzania's capital of Dar es Salaam on February 3, 1969 where his life was taken from him by a powerful parcel bomb sent to him from Japan by PIDE agents. An equally energetic and charismatic young man, Samora Moses Machel, took over the Presidency of FRELIMO. The late Samora was, before that, an overall Commander of the military wing of FRELIMO. In his position as Commander, Samora proved to be a courageous and brilliant military strategist, spending most of the time with his fighters on the front lines.

Under his able leadership, FRELIMO opened new war zones in Manica, Zambezi, and Sofala Provinces in the south and close to the seat of imperialism, Laurenco Marques (Maputo). This dealt a devastating blow to the Portuguese forces and their NATO allies. With massive support from people of all walks of life throughout Mozambique, within only a few years new fronts were established in the remaining strategic provinces of Inhambane and Gaza in the south where the Portuguese had vowed to defend their interests to the last drop of their blood.

FRELIMO's brilliant successive victories sent jittering messages to Lisbon that soon caused pandemonium within the ranks and file of the Portuguese military establishment. Despite the ignorance of the rest of the world, and connived at by the Portuguese authorities, the war of liberation in Mozambique was then being fought with increasing success on several of the last remaining vital fronts, but the fighters faced stiff resistance in their last leg to liberation. South Africa, Rhodesia and Portugal formed an evil alliance to defend Mozambique at all costs because all three reactionary States had gargantuan interests in Mozambique. They had to be defended and protected. Dr. Alberto Noguera Portugal's former notorious Foreign Minister and a personal friend of Malawi's late eccentric despot Hastings Banda, once remarked: "Portugal's African provinces constituted one of the last bastions preserving 'Western Civilization' in that part of the world and it is therefore in the interest of the entire west to help Portugal stay in Africa."

Soon after his cryptic remarks, the Portuguese fascist regime in Lisbon was toppled by military officers led by General Espaniora. With the help of liberal minded people such as Mario Soares, the military junta soon established its authority in the country. General Espaniora was a Commander of the Portuguese expeditionary forces in the colony of Angola. The forces in Mozambique were led by General Kaulza de Arriaga—one of the most cold-blooded military leaders—with offices also in Blantyre. As well he was a personal friend of Hastings Banda. General Espaniora and his colleagues expressed their concerns to Salazar's government that Portugal could not win the war in its colonies and therefore there was no need for further needless loss of lives among their young soldiers nor further waste of resources—even though much of these were contributed by NATO nations. Portugal is the poorest state in Europe, but sustained the most extensive and cost consuming wars in Africa.

Forthwith, after the coup, General Espaniora declared a cease-fire in Mozambique, Angola, Guinea Bissau and the Cape Verde Islands, Portugal's overseas possessions. That marked the end of one of the most brutal and contumacious colonial powers in Africa. Mozambique declared its independence on June 15, 1975 after 500 years of foreign domination—the longest in the continent. And the late Samora Moses Machel became its first black Head of State and immediately Mozambique was admitted into membership in the now defunct OAU.

1. Meanwhile, the membership of the Frontline States expanded from three to five, Malawi exclusive. The independence of Mozambique in Samora's views, was meaningless unless it was linked up with total liberation of his neighbors, echoing Nkrumah's cry that the independence of Ghana was meaningless unless it was linked up with the total liberation of Africa. Within six months of gaining its independence, Mozambique closed its borders with the white supremacists in neighboring Rhodesia setting a paradigm case for the unshackling of "Portuguese" Africa.

Indeed, the move revolutionized sanctions against Ian Smith's minority regime, but at a tremendous cost, as landlocked Rhodesia relied mostly on the Mozambican ports of Beira and Laurenco Marques (Maputo) for its foreign trade. This use of Mozambican ports brought into Mozambique much needed foreign exchange. It was estimated that the newly independent state lost between US$300-400 million a month in port revenues. Even though sanctions were officially imposed against the rebellious white minority regime, Malawi offered its facilities for the export of tobacco at Limbe Floors, which found its international markets by branding the commodity as "Product of Malawi."

However, the independence of Mozambique hastened Malawi's isolation among African States for its treacherous policies. Apart from reactionary Kenya, which had an Embassy in Malawi, Banda managed to cultivate political relationship with Lesotho's Prime Minister Jonathan Leobua who had a short-term relationship with apartheid South Africa. However, after realizing he had jumped on an evil bandwagon, Leobua snubbed Banda as an imperialist dupe, therefore, Malawi remained with Kenya which had also treacherous policies on Africa's liberation struggle. As expected, Banda was not invited to the independence celebrations of Mozambique, while Presidents Nyerere of Tanzania and Kenneth Kaunda of Zambia, received hero's welcomes by the jubilant people of Mozambique in appreciation for their unflinching support during the liberation struggle.

After the fall of Mozambique, PIDE, which had a strong tradition of violence (its officers were trained by the Gestapo and it enjoyed a considerable measure of autonomy that allowed it to act outside the control of the official law), saw its activities in Malawi had become irrelevant and the majority of the operatives had left for Portugal, South Africa, and Rhodesia. Some of the operatives remained in the country where they continued to work for Banda as personal bodyguards and in the State Security Division. Banda relied heavily on white officers rather than his own African citizens.

As Mozambicans were consolidating their gains, Malawians saw an influx of different friends, this time, from South Africa, Rhodesia and Israel in anticipation of a new chapter in the liberation endeavors. ZANLA, ZANU's military wing and UMKONTHO WE SIZWE, ANC's military wing, moved to Mozambique to be closer to their respective countries. This sent shock waves to the fascist minority regimes in the south and west of Mozambique. Despite the fall of Mozambique into the hands of the indigenous people, Malawi was still regarded as a vital rear base for counter insurgency. BOSS from South Africa, the Rhodesian Secret Agency and Israel's MOSSAD, took control over Malawi's intelligence services to deal with ANC, ZAPU, and ZANU movements.

ZIPRA AND ZANLA sent thousands of young fighters from their bases in Mozambique and Zambia into Rhodesia for the first time after the defeat of the Portuguese forces. Consequently, Zambia became a prime target for BOSS and Rhodesian Secret Police. ANC's offices in Lusaka were frequently bombed, ZANU and ZAPU offices were not spared either. The President of ZANU Albert Chitepo, a distinguished lawyer and foremost African nationalist, was killed by a remotely controlled bomb on his driveway in Lusaka in 1974. The killers were believed to be whites poised as tourists holding diplomatic Malawian passports. The same year, another top militant nationalist Jason Ziapapa Moyo of ZIPLA High Command, was assassinated in the same way at his Lusaka home. The suspects were also whites believed to have, at will, crossed the Malawian border with Zambia at Chipata and into Zambia. In essence, President Banda compromised both the independence of Malawi and, to a large extent, the dignity of its people who were once filled with Pan-Africanist sentiments. But, under a Gestapo, Malawians had no choice other than submit to the status quo.

The independence of Mozambique left two major and controversial conflicts in limbo. The struggle in Rhodesia had just entered a new and decisive phase. In South Africa, the Nuclear Arsenal had just been completed at Pelindaba with the help of the Jewish state and, the largest Naval Base in southern Africa, in Richards Bay, was in the processes of modernization and being made ready for a perceived invasion from the north. At the onset of an armed struggle, South Africa, Rhodesia, and Mozambique formed an "evil axis" with Malawi as a "rear base" against the rising billow of African nationalism.

The advance earlier of the FRELIMO forces, instilled an enormous sense of nervousness in South Africa's ruling clique that prompted the former to sign a military pact with Banda's regime in 1971. Another motive behind the signing of the treacherous pact was that South Africans, who viewed Malawi as their greatest ally in Africa, were quite worried that Masauko Chipembere, a radical former rebel minister, and his colleagues could take over the reigns of power in Malawi and that could alter the status quo. Therefore it was not a surprising scenario that Foreign Minister Pick Botha was dispatched to Lilongwe to test the water soon after the pact.

It was not known, however, how Botha regarded the situation. Nevertheless, Pretoria feared that if there were free elections to find someone to step into Banda's shoes, his replacement might not be as well disposed to the apartheid regime as the Machiavellian Banda had been over two decades—much to the chagrin to the rest of Africa.

The military pact had been initiated and agreed upon after Malawi had established a diplomatic mission in Pretoria two years earlier, the first of its kind by an independent African State. This treacherous move was widely condemned throughout independent African States, hastening the isolation of Banda's regime which was then largely controlled by apartheid South Africa on one hand and western imperialists on the other. After the downfall of Portuguese East Africa (Mozambique) in 1975, PIDE and Portugal's Military Attachés were subsequently replaced by the equally notorious South Africa's BOSS and a Military Attaché Colonel Peter Van der Pretorius in Lilongwe. This sort of trend turned Malawi, an independent nation, into virtually a South African "Bantustan" with equal status to Kwazulu or Baphutotswana.

With the successes recorded by ZIPRA and ZANLA forces inside Rhodesia and the biting of international sanctions, Malawi played a devastating role by facilitating Rhodesian exports through its systems to world markets—even though it brought in badly needed foreign exchange for the beleaguered racist regime. As expected, the signing of a military pact between Malawi and South Africa saw the acceleration of sabotage against the Tanzania-Zambia railway (TAZARA), which was then under construction by the Chinese Government from the Port of Dar es Salaam to Kapilimposhi, northern Zambia. The railway, though, was passing through Tanzanian soil into Zambia–but a stone-throw distance to a Malawian border–thus making it easier for South African saboteurs to blow up the construction at will.

The Railway was meant primarily to lessen dependence on South African and Rhodesian transport systems by landlocked Zambia. Like Zambia, Malawi was to benefit from this project because it was only about 80 km to the Tanzanian soil where the railway was passing at Tunduma. When the feasibility studies were underway in the mid-60s, former rebel ministers urged Banda to join the venture that could eventually free Malawi from the grip of the minority regimes' transport systems. Banda, as expected, aggressively refused because the railway was being constructed by "Red-China." Once, South Africa's most ferocious Prime Minister John Voster remarked on the liberation war in Mozambique thus: "Up there in the north 45,000 Portuguese soldiers are fighting, some are dying, to hold back the Red-equipped terrorists seeping in from Tanzania." Banda harbored similar sentiments towards FRELIMO.

Malawi's foreign policy was largely dictated by foreign powers, it had no independent foreign policy of its own. In the thirty years Dr. Banda was in power, he attended very few OAU meetings and called his counterparts hyenas and hypocrites. On the contrary, he never shunned Commonwealth gatherings where he could sit beside the Queen and feel he was on top of the world. OAU and Commonwealth gatherings were platforms preoccupied with controversial issues about illegal regimes in Rhodesia and apartheid South Africa. However, South Africa's outward policy managed to lure very few friends and those were attracted by economic promises and to some extent, military alliances. The policy brought Malawi and the Island of Madagascar closer to South Africa's sphere of influence. Apartheid South Africa bragged about winning the most vital area that could be turned into a naval base in defense of the Cape route against Soviet massive sea power.

However, the marriage of convenience did not last long. As the wind of change was blowing across Africa, the reactionary regime of Philibert Tsiranana was toppled in a military coup by the progressive General Gabriel Ramanantsoa and forthwith through his articulate Foreign Minister Lieutenant Commander Didier Ratsiraka, declared that Madagascar was canceling the convention under which South Africa was to build a five-star hotel on the Island of Nossi-be.

The reaction following Madagascar's popular revolution, was regarded in South Africa as a great setback of the country's outward policy. However, the changed trend in Madagascar left only Malawi on South Africa's evil bandwagon. Dr. Banda and Tsiranana were personal friends and both were quisling puppets of apartheid South Africa and working to undermine the efforts of the liberation struggle in southern Africa.

Malawi has no common borders with South Africa or Zimbabwe, but has with Mozambique in east, west and southwest. Scholars and academics of African affairs often use this to justify Malawi's cooperation with the Portuguese colony. However, this argument is invalidated by the fact that there are other countries in Africa which have no direct access to the sea (Botswana, Zimbabwe, Zambia, Central African

Republic, Chad, Uganda, Mali, and Niger, for instance). These countries had not been obliged to abdicate their independence as Malawi had virtually done to Portugal, apartheid South Africa, and Rhodesia.

The territorial exchange agreement signed between Malawi and Portugal gave the right of access to the Indian Ocean in exchange for the right to use Malawi territory for military maneuvers. This liberty was used by the Portuguese security forces in February 1966 to bomb a peaceful village in the Mponda district, southeast Malawi, where fifteen innocent Malawian citizens were killed. The Portuguese suspected the village harbored FRELIMO combatants. The sad part, however, was that the Malawian reactionary regime was unable to claim that there had been violations of territory because the terms of the agreement invalidated any protest Malawi might have made to the United Nations, and the Malawi government, instead, chose to ignore the public outcry.

Malawi had diplomatic relations with Portugal at the Consulate level, the only independent African State to do so. The Malawian diplomat in Lourenco Marques, as I mentioned in the previous lines, was a Portuguese himself and one of top political advisors to President Banda. Many of business, security officers, and constructors of Portuguese origin, also acted as the President's advisors. Malawi's identification with Portuguese reactionary policy was at the expense of self-determination of the oppressed people of Mozambique, Angola, Guinea Bissau and the Cape Verde Islands.

The Republic of Malawi had also identified herself very closely with the countries with expansionist territorial policies and planners which made them active satellites of American imperialism. I have also to remind you that Banda also claimed parts of Mozambique which was strongly supported by Portugal and South Africa. As is well known, the United States State Department viewed the anti-colonial struggle in the early 60s as a threat to the United State interests in Africa. The satellite states were used to encourage the policies of neutralism and nonalignment and to mask independence and western control. The role of Israel, is perhaps the most indicative of this.

Banda's policies were both a shame to the people of Malawi and retrogressive to the liberation struggle of mother Africa. On several occasions, Banda asserted that the settlements of whites in Rhodesia, South Africa and the Portuguese colonies of Angola, Mozambique, Guinea Bissau and the Cape Verde Islands were authentic but he denounced the Arabs in the north, especially the atrocities committed by the successive reactionary Arab regimes in Khartoum against African population of southern Sudan. However, much as I disagreed with Banda's countless policies, I agree with him on this point of view, but I strongly disagreed with him that the settlements of the whites in southern Africa were legal.

The presence of South African military personnel and Rhodesian covert agents in Malawi did not slow down the pace of the liberation war in Rhodesia either. As the Mozambican border with Rhodesia was then vulnerable to incursions by freedom fighters, the war in Rhodesia was in its conclusive phase. It was therefore, absolutely clear that the imperialists and their running dogs, such as Banda, were losing the war to the nationalists. In mid 1978, an executive jet was brought down by ZIPRA forces in the area northeast of Zimbabwe killing all eight top military and senior government officials including the pilot, all on a reconnaissance tour in the war zone.

This was a turning point of the liberation endeavors and a major blow to the racist minority regime of Ian Douglas Smith and the white community at large. The emotions were high and talk about unconditional peaceful solutions was the subject of discussions in most white households.

After exhaustive and at times temperamental deliberations at London's Lancaster Constitutional Conference on the Rhodesian independence dispute, it was fundamentally agreed to grant independence to Rhodesia on the basis of one-man, one-vote general elections. The elections were handily won by Mugabe's ZANU PF on tribal and regional lines which still exist in Mugabe's dictatorial regime. Zimbabwe achieved her independence in 1980, and Robert Mugabe became its first African President and ran the nation as his personal estate.

The independence of Zimbabwe left Malawi marooned and virtually surrounded by progressive states. Dr. Banda had no other alternative, but to cling onto South Africa, Israel, and Rhodesian white mercenaries for his survival. Indeed, the fall of Rhodesia (Zimbabwe), left apartheid South Africa in the cold—it was the only remaining colonial power in southern Africa—and Africa as a whole was to see its power effectively challenged by the oppressed. South Africa's influence in Malawi remained largely symbolic. There were few interests to watch, however, ANC's Military Wing UMKONTHO WE SIZWE (Spear of the Nation) was preparing to establish itself in Mozambique.

The scenario brought shock waves to the apartheid regime in South Africa. Geographically, Mozambique has longer stretches of borders with Malawi than any of her immediate neighbors, therefore, South Africa felt it imperative to watch events unfolding from the Malawian territory. To some extent, it used PIDE agents which were still in Malawi (at the request of Dr. Banda) to track down Malawian dissidents.

The independence of Zimbabwe, however, strengthened the membership of the Front Line States in their bid to liberate the last bastion of imperialism, South Africa. Right at the outset, the three prominent members; Zambia, Tanzania, and Botswana, did not in any way trust Banda's Malawi because it had already entrenched itself with the enemies of the African liberation struggle. Malawi's neo-fascist regime headed by Banda, was, therefore, further isolated in the region, making Malawians willing tools of the oppressors of their brothers and sisters in southern Africa on one hand, and Africa in general, on the other. The isolation of the neo-fascist regime was real, to say the fact. Malawians in other African States were treated with suspicion—it was generally taken for granted that they were under the payroll of the imperialists, in other words, they were categorized as outright sellouts.

It happened to me personally in Algiers, Algeria in September 1978. I boarded Russian National Airlines from Dar es Salaam International Airport (Julius Nyerere Airport) to Moscow, USSR and from there proceeded to Havana, Cuba to attend the Afro-Asian International Conference on Youth. In Algiers, we were joined by other delegates from South Africa's ANC, Namibia's SWAPO, Mozambique's FRELIMO and Zimbabwe's ZAPU. I was leading the Socialist League of Malawi (LESOMA), an opposition movement based in exile. At first, my seat was beside two vacant spaces which were later occupied in Algiers by delegates from South Africa and Mozambique. I recognized that they were part of the delegation to the Conference and I introduced myself as a Malawian. Forthwith, I could see the reaction, the atmosphere changed and I noticed a moment of dead silence among us.

We left Algiers at 1:30 PM for Moscow. After we were in the air and I had settled down, I went to the washrooms and on returning to my seat, I found the two seat mates had left. They were talking to the man who had been sent to Dar es Salaam to accompany us (delegates). I had no doubt whatsoever in my mind that the two young men were complaining against me being part of the delegation. Victor Oleg spent a few days with me in Dar es Salaam and he came to understand my unwavering political stand against the Malawian reactionary regime. He assured them that I was part of the delegation with principled commitments and therefore there was no need for them to suspect me as Banda's spy. After sometime, they were convinced to return to their seats. As they settled down, they found me cool and focused on reading a book by Ernesto Che Guevara, a Cuban revolutionary. After a while, one of them was intrepid enough to tell me what they though about me, but after being told who I was by Oleg, they were convinced that I was part of the delegation and they both developed a relaxed mood in my presence. We eventually became comrades in the struggle against the common enemy. After I had shown my passport issued in Dar es Salaam by the United Nations, they felt very free to exchange ideas with me because they carried the same passports.

The isolation of the neocolonial state was so real that Cecilia Kadzamila, Banda's unofficial first lady, embarked on initiatives to make friends through bribery. Kadzamila was the richest woman in Africa and surrounded by the grinding poverty among other Malawians. In Africa, women connected to political leaders, in one way or the other, wield unprecedented powers and influence over their partners. Kadzamila took on Bet Kaunda, the wife of former Zambian President Kenneth David Kaunda. After a spell of telephone conversations, Kadzamila paid a semiofficial visit to Zambia in mid-70s, carrying with her a load of precious gifts for the Zambian First Lady. Bet reciprocated by paying an official visit to Malawi and carried a special message from President Kaunda, then Chairman of the Front Line States, to Dr. Banda. Towards the end of 1970, Dr. Banda paid an official visit to Zambia at the invitation of President Kaunda—"fait accompli."

Malawi's despotic leader was lavishly welcomed and was repeatedly described by Zambian media as Africa's statesman. What hypocrisy? A few years preceding his State visit, the same Zambian media described him as "an imperialist stooge" for claiming part of the Zambian soil. Before his visit, leading Malawian exiles living in Zambia were placed under house arrest until after the departure of Dr. Banda. Soon after his departure, both countries established diplomatic relations at the ambassadorial level.

The establishment of relations between the two neighboring nations was a blessing in disguise for South African intelligence agencies in view of the fact that Zambia gave sanctuary to thousands of South African exiles, and the ANC, South Africa's largest political organization had its headquarters in the capital of Lusaka, Zambia. The Malawi Embassy therefore became a home to South African spies holding Malawian diplomatic passports. Not only that, these spies conducted espionage activities on South African exiles. Malawian exiles living in Zambia were also prime espionage targets.

In October, 1973, Augustine W. Bwanausi (a former rebel minister), Pemba Ndovi, and Nyalugwe died in a very suspicious car accident on a road between Lusaka and Ndola. To the horror and astonishment of the Malawian citizens, Dr. Banda and his henchmen held a dinner party at Colby Community Hall (Kwacha Community Centre) in Blantyre to celebrate the deaths of three Malawian sons deemed enemies of the Life-President Hastings Banda. Since the establishment of diplomatic relations, Malawian exiles in Zambia, especially those who lived in Lusaka, experienced a hard and dangerous life. Their movements were strictly curtailed and closely monitored and they were not allowed to engage themselves in subversive activities against the neocolonialist regime of Hastings Banda. On one occasion, President Kaunda threatened to deport the exiles back to Malawi, but was sharply criticized by the international community and the United Nations Refugee Commission.

The next target on Kadzamila's mission was to win over another influential First Lady, the late Sally Mugabe, the wife of corrupt octogenarian tyrant Robert Gabriel Mugabe. What started as unofficial telephone contacts and ended up with established goodwill gestures between the two highly placed ladies. Sally Mugabe made the first unofficial visit to Malawi to test the waters in 1982. Although the visit was unofficial, the nation's media went into a frenzy with headline stories appearing in government owned newspapers. However, in Banda's era there were no privately owned newspapers operating in the country. On her way back to Zimbabwe, Sally was overwhelmed by the way she had been received. Besides she was given personal gifts by Malawi's unofficial First Lady, Cecilia Kadzamila and the Women's Organization which, of course, was patronized by Kadzamila herself. The gifts included jewels, clothes, handbags shoes and many other valuables including an undisclosed amount of cash. Sally was not only impressed with the gifts, she highly admired how her newfound friend was adored together with her partner Hastings Banda.

Within a month, Cecilia Kadzamila reciprocated with a similar visit carrying additional personal gifts to further cement their dubious friendship. Malawi's former strong lady who had unprecedented influence over her partner's thirty years of brutal repression against Malawians, was given a thunderous welcome at Harare's State House by ZANU PF women wearing colorful cloth depicting Mugabe's portrait.

At ZANU's first convention after independence in 1983, President Banda donated US$3 million to cover the expenses. For the country listed as one of the poorest in the world, US$3 million was an unprecedented waste. It was like taking the water from Lake Nyasa to fill the Indian Ocean. This was an outright waste of meagre resources from an impoverished nation struggling to balance its budget, but Banda knew what he was doing—it was not for the interests of the poor nation, but for his own ego. The strategy hit directly on the nail. President Robert Mugabe paid an official visit to Malawi in 1984. However, because of Banda's past treacherous record during the liberation struggle, some of Mugabe's senior Cabinet Ministers declined to accompany him. Dr. Herbert Usheukunze, then Minister of Health, Edgar Tekere, former Minister of Trade and Industry and Dr. Nathan Shemuyarira, former Minister of Information and Mugabe's high-class henchman, expressed their anger privately at the visit to the person that hobnobbed with the racist regime of Ian Smith.

The state visit of President Mugabe to Malawi highlighted Banda's desire to mend his past sellout policies on liberation endeavors. Indeed, it was Banda's diplomatic triumph after decades of virtual isolation. To the astonishment of the Zimbabwean people and indeed, to Malawians themselves, Mugabe was on record of paying more state visits to Banda's Malawi than to Zambia, Tanzania and Mozambique, the countries that overwhelmingly contributed their meagre resources towards the liberation of Zimbabwe. In fact, without the support of these three Pan-Africanist states, the liberation struggle in Rhodesia (Zimbabwe), would have been both ineffective and impossible.

During Mugabe's first state visit to Malawi, he observed, firsthand, Banda's personality cult at work. He was impressed to see that Banda was not only regarded as the supreme leader, but also a demigod and worshipped by the entire nation. Mugabe had, indeed, analogous sentiments. He loved to be worshipped, and he regarded himself the most learned Zimbabwean. Banda was his best model. On one occasion, Mugabe asked Banda, "What is the magic behind you domesticating the entire population for so long without encountering any resistance?" Banda proudly replied, "It is simple President, pick some troublemakers, deal with them ruthlessly and then, the rest will learn a good lesson. Forget about all this nonsense of democracy, exert stringent control over your subordinates and put in use the divide and rule policy and build around you an unprecedented culture of personality cult, that is how President, I have managed to turn these people into a submissive society for a long time." Banda concluded with laughter. Henceforth, Mugabe graduated with honors from Banda's school of thought.

In May 1990, President Banda paid an official visit to Zimbabwe to attend the country's tenth independence anniversary celebrations. At independence, President Banda had not been invited, instead, the late Dr. Attati Mphakati the militant leader of the exiled opposition, the Socialist League of Malawi (LESOMA), was invited.

On arrival at the Harare International Airport, Dr. Banda demanded that the National Television and Radio Station should address him by his full title, "His Excellency, the Ngwazi Life-President Dr. Hastings Kamuzu Banda." He also asked for the full form of address for his partner, "Mama Cecilia Tamanda Kadzamila," who was always at his heels. His demands in a foreign country, baffled most of his hosts, some blamed senility as a factor to such unbecoming behavior by the visiting Head of State, but in actual fact, this is what he expected. At home in his country some people landed into prison for omitting parts of the title. At the time he was 99 years of age.

As soon as he settled down at the Airport VIP Lounge, he sent out a message through the Malawi Embassy (which had been established during the white minority regime of Ian D. Smith) that all Malawians resident in Harare should line up along the road from the airport to the city centre to cheer him as he drove past. Later, when he realized there were not enough Malawians to line the seven-kilometer route, he ordered them to gather at the Town Hall instead, where he was due to be conferred the Freedom of the City of Harare. Some misguided supporters duly obliged, sang and chanted the scarcely accurate message, "Zimbabwe ndi Malawi Tagwirizana" (Zimbabwe and Malawi are united). But Malawi made an alliance with the oppressors of the black majority during the liberation struggle.

The Malawians in Zimbabwe raised US$5,000 of their hard earned money for personal use of Dr. Banda and his partner, despite the fact that he was one of the very richest men in Africa, though from the poorest country in the world. Sadly, the majority of Malawians in Zimbabwe were finding it difficult to make ends meet.

The US$3 million Banda donated to Mugabe's ZANU PF, had a tremendous political impact. Soon after the Malawian President left after his visit to Zimbabwe, the leader of Malawi Freedom Movement (MAFREMO), Dr. Edward Yaphwantha, was arrested and deported. Malawi's murderous secret agents were allowed into Zimbabwe to work with Mugabe's notorious secret police to track down Malawian exiles opposed to Dr. Banda's regime. Many exiles were duly deported, others including myself, were detained under very inhumane conditions.

After the release of Nelson Mandela the former South African President in 1992 following 28 years of incarceration, President Banda offered Mandela's ANC US$3 million—not with an open heart, but in a bid to appease ANC on one hand, and the people of South Africa on the other. More than once, Banda denounced ANC and other freedom fighters as communist terrorists.

Unlike Mugabe's ZANUPF, Mandela's ANC declined to be cajoled and betrayed by their conscience in preference of financial bribery. Even though Mandela visited Malawi a few months after he was released, it was not motivated by any financial offer but by a congeniality with the oppressed masses of Malawi under Banda's brutal regime. The President of Malawi shocked the entire group of independent black states when he treacherously defied international opinions to visit apartheid South Africa in 1972, while Mandela was still in prison—and after he had signed the infamous military pact with Pretoria which stipulated, among other things, that the attack on Malawi could be interpreted as an attack on South Africa and therefore, the Republic of South Africa reserved the rights to come to the defense of an ally.

Perhaps, the move of the Malawian government to extend unprecedented support to RENAMO bandits fighting the legitimate Mozambican government, was the highest stage of betrayal seen in novel history.

Revolutionary National Movement (RENAMO), was formed during 1976-1977 in Rhodesia, present day Zimbabwe, by Jorge Jardim, a Portuguese multimillionaire and Malawi's former Consul-General in Mozambique and also a PIDE Director. Initially, RENAMO was comprised of disgruntled Portuguese whites who fled Mozambique after FRELIMO's victory in 1975. To be effective enough in Mozambique, Africans were recruited to join forces, these were from different political factions such as Comite Revolutionario de Mozambique (COREMO)—in English, the Mozambican Revolutionary Committee. Andrea Matadi Matsangaise was appointed its overall leader and Radio Africa Livre (Radio Free Africa) which aired anti-FRELIMO propaganda material from Salisbury (Harare) was passed on to him from Portuguese whites.

After the Rhodesian white minority regime of Ian D. Smith was toppled by African nationalists in 1980, Radio Free Africa was transferred to Natal, South Africa where it continued to air malicious propaganda against the Mozambican government under FRELIMO. RENAMO did not encounter problems in recruiting combatants, hundreds were drawn from

Malawi where they were operating under PIDE during the liberation war in Mozambique against FRELIMO. Thousands more were drawn from political prisoners and hard-core criminals freed from government prisons throughout the country by initial RENAMO guerrillas trained in Rhodesia, South Africa, and Malawi. RENAMO, to say the fact, had no political platform, its leaders had no direction, they were merely misguided opportunists and hoodlums used by diehard Portuguese reactionaries to destroy Mozambique and ultimately embarrass the new nationalist government under FRELIMO.

After the demise of Andrea M. Matsangaise under mysterious circumstances, Alfonso Dhlakama, one of the worst of the rogue rebel leaders, took over the reins of RENAMO leadership. The bandit organization never starved from a cash shortage to sustain the treacherous war machinery. Former Portuguese business people, with multimillion dollar investments worldwide, provided substantial financial help to the bandits of RENAMO. Meanwhile, after the collapse of the Rhodesian racist regime, the Republic of South Africa became the main backer and supporter of the bandit movement financially and otherwise. The first passport Dhlama used to travel abroad, particularly to western Europe and the Americas, was issued in Pretoria, South Africa in 1982 under the pseudo-name of Steve Jabulani.

After the Salazar regime fell in Portugal, Jorge Jardim who was then living in Lisbon temporarily and was a wanted man by the new regime of military officers, took refuge in the Malawi Embassy in Lisbon before fleeing to Malawi under a Malawian diplomatic passport. Jardim, Malawi's former "Honorary Consul" in oMz-ambique, appointed in 1964 (soon after the famous Cabinet Crisis) was a Beira businessman and godson of the former Portuguese nefarious dictator Antonio Salazar, the owner of Beira's daily newspaper, Noticias da Beira, and a powerful figure within the notorious colonial secret police, PIDE.

It was Jorge Jardim, after the formation of FRELIMO in 1962, who tempted Banda that if he could help the Portuguese in their fight against communism and FRELIMO, he stood to gain the entire northern half of Mozambique, a territory that surrounds and dwarfs Malawi in the southwest. However, the Portuguese colonists had not bothered to develop the land and therefore, there was little use for this territory anyway–though President Banda had long coveted it. To emphasize the point, Jardim gave Banda an old map of the region, purporting to show the size and significance of the ancient Malavi Empire. Banda later showed the map to the late Julius Nyerere, President of Tanzania and one of the greatest Pan-Africanist of our time, thereby trying to convince him that much of Mozambique belonged historically to Malawi. As expected, Nyerere snubbed him and warned him not to fall into imperialist machinations that could lead to a maelstrom in that volatile region.

But the warning came too late, Banda was already playing into the hands of the imperialists. Malawi had already become an overseas province of Portugal and a Bantustan of apartheid South Africa. When some of the FRELIMO dissidents who had formed a splinter group, COREMO in Lusaka, Zambia, Jorge Jardim supported it and urged Banda to give them shelter in Malawi. COREMO later changed its name to, Uniao Nacional Africana da Rombezia. Rombezia was the name to be given to the new territory, stretching from the Rovuma River on the Tanzanian border to the Zambezi River in central Mozambique, land that Banda anticipated could become part of a Greater Malawi.

The fact that the only potential routes for Malawi's exports and imports are two main railway lines that run across central and northern Mozambique, one to Beira and the other to Nacala, also figured in Banda's thinking. On his first visit to Lisbon in 1962, soon after the attainment of self-government, the magazine, Jeune Afrique reported that he went to trade "Nationalists for the Railway." Malawi had completely abdicated her independence to the Portuguese reactionaries thus turning Malawians into political slaves of foreign powers. Malawi assisted the oppressive colonial army with transshipments of fuel and military hardware. Malawian gunboats were manned by Portuguese and its crews were trained by them to patrol Lake Nyasa which forms part of the borders with Mozambique and Tanzania. They were seeking to halt FRELIMO infiltration. Toward the end of the war, however, the traitor on seeing the direction in which things were heading, finally allowed FRELIMO to use Malawian soil on a limited basis. FRELIMO by then had already liberated more than half of the Mozambican territory and, therefore, Banda's offer was outright rejected.

After FRELIMO gained control over Mozambique in 1975, Jorge Jardim convinced Banda to give sanctuary to the colonial secret police, PIDE, along with some FRELIMO deserters and the President obliged by incorporating them into the Malawian army, police force, intelligence agency and civil services. The ramification was that many Malawians lost their jobs to accommodate Portuguese rogues and their African accomplices.

Meanwhile, the Uniao Nacional Africana do Rombezia, was renamed Africa Livre (Free Africa). However, the name was not strange, it was the name of the Radio Station that Rhodesia had set up for RENAMO when it was launching sporadic armed attacks into Mozambique. Africa Livre remained a minor destabilizing force, and was eventually folded into RENAMO in 1981, after RENAMO's then new sponsors, the South Africans, decided to open a northern front inside Mozambique using their long time client Malawi as a rear base and strategic ground.

What goes around, comes around. RENAMO's attacks on the roads and railways in Mozambique put Malawi in a very desperate situation. More than 65 percent of Malawi's external trade passed through Mozambique. After RENAMO rogues cut the line to Beira in August 1982, South Africa, Malawi's foremost supporter, gave its Bantustan State 55 new heavy duty trucks. However, the trucks were not sufficient to cover the shortfall. Then the line to Nacala was cut in 1984, forcing Malawi to export its entire 1985 tea and tobacco crops by air, at staggering costs. By then, a huge part of Malawi's external trade, like that of its landlocked neighbors, was passing through the Republic of South Africa.

To add insult to injury, the signing of the worthless Nkomati Accord between Mozambique and apartheid South Africa in 1984, exacerbated Malawi's exigency. South Africa transferred RENAMO's remaining bandits to Malawi's main external rear bases. There, the anti-FRELIMO elements in the country's civil service and South Africans training Malawi armed security forces, were apparently appreciative to receive such an assistance. Malawian buses and trains were seconded to provide transport for RENAMO fighters to the battle fronts. RENAMO had exploited the huge number of Mozambicans living in Malawi, by forcing them to join the fighting—all with the help of the Malawian government which was directly involved in the Mozambican internal affairs.

In fact, Malawi had virtually become a Portuguese overseas possession. They controlled almost everything after the British M16 relaxed its influence in Malawi. Heavy and frequent traffic of military jets and helicopters were observed into Mozambique airspace from Malawian air strips in Zomba and other parts of southern Malawi. Injured RENAMO thugs were carried back to Malawi for medical treatment, with the result that thousands of Malawians were denied medical attention—all in preference of RENAMO bandits. RENAMO's petrifying military successes in central Mozambique in 1985-1986, that included the capture of a number of district capitals, could never have happened or been achieved without the express support of the neocolonialist regime of Hastings Banda.

A good number of RENAMO's top Commanders and other top officials, were issued with Malawian diplomatic passports. Alfonso Dhlama traveled with one of these, under the pseudo name of Brighton Lenga, issued in Blantyre in 1984. Banda all along had denied harboring RENAMO bandits. But the late Samora Machel's display of RENAMO leaders' passports issued by the Malawian government, at his meeting with President Banda face to face in September 1986 (where the leaders of Zimbabwe and Zambia were also present at SADCC meeting in Lusaka, Zambia) proved that Banda was lying all along. Also among the documents were transcripts of radio messages sent from Malawi to RENAMO's Commander Alfonso Dhlakama. Most of the radio messages came from a RENAMO representative referred to as "Joseph," but the Mozambican intelligence sources believed that to be the code name of a Portuguese reactionary Jorge Jardim, then residing in Blantyre, Malawi. The messages were sent first in English, and then translated into Portuguese. The most astonishing scenario at the Lusaka meeting, which was meant to tell Banda point blank to cease forthwith from supporting RENAMO bandits, was that President Robert Mugabe remained docile. But his soldiers along side of those of Mozambique died in defense of Mozambique's soverignty. That prompted speculations that the US$3 million that Banda donated to ZANU PF first convention in 1984, shut down Mugabe's big mouth.

The meeting in Zambia was part of a concerted effort to end Malawi's support for RENAMO. Later Samora Machel almost lost his temper and threatened to close Mozambique's border with Malawi and even to mobilize missiles along the border. Even though most of Malawi's trade was passing through the South African ports of Durban and Port Elizabeth, it still had to transit through territories of its neighbors. Though Banda had consistently denied that he had ever supported RENAMO bandits, he at last conceded his involvement in Mozambique's internal affairs. Forthwith, after the crucial September meeting, he expelled as many as 15,000 RENAMO fighters based in Malawi. However, for Mozambique, the expulsion of these thugs meant more trouble in the offing. RENAMO launched one of its most successful onslaught yet, driving toward the coast and Quelimane, with plans to cut the country into two and declare, at last, the northern half of the country, an Independent Republic of Rombezia.

The reaction from the Mozambican government and its ally, Zimbabwe, was swift and decisive. They managed to halt RENAMO short of Quelimane, and in 1987, launched a counteroffensive. By July 1988, government forces with its Zimbabwean allies, had re-conquered towns all the way to the Malawian border.

The aftermath was that the fighting had devastated the whole of central Mozambique sending more than a half-million people flooding into Malawi as refugees, and suddenly making Malawi the host of the highest ratios of refugees to population in the world. But this was Malawi's own creation by supporting RENAMO which had no real political direction. Indeed, the situation created an unprecedented sense of desperation in one of the poorest nations in the world. It attracted a great deal of worldwide attention. Aid and relief groups made their way into Malawi along with foreign journalists, whose presence in the country was disturbing to Banda's murderous regime. But there was nothing that the beleaguered regime could do. Foreign journalists were banned in Malawi, but those who were allowed into the country, were obliged to toe the government's line. Equally, local journalists were no exception. They had to dance to the government's tune otherwise they could end up in the country's notorious concentration camps. After the Malawi government had succumbed to world pressure, foreign journalists poured into Malawi without hassles and immediately learned the reasons why they had been expressly banned by the Police State. However, the RENAMO bandits had finally been expelled. But at what price nationally and internationally?

Banda's close alliance with Africa's arch foe, South Africa, raised unprecedented speculations that Samora's tragic demise in a plane crash a few months after threatening to mobilize missiles along the border with Malawi, prompted violent reactions in Harare, Zimbabwe where Malawi's Embassy was attacked by an angry mob suspecting Malawi's involvement along with that of apartheid South Africa in Samora's untimely demise. In Maputo, the capital of Mozambique, Malawi's Embassy was likewise attacked by angry Mozambicans who believed that Banda, in alliance with the Boer regime, killed their President in cold blood.

Not only was it that RENAMO enjoyed the blessings of the Head of State Hastings Banda. John Tembo, Banda's notorious henchman (after he relinquished his post as the Governor of the Reserve Bank of Malawi, possibly as a result of American pressure on the World Bank) had been working for Banda in the Sanjika Palace and frequently traveling abroad as his special emissary. In September 1987, Banda summoned the top brass of the army and police and intimated that he wanted Tembo to take over after his demise.

It is said that both the army and police told him point blank that it would be impossible to provide effective security for Tembo and his niece Cecilia Kadzamila–Banda's partner for more than two decades.

As a result of that meeting, Tembo and Banda began to seriously consider RENAMO as a better security option after Banda's impending demise. It could not be an accident of history that about this time the RENAMO bandits suddenly intensified their activities in the Angonia District of the Tete Province of Mozambique, an area adjacent to the Dedza District of Malawi (also populated by Ngonis) from which Tembo comes. Whatever the explanation, it was also during that period that Tembo became very active as an emissary of Banda—shuttling between Malawi and the SADCC capitals carrying special messages from Banda on various issues including on RENAMO which was not well received.

However, Malawians saw this as part of buildup for Tembo whose human rights record in the country was frightening. This act which could have certainly delighted apartheid South Africa (with considerable investments in Malawi, much as Tembo had himself invested in South Africa), could be best suited to protect and safeguard their economic as well as military and security interests in Malawi. During the dying days of Banda's regime, Tembo and his niece Cecilia Kadzamila were linking persons between RENAMO and Banda on one hand, and apartheid South Africa on the other. However, as time went by in their bid to usurp national leadership, with RENAMO as a power base, they could no longer be regarded as an asset in view of the concerted efforts of the Mozambicans themselves, supported by Africa, to root them out.

Malawi was not the only African country with connections to RENAMO. The Kenyan regime, itself neocolonial with far right views, supported RENAMO from at least mid-1988—more than a year before the corrupt Kenyan tyrant Danie Arap Moi was asked to mediate in the bloody Mozambican national conflict. As from July 1988, Kenya supplied financial and material support to RENAMO bandits through the Malawi government. Kenya and Malawi, both puppets of western imperialism, did not contribute to the liberation struggle of Africa. Instead, both regimes maintained strong political and economic relations with Africa's oppressors.

The sad part of it, however, is that the former Organization of African Unity (OAU) buried its head in the sand pretending as if nothing went wrong despite the fact that one of its Charters stipulated that its members would not interfere in the internal affairs of other member states. Unfortunately, Malawi and Kenya, clearly meddled into the internal affairs of the independent State of Mozambique, but the OAU remained totally indifferent. Amongst the leaders of Africa, only the late President of Tanzania, Mwalimu Julius Kambarage Nyerere, condemned Dr. Banda for the treacherous path he had taken against Mozambican independence and in defiance of the OAU charter.

It is no secret that Malawi played a devastating role in the destabilization of Mozambique by supporting RENAMO thugs who committed untold atrocities against innocent fellow Mozambicans under the notorious leadership of Alfonso Dhlakama whose activities were related to former Liberian tyrant Charles Taylor and Uganda's heartless cultist rebel leader Joseph Kony. But despite political change in Malawi, no formal apology has been conveyed to the government and people of Mozambique by successive governments particularly, that of Bakili Muluzi, who of course could have known better what was happening then as Secretary-general of the dreaded Malawi Congress Party and the second highest ranking official in the government.

The current political and economic crisis engulfing many parts in the Continent, are attributed to our leaders' lack of vision and commitment. As soon as these leaders are voted into power, their first priority seems to be to amass wealth and manipulate national Constitutions to suit their political agendas. Alas, it is Africa's leaders who have failed Africa.

But it is not too late to rescue Africa from these deep-rooted problems created by greedy individuals. Empires have collapsed, walls have crumbled, and indeed, despots have fallen. When the masses of Africa finally emerge victorious over their oppressors sooner rather than later, Africa will reclaim her rightful place among friends of our world.

Chapter Ten

THE STRUGGLE FOR DEMOCRACY

The struggle for democracy in Malawi had been long, risky, and painful. In reality, it had been spearheaded by exiles under most daunting circumstances while the majority of the present leadership were part and parcel of the most despicable regime in the Continent of Africa. Soon after the attainment of self-government in 1961, the late Dunduzu Kaluli Chisiza saw the need for a radical change of leadership in the view of the fact that the country was heading in the wrong direction under Hastings Banda's leadership.

On September 9, 1964, the revolt by cabinet ministers against Banda erupted into an open crisis signifying a new chapter in the country's political history. Even though Banda's henchmen and sycophants treated the revolt with derision, the exigency was most unique in the African context in the sense that it is highly unusual for cabinet ministers to covertly, or overtly, challenge feared despots who also wield unprecedented powers.

The revolt, as I have endeavored to explain in previous chapters, was ignited by principled desires for political emancipation and a sense of self respect which were, apparently, on the verge of disappearing entirely. The revolt, however, had nothing whatsoever to suggest that the able ministers attempted to usurp power or leadership of the dreaded Malawi Congress Party (MCP). In essence, these true sons of our soil, were driven by their convictions to establish a truly independent and democratic nation.

After the rebel ministers were convinced that there was no chance to resolve the crisis for the interest of the people of Malawi on one hand, and Africa on the other, they agreed in principle to form a political party that would represent the aspirations of the people and placed itself as an opposition Party on the national level. They were strongly convinced that any effective opposition activities could be based within the country. The concept was received with unanimous consensus among the majority of the people of Malawi. Even before the notion was made official, Banda realized his position was threatened. Hence he embarked on a Mugabe-style approach—he organized political thugs and militias to intimidate supporters through state-sponsored violence. Real and imagined supporters of the rebel ministers were beaten up, their homes burnt down. Their meetings were frequently disrupted by rogue gangs organized by the Malawi Congress Party (MCP) under the leadership of Aleke Banda and Gwanda Chakuamba Phiri—both later becoming Commanders of the most feared Young Pioneers (Banda's personal thuggish militias).

As the crisis deepened each day and the support for the rebel ministers gained increasing momentum, their lives were exposed to real danger. New ministers that Banda had appointed after the crisis were of questionable merit, most of them being academically decapitated—men such as Albert N. Muwalo, Gwanda Chakuamba Phiri, Q. C. Chibambo, Gomile Kumtumanje, and Aleke Banda. John Tembo, though a graduate from an Indian university, fell below intellectual standards. Also among the appointees was John D. Msonthi, a promising star, but he betrayed his talents and conscience for personal gains. He died a mysterious death while serving in Banda's cabinet.

These misguided people engaged in covert plans under the leadership of President Banda to liquidate the rebel ministers—Banda's prime targets. They were followed wherever they went and watched at whatever they were doing. Finally, they reached a conclusion that they could do something better in exile than in their graves. Chipembere's popularity had no bounds, being extensively popular among students, civil servants, teachers, farmers, factory workers, and rural populations.

The support the rebel ministers received from the masses of our people worried Banda and his sycophants and he made it quite clear that his foes were to be ruthlessly dealt with once and for all. It was this scenario that led to the rebel ministers' exit. They had no choice. They had to flee into exile.

During the first multiparty general election campaigns to be held in thirty years, the same people who conspired to eliminate the rebel ministers, told their ill-informed supporters that Kanyama Chiume and Masauko Chipembere brought Hastings Banda into the country only to dump him on us while they themselves lived sumptuously in exile. Though this piece of cheap propaganda resonated among the voters, it ignored the realities of exile life.

Back in Dar es Salaam, Tanzania in 1973, Masauko Chipembere, to his uttermost astonishment, found his colleagues divided. At first, he thought ideology could be the factor. He wasted no time in trying to reunite them as he strongly believed that unity at that trying moment was more crucial than anything else. However, it was later apparent to him that ideology was not the issue at stake. His colleagues had revisited old differences created by Banda in order to divide and rule them.

The worrisome scenario Chipembere encountered was the extent to which Kanyama Chiume and Yatuta K. Chisiza had separated due to their differences. Both men came from the north and were Tumbuka speaking. The late Orton C. Chirwa and Yatuta Chisiza were good friends since both were in the cabinet and the late Augustine W. Bwanausi had left for Zambia where his brother Dr. Harry Bwanausi had lived after a bitter disagreement with President Banda and before the crisis erupted.

To make things worse, there was pressure from one group of Chipembere's supporters urging him to dump Kanyama Chiume and from another group pressuring him to dump Yatuta Chisiza. Indeed, Masauko found himself with a dilemma in trying to make a decision on that divisive issue at the precise moment in the struggle when unity meant either we destroy or build. The obvious case was to remove Banda. The exiles and Malawians of goodwill would then have to embark on an armed struggle reminiscent of Fidel Castro's revolution against Cuban dictator General Fulgencio Batista in 1959. Masauko, therefore, needed the expertise of both—Yatuta Chisiza on the military front and Kanyama Chiume playing a vital diplomatic role.

Before Chipembere arrived in Dar es Salaam from the US where, after a spectacular escape from Malawi in 1965, he was living with his family, Yatuta Chisiza had gone to China for military training that took him nine months to complete.

As differences dragged on and chances of resolving them appeared remote, Yatu, as he was popularly known to his supporters, was left with two options; to remain in Dar es Salaam and engage in further fruitless talks to end the dispute, or, go ahead with the revolution without his colleagues. Ultimately, the latter was his decision.

Yatuta led a group of 16 strong and highly trained combatants into Malawi in September 1967, through eastern Zambia. The tactic which the fighters had followed was that of the "foco" system, a pattern of revolution applied by Major Ernesto Che Guevara (who died in Bolivia the same year as Yatuta Chisiza). Yatuta died on October 12, 1967 in a battlefield at Mpatamanga Bridge, a battle described by white mercenaries recruited by Banda from apartheid South Africa and racist Rhodesia, as "fierce and heroic." Certainly, the tragic demise of one of the illustrious sons of our soil escalated Banda's propaganda image of invincibility—it added credence. There was everything to suggest that the policies of Banda had solidly taken root in Malawi.

Yatuta's heroic determination to fight for the liberation of his people had been in vain. There was not even a popular uprising, indicating that the people of Malawi had been completely tranquillized and succumbed to their own slavery.

Combatants who fell in action with Yatuta were C. J. Lutengano Mwahimba (former top civil servant in the Ministry of Commerce and Industry and one of Malawi's early university graduates) and Felix Mwaliyambwile. Those captured and found guilty by the Malawi High Court were executed in early 1969, including: G. Bonongwe, Tomango Chidawati, Suwedi Masamba, James Kamanga, M. Moyo, G. M. Mwakawanga, M. 1. Mphwanthe and Harris Phombeya.

The casualties on the part of the government were said to have been considerable. The (unofficial) information leaked out of Malawi and confirmed by one government official (who remained anonymous) was that there were about 200 government troops killed and 100 Young Pioneers. Widows and dependents received monthly salaries and were told that their husbands or sons had been sent abroad for further training.

Yatuta Chisiza's bold attempt to unseat a neocolonialist and a most brutal regime, marked the end of physical opposition. Still, the exiles were not disconcerted. They spearheaded the struggle for democracy diplomatically and by means of organized covert political cells in the country—always ready for another push. The stratagem of the exiles was at times futile and disappointing but in a small way it managed to isolate Malawi diplomatically—especially among progressive African states—leaving the puppet government stuck to apartheid South Africa, racist Rhodesia, and fascist Portuguese East Africa (Mozambique).

The defeat of Yatuta left Banda in tight control of the sadistic regime and with tremendous support from his masters in the so-called western democracies. At one of his humdrum public meetings, he did not mince his words. He told his people (to the accompaniment of wanton ululation and clapping) that he was in full control of the State and that he could go so far as to reside in London and still rule the country from there with precision. Admittedly, Malawians are best known to have courageously and indomitably fought against the imposition of the Federation of Rhodesia and Nyasaland and also against

British colonialism. It is therefore amazing that they would wittingly sink so low under the abominable abusive of power and the brutal atrocities of Hastings Banda—a charlatan acting against innocent masses of our people.

However, the fall of Yatuta did not in any way or form create a dent on the morale of the exiles despite the unprecedented difficulties met in the course of carrying out an effective opposition against the so-called independent state. Revolutionary activities were kept very much alive.

To this effect, Masauko Chipembere formed a political party known as Pan-African Democratic Party of Malawi (PDP), based in Dar es Salaam, Tanzania, and with a powerful branch in Zambia represented by the late Augustine Willard Bwanausi (a brilliant mathematician and former senior Minister of Social Development and Housing). The Party enjoyed massive support among a million Malawians living in Tanzania and an equal number in Zambia. In Malawi itself, circumstances hindered significant progress in recruiting potential members. However, in Karonga and Chitipa Districts, both border towns with Tanzania and Zambia, impressive recruitment drives were recorded. Clandestine cells were established to discuss programs and strategies. I was astonished and encouraged when I attended a secret meeting in Kapolo, Karonga on March 6, 1974, to find youths there from as far away as Mangoche and Blantyre (some 600 km south). (To get to the meeting, I passed through the official border post disguised as a local Muslim trader with hundreds of pieces of propaganda material in my possession.)

Such was the situation at the official crossing at that time. It was, indeed, an ideal situation for infiltrating armed cadres and preparing the ground for protracted revolutionary warfare. One thing I observed after two nights of secret meetings—the majority of people lived under absolute fear and had good reason for that. Practically speaking, Malawi had virtually become a Gestapo state, people could not trust even their own shadows. Generally, I left with the impression that people inside the country were ready to sacrifice their lives for a noble cause—provided they were led by trustworthy and committed leadership that, in the end, could produce fruitful results.

Innuendos, intrigues, and mistrust continued to flourish among exiled Malawians and, most importantly, within the party structures. Masauko Chipembere was, more than ever before, convinced that any real and sustainable struggle against the Banda regime had been outright betrayed and there was no chance to dislodge Banda in the near future—he was too strongly backed by western imperialist nations for their own economic and political interests.

The infighting, unfortunately, had reached unstoppable proportions. It appeared highly probable that external forces had infiltrated the inner circle and sown seeds of confusion within the party. The most damning accusation was that Chipembere was not a Malawian in view of the fact that his parents and grandparents had lived outside Malawi and therefore this disqualified him from becoming a leader. That such an irrelevance could be used to discredit a leader and distract attention away from problems of increasing significance was amazing. Indeed, the biggest problems were the continued oppression of Malawian people on one hand, and, the exploitation of the Malawi resources for the benefit of overseas lords, on the other. Indeed, the accusations made against Chipembere could be more appropriately leveled against Hastings Banda who had no roots in Malawi and his parents and grandparents were virtually unknown. Chipembere had been involved in the front lines of the nationalist struggle since he was in his 20s—and right along side his friend and brother Kanyama Chiume who was one year older than him. He suffered the most at the hands of colonialists and, yet, he didn't enjoy the fruits of his sweat.

From the time of his arrival into the United Republic of Tanzania from the US in the early seventies, President Banda increased espionage activities into that country by using the dreaded CIA and MOSSAD to his advantage.

In early 1974, Chipembere published a pamphlet entitled "My Malawian Ancestors" in which he elaborated on his roots and, thereafter, he hurriedly left for the US with all members of his family. His departure to say the truth, left a big dent, not only within the party, but also in the liberation struggle against Banda's puppet regime. For a little while, Kanyama Chiume took over the leadership of the Party (PDP) which was then on the verge of collapse. And it did not last long. It met its demise during the early stage of his leadership. As expected, the departure of Chipembere was good news to Banda because he had been a thorn in the dictator's flesh. He hurriedly told his people, "Masauko Chipembere has ran away back to the US and his PDP is dead. He is a coward." He further warned Malawians, especially Chipembere's supporters, that rebels would not succeed with toppling his government as long as he was still alive. The warning, however, had an irreversible impact on Malawians, the majority of whom longed for political change.

The most devastating news to the exiles, and indeed, all Malawians back home, was that of the tragic and untimely demise of Masauko Chipembere in the US in 1975. He had been undergoing studies for a doctorate and teaching. In an apparent mood of jubilation, Banda officially announced the death to his people at a public rally in Rumphi, the rebel stronghold in the north. Indeed, Chipembere's untimely departure at the moment when Malawians most needed his gallant leadership, instilled within them an intense sense of fear and desperation. The defeat of Yatuta Chisiza on a battlefield and the death of Masauko Chipembere, both gallant and illustrious sons of our soil, gave Banda an upper hand in dealing with internal dissent.

In March 1976, Kanyama Chiume launched his own party in Dar es Salaam, Tanzania, and named it the Congress for the Second Republic of Malawi (CSR). The party's objectives were to continue with the struggle for democracy and thereafter create an independent free society in a Socialist State based on cultural heritage. The party also envisaged a nation free from the entrenched tribalism created by Banda and his Malawi Congress Party. It anticipated leaving the doors open for liberation movements to operate from Malawian soil. The CSR also aimed to break the colonial and artificial boundaries and work for unification and regional cooperation.

As divisions escalated within the exiled camps, another political party was formed in July 1976, this time by Orton E. C. Chirwa, QC. He was a former powerful Minister of Justice and Attorney General and founder, and first President, of the Malawi Congress Party (MCP). He named his new party the Malawi Freedom Movement (MAFREMO) based in Dar es Salaam, Tanzania and with branches in both Malawi and Zambia. MAFREMO was among several exiled movements opposed to President Banda's deleterious policies. A stalwart of the pre-independence nationalist movement, Chirwa was, apart from holding senior cabinet posts in Banda regime, Chairman of the Disciplinary Committee of the Malawi Congress Party and one of the nationalist politicians who gained Banda's grudging respect because of his education and his status as a distinguished lawyer.

MAFREMO promised to establish a free democratic state and put an end to the unprecedented tribalism and regionalism Banda and his dreaded Malawi Congress Party had institutionalized in the country—detrimental to both national unity and developmental progress. MAFREMO could also commit the nation's meagre resources to enhance the liberation struggle in Southern Africa and to maintain closer ties with liberation movements in order to realize and hasten meaningful achievements in their endeavors.

Earlier on, the Tanzanian authorities had expressly warned the Malawian exiles of divisions which could disastrously impede their efforts to defeat Banda's reactionary regime—which had become a launching pad of the western imperialist blocks. It also warned them of suspicious activities by some people masquerading as refugees from Malawi.

On Christmas Eve of 1981, Orton E. C. Chirwa, his wife Vera Chirwa (a lawyer) and their son Fumbani C. Chirwa, a mechanical engineer, were seized by Banda's foreign-dominated security services on the Zambian-Malawi border. Their seizure served as a virtual stumbling block for democratic change in Malawi.

In 1983, Orton and Vera, both prisoners of conscience, were convicted of treason after an unfair trial in a traditional court presided over by illiterate judges with connections to the Malawi Congress Party. They were initially sentenced to death, but the sentences were commuted to life imprisonment with hard labor after intense pressure from the international community on their behalf. A few months later, President Banda made a scathing remark in a speech in Blantyre, the commercial hub, in which he accused Orton Chirwa of continuing his political activities in prison and of circulating critical leaflets from his prison cell. The President was reported to have said that Orton and Vera did not deserve the clemency that had been shown them.

On July 17, 1987, Orton and Vera were transferred from Mikuyu Prison (dubbed "Auschwitz" for its notoriety) to the equally brutal Zomba Central Prison, built by colonialists in early 40s, where the conditions were also beyond man's endurance.

During an earlier period of incarceration at Zomba Central Prison, Orton and Vera were manacled for long periods each day and handcuffed to an iron bar at night—thereby deprived of sleep. Neither could they move freely in their separate tiny cells—lit by only a small hole above their heads that served as a window. Under these brutal conditions Orton, then in his late 60s, suffered adverse health. His wife Vera, who had suffered poor health for some years, suffered further deterioration in prison. Her acute high blood pressure worsened and she was at times even denied her usual dosage of medication. Orton Chirwa himself developed severe eye cataracts while in prison and was denied medical attention.

Vera Chirwa, as a woman, endured the same painful conditions in prison as if she were a criminal felon. For three months in 1986, and again between January and March 1987, she was locked-up and chained—both arms and legs. She was repeatedly chained day and night with handcuffs attached to a metal peg in the ground so that she could not stand or move. Her cell by all standards, was inhumane. It was like a matchbox. It was five to six feet wide and nine to 12 feet long. Equally, Orton Chirwa endured unprecedentedly severe treatment. He was frequently brutally beaten by uncouth prison warders, subjected to frequent electric shocks, and worse still, frequently starved.

Mr. Orton Chirwa was found dead in his small noxious cell in early 1992, shortly before all political prisoners were ordered to be released as part of demands by the opposition parties and the international community. The circumstances surrounding his tragic demise indicated, beyond reasonable doubt, that Chirwa was murdered and had not died of natural causes as the sadistic government suggested. The government's attempt to conceal or suppress news of his death, and the circumstances surrounding it, therefore, put a massive question mark over Banda's sincerity when it came to political dispensation.

There was a massive display of opposition to the government when an estimated 55,000 people marched to the funeral of Orton Chirwa, the veteran leader of MAFREMO. One report suggested that during the funeral procession a suspected provocateur was beaten to death when the crowd descended on him thinking that he had planted a bomb in the car carrying Chirwa's children. Orton was laid to rest in his home village of Manola in the Nkhata Bay district in the country's northern Region. Banda's government, though it allowed the Orton's children to return from exile for the funeral, did not allow his wife Vera, then still in prison, to attend the funeral

After Chirwa's death, Dr. Edward Yaphwantha took over the leadership of MAFREMO. With assistance from a middle-east nation, Dr. Yaphwantha in March 1986, sent a group of ill-equipped young fighters into northern Malawi through the Kyela-Karonga border post. During these skirmishes two policemen were killed before the young fighters fled back into Tanzania. The Tanzanian government under the corrupt leadership of President Ali Hassan Mwinyi started to cultivate political relations with Malawi (after decades of hostility between the two neighboring states because of Malawi's treacherous policies over Africa's liberation struggle). At the same time, Dr. Yaphwantha was hurriedly issued with a warrant of deportation that took him to Zimbabwe—a risky choice for anti-Banda activists. Indeed, Robert Mugabe, a cold-blooded thug, was the strongest supporter of Hastings Banda in southern Africa. He adored him and embraced his autocratic stance. As expected, Yaphwantha's stay in Zimbabwe was unwelcome and he was ordered out of the country within 24 hours of his arrival, otherwise he would be sent back to Malawi to meet his final fate.

The leader of MAFREMO headed back to East Africa—to Uganda, under President Yoweri Mseveni. When Malawi was gripped with multiparty winds of change in 1993, Dr. Yaphwantha, instead, went to Zambia leaving MAFREMO leaderless and hence precipitating its natural demise. Meanwhile, two exiled-initiated movements, the Pan-African Democratic Party (PDP) and the Malawi Freedom Movement (MAFREMO), dropped out of the struggle leaving CSR alone and on the move.

In March 1977, another movement was formed and joined the fray—the Socialist League of Malawi (LESOMA) led by a young, charismatic, and brilliant economist Dr. Attati Mphakati. It was based in Dar es Salaam Tanzania, with branches and cells in Zambia, Malawi, and Mozambique. Of all the exiled movements, LESOMA proved both militant and focused and its members and leaders were largely drawn from the younger generation throughout the country.

As other movements before it, LESOMA strived for a new and fair deal for all the people of Malawi, to create a new society, and to build a new nation that could strive for the unification of mother Africa. LESOMA also promised to introduce into the country a socialist system based on our cultural heritage and against the man-eat-man society which was consistently encouraged by the former cold-blooded despot Hastings Banda's Malawi Congress Party (MCP). LESOMA also aimed to encourage that the resources and wealth of our country be equitably shared among its people and to guarantee the formation and full participation of workers, students, professionals, peasants, and intellectual organizations. Grass-root women's movements were to be encouraged and would replace the elitist feminist movements which were led by mistresses of politicians and served no useful purposes. Women could participate in politics at the same level as men in order to hasten the steps for their own emancipation. (Women in Malawi had been virtually turned into political tools for their own oppression and slavery.)

LESOMA was convinced that only armed struggle could remove Frankenstein Hastings Banda from power. In this regard, the movement wasted no time in establishing a military wing to carry out that sacred duty. The wing was called the Malawi National Liberation Army (MNLA) under the leadership of John Chikwakwa, a former youth leader. Forthwith, recruitment exercises were undertaken and hundreds of young men were recruited from within the country and sent to Libya and other Middle East nations for military training. Additionally, the movement's Education Committee sent other hundreds on scholarships to study in different fields in eastern Europe. I was among the successful candidates who went to the former Soviet Union (Russia) to study journalism.

Meanwhile Dr. Attati Mphakati the late charismatic leader of LESOMA moved to Mozambique and lived in Maputo amid an insurgency initiated by RENAMO thugs in Mozambique. There were multiple advantages for Attati to operate from Mozambique. First, he spoke fluent Sena, the dominant local dialect of northern Mozambique and the bordering populous districts of southern Malawi. He also spoke Lomwe, another of the dominant dialects in southern Malawi.

With free movements of people along the border Attati quickly established potential contacts that resulted in the express formation or establishment of powerful covert cells or nuclei to hasten the processes of armed revolution. The leader of LESOMA also miraculously succeeded, to a large extent, in recruiting cadres from such vital sources as armed forces, police, intelligence agencies, and the civil service sector. This put LESOMA closer to a position for armed rebellion, the movement's ultimate stratagem.

Attati's successes in his new front caused a commotion in the enemy camp that prompted Banda's western imperialist friends to track Attati's activities and movements by means of the watchful eyes of the dreaded CIA, MOSSAD and South Africa's BOSS.

On April 19, 1977, Dr. Attati Mphakati, the militant leader of LESOMA, was attacked by a powerful parcel bomb in the capital of Maputo, Mozambique—an explosion that blew off eight of his fingers. The following day, Banda, boastfully told his boisterous rubber-stamp Parliament that one of the most cunning dissidents, Dr. Attati Mphakati, had been killed in Maputo by a bomb—foolishly unaware that Attati had escaped death. Dr. Banda further told his henchmen, "My boys carried out this attack." Having said that in a jovial mood (in public and quoted by international news media) the Mozambican government, surprisingly, remained silent and indifferent to this brutal and provocative act of violence carried out against the integrity of the state. Not only did Mozambique remain indifferent, the defunct Organization Of African Unity (OAU) and the rest of independent African states also buried their heads in the sand as if nothing serious had happened that deserved the condemnation of the continental watchdog.

Finally, Dr. Attati Mphakati was murdered in cold-blood on February 20, 1983. His mutilated body was found in a storm drain in the city centre of Harare, Zimbabwe. Attati vanished as soon as he finished clearing with airport immigration at the Harare International Air Port at 1:30 PM from a

Maputo-Harare flight by Mozambican Air Ways (LAM). It is widely believed that Attati was abducted by professional MOSSAD assassin-agents in league with Malawian notorious Secret Police which operated freely in collusion with Zimbabwe's most feared State Security Agents. At the head of the Malawi agents was an Israel-trained assassin attached to the Malawi Armed Forces, the late Colonel Liyabunya, who traveled from Malawi earlier by road via the Chirundu border post on the mighty Zambezi River which separates Zambia and Zimbabwe. Liyabunya stayed in a hotel near where Attati's body was found.

In the aftermath of Dr. Mphakati's death, Brighton Matewele, a radio announcer with the Zimbabwe Broadcasting Corporation (ZBC) (who also happened to be Attati's tribesman) and Greenson M. Mhango, a Malawian diehard opportunist working in Zimbabwe and recruited by Malawi Secret Police, were subsequently arrested in connection with Attati's tragic death. In fact, Dr. Attati Mphakati stayed in a city hotel where Greenson Mhango was working as a manager.

Mr. Brighton Matewele and Greenson Mhango were released without being charged and Colonel Liyabunya escaped via Bulawayo—the second largest city in Zimbabwe—and then into the apartheid Republic of South Africa. Attati's left hand was severed, for reasons nobody knows. In view of the fact that two of the suspects were set free and the third one knowingly fled to escape justice, it seems clear that the Zimbabwean government was directly involved in Attati's mysterious demise. One of the most critical of Banda's regime in Mugabe's cabinet was the late Hubert Usheukunze. He described Attati's death as "brutal" and asserted that in Zimbabwe someone can be slaughtered like a "chicken." However, Usheukunze's assertion was also echoed by a large number of Mugabe's senior members in his ruling ZANU PF and equally by exiled activists who also condemned the government's handling of Attati's death.

However, the tragic death of Attati Mphakati, the young charismatic and visionary leader, created a sense of uncertainty among exiles and the majority of our people back home. Grey Kamnyembeni, a neophyte and little known in the country, was elected as the new leader of LESOMA—a fractured movement.

Another victim of Banda's evil campaign against the exiled communities was Journalist Lifford Mkwapatila Mhango who was based in Lusaka, Zambia and worked for the Zambian "Daily Mail." He was killed on October 17, 1989, only three weeks after Banda had publicly denounced him. Lifford died of severe burns, along with nine members of his family, including a six-month old baby girl, as a result of a firebomb attack on his Lusaka home.

The motive behind the horrific murder was that Mkwapatila who lived in exile in Zambia, had published an article exposing corruption in the national women's organization, the CCAM which was led by the richest and most wicked woman in the country–Cecilia T. Kadzamila—who purportedly acted as "Official Hostess" to the cold-blooded tyrant Hastings Banda. Unofficially, they lived as husband and wife for over thirty years. Kadzamila and her uncle John Tembo who wielded unprecedented influence and power under the Banda regime, were behind concerted atrocities against Malawians especially the Tumbuka-speaking people of northern Malawi. They bore the brunt of Banda's tribalistic administration.

In a deathbed interview, Mkwapatila asserted that he had no doubts whatsoever that it was the notorious agents of the Malawian regime who carried out the heinous attack. In February, 1991, Mkwapatila's brother, Dr. Goodluck M. Mhango was brutally assaulted by state-sponsored militias and subsequently imprisoned at the Mikuyu death camp without charge. Both the Mhangos hailed from northern Malawi. Lifford was secretary for the exiled MAFREMO in Lusaka, Zambia.

Within a few months of Lifford's horrific murder in Lusaka, the suspected killers were arrested in different parts of

Zambia. They were all Malawians connected to a government-sponsored murder squad trained at the military base in Salima, Central Malawi by military experts from Rhodesia (Zimbabwe), apartheid South Africa, and fascist Portugal. It is reported that they were in Lusaka for a number of months for reconnaissance led by Lifford's home-boy who had gone to Lusaka earlier on for surveillance.

The suspected killers were named as, George Kuntepa, Bright Phiri, Kelly Nkhoma and Ishmael Zimba. What is generally known is that one of the criminals, Ishmael Nkhoma died in a police cell in Lusaka on November 20, 1989. There is no information whatsoever pertaining to the other three. There is speculation that they were handed over to the Malawi government covertly and prior to any wind of change sweeping across Africa. If this information were correct, then it was a mockery of a humanist belief that was embodied in President Kenneth Kaunda's government.

Fundamentally speaking, the exiles, though few in numbers, kept the banner of the revolutionary struggle high and sustainable despite brutal and ruthless reprisals from the Banda regime which was tightly controlled by former colonial powers—Britain on one hand and apartheid South Africa, Israel, Rhodesia and other western imperialist nations on the other. As for other African nations, especially Malawi's neighbors, only Tanzania under the progressive leadership of late Julius Kambarage Nyerere came forward to help politically and materially. However, the Tanzanian government alone, with its meagre resources could not be expected to do much as it was also preoccupied with the hot issue of the liberation struggle of southern Africa whose entire movements were based in Dar es Salaam, Tanzania.

In east Africa, Kenya, a neocolonial state was in place under Jomo Kenyatta's leadership. In March 1965, two prominent exiled leaders and former cabinet ministers Kanyama Chiume and Augustine Bwanausi traveled to Nairobi, Kenya, to meet government officials there and to explain to them the political situation in Malawi and the reasons why they disagreed with President Banda on major foreign polices pertaining to southern Africa. Kenya itself, like Malawi, did not recognize or help liberation movements from Southern Africa such as ANC, ZAPU PF, ZANU PF; SWAPO, PAC, FRELIMO, FNLA and MPLA. Kenya and Malawi both established economic and political relations with evil regimes that violated fundamental human rights and which were condemned by all the peoples of our planet. Kenya's Vice-president Jaramongi Oginga Odinga, a fervent African nationalist, was very much willing to receive the exiled Malawians and to have a chat with them, but he was also in a precarious political situation similar to what the Malawians had gone through.

As expected, Kanyama Chiume and Augustine Bwanausi had their request rebuffed and the President, the late Jomo Kenyatta, issued stern warnings to the Malawian exiled leaders to leave the country within twenty-four hours otherwise they could be deported directly to Malawi. The two ardent Malawian nationalists, however, were not taken aback in view of the fact that the neocolonialist regime of Jomo Kenyatta, had started harassing promising and emerging young nationalists who agitated for an unadulterated Pan-Africanist image in Kenya—in line with other progressive African States.

As in Malawi, Kenyan reactionary authorities felt threatened by young progressive nationalists steadily attracting a potential following from among a disgruntled majority of the people who strongly felt that Kenya's independence had been betrayed by Kenyatta's leadership. Politically motivated assassinations began to show its ugly head in Kenya, prominent nationalists such as Tom Mboya, James M. Kariuki, Gama Pinto and many others, were brutally murdered in cold-blood. Moreover, there are unprecedented suspicions that the gallant leader of former Mau Mau Liberation Movement, Dedan Kimathi, was betrayed by KANU top insiders.

It is generally accepted that it was easier and less risky to fight former colonial establishments than to fight African dictatorial regimes. The former were, to some extent, democratic and tolerant—apart from apartheid South Africa and the Portuguese colonies—while the latter are led by rogues and kleptocrats who are void of moral principles. It has taken Malawians almost thirty years to see their dreams come true. Inside the country, the masses were completely subdued by Banda's reactionary regime which was awash with money from western nations—money granted to protect their economic and political interests.

The struggle for democracy in Malawi had passed over enormous stumbling blocks. But the fall of the notorious Berlin Wall in the early 90s opened a new chapter in the world history. In no time, oppressed masses around the world—Malawians included—seized the golden opportunity for their conclusive advantage.

In Malawi, Catholic bishops hurriedly issued Lenten Pastoral Letters which were read on the first Sunday of Lent on the 8th of March 1992 in all Catholic Churches throughout the country. The letter was an open and strong challenge to Banda's obnoxious regime of thirty years following the famous Cabinet Crisis of September 1964, when the illustrious young nationalists revolted against Banda. In their letter, the bishops strongly denounced the increasingly unjust distribution of the nation's wealth, the widespread economic and political corruption, and the acute inadequacy of health and education services. The letter, however, was received with unprecedented jubilation and determination by an enormous number of Catholic followers on one hand, and by the majority of Malawians, regardless of their faiths, on the other.

The reaction from the oppressive regime of the charlatan, was swift and panicky in a sense. Banda could not, in any way, believe that such a challenge could come in his lifetime. Two days after the release of the letter, the notorious police summoned the letter's signatories for what turned out to be an interrogation during which the bishops were repeatedly accused of sedition. Though all known copies of the letter were confiscated, they had served their purpose even though the government-controlled Malawi Radio announced that possession of the letter was a criminal offense. However, the vehement nature of the response by the nation's atrocious establishment and the reported threats to lives of the bishops, prompted countless religious leaders throughout the world to express their strong solidarity with the Catholic Church in Malawi.

Among others who expressed their solidarity with the bishops of Malawi were; the Bishops' Conference of England and Wales, Missio (Munich and Achen), the Flemish Justice and Peace Commission for Internal Church Affairs (Germany), the International and Development Affairs Committee (Church of England), Miserior (Germany), Commission of Justice et Paix (Brussels, Belgium), Canada Religious Conference, and the Missionary Sisters of the Holy Rosary (Ireland). However most of these organizations either remained unconcerned about violations of human rights in Malawi during the cold war or they supported Banda's inhuman regime.

After all, President Banda was an Elder of the Church of Scotland and highly respected and exalted as Africa's wise statesman. One of Banda's strongest weapons in his whole political career was his policy of "divide and rule" and the outright lies which characterized his rule. However, the shock-wave of the fall of the Berlin Wall was irreversible, it was felt thousands of miles beyond its borders and with progressive effects.

Old habits die hard. Amid the crisis Banda tried to divide the Roman Catholic Church in Malawi and Church of Scotland by driving a wedge between them. Banda alleged that the two prominent denominations had bad relations existing between them. To this effect, the Church of Scotland reacted angrily over the President's remarks and issued a strong rebuttal through its Department of World Missions and Unity on March 16, 1992. It insisted that the freedom to teach the Christian faith, including its social aspects, must be guaranteed and respected by the government. The Church went on to warn Banda that the two churches were sister churches with proficient working relationships at all levels and, therefore, his policy of divide and rule was a nonstarter.

Perhaps, the church's stern warnings against any threatening actions taken against the Catholic bishops in Malawi gave Dr. Banda second thoughts. As the crisis heated up, the Church of Scotland made it a matter of public record that President Banda had been excommunicated and emphasized the fact that it was not correct to describe Banda as an Elder of the Church of Scotland. It made no meaningful sense. However, the denial of the Church of Scotland could not hold water in the sense that during the quarter of a century Banda had been in power, he was expressly known as an Elder of the Church of Scotland. In Scotland too, he was known as such. The excommunication which was long over due, was put in place to mollify the international community. The Church of Scotland (quoted from an anonymous source) claimed that the Church excommunicated the tyrant because he was living with a concubine in violation of the Church's norms and there was a growing international outrage about his abysmal human rights records that were contrary to Christian beliefs.

The Lenten letter appealed to Malawians from different walks of life that the issues juxtaposed in the letter required ongoing and more in-depth reflection. It added that it was the Church's mission to preach the gospel which affected the redemption of human race and was the liberation from every oppressive situation, be it hunger, ignorance, blindness, despair, paralyzing fear, and so forth.

The letter was collectively signed by;

Archbishop: James Chiona of Blantyre Diocese,

Bishop: Felix E. Mkhori of Chikwawa Diocese,

Bishop: Mathias A. Chimole of Lilongwe Diocese,

Bishop: Alessandro Assolari of Mangochi Diocese,

Bishop: Allan Changweza of Zomba Diocese,

Bishop: G. M. Chisendera of Dedza Diocese, and

Monsignor: John Vincent Roche, Apostolic Administrator of Mzuzu.

Msgr. John Roche was Irish-born and based in Mzuzu, northern Malawi. He was singled out as the ring leader and author of the Lenten letter.

In subsequent weeks, the dreaded Malawi Congress Party (MCP) leadership, at their meeting on March 27, 1992 in Lilongwe, and chaired by President Banda himself, conspired to abduct and kill the Catholic bishops. Roche was the prime target. But by the grace of God, the plans were botched at the last minute when he was called out of his Cathedral in Mzimba, northern Malawi. There he had been giving a sermon for Good Friday. He was forthwith deported. Roche had lived in Malawi for twenty years. In all, more than a hundred thousand copies of the letter were distributed across the country.

Fundamentally and realistically, the Pastoral letter ignited the engine of change, change that had been badly sought for thirty years under the most oppressive regime in African history. The international religious groups, indeed, hastened the pace of political change in Malawi and instilled into the people an immense sense of fearlessness that enabled them hold the bull by the horns.

After a month or so of the Pastoral letter which was extensively read in the country, not only by members of the Catholic Church, but also by members of all denominations across the country, political pressure mounted against the Banda regime. Exiled movements which spearheaded democratic change even before the publication of the Lenten Letter, buried their hatchets and agreed to operate under one united front to enhance the vehement political challenge over the visionless Malawi Congress Party regime which was uncompromisingly indifferent to multiparty democracy.

In March, 1992, the United Front for Multiparty Democracy (UFMD) was inaugurated, encompassing exiled factions in Lusaka, Zambia. On March 10, 1992, the Southern Africa Regional Institute for Policy Studies based in Harare,

Zimbabwe, the Fredrick E. Foundation, and the United Front for Multiparty Democracy (each representing different political persuasions) met in Lusaka, Zambia, with the tacit support of Fredrick Chiluba the former disgraced Zambian President. Robert Mugabe had refused permission to hold the conference in Harare, Zimbabwe, in view of the fact that he would enrage President Hastings Banda—whom Mugabe held in high esteem.

It is alleged that the UFMD had sent eleven airline tickets to enable activists from inside Malawi to attend that historic conference in Lusaka. The said tickets were alleged to have been sent through the late Chakufwa Chihana who, according to an anonymous source of information, was not duly invited to attend the conference. To the utter astonishment of the conference's organizers, Chakufwa Chihana arrived alone and when asked the whereabouts of the remaining ten tickets, Chihana could not give a convincing explanation. The mystery surrounding the ten tickets, however, still remains unsolved hitherto. To be fair to Chihana, he presented a well-prepared speech in the conference. He cited greed, the lust for power, and tribalism as causes for the economic and political instability in the country. He also condemned narrow-mindedness and lack of patriotic interests to overcome rational and sober approach to national issues. However, Chihana could not propound the mechanisms that could be established in a new Malawi—politically and economically. Instead, he openly advanced his own political ambitions in the corridors of the Conference Hall.

Chihana was forthwith advised to deal with the pressing issues affecting the future of the nation and leave the question of leadership for the people to decide at a national convention to be held at a future date inside the country. The conference had no rights whatsoever to impose a leader on the majority of the people from outside their country. To quote his own words, Chihana had this to say: "Some of us may have high expectations and political ambitions." After his bid for leadership of the national multiparty movement had been ignored, rumors swirled within the Conference Hall that Chihana would return to Malawi soon. He was sternly warned not to launch a political party while in Malawi until the conditions were absolutely ripe.

Chihana quietly left Lusaka on March 21, 1992, before the end of the conference via the Jan Smuts (Oliver Tambo) Airport in Johannesburg, South Africa. He finally returned home on April 6, 1992 where he was forthwith arrested at the Lilongwe International Airport by the notorious undercover agents as he was preparing to read his speech to awaiting reporters.

Mr. Chihana remained behind bars until December 14, 1992, when he was sentenced to two years imprisonment for possession of seditious material and 18 months (to run concurrently) for the importation of seditious material. Originally, he faced five counts of sedition and two counts of acting to undermine confidence in Banda's government—including saying that 90 percent of Malawians wanted a change of government and that President Banda was too senile to run the country. These five charges, combined, carried a sentence of 35 years in prison. Banda hired two British lawyers at the expense of taxpayers to lead the prosecution against Chakufwa Chihana.

Chihana did not receive a fair trial in the sense that the court system in Malawi was also held prisoner by Banda who ran the nation as his personal estate. The nation had two court systems as I have already indicated in previous chapters, the traditional court which tried Africans only and the conventional courts for all races. There was no legal representation within the traditional court system, yet it was here the government directed most cases involving murder, sedition and treason. Sometimes President Banda or his office just decided that no court should entertain a particular case.

As the struggle for democracy intensified and appeared unstoppable, the US government, the traditional supporter of the Banda regime, sent a stronger and more public messages to the Malawi government about human rights concerns.

Though the US cut its aid to Malawi from US$38 million to $22 million in 1992 because of the nation's horrendous human rights records, the Lawyers' Committee wanted the IMF and World Bank to likewise suspend new loans to Malawi until Banda's government changed its policy on human rights.

After the fall of the wanton Berlin Wall, Britain and the US became irritated with the Malawi's vicious policies and began to act positively towards democratic change in Malawi. However, untold damage had already been done. western democracies had remained indifferent to the plight of the Malawian people for a solid thirty years.

Due to international and domestic pressure, Chihana was released earlier than expected. During his incarceration, he was subjected to inhumane conditions as most political prisoners before him had also experienced. On his first night of freedom he complained that a wild cat had been put in his small cell that looked like a small leopard which grew in size as it became angry. The motive behind putting a wild beast in the cell was to scare Chihana and deprive him of his sleep. The cell was too tiny and with the size of Chihana's body and with no ventilation, there was a risk of suffocation. He was also held for almost a month in leg irons that had been imported from Sheffield (UK) for that purpose. As a result, his legs were badly swelled and he was also incommunicado from family and friends.

Chihana's return to Malawi on April 6, 1992 to challenge the Emperor of Malawi who had ruled the Southern African nation with a brutal iron fist for thirty years, was seen by Malawians of all walks of life as both courageous and heroic. However, Malawians would have welcomed anybody who spoke the language of liberation from Banda's rule. Chihana made the courageous move knowing full well that Banda could not harm him physically as the vicious tyrant had previously done to countless other political activists.

As socialism was steadily loosing its influence globally, the Americans did not want Malawi to fall into the hands of radical or extremist nationalists with connections to socialist camps or with left-wing views such as Kanyama Chiume, G. Akogo Kanyanya and to some extent, Dr. Harry W. Bwanausi. Chakufwa Chihana therefore, was singled out as America's good friend who could safeguard their economic and political interests in southern Africa. In this connection, the American government forewarned Banda not to, in any way or form, harm Chihana should he return to Malawi to present his case.

When Chihana made the decision to return home to challenge the monstrous despot, he knew already that he was in safe hands a soon as he arrived into the country–the big brother was there to defend and protect him from any harm that could be waiting for him. In thirty years, apart from the famous Cabinet Crisis of September 1964, no Malawian politician had ever challenged the omnipotent ruler in the open. The return of Chihana, apparently prearranged by the Americans, was massively construed as heroic and selfless which led him to believe that he had an overwhelming support of the Malawian people.

Believing that with the support of the superpower, he was going to be the next President of Malawi, Chihana hurriedly launched his Alliance for Democracy Party (AFORD)—contrary to the admonishment he was given at the Lusaka Conference for Multiparty Democracy. Soon the party received massive financial support from the US government to fund its campaign activities. Within a week of AFORD's formation, another party was formed under the name of United Democratic Front (UDF) under the leadership of Bakili Muluzi. He was a Muslim and a former Banda henchman and hand-picked as the Malawi Congress Party (MCP) Secretary-general. Chihana forthwith branded UDF as Malawi Congress Party "B" and UDF hit back with forceful strategic accuracy, appealing to Malawians, especially those from vote-rich Southern Region that AFORD was the Party for minority Tumbuka speaking of the north.

Chihana's dreams were shattered and that marked the beginning of the end of once mighty AFORD. It seems to me, however, the American's notion of propping up Chihana was a nonstarter. Being himself a northerner from a minority ethnic group, he could not win in any national general election in Malawi—whether rigged or transparent—in view of the fact that Banda and his Malawi Congress Party (MCP) government, had deliberately divided the country along tribal and regional lines to enhance their own political and economic self-interests.

The formation of AFORD drew immediate condemnation from exiled UFMD which had just been mandated to represent several factions in exile. A press statement signed by its interim President George Akogo Kanyanya (the veteran former MP from Karonga who resigned his seat in support of the rebel ministers during the Cabinet Crisis of September 1964) had this to say: "UFMD has dissociated itself from a group of ten Malawians who mandated Chakufwa Chihana to organize an interim committee of UFMD under the name of AFORD inside Malawi. Kanyanya went on to say that he was aware some participants to a recent seminar on prospects for democracy in Malawi, had elected Chihana to represent the UFMD in Malawi, without the organization's knowledge. The statement went on, "There have been a lot of distortions pertaining to the leadership of UFMD, but at no time, did we elect Chihana to spearhead political activities under the auspices of UFMD in Malawi."

The leadership of UFMD which had accused Chihana of political ambitions at the Conference for Democracy in Lusaka was ultimately vindicated when Chihana formed AFORD behind its back and became its President. This spelled deep trouble for Chihana and his party during a crucial transition period.

When Banda succumbed to pressure from the exiled UFMD and international groups to declare an amnesty for the exiles to return home to participate in the political transformation of new Malawi, UFMD returned home as a unified movement. It represented; the Socialist League of Malawi (LESOMA); the United Democratic Party (UDP); and the Malawi Freedom Movement (MAFREMO)—under the leadership of Dr. Y. E. Yaphwantha, the former archenemy of Banda's regime and with George Akogo Kanyanya as Vice President on an interim basis. Two prominent members Dr. Mapopa Chipeta and Frank Mayinga Mkandawire defected to join their tribe's man, Chakufwa Chihana, in the AFORD ranks. Astonishingly, the late Kanyama Chiume, the leading exile personality and an ardent anti-colonial nationalist, was not invited to attend the Conference for Democracy in Lusaka and, therefore, his Congress for Second Republic of Malawi (CSR) returned home as a separate political movement.

The reason why Kanyama Chiume was not invited to attend that historic Conference on the future of our nation, was not known, but there were speculations that some of the organizers, who themselves harbored leadership ambitions, feared Kanyama's charismatic stature and his fiery oratory. But this was not a good omen for the country which was aspiring for a decent and democratic society.

Finally, UFMD and CSR returned home toward the end of 1992 after 30 years of torturous and uncertain life in foreign lands, to put up the fight of their lives. Their return was received with mixed sentiments. Some regarded them as heroes and some alleged that they were traitors for having abandoned their people in order to live voluptuous lifestyles in exile. Having lived in exile myself for three decades, exile life is next to life imprisonment.

While it was triumphant to return home to participate in a final push for freedom and democracy, the exiled movements faced another hurdle, this time, lack of financial strength which is crucial to any election battle. The Organization of African Unity (OAU), did not recognize their status in view of the fact that Malawi was an independent state, therefore, the exiled movements were ineligible to receive the Organization's funds like the liberation movements under the racist minority regimes. This had a devastating impact on both former exiled movements while, at the same time, AFORD AND UDF had an impressive financial standing. AFORD received substantial financial assistance from the US and other powerful western nations, while UDF had its source of funds from fundamentalist Muslim countries in the Middle East. Both sources of assistance had dubious motives behind them. The Americans and other western nations wanted someone to follow Banda who would safeguard their political and economic interests. At the same time Muslims wanted to introduce Islam into Malawi and to make it a bridgehead into southern Africa.

Even though political parties had been allowed to operate, Banda still resisted the wind of change which was sweeping across the valleys and mountains of Africa with irreversible alacrity. The brutal despot had in mind that his western masters would come to his support as usual. Unfortunately for him, he was living in a cocoon of self-deception, outdated, and out of touch with prevailing realities.

Old habits die hard. Banda would not go down without putting up a last fight. He and his Malawi Congress Party (MCP) still remained opposed to multipartyism and launched into politically motivated violence that gripped the nation at a larger scale. There were indications that the government had been expecting something was going to happen. Rogues and hoodlums were hired by the government (in addition to Malawi Young Pioneers [MYP]) Banda's personal unruly militias who went on rampages beating up people, arresting opposition activists, and spreading a sense of fear and hopelessness among the population. Indeed, it was a scenario akin to Robert Mugabe's campaign of violence spearheaded by government-sponsored war veterans and street thugs.

In May 1992, a large amount of riot control equipment, including tear gas, guns, shields, padded jackets, truncheons, and training manuals were brought in from racist South Africa and distributed to Banda's militias and other security forces. The equipments were manufactured by the country's leading company—Strategic Concepts. Hundreds of young people had returned from South Africa after they had been trained in combat, especially in dealing with unarmed civilians.

As emotions burst into the open and the zest for freedom and justice, which had been virtually denied to the people of Malawi for three decades, reached a zenith. Crowds and mobs surged through the streets of Blantyre, Lilongwe, and Mzuzu looting shops and demanding pay rises and an end to one-party rule which was the major and fundamental issue. By the end of the day, over 50 people were counted dead and 375 injured. The following day other towns and locations throughout the country were exposed to violence and general disorder where also hundreds of civilians were murdered in cold-blood by trigger-happy police and other brutal agents of death.

Before the deadly riots, the Malawians' reputation for timidity and passiveness appeared to be justified. For 28 years they had allowed themselves to be ruled by a single madman without protest. The last time there were protests was in September 1964. Tom Carver, the first foreign journalist to arrive at the scene of Malawi's first uprising in May 1992, described the extraordinary rite of passage of a previously timorous and passive population.

Nonetheless, in spite of the riots (the first of their kind in the country in almost thirty years) the regime continued unblinkingly defiant in the eyes of the international community. A week after the riots, the Minister of State, John Z. Tembo, Banda's notorious henchman, issued a statement that the Malawi government would not allow pluralism in the country because the system would bring tribal wars like those in the Congo and Uganda.

Tembo seemed ignorant of the prevailing cause of the civil wars in both countries—tribal sentiments had nothing to do with the wars in either countries. In the Congo, for instance, the civil war was precipitated by foreign powers (soon after that country achieved independence from Belgium on August 15, 1960) seeking to control gargantuan mineral resources (gold, diamonds, copper, cobalt, petroleum, just to name a few). In Uganda, the brute Idi Amin Dada overthrew the civilian democratically elected government of Dr. Milton

Appolo Obote for his own selfish ends and plunged the nation into bloody conflict.

It wasn't until powerful international financial institutions joined the fray and flexed their muscles, that Banda came to his senses. On May 11, 1992 the World Bank and western donors, meeting in Paris, France, froze US$74 million of aid to Malawi—this after decades of turning a blind eye to the excesses of the self-declared Life-President Banda's regime. The donors decided that the Malawi regime no longer deserved foreign aid because of its contumacious violation of human rights and tenacious refusal to accept democratic change.

Donors were convinced that these events could ultimately trigger the long awaited turning point in Malawi's 30-year, one-party, obnoxious one-man rule. This came as a bitter blow to Banda and his horde of self-seekers. The donors had agreed that the Malawi government had failed to fit their criteria of "good government" and they decided to follow the example in Kenya, another corrupt and neocolonial government, and used further aid as leverage for political change.

During this meeting, donors demonstrated a significant change of heart toward Malawi. They no longer viewed it through their cold-war-tinted glasses. Before that meeting, a few years earlier, Malawi received unprecedented praise, especially from the US and Britain since the despotic regime had not followed the socialist path of its neighbors; Mozambique, Zambia, and Tanzania.

The fact that hundreds of Malawians had fled into political exile around the world, other thousands of political dissidents crowed Malawi's concentration camps (living in repulsive conditions), and that many government opponents had vanished, was conveniently and completely overlooked.

Here too, the Malawian exiles played a decisive role in the struggle for democracy in their homeland. From North America, Professor Dr. Peter Mtalika, the young brother of the late state President Dr. Bingu wa Mutharika, led a strong delegation to the donors' Conference in Paris to urge them to cut economic aid to Malawi which lubricated the engine of oppression against the people of Malawi. In Europe, the exiles sent similar delegations to present a common stratagem to those leaders. To their credibility, all of the exiled delegations traveled on their own personal expenses, while the delegations from Malawi Congress Party government used taxpayers' funds to represent the evil establishment.

For thirty years the Banda government had relied on economic handouts from western powers and had been held up as one of Africa's most successful models of free-market economics. But in addition, growing international outrage about its abysmal human rights record, the World Bank finally slated Malawi's economy as being grossly distorted to squeeze wealth from rural peasants into the pockets of Banda, Tembo, Kadzamila and a select group of sycophants. If it were true that Malawi's economy was the best in an African perspective, that statement was utterly fraudulent because, the skewed economic system had left Malawi with a rural population trapped in grinding poverty and with the world's highest child mortality rate.

According to the World Bank's 1992, World Development Report the mortality rate for children under five averages was 248 deaths per 1,000 births compared to 204 in war torn Mozambique, 89 in South Africa and 72 in Zimbabwe. The sad part of it was that the funds which were meant to feed the poor people of Malawi, were used to build state palaces at exorbitant costs. In one of the poorest countries in the world, President Banda built more opulent palaces than any other country in Africa. However, his sycophants construed all this as pillars of excellent national economic development.

In a Pastoral letter that was distributed to Malawians on March 8, 1992, and reproduced in full in the British paper report said in part: "In our society, many people still live in circumstances which are hardly compatible with their dignity as sons and daughters of God. Their life is a struggle for survival. At the same time, a minority enjoys the fruits of the peoples' sweat and can afford to live in luxury and wealth."

"Though many basic goods and materials are available, they are beyond the means of many of our people."

"People will not be scandalized to hear these things, they know them. They will only be grateful that their true needs are recognized and that efforts are made to answer them. Feeding them with half-truths, only increases their cynicism and their mistrust of government representatives."

The Bishops went on: "For long, we have refused to see that, beside praise of hollow achievements of the last decades, our country still suffers from many evils: economic and social progress do not trickle down to masses of the people, academic freedom is vehemently restricted, exposing injustices can be considered a betrayal; revealing some evils of our society is seen as slandering the country; monopoly of mass media and censorship prevent the expression of dissenting views; some people have paid dearly for their political opinions; access to public places like markets, hospitals, bus depots, etc.. is frequently denied to those who can not produce a party card; forced donations (when the life President visits an area) have become a way of life."

Malawi is one of Africa's least urbanized countries with 85 percent of the population living in the rural areas. The small country is also one of Africa's mostly densely populated, meaning that each family has only relatively small three to five hectare plots.

Rural life did not mean being free from politics as Banda's Malawi Congress Party (MCP) was built on a network of women's leagues and thuggish Pioneer Youth leagues which reached into villages. Very few Malawians were brave enough to refuse purchasing membership cards of the sole Party, for which they were coerced to pay in cash, and whenever the Party official visited an area, the residents were obliged to give cash donations. With these woes fresh in their minds, Malawians vowed to liberate themselves from the shackles of a fascist regime, the worst in the history of our country.

The economic fragility of the Malawian government could not resist the impact of concerted sanctions imposed by donor nations and powerful financial institutions for its intransigency. Within a month of economic pressure, cracks were visibly seen. Banda was therefore coerced to align himself with the prevailing realities. The forceful wind of change finally caught up with Banda's heinous policies and desires to thwart national aspirations toward democratic reforms, but he was still convinced that the majority of Malawians preferred a one-party system to pluralism. Therefore instead of sending Malawians straight to national elections, he chose to send them to a referendum which the opposition forces criticized as a waste of time and meagre resources.

After months of political turmoil in which Banda confronted the most concerted political opposition in thirty years, on June 16, 1993, Malawians went to the polls to cast their votes on the referendum to choose whether they wanted to live under one-party despotic rule or under pluralism.

As in most of African governments, the "culture of election rigging" is prevalent, and Malawi was no exception in this case. A statistical and demographic analysis of the voters' roll released by one of the major opposition groups asserted very strongly that the voters roll in the country could not exceed 3.2 million. The group further alleged that the register of 4.6 million Malawians, representing 50.5 percent of Malawi population, was loaded with multiple and bogus voters that could give the ruling party an advance victory of over 40 percent before the actual voting started. In other words, the multiparty verdict needed 90 percent of the vote to absorb the anomaly and achieve victory.

True to the suspicions of the opposition groups, 1.5 million Malawians did not vote. In its analysis, the United Democratic Front (UDF) reports asserted that the indelible ink obstructed multiple voters who had more than one registration certificate. In many areas, ink was washing away, but it required another hour of washing and another two and half hours of queuing to vote again.

As such, the maximum a vote-rigger could vote was four times and it required a massive operation to render the rigging effects significant. By and large, intimidation and harassment of the voters at polling stations were rampant, but this could not wear down the morale nor the desire of the long enslaved people to exercise their long awaited rights.

The referendum question was officially framed by the MCP government which did not consult the other interested parties. The referendum question to the voters read thus: "Do you wish that Malawi remains with one-party system of government with the Malawi Congress Party (MCP) as the sole political Party or do you wish that Malawi changes to the multiparty system of government?" This is how the referendum question was officially framed. As the question stood, there was no doubt that had the voters said "YES" to single party, it would have meant yes to the continuation of the MCP rule as the sole political party for another millennium. The voters, however, rejected that prospect and instead chose pluralism by an impressive 63 percent of the total votes cast. It was also significant that out of 3.2 million Malawians who cast their votes, 2 million opted for pluralism while a little over a million settled for no change. At a regional level 89 percent of voters in the north voted pluralism while the south 82 percent and in the central region 34 percent. The reason why the Central Region recorded a low percentage favoring pluralism is the fact that President Banda and his notorious dupe John Tembo hailed from the Central Region which was perceived as the stronghold of the dreaded Malawi Congress Party and its tribal base. Attempts at corrupting the votes were also revealed by the fact that of 70 percent of the votes (90 percent of these votes declared null and void) 54 percent were in the Central Region. In particular, Lilongwe had the highest number of votes nullified in the whole country.

What was the final significance of this historic aftermath? It simply meant that the MCP and its system of government no longer enjoyed the popular support from the masses of our people. It meant the Malawi Congress Party had no mandate to initiate new policy decisions for the nation on their own because they lacked the requisite legitimacy.

Soon after the results had been published, the Public Affairs Committee (PAC) under the Chairmanship of Rev. Emmanuel Chinkwita Phiri, called for the immediate formation of an interim government for the period leading to the national general elections following the landslide victory by the pressure groups. The fact that the government went to the populace made it absolutely clear that it was seeking a vote of confidence from the people. But the masses voted overwhelmingly against it and it had to face the consequences. As expected, President Banda rejected the call for an interim or government of national unity saying that the notion was not on the table. However, because of the fact that the majority of the people had overwhelmingly voted for change, it was clear that Banda and his MCP government were fast approaching the disgraceful end to an era.

The final push for long awaited democracy was imminent. Malawians had thrown away their culture of timidity and grasped a new sense of confidence in themselves aimed toward the ultimate victory for humanity over the dark forces. They gained unprecedented momentum sufficient to break the shackles of fascism once and for all. Still, the diminutive demon, he who had the touch of magic, seemed not to have gotten the message. For Banda, at the age of 103 and by far the oldest leader in the world, it remained business as usual. As in the referendum campaign, the struggle ahead was similarly full of huddles. The opposition groups were not allowed to use the state-controlled Malawi Broadcasting Corporation (MBC) to air their views. As the struggle reached unstoppable dimensions, Banda was ultimately coerced into announcing the date for national general elections.

Local multiparty movements encouraged by the previous referendum's overwhelming aftermath, gained strong momentum to drive home their unstoppable quest for freedom and justice. Meanwhile, Banda's former backers, Britain, Germany, and the US toughened the existing economic and political sanctions against the murderous regime. Finally, the so-called Messiah, as he loved to be known by his people, announced that Malawians would go to the polls in a national general elections on May 9, 1994, after precisely 30 years of brutal dictatorship. Old habits die hard. The savage despot resolved to go down fighting. As such, he let loose his thuggish paramilitary militias to intimidate, beat up voters, and in some cases to kill innocent people. Political rallies held by opposition groups were violently dispersed. However, this undemocratic tactic only served to harden people's resolve to end their long sufferings.

The isolation of President Banda and his discredited Malawi Congress Party (MCP) increased each day. Mozambique, hard hit by RENAMO thugs trained in Malawi and with numerous military bases there, prayed for change in Malawi. Former President, Joaquim Chissano and the government of Mozambique bore a deep grudge against the regime because Malawi was also used as a logistic and transit point for RENAMO bandits. The Mozambique government also suspected Banda was involved in the tragic death of Samora Machel in collusion with the notorious apartheid South African Bureau of Secret Police (BOSS) in 1986. Zambia and Tanzania were also praying for change. Zimbabwe's President Robert Mugabe was the only leader in the region to keep warm personal relations with his Malawian idol. However, he was unlikely to find many colleagues within his corrupt government who could support Banda.

To cement their perfidious relations, Mugabe's ZANU PF donated 65,000 white T-shirts with cockerel imprints from Zimbabwe (cockerel is MCP's symbol) to be used during the general elections campaign in May 1994. Ties between the two kleptocratic Presidents (Banda and Mugabe) were said to be far beyond what an ordinary Malawian eye could see. It must be noted, however, that Banda had an excellent political relationship with Ian Smith's minority regime and at the same time, Mugabe along with Zimbabwean freedom fighters were barred from entering or visiting Malawi. They were called communist terrorists. Besides the donations of T-shirts, Mugabe also donated US$4.5 million to Banda's Malawi Congress Party to facilitate election campaigns.

Apart from Mugabe's Zimbabwe, apartheid South Africa was directly involved in Malawi's internal affairs by siding with an old ally. As the election campaigns gained momentum and the opposition groups attracted thousands of supporters at their rallies, Banda and his henchmen launched a desperate attempt to remain in power by all means possible. President Banda called on South African police expertise to beef up his police force's ability to intimidate and harass the populace.

Lieutenant-General Basil Smith, a notorious individual (stained with the blood of Soweto kids) and Colonel Andre Beukes (also a brute) arrived in Malawi amid election campaigns in April 1994. The visit by these top Police Officials was described by the Malawi regime as an investigation into the dagga trade between Malawi and racist South Africa, but according to the reliable sources, the two officials were experts in counterinsurgency and political surveillance and would not likely be used for low level narcotics work. After all, there were no wide spread drug activities in Malawi to warrant such a high level visit. To make things worse, the two Police Officials, were in charge of the security police while it was covertly backing Inkatha hoodlums during South Africa's turbulent transition to democracy and justice.

Despite all attempts to intimidate and frustrate the opposition movements, it was a foregone conclusion that the days of Banda's evil rule (wherein Malawians were like sheep before their shearer) were fast approaching an end. But a big question still lingered among the majority of the people: "Could the three major parties; the Malawi Congress Party (MCP), the United Democratic Front (UDF), and the Alliance For Democracy (AFORD) establish a progressive government that would enhance; transparency, democracy, justice, and equilibrium within regional development—key features which were brutally denied to Malawians for thirty long years?"

Generally and fundamentally, all three Parties lacked key qualities of focused and progressive leadership. After thirty long years of misguided political and economic policies, Dr. Banda's MCP government had lost absolutely all touch with the people. He had instituted a countrywide personality cult without rival anywhere else in Africa. His supporters had completely lost all sense of direction. An MP, Kaphwiti Banda (no relation), who defected to the UDF during the multiparty struggle, once asserted in the rubber-stamp Parliament: "I respect the life-President Ngwazi Dr. Hastings Kamuzu Banda as the young brother of Jesus." This was not a mere joke. It is quite clear that this brainwashed MP spoke sincerely from the bottom of his heart.

As to the UDF, Malawians did not expect miracles or progressive change either. But they deeply desired political change, believing that everything else would follow in due course. All members of the UDF leadership were former henchmen and sycophants of President Banda and some were known to have committed repulsive atrocities against innocent civilians. The leader himself, Bakili Muluzi (hand-picked from the streets by Banda to be the Secretary-general of the MCP) lacked significant academic achievements. He was of the type Banda most cherished for the ease by which he could push them around. Not only did Muluzi lack an even modest education, he was an ex-criminal. He was convicted in 1968 of theft by a government civil servant and sent to prison for a number of years where he was known as Convict No. CR04517/68. However, the qualities of his leadership were to be seen in the future.

Neither did AFORD impress the majority of Malawians. It was perceived as a tribal group with a leader extremely hungry for power. For this reason the two regions (Central and South), with commanding majorities, resented AFORD. But on the other hand, the Party was comprised of young and highly educated personnel. However, right from the outset, AFORD shot itself on the foot by refusing to heed the advice from the UFMD-sponsored democracy conference in Lusaka,

Zambia, that the formation of any political party or movement by Chakufwa Chihana could be construed as a tribal oriented group. And this is what precisely happened. President Banda and his Malawi Congress Party had intentionally through unprecedented hatred of the northerners divided the country along tribal lines in order to suffocate the minority and deny them their political and economic basic rights.

To make things worse, the leader of AFORD appointed Ahmed Dassu (an Indian with very limited political experience and lacking any sense of the moral values and culture of the Malawian society) to be his political adviser. Throughout the campaign, Chihana portrayed himself as the redeemer of the long-suffering people of Malawi. Though lacking a sense of vision for a new Malawi, he was completely misled by false beliefs that he would be the next President of Malawi. After his backers, the Americans, concluded that he could not win the elections at the poll, they advised him to unite with the UDF. This he categorically refused to do so because he regarded the UDF as Malawi Congress Party "B"

In the UDF Camp, Bakili Muluzi was a nonstarter because of his close relationships with Asians of Indian origin. Following his unceremonious expulsion from the Malawi Congress Party (MCP) as its Secretary-general in 1982 (in order to pave the way for John Tembo, Banda's former notorious dupe) Muluzi had gone into the transport business with Asians. Moreover, having been propelled to power after the first multiparty general elections on May 17, 1994, he thoughtlessly appointed Lillian Patel, an Indian, as Minister for Foreign Affairs—the most strategic and prestigious position in the government. Like Ahmed Dassu, Lillian Patel was a neophyte and lacked political and economic visions of the country. This should be no surprise since she was ignorant of African values and culture and completely unqualified to represent the nation in international forums.

It is of significance that Asians of Indian origin have dominated economic establishments in Africa, particularly in East Africa, for over a century and half. In this regard, they have entrenched themselves in Malawi's political and economic spheres and thereby they gained direct accession to our leadership—at the same time making themselves the richest single group in Africa. Their closeness to the Presidents and top government bureaucrats has enabled them to smuggle millions (if not billions of dollars) to Europe and the Americas where they have established impressive businesses. Meanwhile the majority of Africans back home, their very neighbors, languish in grinding poverty.

The two former exiled movements, the Congress for the Republic of Malawi (CSR) led by Kanyama Chiume (first Minister of Education and Foreign Affairs in post-independence Cabinet) and the United Front Movement for Democracy (UFMD) led by Dr. Harry W. Bwanausi (former Director of Medical Services) were both focused and visionary. Nevertheless, they lacked funds to run effective campaigns. When Malawians went to the polls on May 19, 1994—in a massive show of defiance—more than 3 million citizens cast their votes. As expected, however, the results were based on tribal and regional grounds.

The UDF (southern-based) emerged victorious followed by the Malawi Congress Party (MCP) (central region) and the third-placed AFORD (northern region). Had it not been for UDF, the MCP could have been reelected and Banda (then at the age of 105) could have remained in power for another a million years. Both the CSR and the UFMD were completely wiped out and forthwith rendered their support to the UDF which was ready to accommodate the exiles—at least for the moment. Some of the members were appointed to ministerial posts and other positions. But, after three decades of misery and slavery, would the new political structure bring hope and a sense of foresightedness to the majority of the people?

In his inauguration acceptance speech in May 1994, Bakili Muluzi emphasized unity, transparency, and democracy as the steppingstones to building the new Malawi. To follow up his own words he immediately formed: (a) a poverty alleviation program to help poor Malawians earn decent livings,

(b) a society corruption bureau to uproot corrupt elements, and, (c) a truth and reconciliation commission to bring to justice those who committed acts of atrocities against innocent citizens and, indeed, all those who violated basic human rights. These moves were highly applauded and gave real hope to the nation's dehumanized souls.

However, sooner rather than later, Muluzi lost clear direction and things started falling apart. None of the proclaimed programs gathered momentum. The truth and reconciliation commission (reminiscent of post-apartheid South Africa) was composed of the very same people who were allegedly engaged in atrocities and ghastly abuse of basic human rights. After all, the President had himself been part of the murderous establishment that existed for thirty uninterrupted years. In his tenure as Secretary-general of the ruling MCP, Muluzi held the second highest position after Banda. It was in that era that cross-border attacks against unarmed Malawian exiles were increased at an alarming speed. Dr. Attati Mphakati (the charismatic and prolific economist and leader of the opposition LESOMA movement) was murdered in cold-blood in the city of Harare, Zimbabwe. Later, Lifford Mkwapatila Mhango and his entire family were brutally massacred in Lusaka, Zambia. The leader of MAFREMO, Orton Chirwa, QC, his wife Vera (also a topnotch lawyer), and their son Fumbabi were abducted from Chipata, Zambia. Chirwa was brutally murdered in his tiny cell in Zomba prison after eleven years of incarceration. In response to the abduction in 1981, Bakili Muluzi went public announcing that the nation of Malawi had received a wonderful Christmas gift—Mr. Chirwa and his family were abducted on Christmas Eve.

To appease both Malawians and the international community, Banda, his concubine Cecilia Kadzamila, and his closest henchman John Tembo were all arrested and taken before the courts of law to face justice for their crimes. Due to the fact that the government was ill-prepared, all three of these wicked people won their cases on technicalities and were forthwith set free. In stark contrast, South Africa's Truth and Reconciliation Commission (TRC) acted with precision and impartiality to bring the apartheid era criminals and sadists to justice. One such criminal De Kock, then 47 and a former police colonel, was found guilty of six racially motivated murders and a range of other crimes. He was convicted and jailed on October 29, 1996 for a total of more than 200 years—including two life terms.

With regard to the corruption and poverty alleviation programs, the new government of Muluzi failed miserably. Corruption became an institutionalized culture and the new government came to be perceived as kleptocratic. Malawi was correctly regarded as being among the ten most corrupt nations in the world. This prompted world's financial lending institutions, such as the World Bank and the International Monetary Fund, to cut financial dealings with the Muluzi administration. Ultimately, this resulted in far reaching consequences for the already fragile economy. Individual progressive nations such as Sweden, Norway, and Denmark also cut vital economic aid to Malawi in protest against the rising levels of graft. Funds which were intended for the fight against poverty, were diverted into the pockets of Muluzi's cronies with impunity. At one stage, thousands of metric tones of maize were covertly sold to Kenya. In Malawi at the same time there was an acute shortage of food due to a severe drought that gripped the region. As a result there were dozens of deaths due to starvation. Unprecedented speculations went around that President Muluzi was directly involved—Muluzi himself appeared to be part of the scam.

In 2000, Muluzi's government bought his good-for-nothing Ministers, a fleet of 39 new S-Class Mercedes Benz automobiles, worth a total of US$3.9 million. It had been customary for our governments' ministers to turn official trips into shopping expeditions for bulk-buying of beluga caviar. A journalist with the London Daily Telegraph once observed that so many stereos and televisions had been purchased that the homebound plane found it difficult to take off. With 75 percent of the population malnourished and government medical stores empty of vital drugs for malaria and other curable maladies, a third of all government revenues disappeared into the pockets of Muluzi's henchmen and top civil servants. Money that went astray actually escalated at this time because of a shift from project-based funding (where there is more control) to the more politically correct sector-based funding—like putting money directly into the Health Department, for example. However, when money goes into a large pool in this way, it becomes much more difficult to track how it was spent.

In the mid-term of Muluzi's administration, the general morale began to shrink and political and economic activities started to hit stone walls. The high expectations among the populace were frustrated. Prices for basic commodities such as sugar, bread, maize-meal (the staple food for the whole of Southern Africa) reached unprecedented levels and well beyond the reach of low-income families. Even though Muluzi inherited a very infirm economy from Banda's regime (one that had been wildly praised by the western capitalist nations as a shinning example), he was nonetheless totally ignorant of economic aspects. Coupled with institutionalized corruption in the government departments and parastatal establishments—all packed with maladroit cousins, nieces, nephews, girlfriends, tribesmen—Malawians appeared to be destined for another era of dark days. Indeed, the Muluzi administration exacerbated the economic situation. His government had no funds to run the vital sectors because Muluzi's predecessor Hastings Banda had left Malawi with staggering debts of US$3 billion and more than US$55 million in domestic borrowing. The education system and health sectors were the hardest hit. Schools were lacking basic teaching materials. Hospitals were literally bankrupt. Candidly, Muluzi had absolutely no clue about the art of the government. He ran it as his own fiefdom.

AFORD, which after the elections was widely expected to effect a credible opposition stance, soon became embroiled in a power struggle and Chihana lost direction. Chakufwa

Chihana, once a hero in the multiparty struggle, shocked Malawians when he portrayed his true instincts and aligned with the Malawi Congress Party (MCP)—a party he once described as the "Party of death and darkness" (and a very fitting term). His move sparked a considerable number of additional defections from his (AFORD). It became very obvious to him that his actions had met with unprecedented disapproval. All along, AFORD had presented itself as an unadulterated party, run by leaders untainted by questionable pasts and banner-holders of the democracy to come in Malawi. Chihana's leadership soon started to affect the smooth running of the party once described as the "Clean Party" that spearheaded the multiparty struggle. He became more and more a control freak rather than a commendable national leader. He absolutely abdicated his earlier commitment to the welfare of the poor people and engaged in extreme self-seeking exercises that visibly began to wear down his political destiny with alarming speed. However, Chihana and Banda had similar instincts—both were greedy, power hungry and dictatorial—a fact that Chihana himself openly acknowledged. Some of his supporters openly conceded that if he were elected as the President, he could be worse than Banda himself—a perception that was also shared by most Malawians.

The alliance between AFORD/MCP—unanimously considered as "unholy" by the majority of the people—did not last long. As predicted by many, it met certain demise before it could even learn to crawl. The marriage of convenience was over once and for all. The defection from the marriage with the MCP had not come as a surprise to most people. It was widely believed that Chihana did not receive the rewards agreed upon and that he was uncomfortable with the MCP Vice-president Gwanda Chakuamba Phiri and Treasurer-General John Z. Tembo. It was obvious that Chihana, with his high ambition to hold the country's highest office, could not go along with these two rogues with similar ambitions.

Chakufwa Chihana, literally worshipped by his supporters in northern Malawi, and who cherished the politics of a personality cult similar to that of the late Hastings Banda, went into yet another marriage of convenience. This time it was with the United Democratic Front (UDF), a party which he once termed the "Malawi Congress Party B" because of its former exclusively MCP leadership. His move, further eroded his short-term political career. He was forthwith seen by people as lacking political principles and anticipated getting rich fast—and much before addressing the welfare of the poor majority. Not only was Chihana's political future uncertain, the AFORD Party also was losing support at an alarming rate because of his opportunistic behaviors.

In the new marriage, Chihana was appointed Second Vice-president and Minister of Agriculture and Irrigation. Two of his colleagues were also given Ministerial posts. However, the appointment of Chihana to the Vice-presidency caused an uproar. The country's top lawyers threatened to take the matter to the Malawi High Court to reverse the appointment which they deemed as both unconstitutional and illegal. Despite the criticisms from the lawyers and the majority of citizens, President Muluzi went ahead with the appointment.

Again, the marriage of convenience with the UDF was short-lived. Chihana made an exit from the alliance and accused the UDF government of corruption and mismanagement. He expected his colleagues to do the same. Though some followed him out, two of his senior AFORD colleagues—Mr. Frank Mayinga Mkandawire and Dr. Mapopa Chipeta, both former UFMD activists—refused to dance to his tune and both remained with the UDF cabinet. Earlier Chihana had been heard to say that Muluzi was a good and competent leader who did not make mistakes. His remarks drew sharp reactions from his supporters, and Malawians in general. Some denounced him as the worst political prostitute ever seen in Malawi's history. UFMD forthwith warned his supporters and the nation as a whole that they were not astonished with Chihana's moves. He had demonstrated his lack of principled leadership at the Lusaka multiparty conference while clearly showing political ambitions imbued with an unlimited appetite for power. This was to be obtained at the expense of the suffering people of Malawi. Indeed, he had no patriotic pride or zeal in him. He was just driven by the desire to enhance his own political and economic self-interests.

I vividly recall some few years back writing a letter to several AFORD MPs—not as its member, or a northerner for that matter—as a Malawian patriot and above all, a Pan-Africanist. In that letter, I urged them take a decisive move to ostracize Chakufwa Chihana from AFORD's leadership as his actions and behaviors would eventually destroy the party from within. As expected, not even one MP bothered to acknowledge the receipt of my letter. Nevertheless, my prophetic letter proved right. A decline from 36 MPs after the first multiparty elections on May 19, 1994, to one MP in the following election speaks volumes. AFORD, once a popular Party, is now history—both it and its leader.

As I have mentioned previously in this chapter, the major parties; the UDF, the MCP, and AFORD had no political vision capable of transforming the nation, as it was, into a truly progressive and democratic society. All three parties were largely preoccupied with political opportunism and lining their pockets while the masses of our people remained trapped in the dreadful grinding poverty inherited from Banda's kleptocratic government.

In the middle of the second term of Muluzi's rule and after having tasted the sweetness of power, things began to dramatically fall apart. The President started to meddle with the National Constitution in order to enhance his own political agenda. Constitutionally, the President is limited to only two consecutive terms in office. His activities aroused suspicions among the people including some of his own MPs. National news outlets quickly picked up the widely discussed rumors of Muluzi's intentions. But he strongly denied the rumors as being concocted by his political foes. Where there is smoke, there is usually fire. Toward the end of his second and last term, he showed his true colors. He covertly channeled millions of dollars into a reelection campaign. Some of his closest sycophants put the figure at US$2.5 million—all used to bribe his MPs and others from the opposition parties to support his bid for a "third term" Presidency.

When this contentious issue was introduced into Parliament for approval, it almost plunged the nation into political turmoil. In fact, the issue came about while the people of Malawi were still nursing the wounds of Banda's brutal thirty-year reign. Immediately, people took to the streets of major cities and towns to protest against Muluzi's bid for a third term—something which was not permitted by the Constitution of the land. The UDF Youth League (the so-called young democrats) went amok beating and intimidating peaceful demonstrators with the tacit support of police–all reminiscent of Banda's janjaweeds (personal brutal militias, the Young Pioneers).

During the October 2002 sitting of Parliament, the government introduced a Constitutional Amendment Bill which sought to amend Section 83(3)of the Constitution to allow the country's President to serve three instead of the two terms as stipulated in the country's Constitution. The Bill, however, had failed earlier in July when it was—to the astonishment of many—tabled by the AFORD Member of Parliament for Karonga-Nyungwe, Khauli Msiska, a former exile and critic of Banda's life-Presidency. In the aftermath, the move provoked unprecedented reactions throughout the country. The Malawi Council of Churches and the Catholic Secretariat unreservedly condemned the move as evil and divisive and intended to benefit a few greedy and corrupt elements in the society. Robert Mwaungulu of the Catholic Commission for Justice and Peace at the Secretariat in Lilongwe, urged leaders of AFORD, UDF and MCP, to give way to new blood. Sadly, it is presently the case that Malawian politics is, to a large extent, dominated by old and visionless politicians who are largely supported by tribesmen.

Those who knew Bakili Muluzi were not surprised by his moves. Apart from being a convicted criminal, he had also joined the most feared sadistic organization, the Malawi

Young Pioneers (MYP). Generally, youths who joined this militia group were normally uneducated or primary-school leavers who could not get employment anywhere. He showed dedication and ruthlessness while carrying out instructions from his seniors and quickly rose to the rank of Commander before being appointed Secretary-general of the dreaded Malawi Congress Party (MCP) by life-President Hastings Banda.

As the issue of a "third term bid" heated up, the country's major aid donors; the US, Norway, Britain, and the EU warned Muluzi not to manipulate the Constitution to permit him a third term of office. Meanwhile Chakufwa Chihana the leader of the then troubled AFORD, supported President Muluzi's bid behind the backs of his colleagues and the party. Chihana had then reached a tipping point in his controversy-laden political career which threw his once mighty Party (AFORD) into hubbub and was almost wiped out in the General Elections that followed within a few months. He himself as the Presidential running mate with Gwanda Chakuamba Phiri, a brute and political self-seeker, lost the elections. AFORD, his party, garnered only one seat and that was won by Chihana's dubious daughter-in-law.

Mr. Chakufwa Chihana and MP, Khauli Msiska, who both supported Muluzi in his third term bid, were alleged to have been bribed with unlimited amounts of money from government coffers. However, President Muluzi, despite using badly needed meagre public funds to buy support for his circuitous and unconstitutional move, met petrified and concerted resistance from Christian Churches, Civic Groups, students, and indeed, the broad masses of our people. The only group which supported him actively was the Islamic community which accounted for less than five percent of the total population. Muluzi was himself a devoted Muslim with vast connections to Islamic fundamentalists and radical Islamic regimes in the Middle-East from whence he acquired his financial support. Finally, Muluzi succumbed to overwhelming pressure—even his own children pressured their father to give up the bid and step aside for the good of the nation.

In December 1998, and toward the end of his second term, Muluzi conceded defeat. This after having plunged the country into a political and economic quagmire. One thing was certain, he could not reverse the emergence of the democracy for which Malawians had so gallantly fought. No leader in Malawi today would dream of turning back the clock and destroying the young democracy in order to realize his own personal agenda. After all, after 30 years of the thuggish rule of Hastings Banda, Malawi has emerged from a dark tunnel to create one of the strongest democratic states in the Continent—something never seen before. But we must not be contented with fragile gains. We need to do more to educate our people in the principles of democracy within our society.

On the economic front, the third term bid, created a tremendously gloomy economic situation that almost tore the country apart. Muluzi faced a formidable challenge to reshape the image of his Party on the one hand and to win back voter and donor confidence on the other. Increasingly, donors began to withdraw aid to Malawi in 2001 citing a lack of transparency, institutionalized corruption, and political intolerance reminiscent of Banda's reign. Muluzi saw his name being linked to some of Malawi's biggest corruption scandals in history. Close to US$17 million vanished from the education Ministry. This led to three Cabinet Ministers being removed from office in November 2001.

The "Third term" bid not only paved the way for yet another rebirth of a dictatorship in the country, it was also vividly seen as Muluzi's desperate move to protect himself from possible prosecution for alleged involvement in extended corruption scandals. Not only were Malawians caught in the middle of the controversy, Africans elsewhere were amazed with a sense of disbelief that, after suffering the rule of a doddering old fool for 30 years, Malawians would contemplate sticking their foot back in the mire of yet another President for-life. The majority of Malawians conceded that Muluzi wanted to remain in power to perpetuate his evil agenda of enriching himself and his fawning sycophants. It occurs to me in the final analysis that Africans have a serious "power problem." Once an African has had a "taste" of power, he not only wants more of it, but he wants it for life. Dr. Banda, whose footsteps Muluzi seemed to be wanting to follow, was an exemplification of this atrocious African malady.

After Muluzi's shameful defeat to manipulate the Constitution for his own personal aggrandizement, we saw further pathetically frantic efforts by him to hang on. He saw a chance to advance his desires by proxy—by fighting to place in power a man he thought he could control and turn into a dupe in order to retain control over the ruling Party. To this effect, he hand-picked Dr. Bingu wa Mutharika a highly ambitious, opportunistic neophyte to run as the Presidential candidate for the ruling UDF. This was in spite of the fact that he was not an insider of the Party. The move prompted unprecedented criticisms from potential contenders and members at large in the UDF camp. The move resembles that of his former disgraced Zambian President Frederick Chiluba. He hand-picked the late Levy Mwanawasa to be his successor in the belief that he could turn him into a bootlicker and thus protect him from prosecution for his alleged corruption scandals and abuse of office.

In the May 2004 elections, President Bakili Muluzi tirelessly campaigned for his hand-picked Presidential candidate Dr. Bingu wa Mutharika, especially in vote-rich regions of south and centre.

Dr. Bingu's first priority soon after he had been propelled into power, was to erect a Mausoleum on the grave of the most cold-blooded tyrant in the history of our nation, Hastings Banda. This despite nation-wide disapproval in the sense that at the time the country was in despair of food supplies due to an unprecedented drought of a magnitude never before seen in the country. The President spent US$1.5 million of public funds that could have been used to purchase much-needed food for the starving population, mainly children and the old. However, according to the United Nations Human Development Index (UNHDI), Malawi is one of the poorest nations of the world, number 165 of 175. Unbelievably, for a leader, who committed repulsive human rights abuse against fellow citizens for thirty solid years under a "Police State" and pursued a naked and cavalier alliance with the brutal racist minority regimes in Southern Africa, to be rewarded with such high profile symbol is painful to contemplate. President Bingu is known for his unswerving hero-worshipping for the late monstrous Hastings Banda.

Dr. Bingu wa Mutharika lived in self-imposed exile for more than half of his life and decided to bury his head in the sand during Banda's bestial despotic rule. In contrast, his brother Prof. Peter Muthalika was an active member of an exiled Pan-African Democratic Party (PDP), led by late Masauko Chipembere, Malawi's leading nationalist. During President Bingu's tenure as Secretary-general of the Common Market for Eastern and Southern Africa (COMESA) based in Harare, Zimbabwe, he was accused of mismanagement of the organization's funds. In January 1997, he was sent on a three-month forced leave by an extraordinary meeting of COMESA's Council of Ministers. This leave of absence paved the way for a probe which included allegations that he was using COMESA's resources to boosts his own political goals and ambitions. He was unceremoniously fired toward the end of 1997, and forthwith he returned to Malawi where he formed his short-lived United Party of Malawi (UPM) the same year. The Party's failure in two national general elections were attributed by his suspicious past records in (COMESA) on one hand and his unpatriotic demeanor on the other.

In the midst of his first term in the government, Bingu broke away from UDF and formed his own Party, Democratic Peoples Party (DPP). The relations betwixt him and his former mentor Bakili Muluzi, became acrid and finally, dirty politics became the order of the day.

On May 19, 2009, Malawians went to the polls to elect a new government for another five-year term. The elections were described by independent foreign observers as peaceful, free, and fair, which is unique by African standards. In fact, this was an election that inspired the long suffering people of Malawi and instilled into them sense of hope and pride.

As expected, President Bingu and his Party (DPP) were catapulted into power with a landslide victory, particularly in the north where the Party garnered hundred percent of the votes in the hope that Bingu could, at least, endeavor to uplift the "dead north" economically by taking into account the negligence and failures of the former two nefarious leaderships which hailed from South and Central Malawi. In his campaigns, Bingu promised the people of the north that he would inject massive economic development projects in the region which had been ethnically ignored by the two previous regimes.

Soon after swearing the oath, the people from the north, woke up in disbelief and amazement to hear that the charlatan President had impulsively introduced a "quota system" on par with the apartheid system of medium of education (Afrikaans) that sparked determined resistance by South African Youths leading to Mandela's release from prison and finally, to "independence." In Malawi, the system curtails the selection of students from minority north into Universities, Colleges and Secondary Schools based on a merit-based system. However, the system met with formidable resistance from the north that led to four progressive MPs ditching the DPP government in protest against a divisive and tribally motivated system.

In his defense of this evil system, Bingu, himself a political neophyte and diehard tribalist, maintained that students from the north cheat on examination and that's why they pass with flying colors. Astonishingly, Bingu and his supporters, have never ever produced any piece of evidence or proof to justify their accusations. The worse case scenario is that many northern students were depressed and traumatized leading, to some extent, to suicides. One young girl of 19 years, committed suicide when she learnt that her counterpart from the south who scored 21 points was selected to enter University while she was not with nine points (highly impressive).

The successes of the northerners emanate from way back in the 18th century when early Missionaries set foot in Nyasaland (Malawi). They established Missionary Institutions in the South and Central Malawi, but were circumvented by the reactions of local Muslim Chiefs who favored "Madarasas" over a western type of educational system. To this end, the Missionaries moved their resources to northern Nyasaland and, established a number of Institutions in Livingstonia (Mumbwe), Bandawe, and Ekwendeni.

It is Livingstonia that later on became a cradle of education in East, Central and Southern Africa. In Nyasaland, Missionary Institutions—Livingstonia in particular—produced potential and intellectual national leadership such as: the late Orton C. Chirwa, QC (a top notch lawyer); the late Dunduzu K. Chisiza, a brilliant professional economist; the late Yatuta K. Chisiza, former top police chief in Tanganyika (Tanzania); Vera Chirwa, first woman professional lawyer; David Kaunda, father of the former President of the Republic of Zambia; Clement Kadalie, the founder of novel Trade Union (SACTU) in South Africa in 1919; Wellington Manoah Chirwa, one of the first professional lawyers in Southern Africa; and Mr. Kamanga, the first senior cabinet minister in Congo's Patrice E. Lumumba African Government (Kamanga hailed from Mzimba District, northern Malawi). However, all the captioned names are for those from the minority Tumbukas of the north. It must also be noted that these names are but a tip of the iceberg.

Fundamentally, I have pinpointed these names to highlight the President's lies and his tribalistic sentiments he harbors against the minority section of the society.

Tragically, the quota system turned to be a "tribal holocaust" in the sense that education is a predominant way of life taking into account that there are no economic activities for people there to engage in. After almost 50 years of independence, the north has been unfairly treated despite the fact that it is the epicenter of the country's brains. northern Malawi, popularly known as the "Dead north," has been neglected by three Presidents all of whom hailed from South and Central Malawi. northerners are expressly regarded in the country as outlandish, mainly by national political leaders who themselves fear competition from the north. This ethnically motivated economic strangulation in the north has created a strong will for academic successes among the overwhelming majority of young people who find it virtually impossible to secure job opportunities in their own province, hence, education has become their dominant occupation unlike their counterparts in the south and central regions who enjoy unprecedented job opportunities due to the inequity of national development opportunities.

In late 80s, former fascist tyrant Hastings Banda introduced the very same system claiming that, in his own words: "If the government does not take drastic steps to curb the entrance of the northern students into the Universities, Colleges and Secondary schools, our national institutions would be overwhelmingly dominated by students from the north." Tragically, these were words directly from the mouth of the Head of State. This was followed forthwith by purging teachers, top civil servants, and parastatal directors. However, the victims of this tribalistic move were students from the south and central regions because they found themselves without adequate teachers in their schools. As for the civil servants, they were replaced by white expatriates that Banda most trusted over Africans. The divisive and unfair system was outlawed by the High Court Judges amid multiparty struggles in 1993.

In almost 50 years of independence, Malawians have been reckless in electing their national leaders. The late President Bingu wa Mutharika had never been tested or tried in any form or shape of political struggle. He came to power like manna from heaven and had no political or economic vision of the country. While the country is in an economic quagmire, he chose to live in a capacious Legislative building for his residence, purchasing a private jet at a cost of US$75 million and 22 Mercedes limousines at a cost of US$3. 5 million. It is alleged that he spends US $250,000 a year for his children and grandchildren in schools abroad while back home, our children are packed like sardines in inadequate classrooms with limited books and other instruments of learning. Most recently, his wedding to a woman 40 years younger than himself cost taxpayers US$3.4 million. He invited to the affair 25 Heads of State as his guests, but to his disappointment, only a handful attended. Those who did not, sarcastically described the wedding as needless and a waste of meagre resources in one of the poorest nations on the face of our planet—while millions of our people are trapped in grinding poverty, the overwhelming majority living below one dollar a day, and unemployment at 65 percent, the highest in the region.

President Bingu has a deep-rooted hatred for the minority northerners akin to the genocidal Hutus of Rwanda toward the Tutsis. His leadership, for his own naked political and economic interests, had dangerously plunged the once united country into an ethnically polarized State never seen in almost 50 years of nationhood. He was also on record for his unequivocal support of the neo-fascist murderers, Zimbabwe President Robert Mugabe, the Iranian infamous brute Mahmoud Ahmadinejad, and former Malawian brutal tyrant Hasting Banda.

In more than four decades, Malawians have been locked into electoral recklessness, electing criminals and tribalists. The late President Bingu, in particular, has been openly showing his true colors by ridiculing the minority (but academically strong) Tumbukas of the north. As his idol Hastings Banda, he purged Tumbukas (the backbone of the nation's civil service) from senior positions and replacing them with deadwood tribesmen. Indeed, Malawians of patriotic humor, regardless of tribal or ethnic affiliation, must fight this cancerous trend which is beginning to circulate in the veins of our people—and very detrimental to their unity and stability. Our Rwandese brothers, have learnt that in a hard way. We must not in any way, shape or form, think that one group of people would triumph in the event of national disorder and tumult. To the contrary, God forbid it. It would be a national cataclysm followed by unprecedented ramifications.

Sadly, the present leadership, which is largely dominated by people from Central and Southern Malawi, condones the trend in which, unfortunately, our nation finds itself for the simple reason that they are in majority and obviously in position to win in any national general elections—though it be detrimental to national interests. We are not angels and it seems to me that we do not learn from mistakes made by our brothers elsewhere in Africa (wise people learn from mistakes, but fools do not). For instance, in Rwanda, Hutus ran amok and slaughtered close to a million Tutsis in a 100 days in a genocide never seen in the modern history of the Continent. Though, animosity between the two ethnic groups existed for a long period of time, their leaders played a dangerous political game that added gasoline to a fire that resulted into despicable consequences.

The danger at the moment in Malawian politics is that those people in positions of influence, have been there for generations and are now obsolete and unable to champion progressive political and economic policies that fit into 21st century realities. They are there only for power and to line their purses, all the while leaving the overwhelming majority of voters locked into the grinding wheel of poverty and never letting them catch glimpses of light at the end of a long tunnel of despair and degradation. But after 30 years of bestial dictatorship, Malawians must be in a better position to consolidate their democratic gains by defending the national Constitution that is always vulnerable to manipulation by greedy and power-hungry elements. Malawians and other African people in the Continent must not sit with their hands and legs folded. They are duty bound to defend their birthrights and those of the future generations at any cost—in Africa, if leaders taste power, it is next to impossible to let it go. They want to retain their power until their last "breath."

In late November 1997, Hastings Banda died of pneumonia at South Africa's Garden City Clinic. He was officially

105. In his last Presidential candidacy, Banda was 97, and clearly blind and deaf. He was treated at government's expenses despite the fact that he siphoned more than US$500 million from national coffers. But why is it that evil men live long? His demise closed a chapter in Malawi's and Africa's history. However, his downfall was received with mixed sentiments throughout Africa. In Lusaka, Zambia, one national Newspaper put its headline thus: "Another African dictator has gone beyond the veil of death." Others asserted that Malawians under his rule were like sheep before their shearer. He destroyed the self-esteem of his people in the same way that apartheid in South Africa dehumanized blacks.

Astonishingly, many Malawians, themselves victims of Banda's ravenous highhandedness, described him as their demigod and father who will always remain in their heart of hearts. As I have already said, the monstrous despot was very old when he died and walked supported only by a walking stick and ear-devices to enable him hear and yet, his roar of "Kwacha" (dawn) elevated Malawians to a hysterical pitch. Then he would declare: "Mtenderee" (freedom) and the response from his subjects (for that's what they were) was deafening. While Malawians, especially those from the Central Region (Banda's adopted region) showered words of praise for their messiah, other people, however, described him as a "heartless cold fish." Banda escaped judgment on earth, but is he ready to face God's heavenly judgment? He knew a lot as a self-acclaimed Elder in the Church of Scotland, however, much will be required of him before the judgment seat of Christ.

After his demise on November 25, 1997, the eccentric despot was buried before a crowd of about 80,000 mourners in the capital of Lilongwe (central Malawi). His lifeless body was laid in State at his US$250 million State House where the funeral procession started. He owned several palaces worth more than US$800 million which most of the country's leaders described as monumental development while more than 85 percent of Malawians live below poverty line on less than a dollar a day. People, especially in rural areas and much of the country, are still battling obdurate grinding poverty.

As a matter of fact, his legacy will have a long term impact on Malawians. People visibly lived in fear of his terror machine, especially the notorious paramilitary Malawi Young Pioneers (Janjaweeds) who enforced strict observation of Banda's nation-building so-called cornerstones: Unity, Loyalty, Obedience and Discipline. Yes, to a true form, Malawians were obedient like school children and this made them the laughingstock of the world and political lepers within Africa. Indeed, fear and despair ruled as Banda consolidated his reign and because he was convinced that Malawians were under his heel, he owned everything he wanted to own during his obnoxious single-party dictatorship. He and the woman with whom he shared a bed, Cecilia Kadzamila, and her uncle John Tembo, Banda's former notorious henchman, wielded enormous power, shunting everybody else to the periphery.

The body of the former evil tyrant had been bedecked in a bronze casket guaranteed to last 100 years in a cemented grave. Whether the technology really guarantees the casket to last that long, remains to be seen. The coffin cost the poor taxpayers US$59,500 and was flown from the US to South Africa. His body, according to his former loyal dupe and personal physician Dr. Hatherwick Ntaba, was embalmed so that it would never disintegrate with time. Whatever the despot's former supporters and sycophants say, Banda's legacy remains both shameful and despicable. No Malawian of goodwill and integrity would be proud of him. He has left the nation more divided on ethnic lines than before he resumed the country's political leadership in July 1958. He instituted into the country a personality cult that left Malawians brainwashed, tranquilized, and ineffectual, like an automobile that moves with flat-tires. In spite of this degradation, the majority of Malawians still adore him—even in his grave, Banda laughs.

Worst of all, the man who ruled Malawi with impunity for 30 years, may not have been a Malawian after all, he died not knowing his own dialect. Dr. Banda (Richard Armstrong) was born from freed slaves in Monrovia, Liberia, on July 6, 1896. He had blood connections with local tribes in Gold Coast (Ghana) where he later settled after he had been declared persona non-grata in the UK for criminal offenses before he dubiously discovered his new home in Nyasaland (Malawi). Nobody in Malawi, including the so-called relatives of his, would write even one line of his ancestral lineage. The charlatan had to convince some political friends that he was a citizen of "Kasungu," Central Malawi. With their help he bought relatives there and claimed that he was born at "Chiwengo" village, but would not tell who were his parents.

Dr. Banda had been surrounded by controversy about his roots and ethnicity from the time he arrived in Nyasaland, on July 6, 1958. In Malawi, people are celebrating July 6, for Banda's birthday (July 6, 1896); Independence Day (July 6, 1964) and July 6, 1958, his arrival into Nyasaland. What a coincidence? However, it is no secret that some highly positioned members of the Congress doubted about his nationality openly. Later on, he became personally very sensitive over this controversial issue. His failure to write memoirs to clear the air of suspicions about his outlandish roots, clearly authenticates claims that, indeed, Banda was not a Malawian and, I would strongly challenge anybody with different views to come forward and dispute my claims. In sharp contrast, his former counterparts such as Kwame Nkrumah, Nnamdi "Zik" Azekiwe, Jomo Kenyatta, Julius Nyerere, Kenneth D. Kaunda and Nelson Madiba Mandela, all wrote personal and impressive memoirs to enable their fellow citizens appreciate what they went through and who they were.

In the absence of Banda's memoirs, the people of Malawi and the future generations will not know the true history of their country. For a man of his status not to leave a line or two of his personal memoirs, suggests that something had gone terribly wrong with him.

Above all, Banda had no due respect for his fellow citizens nor Africans in general, his private secretary for decades was a former British expatriate with dubious behaviors. He arrogantly turned Malawian women into his dancing robots and regarded Malawians as uncivilized and unintelligent. One of his henchmen lamented that they were treated like "office boys." For all of the 30 years he was in power, he let loose white expatriates to dominate and run the affairs of an independent state. Astonishingly, they also had immense powers and Banda listened to them at anytime. He openly said many times that he did not trust Africans to hold senior positions in his government.

Although Banda's funeral was well attended by local Malawians—especially those from his so-called ethnic group (Chewas), only two foreign leaders represented their governments at the funeral. They were President Robert Mugabe, an ardent admirer of the murderous fascist and Dr. Quett Masire of Botswana, as well as Joshua Nkomo, former Vice President of Zimbabwe who became Mugabe's henchman after joining the so-called unity government. In a sharp contrast, President Nyerere's funeral was attended by hundreds of foreign leaders who converged in Dar es salaam, Tanzania, to bid farewell to one of the greatest sons of Africa. The low attendance of foreign leaders for Banda's funeral, demonstrates how isolated the heartless tyrant of Malawi had become.

Chapter Eleven

AFRICA IN TURMOIL

The continent of Africa is the second largest after Asia. It encompasses 11.7 million square miles (30 million sq. km), almost one-fifth of Earth's land. It is separated from Europe by the Mediterranean Sea and from Asia by the Red Sea and Gulf of Aden. From Cap Blanc in the north, it stretches about 5,000 miles (8,000 km) south to Cape Agulhas in South Africa. The northern half of the Continent, is far wider than the south, spanning 4,600 miles (7,360 km) between Cap Verde in Senegal and Raas Xaafuun in Somalia.[xiii]

Africa has a population of 850 million people divided into two major groups: the culturally homogenous—predominantly Arabic and Islamic peoples of the north—and the numerous culturally and linguistically diverse indigenous people of the South. The Continent has 53 independent States speaking more than 1,500 dialects. Before Islamic Arabs trekked to the south from Arabia—the present day Morocco, Algeria, Tunisia, Libya, Egypt and Mauritania—the land was occupied by Black Africans. In essence, virtually the whole of the continent was the home for "Black Africans." Apparently, Afrocentric Egyptologists argue that ancient Egyptians from King Tut to Cleopatra were Black Africans. This is apparently supported by the fact that the ancient Nubians of the Sudan ruled from Egypt to Syria undisturbed for 75 years.

Africa is commonly acknowledged as the genesis of the human race. Discovery of human fossils there lends weight to the hypothesis first put forward by Charles Darwin in the last century that the human species emerged in Africa. Darwin reasoned that since man's closest primate relatives, the chimps and apes, were found in Africa then it was the most likely

---

[xiii] *The Illustrated World Atlas.*

place for the emergence of humans. Following that line of thought, it can be argued that Black Africans held the keys for the major early civilizations such as those of the Nile Valley and Great Zimbabwe. In the Middle Ages, powerful kingdoms arose along these trade routes in the western interior. It is also generally acknowledged that all the present day human beings (Homo sapiens) trekked out of Africa (Eastern Africa) more than 65,000 years ago, heading north where climate patterns changed their physical appearances.

Yet, despite Africa's lucid ancient history, Africans have suffered terribly. The trans-Sahara and transatlantic slave trade (some say thanks to the Arabs and the Europeans) took 10-15 million Africans out of Africa and into the Middle East, Western Asia and the Americas in addition to some 20 million others who never lived to complete the long and arduous journeys along the slave-trading routes. This incalculable loss has had devastating effects on Africa in that it has deprived the continent of some of the best brains—intellects that could have made a great deal of change.

Then came imperialism and colonialism which sought to control the continent's gargantuan natural resources. A Conference in Berlin, Germany ended with the partitioning of Africa between 1884-1885. Out of this Conference Africa was divided into spheres of influence among the Europe's major powers; Germany, Britain, Spain, Portugal, France, Belgium, and Italy. Colonialism and imperialism took on different shapes and designs across the Continent but most Africans found themselves in a bottomless quagmire. Fraudulent treaties were signed between Chiefs who apparently did not comprehend the wordings of the treaty. Sooner rather than later, Africa became the attraction for colonists, business elites, and missionaries. The arrival of European colonists forthwith precipitated industrial-scale exploitation of Africa's national resources. For instance, vast amounts of timber and huge quantities of minerals were shipped off the Continent and into foreign markets.

Before the end of the 16th century, colonies had already been established in some parts of Africa, especially along the coastal stretches. Angola, Mozambique and the Islands of the Cape Verde fell into the hands of the ruthless Portuguese colonists who treated their African subjects as wild animals. Forthwith, the three colonies were incorporated into the Portuguese Empire. For instance, Mozambique was known as Portuguese East Africa.

However, the colonists encountered unprecedented resistance from the indigenous people under well established kingdoms and empires ruled over by powerful chiefs and kings in the West, Central and Southern Africa. In West Africa, powerful kingdoms were in existence along side each other and with tightly knit administrations in Yoruba and Songhai. One striking scenario was that there were no restrictions to movement amongst the indigenous people in these kingdoms. After all, they were the same people. In Southern and Eastern Africa, a powerful kingdom was in place under the most influential King Munomatapa—headquartered in the present-day Zimbabwe.

After the partition of Africa, tribes and clans were separated. Today, ethnic groups or tribes may be found on both sides of state borders. For instance in my own country Malawi we have Tumbukas who may also be found in eastern Zambia or Yao. Ngoni and Sena may also be found in both Mozambique and Tanzania. There are Luos and Masais in Kenya, Uganda and Tanzania, and so on. Today, however, these people require passports to cross many borders.

The partition of Africa, has had truly devastating ramifications for: (a) ethnolinguistic groups among our vast societies, and (b) the erosion of our once vibrant cultures. But the remarkable fact has been that since independence some 52 years ago, there has been no significant territorial conflict among Malawi's neighbors. But in mid-1978, as Idi Amin's ferocious dictatorship began to weaken, Ugandan forces launched an invasion into Tanzania. In its defense, Tanzania encountered some setbacks at the onset, but forthwith regained stability and launched strong counteroffensives that saw Idi Amin's ragtag army in retreat and vigorously pursued to the gates of Kampala and beyond. This war, the first of its kind in the continent between neighboring African states, not only brought about the downfall of Idi Amin, but also unveiled the nefarious roles that had been played by such foreign agents as Frank Terpil, Edwin Wilson, Bob Aristed and others in support of that barbaric and corrupt regime. Among the African state leaders, Malawi's puppet, Hastings Banda supported Idi Amin as a way of showing his contempt for Julius Nyerere and all the Tanzanians who supported Malawian rebels in their country. The war, of course, altered in fundamental ways the political terrain on which African states would thereafter carry out their future.

The colonization of Africa came about at a very high price. Resistance by the indigenous people against the invaders was both heroic and spontaneous. Horrible massacres by well armed and powerful European forces were committed with impunity in order to instill fear and despair among people. There were unprecedented resistances and rebellions in West Africa (Nigeria/Ghana). Some were short-lived and some were prolonged and with devastating aftermaths. Before the Mau Mau uprising in Kenya, the Nandi people fought courageously against British expeditionary forces—casualties were reported to be high on both sides. The Germans likewise encountered hardened resistance in Tanganyika (Tanzania) before they used their formidable forces to contain the rebellion. One such rebellion known as MAJI-MAJI, was carried out in Iringa in southern Tanganyika under the courageous leadership of Chief Mkwawa of the Hehe tribe.

As the scramble for Africa continued unabated, so too the untold sufferings of the African people at the hands of the European adventurists. In 1884, the Germans colonized South West Africa (Namibia). There, they met with rigid resistance from the Herero tribe led by Paramount Chief Samuel Maherero—one of the slyest leaders that the German colonists ever encountered. Later, on October 2, 1904, the Germans launched one of the most tenacious attacks on the peaceful people of the Herero ethnic group. They were astonished to experience the concerted and heroic defense that the indigenous people (with outdated weaponry) mounted against more sophisticated German firepower. This German offensive was led by Lt. Gen. Lothar Von Trotha, a heartless and notorious cold-blooded murderer.

The Herero offered unyielding resistance for three long years (1904-1907). At the end of this bloody conflict inflicted on Africans, more than 250,000 Herero men, women and children were reported to have been massacred in cold-blood by the German forces. After these frightful and unprovoked attacks the evil German General, Von Trotha wrote out a, still-reverberating declaration which, scholars widely believe, sowed the seed of the holocaust.

After putting down the heroic uprising by the Herero warriors at the end of 1907, Von Trotha delivered a stunning Auswissungsbefehl, or extermination order that read in part: "Every Herero found within German borders, with or without guns, with or without livestock, will be shot at the spot. I will not give shelter to any Herero women or children. They must either return to their people or be shot at." Men were lynched in scenes reminiscent of those that occurred in antebellum southern US. Emaciated men, women, and children (with chains draped around their necks) were worked to death in scenes reminiscent of Nazi-run concentration camps.

In later years, a German scholar wrote a book about the Hereros that many historians assert was the basis for Adolf Hitler's theories on race—and helped him justify the ferocious experiments against Jewish people. Sadly, the brutal massacres of the people of South West Africa (Namibia) were, and still are, rarely reported or mentioned.

Throughout the 16th-19th centuries, the African continent saw its soil soaked in blood from both slave trade and imperial designs. In Mozambique and Angola, people revolted against Portuguese encroachment with its brutal and inhuman actions against the indigenous people. For three years straight under the courageous leadership of Chief Ngungunyana from Southern Mozambique, people mounted fierce resistance against the Portuguese. After the Portuguese strengthened its forces with both additional men and more sophisticated weaponry, Ngungunyana was captured on a battlefield alongside his most trusted commanders. They were transported to Lisbon, Portugal toward the end of the 18th century where after death, their bodies were kept in the Lisbon's Museum. In Angola, people resisted the tyrannical Portuguese system that led to bloody wars led by Queen Nyango who fought beside her fighters with unprecedented intrepidity. Nyango declined to acquiesce and fell on the battlefield while defending her land and her African dignity.

In my own country, Nyasaland (Malawi), things were no different. People resented foreign domination. On January 23, 1915 a Nyasa native, Rev. John Chilembwe, led an uprising against British rule. He strongly opposed the way the British people treated his fellow natives—particularly by enlisting young Malawian men into the Kings African Rifles (KAR) and sending them to fight on their behalf in World War I (a war they did not understand). However, the uprising lasted only a month. Chilembwe and some of his supporters were killed on the battlefield—Chilembwe being killed as he was trying to cross the border into Mozambique. Sad though it was, his heroic downfall inspired the subsequent generations to stand up for their rights.

Indeed, there had been several other bloody conflicts especially in southern and central Africa. In the Congo (DRC) in 1879, King Leopold of Belgium declared the Kingdom of Bakongo as his own personal property. That declaration infuriated the people of the Bakongo Kingdom and they took up arms to defend their well established society. In response, King Leopold unleashed a series of prolonged massacres on the poorly equipped indigenous people. It has been estimated that at the end of the conflict, over a million Bakongos were massacred. In South Africa and Rhodesia (Zimbabwe), similar defensive encounters occurred under the heroic leadership of such powerful kings as Tshaka of the Zulus, Dingan, Lobengula, Mushoeshoe, Mzilikazi, Mbuya ne Handa, and many others.

But yet, in his book, "Inside Africa," John Gunther Harper asserts that the benefits the colonial system brought to Africa are incontestable—even though it also brought many abuses. He went on to say that perhaps much of what the white man did was selfish, since it was for the exclusive benefit of the white communities; nevertheless, the record of overall benefits stands for itself. He admitted that while Europeans may have ravaged the continent, they also opened it up to civilization. However, Harper here might not have recalled his history in the sense that when Europeans first set foot in Africa, they found that Africans lived in communities with their own brand of civilization—and they worshipped God. Indeed, the name God existed in every African dialect and that they used fire to cook their food long before Europeans came to Africa.

As a matter of fact, some Europeans were at odds with reality. To them, Africa, should remain an overseas domain for ever. In 1947, for instance, after the end of World War II, Britain's war hero, Viscount Field Marshall Bernard Montgomery, quietly toured Africa and came away with a rueful view of its potential for self-determination. Records made public after his trip divulged that his plan was to turn the continent into a white-supremacist bulwark against communism. This racist master plan that so embarrassed the postwar government, was watched with keen interest and fought to discourage it at all costs. Popularly known as "Monty," he was not the only European with such an evil mentality. John Cecil Rhodes, the father of imperialism and colonialism in Southern Africa, espoused the same notion and suggested that region must remain a part of the British Empire.

A covert two-month tour of eleven African countries in 1947, before many countries had attained independence, led Montgomery to conclude that the African, "Is a complete savage and is quite unable of developing the country himself."

However, his controversial remarks remain open for a continental debate. His attitude to African independence movements was shown in a recommendation to the government that said: "We should have no nonsense with the United Nations Organization (UNO) about Tanganyika; it should be absorbed into the British bosom."

By stereotyping Africans, Monty had, to some degree, gone out of his way. Idiocy has no borders, there are idiots in African societies and there are idiots in European and other societies for that matter. As a former military icon, at that time in point, Monty should not have harbored such despicable sentiments against the African people. He was better positioned than anyone else to acknowledge the fact that thousands of African troops were recruited—some times against their wish—for war services. This in spite of the fact that they did not have anything to gain. Moreover, most did not even know what the war was all about. From British possessions alone, more than 350,000 Africans served in the British army. Their units helped to defeat Italians in Ethiopia and to restore Emperor Haile Selassie to his throne. Forty-five thousand Africans were shipped to India where they fought with distinction in Burma. Disturbingly, from French Africa, about 75,000 Africans were shipped to France to fight the Germans. Again, it must be noted that these young African soldiers died for a cause they did not know or understand. More than half of these young people did not return to Africa and those who returned did so under a cloud of indignity and despair. At the same time, their European counterparts were treated with respect and dignity.

However, one significant fact that African soldiers learned in India and Burma (Myanmar) was how nationalist movements there had served to influence the British government to recognize their rights to self-determination. This even though the people were engulfed in vicious circles of poverty and illiteracy. Upon arrival back home, these soldiers had enormous political influence over their populations. They passed along to their fellow countrymen the hard-won observations gained while abroad—and the impact was extremely encouraging.

From slave trade, to a scramble for Africa, and then to Africa's partitioning, the African people endured unprecedented degradation and equally inhuman treatment at the hands of foreign adventurers. During this epoch, millions of lives were lost through bloody wars, tribal conflicts, and, to some extent, by imported maladies such as syphilis, gonorrhea, and smallpox. From the very beginning of the scramble for Africa, gargantuan fortunes were made from gold and diamonds—as in Southern Africa by people like John Cecil Rhodes. These fortunes, unfortunately, were shipped back to Europe to build economic empires and to lubricate the industrial upswing. Meanwhile, back in Africa, Africans were left to fend for themselves. They received no benefit from their rich resources.

South Africa's gold mines flourished at the expense of the African laborers who worked deep under ground, and under most appalling environmental conditions, conditions that would not, in any way, have been tolerated by miners in Europe. In essence, one may readily see why Europeans targeted southern and central Africa—it was expressly to establish their unbridled domain in order to control vast mineral fortunes which they anticipated to last for centuries. Europeans therefore, established with care for the exploitation of resources from Africa at the expense of black people. Most of the expatriation of resources was handled by major European financial monopolies such as the Société Générale. This establishment controlled a most significant subsidiary—the Union Miniere de Haute-Katanga (first known as the Companie de Katanga)—which has since 1889 monopolized copper production. Union Miniere at times made profits as high as 30 million pounds a year. This fabulous profit benefited the Europeans the most. This grabbing of resources also sparked Congo's unending instability when Moise Tshombe, Congo's traitor, declared independence for Katanga Province and separated from the rest of the Republic of Congo. The Republic of

Congo received its own independence from Belgium's rule on June 30, 1960.

At the end of the World War II in 1945, Africans through their political movements, began to prepare themselves to battle foreign domination and the injustices meted out to them by colonial masters. This road to freedom and justice, however, was bumpy and perilous with massacres and imprisonments carried out with impunity and brute force in many places across the Continent.

Through relentless efforts to break the chains of bondage, Gold Coast (Ghana), won her independence on March 6, 1957 and Dr. Kwame Nkrumah became the first African Prime Minister south of the Sahara. By mid-70s, all African countries were independent apart from Rhodesia (Zimbabwe) and South Africa. Fundamentally, Africans were filled with high expectations and anxious to live under democratic societies where they could chart their own destinies.

But did independence bring hope to the overwhelming majority of our people? The answer is a big NO! Unfortunately, our governments are far worse than the colonial establishments they replaced, thus making the continent a cradle of inhumanity with soils drenched in the blood of our own people. Many of our leaders are best known for greed, tyranny, corruption and kleptomania. These four factors, together with tribalism—the scourge of Africa—are the major causes of the continent's retrogressive trend which is strongly and unfairly blamed on external factors by the failing leadership.

After Gold Coast (Ghana) achieved independence, it was followed by dozens of countries in the continent. Africans were confidently filled with an overwhelming sense of expectation and hope. They expected that African governments, unlike the colonial establishments, would deliver the goods and treat them with respect and dignity under a democratic atmosphere. But would "dreams come true" or was it a false start? The truth of the matter is that African leaders plunged the continent into an unimaginable shame and despair and, finally, betrayed the aspirations of our people.

Dr. Kwame Nkrumah, Africa's greatest Pan-Africanist and an undisputed visionary of our time, in league with Sekou Toure of Guinea, Modibo Keita of Mali, Gamal Abdel Nasser of Egypt, Patrice Lumumba of Congo and Haile Selassie of Ethiopia, formed the Organization of Africa Unity (OAU) in the capital of Ethiopia, Addis Ababa in 1963. This was done to help the still colonized countries fight for independence and forge ahead with the struggle to liberate the whole of Africa. For 39 years of its operation the OAU conducted its businesses from the former notorious prison in Addis Ababa which was donated by Emperor Haile Selassie. To this day, Africa's premier organization still operates from unfinished Headquarters—46 years after its inception.

However, the choice of Addis Ababa as OAU Headquarters, some say was wrong in the sense that Ethiopians do not regard themselves as "Africans," but as "Ethiopians." This applies equally to north Africa's Morocco, Tunisia, Libya, Egypt, Mauritania, and north Sudan. However, during the reign of H. Mariam Mengistu, Ethiopia took a different turn in that, it unequivocally supported the liberation movements in Southern Africa, including Mugabe's ZANLA forces. It is also reported that the African Community in Addis Ababa (working at the OAU, ECA, and the Embassies, and so forth) complain bitterly of the shoddy treatment they normally receive at the hands of the Ethiopian brethren and authorities.

Adding salt to the injury, Ethiopian authorities had been demanding visas from member states for more than 30 years despite the fact that one of the objectives of the Continental's Organization was to enhance closer ties amongst its member states. It is frustrating that OAU officials traveling to Ethiopia for official business, were required to have visas in order to be allowed entry. The scenario, however, casts doubts as to whether the Organization was serious enough about its commitments and worth its formation anyway. Moreover, the Ethiopian government stood to benefit a lot from the presence of the OAU, the Economic Commission for Africa, and the Embassies. By the host agreements, all the supporting staff of these organizations and embassies (except the professional elite) must be Ethiopian. The Economic Commission for Africa (ECA) alone, employs 500 Ethiopians out of its staff strength of 800.

Soon after the Organization adopted the charter of "non-interference" into the affairs of other States, it lost its moral compass and issued a "blank cheque" for Africa's brutal tyrants who hide behind the facade of a treacherous and infamous charter that has tragically contributed to the polarization of Africa. The rampant abuse of human rights is a culture beyond imagination. African rulers carry on atrocities, massacres and genocides at will to protect their own selfish ends. One African writer put it rightly when asked: "How can Africa twist Pretoria's bloody hands while our own are covered with blood of our own?" Note, this was written at the height of the liberation struggle in Southern Africa. It was during the long administration of the OAU that Africans experienced untold sufferings under their own governments—governments of the Tanks, by the Tanks, and for the Tanks. There was blood everywhere, worse even than during colonial era–in Mozambique, Angola, Zimbabwe, Malawi, Kenya, Uganda, Sudan, Chad, Congo (DRC), Congo (Brazzaville), Sierra Leone, Liberia, Ethiopia, Central African Republic, Somalia, the list goes on and on. More than eight million peasants fled their villages to escape generalized conditions of terror and violence from these unstable states and yet, Africa is often called the cradle of humanity. Where is humanity there? People displaced by their own governments are more numerous in Africa than on any other continent. Indeed, the people of Africa have an enormous task to set things on their right perspective as opposed to continuing the status quo.

However, there were controversial remarks, by white extremists and black moderates, that Africans were not ready for self-government. These people, in the case of whites, were usually branded as "racists," while blacks were seen as "stooges" of the colonial administration. On the contrary, I am in support of the views expressed by these people because of what I have seen and experienced under our own institutions. Even prominent African nationalists acknowledged that fact. For instance, during the "Rhodesian (Zimbabwe) crisis, James Gichuru, representing Jomo Kenyatta at the Lagos Commonwealth Prime Ministers' Conference in the mid-60s, in an interview on television, he is alleged to have said, when asked whether he thought that Rhodesia was ready for immediate majority rule: "It would be very stupid if we were carried into an immediate takeover." He continued, "The Africans in Rhodesia are not as well organized as they are here in West Africa and East Africa, if I might claim that much."[xiv] To day, most of the Zimbabweans, I have spoken to, fervently share that view. You cannot dispute that fact when you look back on Zimbabwe and see what one heartless corrupt tyrant has done to the nation and its people.

In the Democratic Republic of Congo (DRC) the cry is the same. The majority of the Congolese people overwhelmingly believe that it was untimely for the Belgium authorities to hand over the government to the African people even though the former colonial masters had a hand in Congo's endless instability. Look at Somalia where the people there had been without functioning institutions for more than 25 years while the OAU/AU watch helplessly the nation's falling apart. Is this the work of foreign powers as African leaders often claim? In Somalia, as in many other places in Africa, tribalism or ethnic violence plays a major role.

At no time, since independence era, has Africa been beset by so many and such dangerous problems as at present and at no time in its history had the OAU seemed so extraneous. The cold-war was over and the United Nations had taken a new lease of life, but Africa was still exposed to the danger of a new big power "free-for-all." Yet, at such a dangerous time, almost no one outside Africa, and not many inside it, seemed any longer to be aware of the OAU's or AU's relevance.

---

xiv Source: House of Representatives Official Report.

It was at precisely this time that the OAU could have been in the forefront of African affairs, making efforts to solve some of the continent's debilitating problems. Not only was that not the case, but African leaders seemed to have lost the will or courage to endeavor themselves to solve the continent's obvious problems. Such a state of affairs enhances the urgent need for reversal and that reversal, had better come sooner rather than later, or else, the desire for renewed imperial factors are likely to get their way as former Britain's Foreign Secretary, Douglas Hurd, espoused earlier in the 70s.

On the other hand, the OAU principle of noninterference into the affairs of its member states may have made sense and been appropriate to the newly achieved independence and sensitivity of the organization's founding fathers—but, it can not make sense today. It is not simply that we have suddenly entered into a novel period where intervention has taken on a different phase after the fall of the cold war, but also because some of the Africa's internal woes have been driven to the extremes—like in the Congo (DRC), Rwanda, Sudan, Somalia, Sierra Leone, Liberia, Zimbabwe, for example—that threaten the whole foundation of continental stability.

Sadly, and shamefully, Africa's approach to apartheid South Africa had long made a rigmarole of the principle (continental stability). Africa's condemnations of apartheid and its support for the liberation movements were always entirely justified; how much more effective they would have been had African leaders also been ready over the years to condemn unequivocally the excesses of the continent's more unsavory evil empire—Idi Amin's Uganda; Mugabe's Zimbabwe; Mobutu's Congo; Al Bashil's Sudan; Banda's Malawi; Nguema's Equatorial Guinea, and so forth.

Africans now ask, "Where is the freedom so parroted by their leaders during the independence struggle?" As a matter of fact, there is a bewildering difficulty with the fact that the OAU left no history of attempting to restrain the continent's more murderous, antidemocratic, or rogue regimes and where such efforts had been made, they had their genesis from elsewhere. For instance, ECOWAS, a West African organization took upon itself the task of intervening in the bloody civil conflict in Liberia and Sierra Leone and thought its military wing, the ECOMOG, could not entirely claim victory, at least, it undertook some responsible endeavors on a regional basis to bring to an end to insecurity and destructive (of human life) civil wars. Indeed, the OAU did nothing.

The change of name in July 2002, from the Organization of African Unity (OAU), to African Union (AU), is a fallacy and nonstarter at best. Effectively, AU came into being in July 2003, under the Chairmanship of Muammar Gaddafi the Libyan who had been campaigning tirelessly after he unsuccessfully attempted to sway the Arab League in his favor for ten years. During this period, Gaddafi cutoff effective relations with OAU and black Africa and threw his weight on the Arab League which is overwhelmingly Arab-oriented and engulfed by corruption, internal divisions and lack of sense of direction.

However, Gaddafi did not encounter problems in his ambitious endeavors to lead a faltering continental organization, he had the resources and willpower. Muammar Gaddafi was unanimously elected in July 2003. Frankly, the election of Gaddafi to lead the continental organization (OAU) in the 21st century, was both shortsighted and lacked any sense of commitment. First and foremost, Gaddafi's human rights record is among the worst since the end of the second World War II. A violent revolutionary, he staged a putsch in 1969 against King Iddris a pro-western Monarch and has, since, undisputedly remained in power hitherto. He has proved himself anti-democracy and has viciously ruled the oil-rich nation and continues to imprison political rivals under horrific conditions.

Outside his Stalinist regime, Gaddafi supports evil empires such as the Mugabe's corrupt and murderous regime by sending huge amount of weapons which oils the engine of oppression in Zimbabwe. He also has extensive personal investments in agriculture sector there. Being the Chairman of the AU, he is also a potential supplier of arms to the Sudan's brutal racist regime under el Bashir, a fellow Muslim Arab. Like the former OAU, the African Union (AU), has tragically failed to condemn these two rogue regimes for their inhuman treatment of their fellow citizens, all this to absurdly uphold the principle of the infamous "noninterference into the affairs of member states."

Under Gaddafi's leadership, the African Union, as with its predecessor the OAU, lost the battle in the sense that it had no vision to spearhead radical change in transforming the continental organization. It has remained weak and vulnerable. In less than two months after launching a new partnership with the G8 nations in Kananaskis, Canada, in 2003, African leaders were on the verge of failing their countless tests. As Gaddafi was preparing to be officially made the Chairman of the AU by early 2003, African leaders nominated him to a key United Nations Committee on human rights. What a mockery of human rights? This, undoubtedly, explains the qualities of leadership the African leaders possess. In his well-written book, The Fate of Africa; Martin Meredith wrote: "That is why Africa is a mess. That is the tragedy of Africa, too many ignorant people are in positions of power and responsibility." Indeed, there are so many Africans with credible academic achievements (of course not the likes of the Mugabes and Kibakis), but, are unlikely to hold strategic positions in the government simply because they belong to a minority ethnic back ground.

However, since Gaddafi was elected to a powerful position in the continental organization, Africa's reputation has been, once again, tragically tainted and leaves behind a big question, "Africa, what lies ahead?" By electing only the notoriously oppressive Libyan to chair the UN Commission of Human Rights (CHR) (assuring Gaddafi's acclamation) African leaders have thrown themselves into doubt about their commitment to the New Partnership for Africa's Development (NEPAD). However, as I am writing this chapter, NEPAD is obviously dying a slow death—soon to be ready to be buried or cremated. With lots of money, Gaddafi is capable of manipulating greedy African leaders to dance to his tune and keeps other nations in business with him.

Apart from Gaddafi's oppressive leadership, his close association with factional Islamic terrorist organizations has earned Libya notoriety in the eyes of the western nations.

When robbed of his opportunities to enhance his pseudo-revolution among Arab neighbors, he turned his sights and revolutionary fervor south of the Sahara. Confused and visionless African leaders fell prey of his charm and charisma. This time he came with the slogan: "United States of Africa" (USA), which the late Kwame Nkrumah (the true son of Africa, great Pan-Africanist and visionary of our time) espoused as soon as the great people of Gold Coast (Ghana) unanimously elected him their President. The unity, with its own US-style Congress, was to be based on his vision of "Jamahariya" a state of the masses led by him. In his attempts to crown himself as Africa's Messiah, he expressly endeavored to take a practical lead in defusing dangerous and destructive conflicts in the Congo (DRC) and the border dispute between Eritrea and Ethiopia while, at the same time, arming the bloodthirsty despot el Bashir of Sudan—his fellow Muslim. However, neither mission has born fruit although his efforts won praise from his idol, Nelson Mandela.

The failures of AU are closely synonymous with those of its predecessor OAU and further instill the sense of hopelessness among the millions of our wretched populations. First and foremost the change of name has not in anyway or form changed the status quo. In practice, it is still OAU. The players are the same and the rules and policies are the same. Gaddafi's bid to shed his radical image looked like a public-relations headache. On September 1, 2009, Muammar Gaddafi marked the 40th anniversary of the bloodless coup that brought him to power—joining the line of life-presidents with celebrations attended by African, Arab, and Latin American leaders; but largely ignored by the west.

Since Gaddafi became the Chairman of the AU, he has been tirelessly espousing the notion of "Federal Union" akin to the United States model. On the contrary, other leaders favor the European Union model, with economic integration the main motor for change. However, in Africa, regional groupings such as ECOWS (in West Africa) East African Community and SADC in Southern Africa, could be the steppingstone for closer implementation of the African Union. Encouragingly, ECOWS plays a pivotal role in enhancing West Africa's stability and prosperity, while East African Community (EAC), once the strongest regional block in the continent with a glimmer of hope for millions of Africans, collapsed through foreign manipulation and intervention due to its lack of commitment and sense of direction.

Britain and the US were prime suspects in the cabal to break the once thriving regional block. It was during the height of East-West cold war that the late President Julius Nyerere of Tanzania introduced "UJAMAA" (African Socialism) and Milton Apolo Obote of Uganda had his own brand of socialism—"Common Man's Charter." Kenya had already abdicated its independence and became a neocolonial state virtually controlled by Britain and the US, both with gargantuan economic and political interests in Kenya, from commercial white farms to a naval base, the largest in the southern hemisphere. The two great powers were convinced beyond any doubt that if the East African Community (EAC) extended its formidable influence and continued to grow extensively and efficiently, Kenya could fall and tow the line of its two progressive partner states which, in turn, could jeopardize the well established western interests in Kenya. Kenyatta therefore, was cajoled into pulling out of the "dangerous communist plot."

From out of the blue, Kenya, under the leadership of late Jomo Kenyatta, began confiscating aircraft belonging to all three states–then rail trucks and coaches. Nyerere and Obote were caught unaware. They had no time to negotiate or to find out what had led to the conflict. Both leaders joined the fray and took what they could lay their hands on. Tragically and amazingly, the once inspirational regional block fell apart thus dashing the hope of continental unity. Sooner rather than later, EAC workers headed to their respective States. However, there remains a glimmer of hope in the sense that there are efforts in all three states (Kenya, Uganda and Tanzania) to revive the East African Cooperation. Some potential differences still exist, but at least something is being done and we shall wait and see how far these efforts will go.

However, OAU did not fail on everything. In the liberation struggle of Southern Africa, the Continental body performed well. With its Liberation Committee based in Dar es Salaam (Tanzania), the leading Pan-Africanist State under the leadership of Julius Kambarage Nyerere, one of the greatest fighters of African liberation, made sure that the liberation movements were well financed and armed even though there were some irregularities here and there. Most recently, the African Union (AU) in Addis Ababa, Ethiopia, came forward with a progressive notion to help our long lost brothers in Haiti by offering help and giving land for resettlement of Haitians in Africa. But with its own eight million or more refugees in Africa it is hard to understand where would the AU might get the resources to accomplish its ambitions.

Fundamentally, the political and economic woes in Africa are largely self-inflicted. There are major factors which attribute to the continent's decline: corruption, tribalism, dictatorship, greed, and lust for power, and the list goes on. Sadly, the majority of African leaders prove to be more cruel to their fellow citizens than the former colonial oppressors. Truly speaking, the colonial powers had their share in Africa's turmoil whether it was economic or political. The continent had been hit by economic stagnation in many parts, weak currencies, lack of technological development, little investment, and few skills. Sadly, African leaders quote these as excuses for their countries' disastrous economic and political performance, although, partly, the former colonial powers are to blame. Nevertheless, African leaders themselves have exacerbated the situation and destroyed Africa beyond repair. Over the years, the majority of African leaders have become richer than their respective countries and many, have misappropriated money and defrauded their national coffers.

In Liberia, late President Samuel Doe used national funds to purchase US$60 million of arms at the outbreak of the Liberian civil war in 1990. Later he confessed to having stashed away US$25 million Liberian funds in foreign private bank accounts. Sadly, none of the loot has been recovered. Not a single foreign account has returned the money to the long-suffering Liberian people, the money has been quietly spirited away by Doe's foreign bankers. Samuel Doe came into power through a violent coup d' etat. together with a dozen colleagues. They machine-gunned their way to power in the capital of Monrovia in 1980, assassinated President William Tolbert, and forthwith spoke of the need to end the corruption and nepotism practiced by previous rulers. This meant that they intended to rid the country of the traditional elite of American-Liberians who had dominated the small West African country since the time of its establishment in 1847 as a haven for freed black-American slaves. Indeed, this largely succeeded.

In fact, what followed was far more barbaric than anything the country of four million had previously witnessed. Sergeant Doe became President Doe following a rigged 1984 election and then presided over a decade of covert executions, public mutilations of opponents, and disappearance of thousand of citizens. Several attempts to overthrow his regime were mercilessly crushed.

In the long run, it appeared that Doe was unable to counter his country's accelerating revulsion. The rebels who began the second military campaign against him had grown from 200 men to several thousands within a few months and took several strategic positions in a 50 km radius around Monrovia. The rebels were led by Charles Taylor, a criminal thug who had been trained and financed by Muammar Gaddafi of Libya. As the rebels advanced at lightning velocity,

Doe made one last pathetic attempt to cling to power by announcing that he would not stand in the election scheduled in 1991. The announcement was not welcomed in the rebel's camp and was hardly enough to halt the juggernaut.

The United States under Reagan's administration was largely responsible for keeping President Doe in power, despite vivid evidence of large-scare corruption and violence. The US gave Liberia more than US$600 million between 1980 and 1985, making it the largest per capita recipient of US foreign aid in a bleeding Africa. Asked why Reagan would pour such an amount of money in a "black hole"? His advisers argued then that Liberia stood at a very strategic position for refueling rights for US military aircraft and ships, and its navigation port for its nuclear submarine fleet, were too significant to ignore.

Charles Taylor (who happened to be Doe's adviser and who fled the country after being charged with embezzling more than US$2 million) appeared on the verge of grabbing power from his former boss. With four ships and 2,100 Marines off the coast of Monrovia, the situation exacerbated. The beleaguered President Doe was trapped in his fortress-like mansion in the capital and was captured by Taylor's merciless fighters. What goes around comes around. Doe's ears and lips were cutoff by rebel soldiers on Taylor's orders and in his presence. While Doe was screaming and crying amid terrible pain and unstoppable blood flow from his unimaginable wounds, Taylor kept on asking his victim, "Where is the money?" Doe collapsed in a pool of blood and died in his mansion. This shows how cruel and barbaric African leaders can be.

Taylor's National Patriotic Front of Liberia (NPFL), like Doe's Revolutionary Front, plunged the country into bloody tribal feuds between Manos and Krahn. The former supporting Taylor and the latter supporting Doe. Tragically, the country was thrown into bloody chaos and anarchy the likes of which were never seen before or since the establishment of nationhood in 1847. Former President late William Tubman, an America-Liberian who ruled from 1944 until his demise in 1971, studied the tribes very well and articulated unification. Indeed, it worked miraculously well until the advent of Doe and Taylor.

On the economic front, Liberia was dealt a big blow. The only viable foreign exchange earner in the country was the 52,000 hectare Firestone-Bridgestone plantation that brought in badly needed foreign exchange ranging from US$75 million to US$120 million a year. Of this, a large percentage went to the government as taxes. This enterprise was largely destroyed and, as a result, thousands of workers lost their livelihood.

Taylor's violent takeover of power from Doe, exacerbated the situation. However, sooner rather than later, Taylor's regime faced a hard-pressing rebel onslaught. To placate the international community, Taylor held a national election in which he won impressively—though the majority of Liberians and world leaders conceded that the election results were false and unreal. Meanwhile, the rebels continued their attacks with unprecedented precision, turning Monrovia into a Stone Age city. In the middle of the bloody conflict, the Bush administration pressed hard for Taylor's removal from power as he was the stumbling block for peace initiatives.

In August 2003, as rebels shelled the Liberian capital, Monrovia, Taylor was coerced into abdicating power and he fled to Nigeria—but vowed to return because he had tasted "power" which is sweet to African leaders.

As his prime desire, when he usurped power, Charles Taylor fled Monrovia with an unprecedented amount of money; some suggested in the range of US$400-500 million all stacked in suitcases and jute-bags, while the national coffers were left bare and empty. In Nigeria, he settled in an opulent neighborhood with his family. Both rights groups and George Bush pressed for his arrest and trial for his violation of human rights. However, as usual, African leaders were reluctant to let one of their bedfellows face justice as that could open the door for others with similar records.

Finally, President Oleseguni Abasanjo of Nigeria reluctantly succumbed to international pressure and Taylor was arrested at a Nigerian-Cameroon border post while trying to flee with bags of stolen money from the Liberian treasury which was apparently entirely cleaned out.

Currently, Charles Taylor is formally charged with eleven counts of war crimes allegedly committed during Sierra Leone's 1991-2002 civil war, which left over 85,000 dead and more than a million displaced. Taylor is now awaiting his fate in the Hague UN sponsored International Criminal Court (ICC).

Even though his arrest had come too late, it still serves as a warning to other brutal tyrants in the continent. He plundered the country's unique resources: its maritime registry system created by the US in 1948 to enable ships to fly under a flag of convenience, circumvent American wage and labor laws and to be available to the nation in times of war. The Registry generated US$30 million per year for the government. Much of that found its way into Taylor's personal bank accounts and when he became a leader, he showed himself to be extremely avaricious, trying to put his hands on every loose piece of change and every resource he could find.

The Liberian tyrant's case is a rare instance of an African despot being brought to justice. A former notorious Chadian military leader accused in the deaths of thousands of people, lives in a pleasant, seaside mansion in Dakar, Senegal. The infamous Uganda's Idi Amin Dada, perhaps the most brutal of all despots, died peacefully in his place of refuge among fellow Muslims in Saudi Arabia. Robert Mugabe, one of the most cruel and corrupt thugs continues to enjoy unprecedented support from his counterparts in the continent, especially those from Southern Africa.

In Sierra Leone, Charles Taylor committed similar atrocities in collusion with Foday Sankoh, the country's most notorious killer in modern history. The memories are still fresh and disturbing in our minds. What was the cause of the macabre atrocities that pitted Africans against Africans? Of course, it was motivated by utter greed that has become Africa's catalyst for bloodbaths and endemic corruption. In the case of Sierra Leone, the abundance of diamonds attracted Charles Taylor to align himself with Foday Sankoh in order to dominate the illicit "diamond trade" (blood diamonds). However, the overwhelming majority of Sierra Leoneans have never seen or touched the gemstones in their lives and yet, they were the victims of greed perpetrated by few misguided hoodlums in search of self-enrichment.

In a conflict where loyalties shifted, peace accords fizzle out, and diamond fields changed hands, brutality against innocent civilians was almost the only constant. Rebels under the influence of drugs, used amputations on children and adults alike to cower the civilian population. They hacked off lips, ears and limbs. Pro-government militias employed equally wanton tactics with initiation rites that included cannibalism. Indeed, the people of Sierra Leone were caught up in a situation where only rogues and brutes could enjoy inflicting such pains on fellow citizens in order to enrich themselves. Corporal Foday Sayhana Sankoh, the man behind such macabre atrocities against his people was described as corrupt, heartless, greedy and a womanizer—the qualities that also fit his former friend Charles Taylor. Sankoh, like his accomplice, was trained in Libya in the art of revolution.

To further his objectives, Sankoh recruited more than 10,000 child soldiers ranging in age from 11-13 years, making Sierra Leone's record one of the world's worst for recruiting child soldiers. United Nations Children's Funds (UNCF), said at least 4,500 children were used to fight the eight-year senseless civil war. Other aid groups put the number as high as 7,000. Millions of dollars acquired from the illegal sale of diamonds enabled Sankoh and his Revolutionary United Front (RUF) to purchase unlimited amounts of arms and ammunitions that sustained the bloody civil war for eight years.

Foday Sankoh was arrested in Nigeria on charges of trafficking in arms. He was subsequently tried for treason and sentenced to death. He languished in detention for two years while his rebel thugs sought revenge, mounting their most sadistic assault on Freetown, the capital. Astonishingly, when he was released and repatriated to Sierra Leone to face justice and the firing squad, the brute won a pardon and a place in politics. Thanks to British elite forces which intervened and swiftly defeated the barbaric force of cannibals, rapists and killers. Sankoh was rearrested and died in prison of an unspecified causes in mid-2000 leaving behind thousands of displaced orphan souls. The bloody conflicts in Sierra Leone and Liberia could have been nipped in the bud if Africa was united and committed to the welfare of its people.

In Togo, a tiny West African nation and one of the poorest, a former president, the late Anassingbe Eyadema, ruled for 41 years with a brutal iron-fist after he seized power in 1967 from a democratically elected government. Like many African leaders of his generation, Eyadema ruthlessly crushed opposition groups, nurtured a cult of personality, then clung onto power decade after decade, growing unprecedentedly rich–while his tiny nation remained in a grinding state of poverty.

While in power, Eyadema groomed his son to take over after his death. He died of heart attack on September 1, 2005, and forthwith, the unprincipled military elite took immediate and firm control of the administration closing the nation's borders and naming his 39 year-old son Faure Anassingbe Eyadema as President. He entirely ignored a succession plan written into Togo's National Constitution that would have elevated the Speaker of Parliament, who was in Europe at the time, to the Presidency with elections required within 60 days.

After a few days of tumult, the rubber-stamp Parliament overwhelmingly ratified Eyadema's (Jr.) ascension by changing the Constitution to allow him serve out his father's term, which was to have ended in 2008. As the norm in African governments, Eyadema the father, amassed gargantuan wealth which, if divided among Togo's four million people, could have made each a millionaire. It is conservatively estimated that Eyadema (Sr.), siphoned away US$475 million and deposited it all in his foreign bank accounts. It is also reported that more than 25,000 Togolese were killed during his 41-year reign of terror.

Indeed, the history of post-independence Africa is both tragic and shameful. It will, however, be received with a great sense of disbelief and affliction when passed to future generations after we are all gone. Already, to our young generation, it is a history of disappointment and indignity.

In Gabon, the story is the same. The late President Bernard Bongo, his name change to Omar Bongo to assuage the Muslim world in the north, died in June 2009 at the age of 73. He had ruled his nation for 44 years, becoming the longest-serving President in African history and all the while shamelessly looting the country's oil wealth. He treated Gabon, as a self-obsessed landlord and considered everything inside its borders to be his personal property. He elevated corruption to a method of government.

Bongo embezzled enormous wealth which made him one of the richest men on our planet. His great political achievement was to make sure that the revenues from Gabon's 2.7 billion barrels of oil reserves guaranteed his grip on power. He cleverly allowed just enough oil funds to trickle down to the general population of two million and, to a large extent, to the armed forces—Africa's power brokers, thus avoiding any potential unrest. At the same time, he offered his internal critics a bargain they could not refuse: "Drop your opposition in return for a modest but glittering slice of the nation's oil wealth." By this method, he neutralized every rival and became the most successful of all Africa's Francophone tyrants, comfortably extending his political dominance into a life-Presidency.

The sad scenario, the largest share of the oil money was set aside for Bongo's personal use and slavish glorification of the corrupt tyrant, became "de rigueur"–just as one of the continent's notorious corrupt tyrants, Hastings Banda, had done in my own country of Malawi (that is to say, turned the nation into his personal estate). The people of Gabon were themselves placated with Bongo University, Bongo Airport, numerous Bongo hospitals, Bongo Stadium and the Bongo Gymnasium. The Bongo hometown "Lewai" was expressly renamed Bongoville.

Gabon won independence in 1960, but has remained a French satellite state ever since. Bongo gave the French company, ELF-Aquitaine, overwhelming privileges and rights to exploit Gabon's unlimited oil reserves. Paris returned the favor by guaranteeing the then young President's grip on power for an indefinite future. Furthermore, France extended its military presence in the country and a contingent of paratroopers underwrote Bongo's rule. As in my own country, Malawi, where the cold-blooded despot Hastings Banda could not trust Africans, Bongo also trusted no one—but the French and his own family. He made his son Ali Beni Bongo, Defense Minister and his daughter, Pascaline, Foreign Minister and then Chef-de-Cabinet.

During his tenure, Bongo spent much time in Paris and, as his counterparts in former French colonies, made friendship with a succession of French leaders, particularly Valery Giscard d' Estain and Jacques Chirac. He once shocked his people when he said that: there could be no Gabon without France. At the same time, self-acclaimed Emperor Bokassa, while attending the death of General Charles de Gaulle in 1970 in Paris, wept profusely and repeatedly called de Gaulle "Papa." Some of the Central African Republic elders said that he (Bokassa) had never reacted so emotionally at his late father's earlier demise. The late Felix Dia Houphouet-Bboigny of Ivory Coast used to import water from France. As well, the laundering of his hundreds of suits and shirts were done in Paris and shipped back to Abidjan by Air France—twice a week and at the taxpayer's expense.

The Daily Telegraph of London described Bongo as behaving like an aging sybarite during his long sojourns. An Italian fashion designer testified that he kept Bongo supplied with new suits and shirts every after two to three months. When an international beauty contest was held in Libreville,

Gabon, Bongo took a shine to Miss Peru, who found herself ushered into the Presidential bedroom. However, the would-be victim of rape managed to break loose and fled. With such leadership in power, should we Africans continue to blame outside factors for our woes?

In further deposition, Bongo refused to tell the Citibank the source of the more than $150 million (all amounts in US dollars) he deposited into his account had come from. With no evidence in internal documents, the bank speculated Bongo's loot came from "donations" from French oil companies. The payments were under investigation by French authorities and his fat private accounts in Switzerland had been frozen. Apparently, in 1977, a Swiss judge described Bongo as the "Head of an association of criminals." Astonishingly, he has not been charged with any wrongdoing.

In part, however, former colonizers are also responsible in part for Africa's down turn, even though Africa's buccaneers are far more destructive. As though it were not enough, Bongo also pillaged the nation's treasury. He built his Palace at an estimated cost of US$800 million. Candidly, not even a leader from Germany, France, or the US, to name a few, could have contemplated embarking on that project.

It is, widely estimated that the wealth amassed by Gabon's Bongo, Ivory Coast's Boigny, Central African Republic's Bokassa, Togo's Eyadema, Zimbabwe's Mugabe, and Kenya's Arap Moi would sustain the economies of Rwanda, Burundi, Lesotho, Swaziland, Malawi, and Guinea-Bissau for more than five years respectively—providing infrastructures, hospitals, schools, housing for poor people, roads, sustainable agriculture and fighting Malaria and HIV/AIDS, and so forth.

As expected, Bongo's son Ali Ben Bongo took over the reins with the tacit support or help of the armed forces, that culminated into a bloody resistance by the people who demanded the democratic reforms which had been denied them for more than four decades. To defend his position, Ali Ben Bongo urged his opponents to take up the matters with the country's High Court Judge who himself was appointed by his late father. What a mockery of justice?

Indeed, the history of Africa, since independence, is filled with cruel and unimaginable scenarios. In early 1994, Africa and the world witnessed something grotesquely repulsive that should not have befell in the 20th century.

What happened in Rwanda, still burns in the hearts and minds of the human race throughout our planet. It all started when President's Habyalimana's jet, returning from Nairobi, Kenya, attempting to land at Kigali's International Airport in Rwanda was brought down in a deluge of firepower from the ground. Habyalimana lost his life in the incident. This happened on April 6, 1994. Even though the accident still remains a mystery, the Hutus who carried out the abominable massacres of the Tutsis, assert that it was the work of Tutsi rebels. Forthwith, within hours, Hutu thugs began killing anyone perceived to oppose the Hutu dominated government. In fact, the killings were directed at Tutsi civilians in a highly planned ethnic cleansing. The Hutu majority and Tutsi minority have lived together for many centuries, but each suspects the other. The Hutus maintain that the Tutsis are not Rwandese but hailed from Ethiopia centuries ago. To the contrary, the Hutus regard themselves as the authentic owners of Rwanda. This is blatantly misguided because before the infamous Berlin Conference in 1884-1885, Africans had no borders, our forefathers roamed about over the entire continent.

The brutal killings which were almost certainly precipitated by tribal hatred—the scourge of Africa—spilled into neighboring Congo (DRC). The Tutsi (Anyamulenge) there had been living in Eastern Congo for over 400 years, but were being harassed and expelled by Mobutu Sese Seko's evil regime, which had strong ties with murderous Hutu establishment. Two years after Mobutu Sese Seko fled Congo on the eve of the rebels' victory in 1998, the remains of Juvenal Habyalimana, former President of Rwanda, was found in Mobutu's Mansion in Kinshasa. How the lifeless body was transported from Kigali to Kinshasa, some 2,000 km distance, and why the body was kept in Mobutu's home, remains a conundrum.

The massacres of the Tutsis and Hutu moderates were carried out with an extreme sense of hatred precipitated by tribalism, and within 100 days, more than 800,000 souls or one-seventh of the population perished in cold blood. More than 50 percent of the two million people killed were minority Tutsis, making the massacres the "worst in recent history."

Sadly, the senseless bloodbath could have been averted if the international community had acted swiftly—especially the UN Security Council and the former Organization of African Unity (OAU)—when Lt. Gen. Roméo Dallaire of Canada compassionately and ardently urged the World body in January 1994 to send International Peace Keepers when genocide became imminent. Dallaire's express pleas fell on deaf ears and, instead, the attention was shifted to the Balkan Region where similar slaughters were being perpetrated by Slobodan Milosevic's forces. NATO troops were ordered to bomb Kosovo in order to protect people of lighter skin while Tutsis were left at the mercy of the marauding Hutu thugs. Astonishingly enough, French troops were dispatched to Rwanda, but apparently sided with Hutu killers.

Shocked by the scale of the brutal killings in his homeland, Major-General Paul Kagame, then senior Intelligence Official in Yoweri Museveni's new government, after veteran Milton Apolo Obote's administration fell, invaded Rwanda from Uganda under Rwandan Patriotic Front (RPF) banner in July 1994 with more than 5,000-strong soldiers who had earlier on helped President Yoweri Museveni dislodge Obote's regime in 1985. These battle-hardened RPF soldiers under the command of the American-trained Gen. Paul Kagame fought one of the deadliest civil wars in the continent. However, not only Tutsis fought under RPF, but also a number of patriotic Hutus were among the ranks of combatants.

Thanks to Kagame and his compatriots, after a spell of two months or so the Hutu's army of genocide began to crumble slowly, but surely. Finally, the gallant soldiers of the RPF routed out what appeared to be a ragtag army of the Hutu killers and pursued them across the border into Congo. Thus came the end of mass killings, but, without RPF's exemplary chivalry the entire Tutsi population could have been effaced from the face of our planet.

Meanwhile, genocide suspects managed to escape and settle comfortably in Europe, Canada, and the US. Through unrelenting pressure from rights group, some of the perpetrators of the massacres were apprehended and convicted in UN-sponsored jurisdictions world wide. In Belgium two Benedictine Nuns were charged for their part in killing refugees who sought protection in their Church. The Nuns received long prison sentences ranging from 20 to 30 years. Sister Gertrude, born Consolata Mukangano, and Sister Maria Kisito, born Julienne Makubutela, were with two men, Vincent Ntezimana, then 40, a former University professor, and Alphonse Higaniro, then 52, a former aide to President Juvenal Habyalimana, whose death in a plane crash in April 1994, triggered the Hutu rampage.

However, Belgium's eagerness to stage and finance the US$2.5 million trial reflects its total failure to prevent the genocide in its former colony—failure for which Guy Verhofstad, the Prime Minister, apologized in 2002. Due to its very extensive notion of universal responsibility, Belgium is championing the fight against the impunity of dictators and executioners.

Belgium's zeal also reflects a much deeper guilt about its conduct in Africa. The trials of these suspects are taking place in Brussels' huge neoclassical Palais de Justice, opened by King Leopold II in 1883. He was a notorious monarch who created a private empire in the Congo and himself committed untold genocide as he raped and plundered it. After all, the Belgians, in collusion with US CIA and Mobutu Sese Seko, were directly responsible for the cold-blooded murder of Patrice E. Lumumba in 1961, the first African Prime Minister of the Congo Republic.

So far, after 16 years of the massacres, the hunt for criminals still goes on today. There have been additional apprehensions of suspects who have been convicted and sentenced to long terms in prison. Among them, Jean-Paul Akayesu, a former notorious Rwandan Mayor, Leon Mugesera, a former adviser to a Rwandan Cabinet Minister who openly encouraged the Intarahumwe (Hutu bloody militias) similar to the notorious Janjaweeds of the Sudan directed by the Arab-dominated regime of racist el Bashir in Khartoum, to cut Tutsis' throats before Tutsis could cut theirs and throw their lifeless bodies into Nyabarongo River for crocodile dinners.

Indeed, jokes aside, something is terribly wrong in Africa and every one of us must be concerned for our own future and for that of our grandchildren to come. In Arusha, Tanzania, four top Rwandan Army officials: Col. Theonstes Bagosora, Lt. Col. Anatole Nsengiyumva, Maj. Aloys Ntabakuze and Brig. Gen. Gratien Kibiligi, were convicted of genocide crimes against humanity, rape, and for their roles as the army leaders. In sentencing the criminals, who were supposed to defend the rights of their citizens, were accused by their UN prosecutors of unleashing "a legion of ferocious demons" on the victims.

The Rwandan tragedy has indeed perplexed millions of people, particularly Africans, by the way it was handled. In the US, Bill Clinton's administration seemed reluctant to flex its muscles to prevent mass killings. Ms. Madeleine Albright, US Ambassador to the UN at the time of genocide, refused to appear before a UN-mandated independent inquiry probing into reasons why the world body failed to prevent the tragic genocide in Rwanda in 1994. Albright could have provided key information about high-level decisions that led the US to call on the UN Security Council to dramatically reduce the number of peacekeepers in Rwanda shortly after the killings started in earnest in April 1994.

The humanitarian Lt. Gen. Romeo Dallaire once passionately lamented; "Africans are being treated indifferently by the world community for who they are." In Britain, a

Rwandese army officer implicated in the cold-blood murder of 22 Tutsi children during the height of the genocide, was expressly given political asylum and settled there and granted welfare benefits. Lt. Col. Tharcisse Muvunyi was then under investigation by the UN tribunal after being accused of lynching Tutsi children in a Convent. However, one wonders whether the British government would have extended such humanitarian gestures to someone suspected of being a perpetrator of the holocaust against the Jews? The humanitarian tragedy in Rwanda is a vivid reminder of what lies ahead for Africa if its so-called leaders, through greed and lust for power, condone and encourage ethnic divisions in order to remain in power and plunder our nations for their own naked-self interests.

Burundi, a close neighbor to Rwanda, is also engulfed in bloody ethnic conflicts between the Hutu majority and the Tutsi minority. Out of six million people, 85 percent are Hutu, 14 percent Tutsi and one percent other smaller groups. The Hutus burn with the notion that they have always been oppressed. The Tutsis are haunted by the notion that they are the Palestinians of East Africa and about to be hounded from Burundi, exiles already driven from Rwanda.

In both these tiny nations located in East-Central Africa, bloody ethnic civil wars have been fought since the early 50s under the watchful eye of the colonial powers—Belgium. In fact, the Belgians deliberately exploited the (Tutsi-Hutu) divisions to further rule them. In other words, the colonial power played the politics of "divide and rule," which so far, has been very effective and devastating in nature. The majority of both groups strongly believe that the present-day situation had been apparently exacerbated by the Belgians who touted the Tutsis as a "superior" tribe and made members of both (Hutu-Tutsi) carry identification cards designating the holders as Hutu or Tutsi.

In 1972, after a coup attempt in Bujumbura, Burundi, the minority Tutsi massacred between 100,000 to 300,000 Hutus, including most of the tribe's intelligentsia. Over a million refugees crossed over into Congo, Uganda, and Tanzania. In 1988 the Hutu people's Liberation Front (HPLP) attempted a comeback from exile in neighboring Congo. However, the comeback was nipped in the bud. Ethnic clashes followed the aborted attacks and more than 5,000 people were killed on both sides (Hutu/Tutsi) simultaneously.

Toward the end of 1995, before even the fresh wounds of the genocide in neighboring Rwanda were healed, the Burundi extremist Hutu militia, "Intagohekas" (those who never sleep) attacked Tutsis in the predominantly Hutu countryside killing 5,000 people. In retaliation, the Tutsi extremist militia, Sans Echec, which means "without failure," killed close to 1,000 Hutu civilians in once mixed neighborhoods of Bwiza and Buyenzi.

Failure of the UN to keep peace in Burundi, precipitated a military coup by Col. Pirre Buyoya, himself a Tutsi, in July 1996. He removed a Hutu democratically elected President Sylvestre Ntibantunganya who subsequently sought refuge at the house of the US Ambassador Morris Hughes. Members of his family were guarded by American Marines. This prompted suspicion among Tutsis that the UN had an anti-Tutsi bias as shown when the UN failed to stop the genocide of the Tutsis in Rwanda in 1994.

The hatred between Tutsis and Hutus stems from entrenched ethnic divisions. Hutus accuse Tutsis of being foreigners in Rwanda and Burundi, claiming that they hailed from Ethiopia (and were Ethiopians). Hutus never tell where they came from. This is a senseless and preposterous notion that keeps two people of the same culture at one another's throat, day in and day out, with no end on sight. If these two tiny nations were blessed with potential mineral resources like Congo, it is most likely that foreign expeditionary forces would be present in both countries, not to keep peace, but to rape and plunder the resources. However, it is not too late to avert this disaster. Africans must themselves find a solution to solve this dangerous and endless bloody ethnic conflict. It is our problem and therefore, we must face it and solve it once and for all. In the famous words of President Barrack Obama: "Yes we can."

Sudan, is the largest country in Africa (area 967,000 sq. miles, with a population of 21-million people)—about twice the size of Europe. The most famous Sudanic States were Ghana, Karem, Songhai and Hausa and they were converted into Islam in the Middle Ages but fell into decline at various dates betwixt the 16th and 19th C.E. In reality, Sudan is genuinely an African land which was conquered by Arabs from the north in the 15th century. The Nubians, from present-day north-Sudan, ruled as far as present day Syria.

In 1962, fed up with the perpetual apartheid-like tyrannical rule by Muslim Arabs, Africans from Southern Sudan revolted and took up arms to defend themselves against injustices and racism meted out to them by the oppressors. In 1969, Gen. Jaafar el Nimiery staged a coup d' etat and forthwith introduced a decree of Arab Socialism and renamed the county the Sudan Democratic Republic (SDR) under strict Islamic Law throughout the country. In the south where Islam does not exist, that was an affront to the overwhelming number of Christians of the south.

Starting as a hit-and-run stratagem, the people of Southern Sudan forthwith regrouped and formed the Sudan Peoples Liberation Army (SPLMA). Meanwhile, charismatic John Garang had just returned from the US where he had undertaken military training at a military college. On his return to Sudan, he was appointed second in command in the Sudanese military structure dominated by Arab Muslim officers.

For his first tour of duty, in 1970, he was dispatched to Southern Sudan, his native birthplace, to fight the insurgents who happened to be his brothers and sisters. To him, the mission was bitterly against his deep-rooted conscience (love of his roots). On the second day after his arrival at the battlefront, the late John Garang, together with a few other compatriots (southerners), defected and joined the SPLMA ranks.

The civil conflict in Southern Sudan reached its zenith towards the end of 1970s when the Arab League intervened on the side of fellow Arabs in the north Sudan. Meanwhile John Garang received support from former Kenyan dictator President Daniel Arap Moi, a rare source. As the conflict intensified, President Yoweri Museveni of Uganda, jumped into the fray and supported the SPLA. Much as I have deep-rooted differences with both Presidents (Moi and Museveni), I strongly believe that they exercised brilliant judgment by identifying themselves as African patriots. northern Sudanese, however, see themselves as Arabs and deny the strongly African element in their skin color and physical features. They associate these features with the Negroid race and see it as the mother-race of slaves—inferior and demeaned.

The civil war in Southern Sudan which was racially motivated by the Khartoum government and dominated by the Arab Muslims, cost unprecedented suffering for the African people of Southern Sudan. In a decade of brutal conflicts, one million African Sudanese are reported to have been massacred by Sudanese government forces and its notorious militias (Janjaweed), and an additional three million displaced. Government-sponsored militias, stormed defenseless villagers. Soldiers shot the men, looted the villages, raped the women, some only eight years of age. Slavery which had been outlawed some 400 years earlier, showed its ugly head in the Sudan in the 21st century. Children of both genders from the ages of 7 to 11, were captured by Arab slave traders at will and transported to northern Sudan, north Africa and Persian Gulf States. These children endured the most inhuman treatment in recent history, many were selected as concubines and were genitally mutilated in order to be accepted in their Masters' culture–and then bred.

For more than two decades, the obnoxious Islamic Fundamentalist regime in the Sudan has been using slave raids as the terror weapon of choice in its self-declared holy war (Jihad) on the African population in the South. The goal is to Islamize and Arabize Sudan's Christians and tribalists. The Islamists in Khartoum also devastated the moderate Muslim Nuba peoples. Slaves are given Arab names and forcibly converted to Islam, sadly under the watchful eye of the UN Human Rights Commission and the Organization of African Unity (OAU), which was particularly vocal against the apartheid regime in South Africa.

Charles Jacobs, President of the American Anti-Slavery Group (AASG) in Boston, USA, wrote in the Los Angeles Times November 1, 1999, thus: "Yet the fate of Southern Sudanese Africans has not been of particular concern in the west. Because of scant media coverage or because many people don't know or because this slavery doesn't fit the familiar black and white pattern or because we fear offending the Muslim World, a shameful silence pervades." However, personally, I strongly believe that liberal western policies toward Islam serve as a direct catalyst for the unprecedented upsurge in Islamic violence worldwide.

As in any liberation struggle, the people of Southern Sudan endured some setbacks in their endeavors to free themselves from Arab racist domination. These setbacks were subsequently accompanied by strings of victories by rebel forces over government troops. This in turn, prompted a peace and reconciliation agreement, the "Lafon Agreement," after the capture of Lafon City along with an intact government platoon on March 31, 1995. Strategically, the fall of Lafon was a most significant victory that forced the el Bashir's racist regime to have a second thought.

After almost 17 years of brutal and bloody civil war, the charismatic and brilliant military strategist Major General Dr. John Garang, the leader of Sudanese Peoples' Liberation Army (SPLA), signed a peace accord in Nairobi, Kenya, on January 9, 1995. It gave Southern Sudan an autonomous status. On the government side, the Vice-president Ali Osman Taha signed on behalf of the atrocious President Omar el Bashir.

In 2008, the Vice-president of Sudan, Gen. Garang, was killed in a helicopter crash while visiting in the south. His suspicious demise sparked violent reactions in Khartoum and other cities in the south. More than 60 people were killed in

Khartoum alone by trigger-happy soldiers of the el Bashir regime. Several clashes were also reported between Arabs and Africans elsewhere in the country.

In the same period of time, former Prime Minister of Lebanon Rafik Hariri, and former Prime Minister of Pakistan Benazir Bhutto were killed by assassins in their respective countries. Immediately, the UN Security Council and the US Government ordered an investigation into their suspicious demise, while John Garang's death, then a sitting Vice President, was swept under the carpet. This is a further proof that the World body—the UN—treats its members differently. The fact that the deaths of Hariri and Bhutto were hurriedly acted upon while that of Garang was not even mentioned, speaks volume.

In 2003, the people of Darfur, Western Sudan, took up arms in order to defend themselves against the injustices, oppression, and tyranny by Arab Islamists. Although 85 percent of Darfurians are Muslims themselves, at this point in time, the conflict is based on racial hatred. Darfurians are African Muslims and considered owners of the land.

Indeed, the situation in Darfur is far worse than the former apartheid regime in South Africa and yet, the international community, and particularly African leaders, remained disturbingly unconcerned as if nothing evil is being done to the Darfurians of Sudan. It is apparently clear that the Arab dominated regime in Khartoum is bent on wiping out the black African Fur tribe, a sedentary people living in that part of the Sudan.

By using Sudanese government soldiers and the brutal militias (Janjaweed) against defenseless citizens; women, children, and the aged, the el Bashir regime committed crimes against humanity. But the UN Security Council refused to accept it as "genocide"—until former US Secretary of State Colin Powell declared for the first time, on September 9, 2004, that the wave of atrocities in the Sudan's Darfur region constitutes "genocide." The genocide convention acknowledged the fact that genocide, whether committed in times of peace or bloody conflict, ought to be considered a punishable crime under international law. "Genocide" was expressly defined in the convention as "deliberate acts designed to eradicate, in whole or part, an entire national, ethnic, racial or religious group."

It is estimated that 650,000 Darfurians have been killed and a million of others displaced in their own country during the bloody conflict. In the absence of global condemnation, the Arab dominated regime in Khartoum, accelerated its acts of violence with barbarity and impunity. However, if the Jewish State of Israel had done that in defense of its citizens, the whole world could have descended on them with full force. We have seen it in Kosovo where minority light-skinned Muslims were saved from annihilation by NATO forces spearheaded by the United States of America which contributed 4,000 troops. Although, the former President of Yugoslav, Slobodan Milosevic was arrested for crimes against humanity in mid 2006, Omar el Bashir, despite despicable violation of human rights, has continued to enjoy sizable support from his friends and Arabs alike—and with impunity.

The conflict in Darfur has been rated the "most" bloody and brutal in modern history and on par with the Rwanda genocide. Yet, the people there are left to fend for themselves. In his comment, Dr. W. A. Knight Professor of International Relations in the Department of Political Science at the University of Alberta, had this to say: "The people of Darfur are losing basically all of their possessions. Their possessions are burned or destroyed while their villages are burned and pillaged." The Amnesty International (AI), had this to say: "There is an attempt at "deracialization," a fancy word for a policy of deliberate rape of African women by Arab men

There are a number of factors which sustained the "war of attrition" in Darfur. The government in Khartoum, because it is Islamic in nature, has been getting unprecedented support from the immoral Arab League and most of Islamic countries at the UN. These inhumane countries are supporting the Sudanese regime despite authentic claims of genocide and ethnic cleansing. The former OAU and the present African Union (AU), which have more member states from Sub-Sahara (Africans), failed to voice even a grain of condemnation over the barbaric slaughter of their brethren. At the same time, in former apartheid South Africa and racist Rhodesia (Zimbabwe)—where the conditions for blacks were not as bad as in Darfur—the OAU shouted itself "hoarse" at these minority regimes. In Africa there is a widely acclaimed observation which says: "It is right for African leaders to brutalize their own people, while it is wrong for whites to do so."

Another factor which strengthened the intransigence of Khartoum's genocidal regime is the inflow of war machinery from Arab nations, most notably the Islamic Libyan regime. The Chinese government also played a devastating role by supplying enormous amount of weaponry to defend its vast oil investments. China is not the only country to ignore the flow of bloody-oil in the Sudan. Canada, through its leading oil giant TALISMAN ENERGY INC., also exploits that benighted country's oil reserves but turns a blind eye to macabre atrocities against the African people. This multinational corporation's greed has severely tarnished Canada's reputation as a country concerned about the world's poor and defenseless people.

In October 1999, oil estimates put Sudan's recoverable oil reserves at more than 630 million barrels. It started to export its crude to the world market in early 2000. In 2001, Talisman Energy of Calgary, together with the national oil companies of China (the main supplier of arms to the genocidal regime of el Bashir and Malaysia) built a US$1.4 billion, 1,600 km pipeline from Southern Sudan to the Red Sea. Talisman put up US$400 million, owns 25 percent of the action, and plans to pump 450,000 barrels a day.

However, some Canadians applauded the action in the sense that it could bring petrodollars to a poverty-stricken nation. But there was also every reason to believe this pipeline, and the money it represents, would bring untold destruction and blood to the region. On the contrary, at the time of apartheid minority rule in South Africa, Canada under the able leadership of Prime Minister Brian Mulroney was most vocal against the evil system in the western democracies.

Finally, though too late, the International Criminal Court (ICC) issued a warrant of arrest on March 5, 2009, against el Bashir for war crimes and crimes against humanity. As expected, Sudan's allies, including a string of African States whose brethren were brutally massacred by Arab extremists, joined Arab States and China for calling the suspension of the ICC warrant—warning it could undermine any so-called efforts to end the six-year bloody and senseless conflict in Darfur. However, the genocidal regime in response, vowed it would not cooperate with the Hague-based court which accuses el Bashir of masterminding a campaign of extermination, rape and pillage in Darfur. The regime further mocked the warrant as not being "worth the ink" in which it is written. Nevertheless, the International Criminal Court (ICC) believes that the action against Sudan might bring about a more "humane world."

Much as the global community tends to forget or abandon the wretched people of Darfur, other loving souls like Mia Farrow and her son Ronan Farrow, both westerners, worked for UNICEF in Darfur to help victims of the unparalleled genocide. Mia and Ronan played a remarkable role in feeding thousands of abandoned children and old people who were left for dead. Indeed, thousands of malnourished souls were saved at an amazing rate. In 2004, 22 percent of the children and the elderly were malnourished, by mid-2005, it was cut to 12 percent. Mia comforted miserable and melancholy looking people with words: "We are all a human family."

Mia and Ronan were not the only loving individuals. George Clooney who had witnessed the bloodletting conflict physically with his father Nick Clooney voiced their utmost indignation against what Nick termed: "The first genocide of the 21st century." He further asserted that, "We did not stop Rwanda, this one (i.e., Darfur) we can stop." In his last words at a Mall Rally, George reminded his audience thus: "If we turn our heads and look away and hope that it will disappear, then they will." "An entire generation of people," concluded the noble soul. In Canada, a humanitarian soldier named General Roméo Dallaire, haunted by the previous genocide in Rwanda where close to a million Tutsis and Hutu moderates perished, passionately appealed to powerful nations not to ignore the plight of the Darfurians for the color of their skin.

However, the international community is eagerly awaiting el Bashir's apprehension and his ultimate indictment as this could by itself send a strong message to other brutal tyrants in Africa.

In Kenya, Kenyans too have not been spared of obnoxious government since its independence in 1963. After a ten-year protracted liberation struggle against British colonialism, Jomo Kenyatta became the first African President and the foremost Pan-Africanist Jaramongi Odinga Oginga as his Vice President after the Kenya African National Union (KANU) swept into power with a landslide majority in the 1963 general election—after almost 80 years of foreign domination by the British.

As in most parts of Africa, President Jomo Kenyatta ruled with an iron-fist and surrounded by fellow Kikuyu tribesmen and relatives. It is true that most of the fight was carried out by the Kikuyu (biggest ethnic group) under Mau Mau leadership. A young energetic and gallant Commander Dedan Kimathi led the group—and not Jomo Kenyatta as we are made to believe. In the mid-50s, Dedani was captured by colonial forces and ultimately hanged for his part in the covert organization. He was buried unceremoniously within the prison's precinct in Nairobi, Kenya. After twenty years in power, Kenyatta never bothered to extend a decent reburial for a national hero. It didn't occur until Dr. Mwai Kibaki, a fellow Kikuyu, was swept into power in the mid-90s and forthwith ordered a decent reburial of Dedan's remains—an act that drew sharp criticism from the British government which considered Dedani as a "terrorist."

Again, as in many parts of Africa, independence brought an unprecedented glimmer of hope to the overwhelming majority of our people throughout the continent. However, that hope has distinctively faded due to the general trend of the African leadership. It is sad indeed, that tribalism has become a scourge of Africa, while corruption is a cult. To say the fact, Kenya had been doing well economically, but it remains politically engulfed by tribalistic anomalies that pose potential destruction of our nations. Few other countries in the world, and hardly any in Africa (apart from South Africa) could rival the economic growth rate of 6.4 percent that the country averaged between 1965 and 1980. Such economic prosperity help sustain relative political stability in the country. However, the only problem centered on who got the lion's share.

For almost all of the 20 years Kenyatta had been at the helm, members of his own Kikuyu tribe prospered economically and politically at the expense of other minority ethnic groups. The Kikuyu (the most populous group) also had been the backbone of the then KANU Party which has now been swept into political oblivion. After the demise of Jomo Kenyatta in 1978, Daniel Arap Moi (who hails from the Kalenjin people, one of several smaller, have-not tribes, that inhabit the Rift Valley in western Kenya) took over Kenya's Presidency.

Daniel Arap Moi's economic strategy was based on developing self-sufficiency in grain, especially wheat. Not astonishingly, this was the crop grown by the native people of the Rift Valley. During the 1980s, Kenya's economy continued to do well, but the recipients of the new wealth, and new influence, had shifted more towards the people of the Rift Valley than to the Kikuyu.

As his predecessor Jomo Kenyatta, Arap Moi packed government senior positions from the Kalenjin ethnic group (Moi is Kalenjin). This spilled over to the related groups such as Masai, Samburu, Pokot, and others. Members of other groups are often appointed to senior positions as a camouflage, with some notable exception such as the powerful Secretary for Provincial Administration and Security, Hezekiah

Oyuge, who was a Luo, from a second powerful ethic group in Kenya. In Moi's administration, Ministers were categorically forbidden to implement any policy of national significance without the approval from the Office of the President. Thus, the Head of the Civil Service, Joseph Arap Letteng, himself a Kalenjin, effectively had the power to overrule Ministerial decisions. In effect, this sort of administrative setup was able to sweep aside any issue or notion deemed to be more beneficial to other provinces than the Rift Valley. Indeed, this is one of the reasons that African governments lack transparency, hence, uncontrolled corruption, inefficiency, and large-scale mismanagement are the norms.

President Moi shamelessly packed his fellow tribesmen into strategic positions as if Kenya was a personal estate. Deputy Police Commissioner, Arap Sumbeiywo (Kalenjin), was a brother to Chief Military Intelligence Officer (CMIO), who was directly answerable to the Head of State.

Tribalism apart, during Moi's tenure, corruption tripled. In fact this occurred under the watchful eye of western democracies and was praised for economic achievements which benefitted only a handful of the ruling clique, their spouses, tribesmen, and senior military brass which in most parts of Africa, protect corrupt and evil leaders, leaving the overwhelming majority to perish in the inferno of poverty. From 1980 to 1990, Kenya became the lucky beneficiary of the west's largesse—receiving approximately US$25 billion in foreign aid. But did the majority of Kenyans benefit from this aid? The answer is a big NO! As a matter of fact, some of the funds (US$350 million) ended up in the construction of a private International Airport at El Doret, a remote village in Kenya that apparently happens to be President Arap Moi's hometown.

Since the construction of the airport more than a decade ago, no international flight has landed there, leave alone local flights. At the same time, Kibera Township, a home for more than 5 million residents in the outskirts of Nairobi, remains one of the poorest and the most dangerous places in the world.

Children swim in sewage due to lack of running water. Diseases are prevalent in the absence of a sustained healthcare system. And above all, crime is part of culture there—and nobody cares.

It is widely speculated that between US$1.6 billion to US$2.5 billion remained unaccounted for after Moi's kleptocratic government was clobbered in national elections some few years back. Moi himself is rated as one of the richest men in the world and members of his family have amassed immense wealth through Moi's connection. Yet, after 46 years of independence, the overwhelming majority of Kenyans remain poorer than during the colonial era. This is not good at all, for this is not what Kenyans expected from their own leaders. But what threatens Kenya's future even more than political obstreperousness is a social explosion. The burgeoning unemployment among school and college graduates, housing, healthcare, poverty, and many other social ills remain as monumental problems.

In 2002, Dr. Mwai Kibaki was swept into power on the slogan of good governance and a promise to fight to end polarizing corruption. Kibaki, an octogenarian professional economist has been in the corridors of power for almost 50 years. As his predecessors, he is surrounded by his fellow Kikuyu fawning sycophants and diehard opportunists who are there to loot and plunder the nation's economy. Kibaki led the Rainbow Coalition (NRC), an alliance of the opposition Parties that ended Moi's thugocracy government after 24 years in power.

In his inauguration speech on December 30, 2002, at the Nairobi Park, Kibaki said: "I am inheriting a country which has been badly ravaged by years of misrule and ineptitude." As he spoke, the crowd sang, cheered and clapped. Looking grim, Arap Moi stepped down after reading a short speech that was drowned out by Kenyans pelting the stage with mud and singing, "All is possible without Moi," and "Go away." "Fellow Kenyans, today I hand over the heavy burden of office," Moi told the restless crowd. "I do so with mixed feelings."

Realistically, the people of Kenya were filled with a new sense of hope and high expectations under Kibaki's leadership. However, the expectations were short-lived. The President, like his predecessors, did not live up to his promises–instead corruption quadrupled, and tribalism and nepotism became part of the government's norm. Sooner rather than later, the situation became uncontrollable, and Lailla Odinga, himself a fire brand, refused to betray his conscience and pulled out of the Rainbow Alliance and formed his own political Party; The Orange Democratic Movement (ODM). Lailla Odinga is a Luo, the second largest ethnic group in Kenya and he is the son of the late Jaramongi Oginga Odinga; Kenya's foremost Pan-Africanist who stepped down as Kenyatta's Vice-president because of the former's neocolonial policies.

In April 2004, Kenyans went to the polls amidst economic depression, institutionalized corruption, and widening ethnic divisions. As Odinga's Party was surely and steadily cruising to victory, Mwai Kibaki hurriedly, with his Army General, Police Chief, and Director of Intelligence in tow, declared victory at a Press Conference while, astonishingly, the ballots were still being counted.

As a result of massive vote-rigging, the once peaceful nation was ultimately plunged into tumult, groups of smaller tribes targeting the populous Kikuyu. Confirming the voting irregularities, the Chief of the Election Commission, Samuel Kivuitu declared that altered tally sheets made it difficult for him to determine whether the election aftermath was accurate. The opposition leader Railla Odinga declared the elections were massively rigged and that Mwai Kibaki stole the votes. There was unprecedented pandemonium in the country. Kenyans slaughtered each other on tribal lines throughout the country for the single reason that one person, filled with lust for power and greed, wanted to remain in power for the rest of his life. Prominent Africans such as former UN Secretary-general Kofi Annan and Bishop Desmond Tutu of South Africa hurriedly arrived in Nairobi, Kenya to work for diplomatic solutions, while tribal lynching accelerated at an alarming rate. Sadly, it was the worst national unrest that Kenya, a relatively stable country, found itself in since independence in 1963.

After the storm had passed and peace returned due to intensive diplomatic endeavors, it was found that more than 5,000 innocent souls had perished in a senseless bloodbath, over 25,000 injured, and 65,000 men, women and children displaced. All these avoidable sufferings point to only one conclusion, "Greed and lust for power."

At last, diplomacy prevailed to a certain extent. A national unity government was finally put in place and Lailla Odinga, the leader of the Orange Democratic Movement (ODM) became the Prime Minister while the cheater Mwai Kibaki, remained President, as this is what he desired—but at the expense of the overwhelming majority of the wretched population.

Even though the unity government was put in place, nothing dramatic changed. Odinga's role has been incredibly undermined by President Kibaki and his gang of detractors. Corruption, also the scourge of Africa, is on the rise and so is general instability. In March 2010, it was reported that US$1 million which was allocated to buy books for schools, vanished mysteriously. At the same time, US$26 million which was foreign aid to buy food for the starving people in northern Kenya, due to its severe drought, also vanished mysteriously. This prompted Kenyan women under the Centre for Rights of Education and Awareness (CREA), to organize a "sex ban" against their men in the hope that the government would listen to their concerns.

To add salt to the injury, the wife of President Mwai Kibaki, Lucy Kibaki, stormed into the newsroom of the country's largest newspaper (The Nation) on April 3, 2005, and demanded the arrest of journalists for what she considered biased coverage. To this end, she slapped one cameraman in the face and ordered her security men, who apparently happened to be Police Officers, to prevent anyone from leaving the newsroom and to confiscate the reporters' cell phones.

At an impromptu news conference Lucy Kibaki, from within the newsroom and broadcast on television, was shown berating the newspaper's staff while the Nairobi Police Chief, King'ori Mwangi, stood by her side looking moronic.

The President's wicked wife was protesting reports carried in the Nation and other daily papers that said she tried to pull the plug on a party for a departing World Bank country Director whose residence was next door to the President's private home. She defended herself by saying that the music was too loud and that she was doing her duty as a "senior resident" of the posh neighborhood by trying to halt the party. However, Kenya's newspapers previously had reported on her allegedly heavy-handed dealings with her husband's staff and the power she was believed to wield within the government.

By and large, this was not an isolated case involving Africa's so-called first ladies. In Malawi (which was brutally ruled by the charlatan Hastings Banda for 30 years) Miss Cecilia Kadzamila, the President's concubine, wielded unprecedented powers. She was the second most powerful figure in the country, indeed, as his partner she was above the law. Her words were final. She was a law unto herself and she made many Malawians, especially the hated northerners, victims of injustices.

President Mwai Kibaki's lust for power and his naked self-interest had largely plunged the once prosperous nation in Africa into irreversible economic and political instability. The number of tourists to Kenya dropped by more than a third in the first half of the year, blaming deadly post-election violence. Kenya which relies on tourism to its famed wildlife safaris, beaches, and other attractions, lost up to US$1.5 billion in that period. Ethnic divisions still remain high in a country that has enjoyed national stability since independence in 1963, because of poor leadership and because economic performance has fallen to its lowest ebb. Kenyans and Zimbabweans, both led by wicked octogenarians have learnt it in a hard way.

Kibaki has been in the political leadership for almost 50 years, Robert Mugabe for almost 31 years. If such people are left in power and protected by military, police, and intelligence personnel, then our dreams will not come true and Africans will remain the laughingstock of the world for another millennium.

Nigeria is the most populous country in Africa (150-million), with immense natural wealth, but also it is the land of extremes. Nigeria is the fourth largest oil producer in the world. The populous nation got her independence from Britain on October 1, 1960. In 1966 its first African Prime Minister, Sir Abubakar Tafawa Balewa, was assassinated in coldblood in an army revolt which was put down by the military leaders who then took over power but were also overthrown six-months later by an army mutiny. In May 1967, a dominant Eastern group, the Igbo, were mercilessly massacred in a pogrom which led to the secession of the East from the Federation as the Republic of Biafra. A bloody conflict ensued from May 1967 to January of 1970, slightly less than three years.

What actually led to the horrifying massacres of fellow Nigerians only few years after colonial rule? After the failed bloody coup against the Nigerian Government in 1966, most of the surviving officers were Igbos, one of the major ethnic groups in Nigeria. The Igbos were then accused of having instigated the coup. This accusation spurred the Muslim Hausa people of northern Nigeria to begin a mass killing of the Christian Igbos. By the time the Biafra government fell and its energetic leader Col. Odumegwu Ojuku had fled the country, the number of dead Biafrans was estimated at anywhere up to 3 million. Though of course many of the dead were fighters, the majority are thought to have died through starvation and related illnesses. However, Nigeria's bloody civil conflict was followed by countless military coups in Africa which plunged the Continent into an endless turmoil. As I am writing this chapter, March 2010, bloody ethnic and religious fighting is going on in northern Nigeria where hundreds of people are reported killed.

While the populous nation is blessed with enormous wealth, Nigerians are among the poorest on the face of our planet. Army Generals and politicians with their families and friends, have amassed unprecedented wealth through unbridled corruption unrivaled elsewhere in the world.

The late Gen. Sani Abacha, that military thug, robbed Nigeria of billions of dollars that could have run the budgets of several African countries, Nigeria inclusive. In the first four decades of its independence, impoverished Nigerians were robbed of more than US$500 billion by their leaders. General Ibrahim Babangida, also a Muslim, is believed to have looted US$12 billion on his exit from power in the early 90s.

Sani Abacha single-handedly stole over US$75 billion from 1993 until his death in 1998. However, no one is sure exactly how much money vanished during his brutal reign and how much his family still has stashed in bank accounts worldwide. In 2005, President Olusegun Abasanjo dismissed two Cabinet Ministers and the National Police Chief, accusing them of stealing huge sums of public funds. The sacked Police Commissioner, Tafa Balogun, allegedly embezzled US$12 million during three years in office. In his desperate drive to contain the despicable level of corruption in Nigeria, Obasanjo introduced long awaited reforms. The new Excess Crude Earnings Account (ECEA) was put in place and opened to public scrutiny. Then, high oil prices had given Nigeria a windfall that could once have gone into senior officials' pockets. Before President Abasanjo stepped down after his term ended in 2007, the account held US$10.5 billion. This shows that corruption in Nigeria, and elsewhere in the continent, can be effectively controlled if the authorities are serious enough. But would that fund be channeled to those in desperate need? That answer is hard to come by.

However, there is no place in Nigeria where public funds are safe. At the local level, corruption is also alive and kicking. For instance, in Anambra State, authorities built a specialist hospital and 23 rural clinics, but all medicines and equipment vanished—apparently sold for private profit. Unable to treat any patients, the desperately needed facilities were reduced to empty shelves.

Corruption in Nigeria, and indeed, in most parts of Africa, has reached an alarming level, bringing with it, a man-eat-man society. Across Nigeria for instance, loans are routinely given for nonexistent projects. State assets are appropriated by public servants and sold for personal gain. It is widely believed that US$125 billion of private Nigerian assets languish in overseas bank accounts, enough to repay the country's entire foreign debt more than twice over.

Out of US $125 billion, Sani Abacha and members of his family own perhaps more than half of the loot. In 2002, the Nigerian government recovered US$146 million in embezzled funds from the family of the late corrupt tyrant Gen. Abacha, whose systematic plundering of the state coffers was partly responsible for the decay of the oil-rich West African country's infrastructure. The British government had found traces of some US$1.3 billion allegedly handled by British banks on behalf of the Abacha family and their cronies. Switzerland had frozen US$670 million in bank accounts belonging to Abacha, and other relatives, while his son Mohammed Abacha aged 30, was caught trying to smuggle out US$100 million. Abacha's wife, driven by enormous sense of greed, was arrested at Abuja's International Airport soon after her husband's demise with five suitcases full of US dollars trying to flee the country. Some analysts put the loot at US$150 million.

Among the many disasters and cruelties that have plagued postcolonial Africa, there is no greater disappointment than that of Nigeria, Congo and Zimbabwe. The former, blessed with gargantuan natural resources, especially oil, has become a hell on the continent. I can summarize thus; "In oil lies wealth; in oil lies tragedy." The nation's State oil company, working with partners such as Shell, Chevron, Mobil, Amoco, and Texaco, produces US$35-40 million each day, but very little if any, reached the most needy citizens—the victims of heartless military tyrants and political kleptocrats.

Promises by successive military governments (in power for almost 35 years) to spend fixed percentages of oil revenue, to bring electricity, clean water, low cost housing, decent roads, village clinics, and schools to the oil-belt have failed. This has led to wide protests against the administrations and the oil companies which tacitly lubricate the engine of exploitation and tyranny against the Nigerian people who have been reduced to a state of destitution.

For a decade, the Ogonis, Nembe, Ijaws, and other ethnic groups, engaged in peaceful protests against the governments and oil companies in regard to the irreparable damage done to the farms and people of the Delta. The dire poverty of much of the Delta in contrast to the luxurious homes and lives of the merciless military brutes, their political bedfellows, and the US and European oil firms who are their partners in evil, has left people desperate, frustrated and bitter. They have been left with no other choice but to confront the buccaneers head-on in pursuit of their supreme conviction, "birth rights."

The destruction of farm land, wildlife, plant life, rivers, and people in surrounding areas had attributed to deafness and prone to respiratory diseases. To this end Ken Saro Wiwa, then 54 and an intellectual and fearless environmentalist, protested against the environmental disaster done to his people by the international oil companies in collusion with the Nigerian thugocratic regime. Saro Wiwa wrote to the Abacha government on behalf of his people to the effect that oil drilling and acid rains had poisoned water courses, streams, creeks, and agricultural land—the life-blood of his people. However, there were few concerns or complaints leveled against oil companies in cooperation with military rogues for the irreparable damage they have done to Delta region.

The growing indignation among the Ogoni and other ethnic groups, instilled fear in the Abacha regime. That fear led to the arrest of Saro Wiwa in April 1995 along with eight of his Ogoni compatriots. After nine months in prison where he and other Ogoni leaders were viciously tortured and finally arraigned on murder charges. But the truth of the matter was, and still remains, that Ken and his fellow activists had been campaigning for the rights of the Ogoni people against Abacha and the ravages of "Big Oil." Far from the truth, they did not commit murder as Abacha asserted. The charges of murder were obviously trumped-up in order to get rid of those who dared challenge the evil regime.

Saro Wiwa, his health having dangerously declined, was defended by Nigeria's most prominent and radical lawyers. However, they were considering pulling out because they believed that the verdict was preordained by the military and the evidence fixed by the prosecution. Encouragingly, there were relentless pleas for clemency from the international community to spare the lives of Ken Saro Wiwa and his gallant compatriots. As expected, the brute and his gang of looters, hanged their critics in November 1995. As usual, African States remained gagged to this repulsive act of barbarity against humanity, indicating that Africans abhor the destruction of life perpetrated by whites, but celebrate the lynching of black by black despots and tyrants.

Shell Oil Company, one of the culprits widely accused of complicitly in Nigeria's environmental and human rights abuse, paid US$15.5 million in an out-of-court settlement to relatives of Ken Saro Wiwa and others brutally executed in November 1995, on trumped up murder charges.

However, the issue of oil riches in the Delta Region is far from over. The leader of the Niger Delta People's Volunteer Force (NDPVF), Moujahid Dokubo-Asari, vowed to target the employees of Royal Dutch Shell for attacks. Another rebel group known as the Movement for the Emancipation of Delta (MEND), which appears to be more active than the former, has engaged the Nigerian Army several times and kidnapped a number of foreign oil workers to underscore their motives. However, some of Nigerian politicians who have connections to oil companies, view this trend as gangsterism. Others call them terrorists. The overwhelming majority of the Niger Delta and, indeed, most progressively minded people, regard them as patriotic young people—driven by nationalistic sentiments—who took up arms to defend the rights of their people and protect further environmental damage of their land. There is a popular saying in Africa which asserts: "A good Nigerian is that who is six-feet deep." However, not all Nigerians are corrupt or greedy, there are some who are decent and clean, but find themselves pushed to the stone wall. Among them is Prof. Wole Soyinka, the conscience of Africa and Nobel Peace recipient for his tireless and, at times, risky criticism of corrupt and tyrannical dictatorship. He is an outspoken critic of rogue regime of Robert Mugabe of Zimbabwe and el Bashir of the Sudan. With a part of funds I have indicated in this chapter as being held in private accounts abroad, would Africans still be convinced that their continent is poor? Let's admit it, we have enormous problems and that is lack of decent and patriotic leadership. Unless the masses of Africa unite and get rid of kleptocrats and dictators, our disabilities will be permanent and we will remain the laughing stock of the world. Nigeria is a land of tremendous riches, but only a small fraction benefit from it—the overwhelming majority live under the most grinding poverty ever seen in recent history.

From Angola's Atlantic waters to southern Sudan's swamps, Africa is a new frontier for western oil explorers and with production and revenues rising daily. The continent is crying out for foreign investment but, human rights groups say, the oil companies may be doing more harm than good by enriching undemocratic regimes, fueling civil conflicts, and polluting the environment. Sadly, ordinary people in Africa's oil-rich areas have seen little or no benefit from huge revenues generated in their regions. Instead the funds are each day burgeoning huge private bank accounts abroad leaving behind millions languishing in the inferno of poverty, disease, and starvation.

The Democratic Republic of Congo (DRC), is the second largest country in Africa after Sudan, and about twice the size of Europe. Like Nigeria, Congo is one of the richest nations on the face of our planet—endowed with prodigious strategic mineral resources from gold, diamonds, copper, oil, aluminum, uranium (which it is believed at one stage was sold to the US to help make the first Atomic bomb during the Second World War which helped defeat Japan), lead, coltan, and cobalt. It is also rich in agricultural products: copal, rubber, palm oil, peanuts, and tobacco. Yet, the Congolese are listed among the poorest people on earth—living on less than a dollar a month, on average. If properly managed, Congo could also become the hub for a potential tourist industry at global level. Congo, with the population of over 40 million and despite continuous civil wars, gained independence from Belgium on August 15, 1960. Soon thereafter, bloody civil conflicts ensued throwing the country into chaos resulting in endless anarchy and turmoil.

Fearing the former Soviet Union's dominance of mineral rich Congo, the Belgians did not want to wait for surprises. Though most of the blame for Africa's destruction goes to Africans themselves, former colonial powers also played devastating roles in trying to dominate Africa's vast mineral resources to their own ultimate advantage.

Forthwith, the Belgian Foreign Minister Pierre Wigny between 10 and 14 September 1960 (barely three weeks after Lumumba's inauguration as first black Prime Minister of Congo) sent a diplomat to explore with the Congolese politicians—Justin Bomboko, J. Kasavubu and Joseph Mobutu (Sese Seko)—the possibility of staging a coup. A few days later, the Belgian Minister without portfolio, Ganshof Van Der Meersch, also sent a top Belgian Security Agent to organize the destabilization of Lumumba's new government. From the outset, however, the Belgian government showed an outright reluctance for Congo's sovereignty and it was under this scenario that Congo was targeted for destabilization. This onslaught plunged the mineral rich nation into economic and political turmoil which, unfortunately, persists hitherto.

Belgians had already made up their minds to get rid of Lumumba as they perceived that he was a communist in league with the communist bloc—particularly to make available to the Soviets a share of Congo's mineral wealth. Much pressure was put on Col. Joseph D. Mobutu (after staging a coup only a few months after independence) to arrest Lumumba. Initial reports indicated that Mobutu was reluctant to arrest Lumumba. After consistent pressure in an operation code-named "Action 58316," the traitor Mobutu on October 10, 1960, finally succumbed to pressure and arrested Lumumba who had himself elevated Mobutu to the top military rank in the Congolese Armed Forces (CAF).

Finally, Patrice E. Lumumba was executed (along with his gallant compatriots Maurice Mpolo and Joseph Okito) in cold-blood on 17 January 1961 between 9:40 and 9:43 PM by African Katangese gendarmes and policemen and in the presence of members of Moise Tshombe's secessionist government of Katanga, the Belgian Police Commissioner, and three Belgian Military Officers. It is also reported that Lumumba was brutally tortured while being transferred to Katanga Province to face execution, but according to reliable sources, Lumumba showed no sign of breakdown and told his tormentors: "Torture or no torture, beatings or no beatings and threats or no threats, nothing will make me betray my conscience, my people, and Africa. *If I have to shed my blood, I must shed it in defense of my country, my people, Africa, and the vast wealth of my country for which, I am going to face gallows. I strongly believe that the wealth of Africa must remain in the hands of my people and Africa.*" Indeed, reading these words from someone knowingly heading towards his final breath, one clings to such heroic words. Lumumba was Africa's greatest martyr of our time. It is, however, sad that Lumumba and his fellow compatriots were put down by bullets triggered by fellow Africans commanded by white mercenaries. Like in Ghana, Kwame Nkrumah was overthrown by military officers he had elevated to high positions, but, who had been on the payroll of the notorious US Central Intelligence Agency (CIA). Unbelievably, these coup leaders were ordered to obliterate vital manuscripts assembled by Nkrumah and his brother-in-struggle—the foremost Pan-Africanist Dr. W. E. B. de Bois, an African-American who moved to Ghana after its independence in 1957. The materials had just been completed after ten years of hard work to compile "Encyclopedia Africana" which embodied cardinal information for the black race. Indeed, this was a sad chapter in Africa's liberation struggle and many clear-thinking continental people ask, *"What lies ahead for Africa?"*

The Belgians knew who Mobutu was but wanted to teach the Congolese the "lesson of their life"—Belgians out, Mobutu in. They left before much damage to the economy had been done. The infrastructure was still intact, health care and education systems were impressive, and to speak the truth, Congo was Africa's pride.

There entered Congo's Messiah Mobutu Sese Seko. Within six years, 85 percent of the 150,000 km of fine roads that existed at independence in 1960 had reverted to bush. A satellite earth station had broken down and so had national radio and television. Generally, all the services that the government delivers to the citizens were completely collapsed. Under Mobutu's repressive and corrupt rule, the nation's economy kept on nose diving. To make purchases people carried large bags of money. At one point, US$1 fetched 4.5 million Zaires, then 7.2 million, then 9 million—then the Congolese switched to the American dollar as trade currency.

As Mobutu consolidated absolute powers, Congo started to bleed profusely. The unruly soldiers and corrupt police force became perennial sources of danger. To try to head off further unrest, the military raised the salaries of the soldiers to 2,000 new Zaires a month or equivalent of about US$4. At the same time a family of six needed US$80 a month to at least make ends meet. However, the soldiers felt they were underpaid and were continuously on the prowl. They sent representatives to Mobutu to urge him to raise their salaries. But, this is what Mobutu had to tell them: "You have machine-guns, what are they for. Use them!" This was seen by the disgruntled soldiers as a "green light" to rob the impoverished citizens. They stationed themselves on the roads to levy fines for imaginary traffic offenses and pedestrians were stopped and asked to produce IDs which did not exist. If the citizen did not produce one, he or she was coerced to pay money or any valuable commodity or item in order to pass through. Soldiers also hired themselves out to provide security for hotels and businesses and even visitors. The situation was so desperate that they even resorted to begging for soap and other necessities from poor citizens.

Congo had reached a point of no return. It became, in fact, a lawless State presided over by a tin-pot despot. While his people were engulfed in unprecedented poverty, the Messiah went on an economic rampage against his own country. He imported a consignment of furniture, perfume, wine (US$175 a bottle), panoramic TV sets, and pink marble for his palace. At the same time, the Congolese national economy was collapsing. The loot cost taxpayers US$17 million. The so-called father of the revolution, as he was popularly known to his subjects, bought expensive properties around the world. For instance, he bought a Castle (the Chateau Fond' Roy) set in the magnificent park in Uccle near Brussels at a cost of US$3.5 million. Back home, he constructed a personal International Airport at Gbadolite in the remote Eastern Region where he hailed from. This at the staggering cost of US$500 million. Not surprising, not even one aircraft landed there and the airport has become a tourist attraction for baboons and monkeys and with trees and grass shooting up to 15-20 feet high. In addition to this, he bought a private jet from France at a cost of US$475 million and a yacht costing US$350 million and based on the Congo River. In all, the Congolese brute amassed US$9 billion—while he left the country with US$10 billion in foreign debt.

Since the death of Patrice E. Lumumba 50 years ago, the Congolese people have never enjoyed stability. Civil wars based on ethnic backgrounds have periodically engulfed the nation—at times, with a horrifying aftermath. Millions of people lost their lives in these senseless conflicts and millions others became refugees in their own country.

In October 1998, Laurent-Désiré Kabila launched a guerrilla war against Mobutu's corrupt and tyrannical regime. From a few hundred fighters to thousands of troops, under Democratic Forces for the Liberation of Congo/Zaire (DFLC), the conflict attracted thousands of troops from the powerful neighboring armies of Rwanda, Uganda, and Angola. The armies of these three countries had two major objectives; to get rid of Mobutu's regime which was considered a destabilizing factor in the region, and to lay their hands on mineral wealth (gold, diamonds, coltan).

After several months of fighting, the rebels led by Rwandese troops finally reached Kinshasa after Mobutu fled the country leaving his disgruntled army defeated. Towards the middle of 1999, Kabila formed the government including Tutsi leaders who put him into power. Half way through the next ten months, Kabila expelled Tutsis from the government they had helped to install. Among those who were expelled, were prominent rebels: Bizima Karaha, Kabila's former Foreign Minister (Tutsi); Deogratias Bugera (Tutsi); and former political advisor and top aide Moise Nyarugabo also Tutsi. Soon after the expulsion of former allies from Kabila's infirm government, another conflict ensued—this time rebels against rebels. It was Uganda and Rwanda against Kabila's Congo which was backed by Mugabe's Zimbabwe and Angola. It was understandable for Angola to join the fray for the simple reason that Congo and Angola share 1,500 km of common borders—unlike Zimbabwe which has no common border with Congo. Zimbabwe was invited by Kabila to defend his fragile administration, Mugabe's motive was clearly to have an access to strategic mineral wealth of the Congo. It is foolhardy to believe that Mugabe would defend the Congolese people while back home Zimbabweans were living in terror and in a state of hopelessness.

As expected, Congo became the "gold mine" of Zimbabwe. Army Generals, Intelligence Officers, Mugabe's top aides and henchmen, and ordinary soldiers, smuggled tons of gold, diamonds, timber out of Congo. And the list goes on.

Military cargo planes were used to haul the loot during the night. Some say that it is the funds looted from Congo that accelerated the lubrication of the engine of oppression in Zimbabwe and sustains the high living standard of Robert Mugabe and his closest allies. At the same time, in the Congo and Zimbabwe people live in dire poverty. Thousands of children die each month of rampant malnutrition. It is widely believed that the notoriously greedy and corrupt Mugabe, and his wicked spouse Grace Marufu, amassed between US$300 to US$500 million from the sale of gold and diamonds from Congo into the black market and these spoils have found their way into Asian foreign banks.

In January 2001, President Kabila was assassinated at his Presidential Mansion in Kinshasa. Details of the assassination remained murky. Government insiders said a lone bodyguard shot the President, but some reports suggested a bitter argument with military brass prompted the slaying. Soon after his death, his son Joseph Kabila, Jr. (a former taxi driver on the streets of Kigoma, Tanzania, and with little education) was unilaterally put into power by the military elite to promote and protect their economic and political interests before those of the Congolese people.

In the short period while Kabila, Sr. was in power, he ignored the welfare of the people and advanced before them his own economic and political interests. He was becoming more and more autocratic and corruption became the order of the day. Some Congolese lamented that he was following Mobutu's foot steps and had absolutely no vision for the plundered nation. Unfortunately, Kabila, the junior, also seems unable to deliver good leadership. Alarmingly, the unemployment rate is at 95 percent, law and order do not exist, and corruption is part of the Congolese culture. Gold, diamonds, and coltan (which is used in making cellphones, and worth US$240 per lb.), are controlled by foreign crooks, rebel factions, and Kabila's private armed gangs. Seventy-five percent of the Congolese population do not know their President, even in Kinshasa a city of 10 million people. Rarely do they see their President, even though he controls a small part of the city. In short, there is no effective government in Congo. More than 500 people die of malaria each month in Kinshasa alone due to a stark shortage of anti-malaria drugs. Moreover, there is only one shell of a hospital and that one left by the Belgians some 50 years ago. Nevertheless, Kabila makes trips to Paris to purchase expensive suits, shoes and other luxurious items.

Fighting and chaos are far from over. UN peace keeping forces which were sent to protect civilians under MONUC, the largest UN mission worldwide, seems to have lost its sense of direction. The mission comprised mainly of Indian and Pakistan soldiers is frequently blamed for failing to stem violence in the violence plagued country. Instead of protecting civilians, these peace keepers are engaged in dubious trade, and sex abuse. Many soldiers of Pakistan genesis have been accused of exchanging their guns for gold and diamonds with notorious rebel groups of the Congolese Rally for Democracy (CRD), the Congolese Liberation Movement (CLM), the National Congress for the Defense of the people of Rwanda (Tutsi), and the Democratic Forces for the Liberation of Rwanda (DFL-Hutu). To this effect, the Congolese government had written to the UN General Secretary Ban Ki-Moon asking him not to send any more Indian and Pakistan troops to reinforce its peacekeeping mission. In northern Democratic Republic of Congo, civilians in their thousands stoned UN peacekeeping bases blaming the international body for failing to protect them.

Indeed, the chaotic Congolese situation, which has been going on for generations, is both tragic and a shame to Africa and must not be allowed to continue. An African solution must be found forthwith. From past experiences, we must not rely entirely on foreign peacekeepers to bring peace for us. Lumumba and his colleagues were murdered in cold-blood while UN Peacekeepers were in Congo. The UN estimates that 4 million people were killed in Congo between 1998 and 2003 and fighting continues, particularly in the east of the mineral-rich nation, an area which has a population of 68 million people. However, despite Mobutu's unprecedented corruption that has irreversibly destroyed Congo by his horrendous human rights records, he was not entirely isolated. He had some misguided friends in powerful nations like the US, where late President Ronald Reagan called Mobutu "America's best friend." But soon after the fall of the Berlin Wall in 1989, the Americans abandoned him after having done their dirty job.

Perhaps Mugabe's Zimbabwe is one of the most corrupt and undemocratic nations in the world. Zimbabwe became independent in April 1980, joining a horde of African self-governing states. After winning the first multiparty elections in 100 years, Robert Gabriel Mugabe became the first black Prime Minister under ZANU PF government.

In his inauguration speech, he openly praised his former arch-rival Ian Douglas Smith (the former Prime Minister of the minority white settlers) for running his country efficiently—a remark echoed by former Tanzanian President Julius Kambarage Nyerere, also, Smith's arch-foe.

Soon the honeymoon was over. After a few months in power, bloody factional conflict erupted in Bulawayo the second largest city between ZANU PF of Mugabe (Shona dominated) and ZAPU PF of Joshua Nkomo (Ndebele dominated). The confrontation left more than 800 dead and over 2,000 injured. This led to major questioning among the majority of Africans whether independence had really brought something better than had been the case during the white minority regime. The irony of the matter was that there had been animosity between the two tribal-oriented movements for decades during the liberation war. In fact ZANLA Forces of Mugabe fought two wars; one against Nkomo's ZIPLA and the other against Ian D. Smith's government forces. Nkomo was from a strong minority Ndebele ethnic group. Mugabe, in turn, hails from the majority Zezulu-Shona speaking ethnic group. The two groups do not see eye to eye as is the case in several African countries where tribalism and ethnic divisions have become prevalent and present an alarming trend.

At the beginning of 1981, the conflict was widened to an alarming proportion. Mugabe undertook a violent campaign against the minority Ndebeles in Matabele land south of the country. The brutal and unjustified operation was carried out mainly by Zimbabwe's powerful Air Force against innocent and defenseless rural Ndebeles. The operation was led by a notorious and criminal Air Force Commander, the so-called Field Marshall Perrence Shiri. He was Mugabe's hit-man and a fellow tribesman. Mugabe also let loose the North Korean trained Guku-ra-hundi (Fifth Brigade) who terrorized and committed horrendous atrocities against the people of Matabele land.

The atrocious and barbaric military campaign took six months, on the pretext of routing out terrorists, but all the while striking terror in the hearts and minds of the Ndebele people. Conservative estimate claim that 35,000 women, men and children were massacred, over 15,000 injured, 10,000 others died of related diseases and starvation, while 150,000 became refugees in their own land—all during this unprecedented campaign of annihilation. However, international calls to arrest and indict Perrence Shiri, Mugabe's mercenary, fell on deaf ears. Fundamentally, the extent of such a crime warrants the UN (Human Rights Commission) to take credible action as it did in the Balkans' bloody conflicts. The UN aside, not even a single African nation stood to condemn the scurrilous crimes against humanity.

Soon after the vile massacres of innocent people in mid-80s, Mugabe consistently dangled the juicy carrot of government of the so-called National Unity and the integration of antagonistic forces into the national Army—knowing pretty well that Joshua Nkomo was desperate for power. When he accepted the idea, which of course, was an obvious conclusion, Nkomo was appointed Vice-president and, as expected and to the delight of Mugabe, ZAPU PF and ZIPRA (Zimbabwe Peoples Revolutionary Army) vanished from the national political radar. Hence followed the creation of Mugabe's corrupt and tyrannical one-party State. It was indeed, a tragic blow to the Ndebele minority on one hand, and to the whole nation on the other. Democracy was laid to rest even for his overwhelming strong supporters the Shona-speaking majority who regarded Mugabe as a small-god. Fundamentally, it was the start of Zimbabwe's road to disintegration, and finally, to the establishment of "a rogue state."

Candidly speaking, Robert Mugabe (as he himself acknowledged at an independence inauguration speech) inherited the strongest and most vibrant economy in the continent. Zimbabwe was the bread basket of Southern Africa (before South Africa became independent) and, millions of African immigrants from as far as Congo, Kenya, Malawi, Mozambique, and Zambia lived in Rhodesia (Zimbabwe), attracted there by green pastures. Education and health systems were rivaled by none in Africa and the infrastructure was the most comprehensively viable in the whole of Africa.

Absolute power corrupts absolutely. Mugabe forthwith was drunk with power, corrupt desires, and dreams of dictatorship. Sooner rather than later, things began to fall apart. Corruption among senior officials of the government and parastatal establishments was fast sweeping the nation like bush-fire. One senior Cabinet Minister (Minister of Mines) Maurice Nyagumbo, was the first casualty in a series of scandals. He was named in a major scandal-of-the-year known to Zimbabweans as "Willowvale-gate Scandal" and involved the buying and selling of cars illegally from the State-owned car dealerships. Nyagumbo was one of Mugabe's closest allies. He committed suicide by swallowing DDT—a deadly insecticide.

As scandal after scandal emerged within the government and State-run Corporations, the redeemer's popularity started to wane. The economy, once the envy of Africa, started to take its toll among the workers and people alike. It, therefore, increasingly appeared that Mugabe had lost the moral compass to lead. Democratic institutions were attacked. Critics were harassed and corruption became the nation's culture. The economy was fast declining. It took a century for white minority settlers to build what was seen as a viable and robust economy that attracted millions of immigrant jobseekers from the region and beyond. On the other hand, it took only ten years for a black government to destroy the "jewel of Africa."

It was apparent that the Zimbabwean redeemer had run out of ideas and subsequently lost vision. He had no other choice but to regain trust from his subjects at all costs. He, therefore, embarked on land issues as his last resort to foment nationalistic sentiments among Zimbabweans, and it worked for a while. His Communal Land Act (CLA) came to be known as Local Land Authorities (LLA).

Soon, Mugabe embarked on a land grabbing mission (against an international outcry but with some dubious support from African leaders who themselves could not afford to feed their own people). Mugabe's thugocrat also received some support from misguided African intellectuals notably, Baffour Ankomah one of the senior editors of the influential New African Magazine which was regarded by Africans as the mouthpiece for their democratic aspirations. On September 2, 2002, amid election campaigns, Mugabe ordered the mass eviction of 2,900 of Zimbabwe's white commercial farmers—for many decades, the mainstay of the agricultural sector. Mugabe ordered them to abandon their homes, land, and other means of livelihood by midnight. The same month, control of the Grain Marketing Board (GMB), the Zimbabwe-owned monopoly supplier of commercial maize (corn), was passed to Air Marshal Perrence Shiri—Mugabe's henchman and an alleged war criminal still at large.

The eviction of white commercial farmers for Mugabe's own interests and those of his dupes has had devastating ramifications both economically and politically. Signs of social and political decay were rapidly beginning to appear. Unemployment rates reached 99.5 percent—the highest in the world and on par with stateless Somalia. The high rate of inflation was particularly perplexing, running at 175,000 percent and leading people to use the one million Zimbabwe dollar-bill to wipe their noses. Then came the startling observation that 3 million Zimbabweans had fled the country for greener pastures. Those too poor or too old to leave faced brutal shortages of food, water, electricity, fuel, medicine, and security. However, every report on Zimbabwe ends with the sad statement that the two main causes of death are "AIDS and Starvation." Before Mugabe's contemptible land-grabbing campaigns, Zimbabwe used to be the breadbasket of the region.

Further, the acquisition of white commercial farms rendered 50,000 black farm workers jobless. Four thousand white farmers who used to feed 12 million Africans, were violently evicted from the farms they had owned for five generations. Unfortunately, Zimbabwe now imports 97 percent of its cereals, including wheat and the staple food, maize (corn). And from who? From the very same white farmers Mugabe evicted and who are now reestablished in neighboring Zambia, Mozambique and as far as Uganda and Namibia. Zimbabwe's export crops have all but vanished, thus leading to a chronic shortage of foreign currency for fuel, medicines, and other necessities.

Realistically, the saddest part of "land-grab" policy is that those so-called landless blacks on whose behalf Mugabe acted fatuously and impetuously, have been shamelessly sidelined or ignored all together. The beneficiaries of the landgrab are none other than politicians, judges, military officers, and members of Mugabe's own family. The list includes: Patrick Chinamasa, the Attorney General; Simon Moyo, Mines and Tourism Minister; George Charamba, Presidential Spokesman ,and notoriously known for his arrogance; Perrence Shiri, a mass murder criminal and Mugabe's hit-man and Commander of Air Force; Witness Mangwende, Foreign Affairs Minister; Joyce Majuru, Information Minister and queen of corruption; Emerson Munangagwa, a notorious Security Chief; and several other high ranking Police Officers.

Mugabe's notorious oldest sister Sabina Mugabe, the ZANU PF MP for Zvimba South—Robert Mugabe's home district—evicted Ford from Gowrie Farm and the neighboring Parklands Farm belonging to John Wilde, the nation's leading specialist producer of seed vital for the once bountiful maize crops. Sabina and her equally notorious ally, Agnes Rusike, the leader of the so-called "war veterans," united to lead a violent campaign against white farmers and their workers in Ford's area of Norton in 2001. In that campaign, 25 African farm workers were murdered in cold-blood and a prominent white commercial farmer Paddy Mcleary was lynched alongside them—and his home for 30 years was looted clean, some of the spoils having been divided between Sabina Mugabe and Agnes Rusike.

Perhaps, the greatest miscalculation of Mugabe's political career was the so-called "land reform" which was meant to chastise the whites, but turned out to be a vehement disaster for the black people of Zimbabwe. Many white farmers, to the contrary, crossed over to the neighboring Zambia and Mozambique where they were received with open arms. Within a decade, these hardworking farmers, with their tremendous experience and resources, have transformed the agricultural sector in their newfound home and provide thousands of jobs to local people and have dramatically increased food production to 60 percent. Some of this increased production is exported back to Zimbabwe to offset acute food shortages there. In other words, these white farmers from both countries have increased badly needed foreign exchange into the government treasury by up to 30 percent.

Astonishingly, in the ZANU PF covert circulation of October 1, 2002, the so-called Marxist Party, accused Nelson Madiba Mandela of betraying South Africans for not demanding their land back from white commercial farmers. The highly partisan paper lavishly praised Mugabe, the corrupt octogenarian tyrant, for standing up for landless blacks in Zimbabwe, while Mandela was accused of deserting the black people in South Africa at the most crucial hour. However, it would be completely foolhardy to believe ZANU PF insinuations against Mandela who endured untold hardship for 27 years in defense of his peoples' plight and who emerged from captivity as Africa's foremost Statesman. He had foreseen the dangers of vengeance against his former tormentors and forcefully emphasized forgiveness and reconciliation among the racially divided citizens of South Africa. He has made the nation a model of human races living together in peace and harmony. Mugabe's vengeance against his former political foes has never helped his country—but, rather, it has plunged it into chaos and backwardness. Meanwhile, there are close to 2.5 million Zimbabweans living in South Africa alone, and back home, Zimbabwe relies heavily on South Africa's food supply produced by commercial white farmers. Indeed, who has really betrayed his own people, Mugabe or Mandela? The answer is obvious. Mugabe has betrayed his own people by killing them through starvation and causing an exodus of Zimbabweans to South Africa. And that exodus was under most cruel conditions—hundreds of children, men, and women were offered up as "crocodile dinners" while attempting to cross the crocodile-infested Limpopo River to reach the greener pastures in South Africa.

The land seizures in Zimbabwe has attributed to untold sufferings of the African people. It is reported that more than 15,000 people have died of starvation—mainly children and the elderly. The farms which have been forcefully taken from white farmers and given to Mugabe's fawning sycophants, have been turned into ghost land where wild trees and grass have grown 12-16 feet high. To this effect, government senior officials privately concede that the brutal shortage of food is the consequence caused by race-based farm seizures.

It appears that in spite of whatever happens to Zimbabweans, Mugabe has no sense of remorse whatsoever. While the majority of the people could not afford to buy a loaf of bread at Z$1,50, Mugabe and his wife, 40 years younger than the rogue President, built a US$7 million three-story mansion in the posh suburb of Borrowdale, less than 3 km from Gracelands, where his wicked wife Grace built a controversial house at a cost of US$5.5 million, all diverted from a low-income government housing fund which was later put on sale. The house boasts a gymnasium and entertainment facilities. Security was also a priority, with computerized monitors, checkpoints, and sensors that can detect unwelcome guests. The house is thought to be the country's largest and most expensive residence. In stark contrast, Ian Douglas Smith, former Prime Minister of the white minority regime, built a modest house in his countryside farm and he is widely believed to have died a poor man. As if it was not enough, the Mugabes also have a country estate with a large house costing an estimated US$3 million at Zvimba—the President's home area.

While Zimbabwe is burning, Mugabe and his wife Grace are swimming in evilly acquired wealth. A month before national elections in March 2002, Mugabe is reported to have sent more than US$25 million through banks in the Channel Islands suggesting that he was ready to flee the country if he lost the elections. It is strongly beleived that the elections were heavily stolen from the opposition candidate Morgan Tsvangirai. Financial investigators have actually discovered that most of the spoils, which had been moving through financial institutions, without their knowledge, have ended up in Malaysia and Indonesia, both of which have strong links to Mugabe's murderous regime. These inquiries, on behalf of the British government, have uncovered a complex network of up to US$138 million in cash that had left Zimbabwe by late 2001.

Disturbingly, a senior financial investigator in Harare contended that bank accounts with perfectly respectable organizations in the Channel Islands, had been instructed to channel money out of Zimbabwe. The British foreign office had hired Kroll Associates to spearhead the hunt for Mugabe's loot. Meanwhile, Robert Mugabe is rated as one of the richest men in the world, while Zimbabwe has slipped into one of the poorest countries on the face of our planet. The damage done to the country's economy is irreversible and will take decades of progressive leadership and an unlimited infusion of foreign aid to put Zimbabwe back to its feet.

The most shocking and unbelievable act of brutality any African leader could unleash on fellow Africans was the demolition of squatter shacks in what has been called an urban beautification Campaign. This, following the arrests of more than 10,000 street traders in the capital of Harare in May 2005.

The announcement of "Operation Marambatsvina" which means "drive out rubbish" followed a four-day police blitz against vendors and flea market traders. The motive behind this unprovoked and shameless act (in a stronghold of the opposition Movement (MDC)) was to punish and intimidate the unfortunate people for their unequivocal support for Morgan Tsvangirai and MDC. The illegal evictions saw as many as half a million people homeless. Two hundred died of cold exposure and police brutality. Those who refused to comply with the eviction orders were ruthlessly crushed by bulldozers. Yet, African leaders did not condemn these obvious acts of violence by the government which is supposed to defend the rights of its citizens.

Robert Mugabe inherited Africa's best health care and education systems which, regrettably, no longer exist. The outbreak of a cholera epidemic toward the end of 2008-2009 in Zimbabwe killed more than 25,000 people, mostly children and the elderly. The number of cases surpassed 70,000. Half the country's population of 12 million was at risk of contracting the normally preventable disease during Africa's worst outbreak in nearly three decades. A lack of running water has been the history of countrywide, and especially in the city of Harare.

The cholera outbreak was yet more evidence that Zimbabwe's most fundamental public services, including water and sanitation, public schools, and hospitals were shutting down—much like the organs of a severely dehydrated cholera victim. The capital's two largest hospitals, sprawling facilities that once could have provided sophisticated and decent care in just such crisis, had largely shutdown weeks earlier after doctors and nurses went on strike over their salaries which were rendered virtually worthless by the nation's crippling hyperinflation.

Patients had nowhere to go for treatment, medicines had virtually vanished from Medical Stores and sold privately by hospital workers in order to feed their families. Corruption in hospitals is so rampant that even hospital beds, mattresses, pillowcases, pillows, bed-sheets, utensils, light-bulbs—and the list goes on—were stolen without the knowledge of Chief Medical Officer or the Health Minister. Cholera patients were treated under the trees, in street alleys, bus depots, and private homes. More than 3,500 doctors, nurses, and teachers fled the country for greener pastures. Despite the regrettable death toll, Mugabe blatantly dismissed the claim and insisted that there was no cholera in Zimbabwe, it had been brought under control—a remark that only an insane person could have uttered.

However, despite the stunning state of affairs, Mugabe held a birthday party marking his 82 years at a cost of US$2.5 million. He was surrounded by his fawning dupes and misguided supporters. In February 2009, against the backdrop of the deadly cholera epidemic, and coupled with the collapsed economy, he lavishly celebrated his 85th birthday at a cost to tax payers of US$3.5 million—this amid an acute shortage of food that led to starvation of more than 20,000 people mostly children and elderly. Malnutrition also took its toll, 65 percent of children were rated as malnourished by the World Health Organization (WHO).

Back in 1998, HIV/AIDS hit Zimbabwe harder than any country under the sun. The government of Zimbabwe for the first time in five years estimated that more than 750 people die each week—independent bodies were putting the death rate far too high. Hospital morgues could not cope with the numbers of dead bodies and as a result, Zimbabweans resorted to burning the bodies of their loved ones–despite the fact that cremation is a taboo in African societies. Sadly,

500,000 children have been orphaned since the 1990s, at the same time, inflation officially hit 231 million percent in July of 2004. John Robertson, an independent economist in Zimbabwe, estimated that it had then surged to an astounding eight "quintillion" percent, that's an eight followed by 18 zeros. In the same year, the Zimbabwean rogue President went to London with his wife and two children for shopping. There his wife, nicknamed "Imelda Marcos" of Zimbabwe, spent US$50,000 on shoes, handbags, underpants, sunglasses, watches, perfumes, and dresses, while his two young kids spent US$20,000 on T-shirts, CDs, and videos starring their hero, the late Michael Jackson.

Fed up with Mugabe, Zimbabweans voted en masse for the leader of MDC Morgan Tsvangirai in the March 2008 Presidential election. In the Parliamentary elections, MDC also won handsomely, but Mugabe refused to concede defeat and vowed to go to war if he lost the elections. Indeed, he lived up to his words. He stopped the publication of election results after he found out that he had badly lost the elections to his arch rival Morgan Tsvangirai. The election results were withheld for a month while they were being doctored. It turned out to be the most controversial elections in Zimbabwe's history.

At the end of April 2008, the government announced that Morgan did not win an outright majority and therefore, must go for a rerun ballot. The opposition maintained that there was no need of another election for they won the elections with an overwhelming majority despite massive rigging and state-sponsored violence which left 250 people dead and over 1,000 injured—mostly opposition supporters. This shows that the people of Zimbabwe really wanted change after more than thirty years of tyranny, corruption and injustices.

As state-sponsored violence accelerated, the leader of the opposition Morgan Tsvangirai, sought refuge in one of the foreign Embassies in Harare. Amazingly, only the international community condemned the election results. Only a few African leaders such as Prime Minister of Kenya Lailla Odinga (himself a victim of Mwai Kibaki's election fraud), Ian Khama of Botswana, and Rwanda's Paul Kagame, joined the chorus.

In a follow up African Union Conference on July 2, 2008, in Sharm El Sheik, Egypt, there were contradicting views on Mugabe's Zimbabwe. Some delegates gave him standing ovations especially those from Southern Africa Development Cooperation (SADC) countries led by Thabo Mbeki of South Africa, itself once a victim of an apartheid system perpetrated by the white minority regime of which Mbeki fought against. Others like Kenya's Odinga and officials from Sierra Leone, Liberia, and Nigeria, condemned Mugabe and his tyrannical regime. Botswana's Vice-president Mompati, was outspoken in condemning Mugabe's government and said, the tyrannical administration of Zimbabwe must not be recognized and that the regime should be barred from the African Union gatherings.

The rigged election was followed by brutal torture against both journalists and Mugabe's opponents. The journalists, Ray Choto and Mark Chavunduka, were subjected to severe torture, including electric shocks to their genitals and hard blows to their heads. Others were tied to an iron bar—head down—and whipped by a cable rope. The overwhelming majority of Zimbabweans concede that they had never experienced such inhuman abuse during the white minority regimes of Garfield Todd, Winston Field, and Ian Douglas Smith. They were appalled to see that their own government led by a black man could treat them like wild animals.

Robert Mugabe had vowed earlier never to forgive a white man in his lifetime because he was refused permission while in prison to go to Kumasi, Ghana, to attend the funeral of his first-born son. From thence, his hatred plunged the nation into chaos and anarchy. Meanwhile, the Unity Government which was put in place to avoid further polarization of the country, seems to have stalled in view of the fact that the Prime Minister Morgan Tsvangirai has since encountered immense problems in exercising his authority due to Mugabe's highhandedness. It is commonly acknowledged that Mugabe accepted the formation of Unity government to solicit much needed economic western funds to save his failed state. Mugabe was stupid enough to believe that the G8 nations which he calls "bloody Whites," would be cajoled into releasing the funds into his control.

Apart from Mugabe himself, his wife Grace Marufu is a power force behind the President's arrogance. She behaves as if she owns the earth and is extraordinarily vicious and greedy. She is reported to have physically assaulted news reporters at the Hong Kong International Airport in 2008, for asking her why she would send her young kids to the most expensive schools abroad while millions of other kids could not even afford one meal a day. At Johannesburg's Oliver Tambo International Airport, she slapped a young lady for asking her why she had come to South Africa shopping for food items while millions of people back in Zimbabwe were starving?

Realistically, Zimbabwe is run by a military junta comprised of civilian loyalists and military high ranking officers who use Mugabe as a front-man. These are the people who are keeping the rogue President in power for their own naked self-interests. They are well known figures in Zimbabwe's ruling circles, for example: Emerson Munangagwa, the head of notorious JOC; Gen. Constatine Chiwenga, the leader of the confused Army; Augustine Chihuri, the notorious Police Chief; Air Field Marshal Perrence Shiri, the Head of despicable Air Force, wanted for crimes against humanity by the International Court of Justice; Major-General Paradzayi Zimondi, the Prisons Chief; and Gideon Gono, the most corrupt cretin Governor of Reserve Bank of Zimbabwe. These evil men have amassed unprecedented wealth from Congo's gold, diamonds, coltan, and timber making them the financially richest elite in the country while the majority of Zimbabweans languish in grinding poverty. The assets of these people, including those of Mugabe, had been frozen and they themselves, including Mugabe, had been put on travel ban lists by the British government and the EU Nations. How much effect that will bear on these rogues, we shall have to wait and see.

Uganda is another case for concern. After five years of guerrilla warfare, President Yoweri Museveni came into power in 1986, with the help of former Tutsi refugees who lived in Uganda—including Major-General Paul Kagame the President of Rwanda. The former President Milton Apolo Obote of Uganda fled for the second time. His last departure took him to the Republic of Zambia where he lived for the rest of his turbulent life. Museven accused Obote of corruption and dictatorship. On the contrary, he himself, has become worse than Obote. He is leading one of the most corrupt and dictatorial regimes in Africa today.

Museveni is accused of using massive public funds for personal interests. In October 2003, Museveni sent his pregnant daughter, Natasha, on his Presidential jet to deliver her second baby in a German private clinic at a reported cost of US$250,000. She was accompanied by her mother, also a senior Cabinet Minister in Museveni's government and another pregnant woman who was supposedly the daughter in-law. Ten other people were in the party to take care of the two pregnant women. The President's reason for sending the two pregnant women abroad for the costly delivery (and due to give birth at the same time) was that he could not trust local doctors and medical services. The fact that the Head of State disqualified medical services under his own administrations sufficiently proves that Uganda is being misruled and that Museveni has ultimately joined the club of Africa's fumbling leadership.

Disturbingly, the President has also packed members of his family into strategic government positions: Janet Kataha Museveni, First Lady, MP and Minister for Karamoja Sub-Region; Gen. Salim Saleh (real name, Akadwanaho) brother, Presidential Advisor for Defense; and Lt. Col. Kainerugaba (son of the President), Commander of the Presidential Protection Brigade (PPB), notoriously known for its brutality against civilians. Kainerugaba's is the most trained and best equipped

Brigade in the National Army, the Uganda Peoples Defense Forces (UPDF).

Meanwhile, Lord Resistance Movement (LRM) rebel thugs led by brute Joseph Kony, continues to inflict appalling and unabating massacres against defenseless children and elderly men and women in northern Uganda. Because of the fact that the Ugandan Army is well trained and massively equipped, people wonder how ragtag thugs have continued to exist and instill unprecedented fear among the northern population for more than two decades. At the same time, the Ugandan Army was able to march as far as Kinshasa, Congo (a distance of more than 1,500 km) a foreign country and there defeat Mobutu's well armed soldiers. However, Ugandans cogitate that Museveni plays tit for tat games because the northern people of Uganda do not support his corrupt dictatorial government installed when he unconstitutionally usurped power.

While Ugandans struggle to make ends meet, President Yoweri Museveni is considered to be one of the richest men in the world with foreign bank accounts ranging from half a billion dollars (i.e., US$500 million) to US$2.5 billion and owns more than 3,500 heads of cattle on his huge farm. In stark contrast, Milton Apollo Obote who died a poor man in exile and buried in his homeland Uganda, did not even have a dime in foreign accounts, a very rare scenario for African leaders. However, as Obote lies in his eternal grave, Ugandans now remember and cry for him. Recent polls (2009) conducted nationwide, put Obote far ahead of Museveni. Seventy-five percent favored Obote while only 20 percent favor Museven. This result would make Obote smile in his grave and feel exonerated.

As Uganda is bracing to become an oil producing nation in East Africa, following the discovery of that commodity in northern Uganda, President Museveni has already mobilized his contingent and started campaigning for national elections in 2011. Ugandans have predicted that Museveni has been attracted by Uganda's new and profitable resources which he wants to control for his own self-interests likes Nigeria's military rogues and greedy politicians—while the majority of their people live in grinding poverty and despair. President Museveni has ruled Uganda with an iron fist for the last 26 years, always winning by doctored elections. There is no doubt in my mind that African leaders are a confused lot, inherently greedy, dishonest, cruel, and corrupt.

In the small Kingdom of Swaziland, things are no different. In 2002, the play boy King of Swaziland, Mswati III, bought a luxury jet at a cost of US$72 million or nine times their deficit of US$8 million. In 2004, the 36 year old King—the absolute monarch of a land where two-thirds of the population survive on an average income of less than US$10 a month—purchased a US$690,000 Maybach 62, the ultra-luxurious Mercedes Sedan from Daimler-Chrysler equipped with a television, refrigerator, heated steering wheel, and sterling silver champagne flutes. This was confirmed by the automaker's South African spokesman.

The purchase added to the fleet of 10 BMW Sedans he bought on his birthday in April 2004. The former pupil of Sherborne School in Dorset, England, has already amassed about 16 wives and 27 children.

The annual ceremony, known as "Umhlanga" or the "Reed Dance," is the highlight of Swaziland's traditional calendar. Every Chief in the country of one million people dispatches a group of teenaged girls (virgins) to the Royal Kraal in Ludzidzini. In the year 2004, Mswati cast his eye over the assembly of virgins and chose 16-year old Miss Teen Swaziland, Nothando Dube. At the time his eldest daughter, Princess Sikhanyiso was seventeen. As customary, every wife is offered a new Palace and a new vehicle (in this case a BMW). In 2005, the King blew over US$18.5 million constructing eight new Palaces for his wives and refurbishing three existing ones.

Yet, in this country where 43 percent of adult population is infected with HIV/AIDS, the highest rate in the world, the victims scarcely afford to acquire AIDS related drugs. The unemployment rate is at 75 percent, one of the highest in

Southern Africa—but better than Zimbabwe at 500 percent. Worse still, the tiny Kingdom is among the ten poorest nations on the planet. Evidently, such leadership is wholly responsible for Africa's self-infliction and not the fault of former colonizers as we are daily made to believe by the failed leadership. The problems of Africa (which I cannot narrate in a single chapter) are colossal and found in almost every part of the unfortunate continent.

We have seen appalling situations in Angola and Mozambique where after routing brutal Portuguese forces from their respective countries, they turned the guns against each other and destroyed the lives of the people they were fighting to defend. In the processes, they destroyed the vital infrastructure that was the backbone of the economic strength. More than that, the death toll amongst civilians was astronomically higher than during the liberation wars. Patients in the hospitals were not spared either, nor were the schools which were bombed—inflicting heavy casualties even on school children. In Angola, the civil war lasted almost three decades and it is reported that 1,000 people died each day—either by fighting, starvation, or related maladies. While the national economy of Angola caved in, the rebel leader Dr. Jonas Savimbi amassed unprecedented wealth from the illegal sale of diamonds and gold. It is widely acknowledged that Jonas Savimbi's rebel group had a budget of US$60-100 billion, enough to run five Southern African States without difficulty. On the other hand, the government spent US$30 to US$50 billion a year on its military budget. In Mozambique, the situation was the same. The Renamo thugs destroyed everything in their path, the worst scenario being the destruction of national parks which contained thousands of wild life specimens—a tremendous attraction for tourists which in turn generated billions of dollars in government revenue. The civil conflict in Mozambique took 16 years and the war of liberation took 10 years. However it is estimated that more people died in an independent Mozambique than during the liberation struggle. The reasons behind this carnage in both countries, are: a struggle for power, greed, and tribalism—the scourge of Africa.

Unfortunately, there is also imminent danger of bloody civil conflicts in South Africa, Namibia, Mozambique, Angola, and Zimbabwe. The ruling parties of these States are not ready to give up power democratically because they impetuously believe that they have divine power to rule—for they are the ones who liberated their respective countries. Already we have seen this in Mozambique where FRELIMO has been in power, undisturbed, for 35 years and the same with the MPLA of Angola and of course, we have seen the direction of Mugabe's ZANU PF. In any case, there will be no fair and free elections in these countries for generations to come and ultimately, as in Zimbabwe today, the overwhelming majority of the citizens will be jogged into remembering their former colonizers.

Not only that the soil of Africa is drenched with the blood of innocent sons and daughters, but it is also contaminated with dangerous nuclear toxic wastes dumped either in secrecy or under contracts with international corporations by our greedy and ignorant leadership. In Equatorial Guinea, the ferocious despot Theodoro Obiang Nguema signed a covert contract in December 199, with a British company, UK of Buckinghamshire, to dump toxic nuclear waste on Annobon Island. It was agreed to start with two million barrels and after ten years, ten million barrels of toxic wastes would be dumped on the Island which covers only 15 square kilometers and is occupied by a population of more than a thousand people. It is revealed that despot Nguema received US$10.5 million from the company to allow the chemical waste be dumped on his Island regardless of the far-reaching ramifications to the health of the people (his family members included), and the future generation, nor the neighboring countries. President Nguema came into power through a bloody coup in 1979, and has since ruled Equatorial Guinea with a brutal iron-fist, and along with the wicked members of his family has amassed immense wealth from oil revenues while the people of Equatorial Guinea remain deeply impoverished and oppressed. The President has built for himself an expensive Mansion in California, US, at a cost of US$35 million.

He owns a private jet which he bought at US$375 million and he also owns countless properties in Spain and other European countries. Nguema maintains a huge foreign bank account in Switzerland which could easily feed his fellow citizens for ten years.

In Ivory Coast, 30,000 people got vehemently sick as tonnes of nuclear wastes were dumped on the outskirts of the capital city Abidjan in 2008. More than hundred people lost their lives. Sadly, a number of West African nations have signed contracts with European countries to provide dumping grounds for their toxic nuclear wastes.

According to reliable sources, Benin, in the west coast of Africa, is reported to have signed contracts to receive millions of tonnes of waste products in one deal, and in another, imported two shiploads of nuclear wastes from France in return for extended, special economic aid in 1988. President Kerekou directed the poisonous products to be buried in the Abomey region near the birth place of his arch rival, the late Captain Michel Aikpe who was killed mysteriously in early 1990s.

In Guinea (Conakry), a Norwegian company was found to have imported thousands of tonnes of toxic waste products which were buried on an Island near the capital of Conakry and, sadly, the regime was preparing to import millions of tonnes more every year. Here, it must be comprehended that at the time Guinea was not under the leadership of President Ahmed Sekou Toure who himself was a committed Pan-Africanist. Then there was Guinea Bissau (Bissau), which had signed two contracts for toxic wastes in 1987, amounting to an importation every year for five years of over three million tonnes of toxic industrial wastes. At a price of US$40 per tonne, Guinea-Bissau stood to make US$600 million. The terribly dangerous toxic chemicals were buried at Binta, nine kilometers from the border with Senegal—in terrain that contains a subterranean river.

In Congo (DRC), the corrupt regime of Mobutu Sese Seko signed a deal with four European nations to import a million tonnes of chemical wastes in return for US$84 million which was, reportedly, directly deposited to the President's personal bank account.

Most disturbingly, over 1,000 tonnes of poisonous chemicals and radio active wastes were found sitting quietly in the port town of Koko, Bendel State. It showed that Nigeria was the final dumping ground for this obnoxious cargo which had, earlier on, been rejected by Djibouti, Bulgaria, Rumania, Venezuela and other countries. In actual fact, Africa has become a dumping ground for highly dangerous and toxic substances which will, certainly in the long term, pose unprecedented health hazards to millions of our people—all because of greed and incomprehensible leadership.

At the invitation of Nigeria's First Lady Mrs. Mariam Abacha, in May 1997, Africa's First Ladies gathered in Abuja, Nigeria (the capital of corruption) to discuss Africa's appalling woes. They came for the first summit of the African First Ladies Mission to discuss the so called Peace and Humanitarian Issues. Decorously dressed wives of African Heads of State flew into the capital in expensive executive jets from countries as disparate as Tanzania, Niger, Guinea, Congo (Brazzaville), Ivory Coast (Cote d'Ivoire), Namibia, Ghana, Equatorial Guinea, Gambia, Guinea-Bissau, Burundi, Angola, Sierra Leone and Senegal. Also in attendance was Mrs. Ruth Perry, the interim President of Liberia. In fact, the price of one jet these so-called First Ladies used could feed half a million underfed people for five years or more or build hospitals, schools, provide clean water, or construct good roads, especially in rural areas where community life is unbearable.

The Secretary-general of the defunct OAU, Salim Ahmed Salim accompanied by his wife, blessed the occasion. The Secretary-general of the United Nations, Kofi Annan was represented by Mrs. Angela King, his special adviser on gender issues.

The fact that women who had the ears of Africa's First Men (despots, kleptocrats, thugocrats, emperors, brutes), had at last stepped out of Castles, Palaces and Mansions to address the pressing issues of poverty, conflicts, wars, child abuse, refugees, ignorance and disease, was a welcoming gesture.

Finally, the so-called First Ladies issued a 15-point communiqué as a conclusion to the summit. It was simply a string of platitudes that reduced the gathering to a mere Sunday School picnic. They condemned the use of child-soldiers, civil wars, tribal conflicts, the illegal arms trafficking, child labor, and prostitution. Surely, I think every African knows pretty well about that.

However, having endeavored to impress Africa and the World at large, the women just shed crocodile tears. They had sidelined real causes of conflicts and instabilities in Africa, "their Husbands." In fact most of their men came in to power through bloody coups d' etat, so, on what moral grounds did the women stand when they adopted resolutions on Africa's conflicts? Mariam Abacha's husband Sani Abacha is on record as being the most corrupt and brutal despot Africa has ever seen in modern history and yet, she dared organize the conference to appease the masses of Africa and the world at large. How would they remain unaware of the billions of dollars in public funds their husbands deposited in foreign bank accounts while millions of children in Africa are malnourished, millions die of curable diseases for lack of medicine, and above all, Africa's economies are in shambles?

Realistically, the gathering was a "summit of hypocrisy." However, it may have been a good thing for the First Ladies to address issues affecting their continent, but they deliberately avoided the cold issues of corruption, tribalism, greed, and dictatorship which are the prime causes of wars, conflicts, poverty, and economic disaster—all perpetrated by their husbands. A few years later, after the death of her husband, Mariam Abacha and her son were apprehended at Abuja International Airport with huge sums of money which they were trying to smuggle out of the country.

After all, how many First Ladies have had an opportunity to question their men on the billions of dollars in their foreign bank accounts? How many have chided their men about horrendous human rights abuses?

Chinese penetration of Africa is also a matter of immediate concern. There is no doubt that China's economic upsurge globally, has seen the continent of Africa slowly but steadily becoming China's major source of raw materials and oil reserves—which China, the social imperialist state, desperately needs to drive its expanding economy. In Africa, China focuses its eyes on Southern Africa region: Zimbabwe, Zambia, Malawi Mozambique, Botswana, Angola, Namibia, and Congo (DRC), for its colossal mineral wealth: gold, diamonds, copper, oil, natural gas, coal, uranium, timber, nickel, and steel.

But Africa's naked willingness to become China's dumping ground for its cheap commodities in return for economic aid, is both degrading and reflects a lack of moral standing by our leaders. China, in fact, does not care a dime's worth whether its aid to Africa is properly used or not. Its first and foremost priority is to feed and provide jobs to its two billion people and Africa is seen as the source of all that—while its more than 400 million people live far below the poverty line. However, despotic African leaders hail Chinese gestures as true friendship because it does not attach any strings to its deals, nor does it demand that tyrannical African regimes introduce any particular set of economic and political reforms—not in the way our traditional western partners insist on democratic reforms in return for aid and loans. Nor do they demand an end to human rights abuses and corruption as the industrialized west sometimes pretends to do. However, the west also must not try hiding behind the facade of democratic norms because they also poured unlimited amounts of economic aid into the repulsive and tyrannical regimes in Malawi, Kenya, Congo (DRC) and many others during the East-West Cold-War.

Africans however, must not be cajoled by China's economic successes. We have done businesses with the west for close to 60 years. They are not perfect, but neither are the

Chinese better than them. The Chinese are attracted by our enormous riches for their own interests regardless of our sufferings. China's closest friends in Africa are the genocidal regimes of Sudan and Zimbabwe and they are supplying deadly military equipment to both satanic regimes. For instance, in April 2008, at the height of Zimbabwe's bloody conflicts, China sent a cargo ship full of weapons. However, it was blocked at Durban Port by stevedores and forced to return to China with its deadly military weapons. China treats, of all the people, Mugabe as a "Distinguished African Statesman." During his speech at an Arab League Conference in Cairo, Egypt, November 7, 2009, Chinese Premier We Jiabao promised African leaders an additional US$10 billion in aid—a gesture indicating that China is there to stay and dictates its will.

But with billions of dollars poured into Africa (without a set of strings or guidelines for economic development) more than half will find its way into foreign bank accounts. It is, indeed, a dangerous price that Africans will ultimately pay. Already in Zambia, miners accuse Chinese-owned mines of enforcing inhuman work standards: starvation wages, hazardous conditions, long hours, and no days off. Chinese immigrants have redoubled in ever-growing numbers to work in manufacturing, construction, commercial, and retail industries that China has initiated, thus prompting accusations that Chinese investors are taking jobs rather than creating them. Already cheap manufactured goods are flooding Africa's local markets (everything from clothing to electronics) thus frustrating Africa's would-be entrepreneurs in their attempts to establish a strong industrial base for their economies.

Chinese have also set their eyes on land grabbing in Africa. China which already farms more than 100,000 acres (40,000 hectares) in Australia, is buying or leasing huge swaths of farmland in Cameroon and Uganda. On the Island of Malagasy, deals prompted a peasants' revolt that forced Chinese entrepreneurs to leave the Island. In Luanda, Angola, Angolan Mafia attacked Chinese expatriates in November

2009, apparently to register their outrage against the Chinese presence in the country. There are also similar instances in many other parts of Africa.

A shadowy terrorist group called itself ARFAP (African Resources for African People) had claimed responsibility for the kidnapping of twelve Chinese executives attending a Lusaka Conference on copper extraction. Video has gone global showing the execution of two executives and threatening the murder of two more if China does not withdraw from all predatory exploitation on the African continent.

Above all, millions of Africans will not forget the lynching of African students in Beijing in December 1989, in what it appeared as "racially motivated" carnage. Three African students at the Beijing Language Institute were murdered and more than 50 wounded by Chinese mobs alleging that the students were dating Chinese women. The mobs, including students and workers took part in the melee and in the process, they were shouting: "Kill the black devils" and "Blacks go home." Amazingly, the authorities in Beijing stubbornly insisted that racial prejudice does not exist in China. Nevertheless, the Chinese police acted brutally and discriminately against African students. They used electrical batons and beat any African student they could find.

However, Africans appreciate China's economic aid to Africa, but the overwhelming majority of them remain apparently skeptical and wonder about the motive behind Chinese offers of such ambitious and enormous economic aid to Africa? Many more complain about Chinese attitudes and arrogance toward Africans. "They are very reserved and they do not intermingle with local populations like the westerners," a young Zambian miner retorted. But also we ought to appreciate the role played by China during the progressive leadership of Chairman Mao Ze Dong and Premier Chuo En Lai in unequivocally supporting the liberation struggle in Southern Africa.

In 2006, friendship between rich China and poor Africa reached a turning point when the Chinese government held its historical China-Africa Forum (CAF) in Beijing, the Chinese capital, and attended by almost 50 of Africa's 53 countries and 40 Heads of State. By all standards, it was a unique gathering—a single country hosted an entire continent in this fashion. At the meeting, Chinese leader Hu Jintao made an unprecedented number of specific pledges to his new found African friends. This included: China would build more hospitals in Africa, provide billions in preferential loans, open China's markets to African exports, and train African professionals. In fact, this lengthy list seems most likely meant to lure Africans into surrendering their dignity, and above all, their huge reserves of natural resources to an emerging and ambitious giant.

Whether Chinese aid makes a dent on Africa economically, remains to be seen. The western industrialized and former colonial powers transferred a trillion dollars to Africa after independence some fifty years ago, but nothing substantial on Africa's economic direction has been so far realized. The continent of Africa still remains behind other continents whether economically or politically. Much of the funds intended as aid to the needy, ended up in private foreign bank accounts owned by unscrupulous Presidents, their sycophants, and military high ranking officials. It is estimated that more than US$500 billion owned by these evil people, is stashed in private bank accounts in Europe, America and the Asian countries—yet Africans remain in a hell of poverty, stricken by untold diseases, and greater hunger than during the colonial epoch.

It has been widely asserted by African leaders that Africa's economic disaster is attributed to former colonial powers' intrusion into the continent's affairs. They condemn the imposition by the World Bank and the International Money Fund (IMF) of the Structural Adjustment Programs (SAP). In fact, this accusation is a cover up of their evil and incompetent leadership which has resulted into Africa's downfall. How could our economies stand up against such corrupt and misguided leadership—which see some of the leaders become richer than their own respective governments? The truth of the matter is that when the financial institutions imposed SAP in 1980s, the economies were already in grim tatters. The national treasuries were empty even though private foreign bank accounts continued to burgeon with each passing day.

Some pundits assert that foreign aid would not work in Africa. It is estimated that the United States alone has spent about US$1 trillion since the World War II building agriculture programs schools, and infrastructure in impoverished countries. In Africa, such aid unfortunately; builds private airports, purchases private jets, builds costly palaces for (emperors and dictators), buys expensive cars for Presidents and their sycophants, and sends their children abroad to attend very expensive schools. The list of financial abuses is long.

As a result, there has been a very disappointing scenario. The level of poverty in Africa is still incredibly high and the gap between rich and poor, is indeed, obnoxious. More than 300 million people still live on less than $2 a day and most of the nations have seen neither a rise in longevity or in income in the 50 years of independence. In my own country Malawi (formerly Nyasaland), the first President, one of the most corrupt and ruthless tyrants the late Hastings Banda, ran the country as his own estate. He used aid money soon after independence from Britain 1964, to build a Palace at a cost of US$25 million. He told his enslaved people that the funds came from his pocket. In actual fact, the funds came from Britain and were meant for national development programs. Unbelievably, at that time the poor country had only one big hospital, Queen Elizabeth Hospital in Blantyre, built by the then Federal Governments of Rhodesia and Nyasaland and serving 3 million people. In most parts of Africa, military budgets surpass those of education, health and agriculture despite the fact that there are no threats or territorial conflicts to defend against.

There is also an imminent danger of losing its most treasured African culture which Pope Benedict XVI described as "spiritual toxic waste" of materialism and nihilism sent by the First World, which is called a new form of colonialism. Any nation that abdicates its own cultural heritage has no place in a civilized society. It becomes misguided and eventually, a rogue state. Meanwhile, Africa is engulfed by insurmountable woes which needs strong and visionary leadership to keep the continent afloat. In many parts of Africa, big families are the cultural norm therefore, our governments, especially those of sub-Saharan countries, will need to create millions of jobs and improve health care facilities, schools, and formulate fundamental agricultural policies to increase food output. It is estimated by Population Data Sheet (PDS) that by 205, the population of Africa will soar to one billion people. The population in Congo (DRC), which has been miserably torn by senseless civil wars, could more than triple during the same period to 185 million, while that of Africa's most populous nation, Nigeria, could more than double to 307 million. From my observations, none of these two resourceful giants are in a position to sustain such burgeoning populations.

The best system to ensure the equality of wealth distribution is through the establishment of socialism based on our cultural heritage. The western industrialized nations maintain that capitalism is the only way to build strong and sustainable economies, but the recent global economic meltdown proves it wrong. Pure and unregulated capitalism is not the only way of life. The most successful democracies on the face of our planet, are social democracies such as Denmark, Norway and Sweden. Without socialist ideals, the world would be a much more bestial place in every way, just as without capitalism, socialism is unsustainable.

Either way, the problems are Africa's and it is for Africa alone to stand on its feet and solve these man-made problems. The word independence is meaningless if the continent perpetuates dependence on other people after more than 50 years of independence. We have enormous resources to build sustainable and balanced economies for our countries so long as we detest corruption, greed, dictatorships, and tribalism, the scourge of Africa. It is extremely heartbreaking when you talk of Africa—the overwhelming majority talk of senseless and brutal wars, endless starvation, pervasive and institutionalized corruption, deadwood leadership, widespread and cruel poverty, and uncontrollable HIV/AIDS.

It would be foolhardy to believe that our problems will come to an end naturally without our relentless efforts. We have, above all, to embrace democratic norms in order to create equal opportunities for all our citizens and elect competent and clear-minded leadership regardless of ethnic background. In my own country, for almost 50 years, the national leadership has come from the south and central Malawi, treating northerners as foreigners in their land of birth. In February 201, the late President Bingu wa Mutharika imposed a Quota System on students from the north accusing them of cheating over examinations. The accusation is extremely unfounded and a pack of lies that almost plunged the nation into a political quagmire. However, the President was never forthcoming over the contentious decree which according to an overwhelming majority of northerners, he was driven by an inborn hatred of the minority people of the north who themselves have highly excelled in academic fields for the last century. This is the kind of leadership that drives Africa into senseless conflicts and bloodbaths.

However, the truth is not in doubt. Africa has been pushed to the stone wall and we can see a picture of unparalleled despair of a continent that is beyond emancipation. But I have a dream that some day men and women of integrity, who love Africa, will decide to enter politics. Not for power, ambition, or greed, but from a desire to serve the people and their beloved Africa, to restore dignity, a sense of direction, and decorum to the process of governing our Africa.

Realistically, not all African leaders have disappointed their people even though the overwhelming majority have. The post-independence leaders such as Dr. Kwame Nkrumah of Ghana, Julius Nyerere of Tanzania, Milton Obote of Uganda, Kenneth Kaunda of Zambia and Seretse Khama of Botswana had at least instilled a sense of hope into the minds of their people and individual impetuous nationalists such as Wole Soyinka of Nigeria, Sheik Anta Diop of Senegal, Dunduzu Kaluli Chisiza of Malawi, Theophile Obenga of Congo (Brazzaville), Jaramongi Oginga Odinga of Kenya and of course not to forget our brothers in Diaspora who played a remarkable role in the liberation of Africa such as William E. B. Du Bois (African American) moved to Ghana after independence in 1957 and died there), George Padmore (West Indies), Walter Rodney (Jamaica), Marcus Garvey (Jamaica), Dr. Yosef ben-Jochannan (African American), Dr. Martin Luther King (African American), Malcolm X (African American), Franz Fennon of Algerian descent and Steve Bantu Biko a South African liberation hero who was brutally murdered in Pretoria prison in late 70s and of course never to forget Nelson Madiba Mandela—the lion of Africa.

CRY, BELOVED AFRICA.

For further information, contact the author:

Winston C. Msowoya
Apt. 208, 6120 Stanton Drive,
Edmonton, Alberta, Canada T6X 0Z4
Telephone: 1-780-488-4003